About the Author

FRANCIS L. WELLMAN, one of the great nineteenth century trial lawyers, made his reputation in the musty New York courtrooms of the '80s and '90s as Assistant Corporation Counsel and Assistant District Attorney.

Born in Brookline, Massachusetts, on July 29, 1854, he was a direct descendant of Francis Lewis, third signer of the Declaration of Independence, and of Morgan Lewis, an early governor of New York. He was a graduate of Harvard College and of Boston Law School.

Mr. Wellman settled in New York in 1883. As Assistant District Attorney, he gained prominence in a number of celebrated criminal cases, including the notorious Carlyle Harris case. He became widely known for his spectacular coups in the cross-examination of witnesses, but he often emphasized that he depended not on trickery but on hard work and methodical preparation. In 1894 he resigned to devote his entire time to private practice.

He died on June 8, 1942, at the age of 87.

The Art of Cross-Examination

WITH THE CROSS-EXAMINATIONS OF IMPORTANT
WITNESSES IN SOME CELEBRATED CASES

FRANCIS L. WELLMAN

Fourth Edition, Revised and Enlarged

 COLLIER BOOKS, *New York, N.Y.*

COLLIER-MACMILLAN LTD., *London*

*First Collier Books Edition 1962
Seventh Printing 1970
The Macmillan Company
866 Third Avenue, New York, N.Y. 10022
Collier-Macmillan Canada Ltd., Toronto, Ontario*

PRINTED IN THE UNITED STATES OF AMERICA

A Note from the Publisher

THE PRE-EMINENCE of *The Art of Cross-Examination* in its field is striking evidence of the enduring value of this work to the legal profession and to the general public.

First published by The Macmillan Company in 1903, the book has appeared in four editions and fifty printings during the past six decades.

The Collier Books edition, which makes the volume available in paperback form for the first time, is the fourth—and latest—edition published in 1936.

To my Sons

RODERIC AND ALLEN

WHO HAVE EXPRESSED THEIR INTENTION

TO ENTER THE LEGAL PROFESSION

THIS BOOK

IS AFFECTIONATELY DEDICATED

"Cross-examination—the rarest, the most useful, and the most difficult to be acquired of all the accomplishments of the advocate. . . It has always been deemed the surest test of truth and a better security than the oath."
—Cox.

Preface to the Fourth Edition

THIS PRESENT EDITION—and I think I can say definitely the last edition—has very much enriched the several preceding editions by two strikingly new features. Whereas heretofore the text has been largely limited to the author's own precepts and experiences, he is most pleased to be able to offer a chapter written by Max D. Steuer, in which —speaking from an experience of forty years as a cross-examiner—he points out a few of what he terms its "lurking, if not great dangers." No one at the New York Bar knows more about the way to conduct a trial from an artistic standpoint than Mr. Steuer. Another well-known trial lawyer, Emory R. Buckner, at one time United States District Attorney for the Southern District of New York, has obligingly contributed his personal ideas of how to become a successful cross-examiner in a brief but compelling chapter over his own signature.

In addition, the author is now able, through the kindness of his friends, to offer many new and recent examples culled from the experiences of those trial lawyers who, at the very moment, hold enviable positions as leaders of the New York Bar so far as the conduct of court trials is concerned. These illustrations include the well-earned triumph of Herbert C. Smyth in his conduct of the Mrs. Gloria Vanderbilt litigation to recover the custody of her only child then residing at the country home of her aunt, Mrs. Harry Payne Whitney.

A second absorbing drama grows out of the generalship shown by Lee Parsons Davis, one of the leaders of the Westchester Bar, in his conduct of the litigation where the socially prominent Rhinelander family was trying to annul the marriage of their son to his negress wife.

Henry W. Taft, whose position at the New York Bar is too well known to admit of comment, contributes a striking example of the best method to destroy a hypothetical question propounded to an expert witness in a will contest, where the witness had no knowledge of the mental condition of the testator other than the facts assumed in the hypothetical question which elicited his opinion that the will was not the product of a man capable of understanding how he was disposing of his property.

Lloyd Paul Stryker, who is fast approaching leadership at the local bar, offers an exceedingly attractive instance of how his opponent's honest case can be shattered by ill-advised answers to a skilled cross-examiner.

George W. Whiteside, the equally eminent trial counsel for one of our leading local law firms, gives an illuminating example of how to handle insane witnesses who have all the appearances of normalcy.

Charles H. Tuttle and George Z. Medalie, both ex-United States District Attorneys of the Southern District of New York, who made enviable reputations for themselves in the conduct of that important office, have assisted me with some most instructive illustrations of what the all-powerful weapon of cross-examination can accomplish in the hands of experts in the art.

Joseph H. Choate, Jr., has also sent me some short but amusing and instructive transcripts of some of his court work.

These and a number of others, together with certain additions of the author's own, would seem to justify this revised and much enlarged edition.

I beg to call attention to the Foreword written by John W. Davis, the beloved leader of the American Bar.

Preface to the Third Edition

I AM ENCOURAGED to offer this third edition of my book by a letter from my publishers, stating that twenty years had not seemed to have dulled interest in the subject, either in this country or in England, and urging a new edition.

The reviewers of the first edition drew attention to the absence of any of the author's personal cases although he appeared to have had ample court experience. As a matter of fact, practically all the cross-examinations, not especially credited to others, were drawn from my own practice.

The second edition was much enriched by extracts from the cross-examinations of such celebrated trial lawyers as Sir Charles Russell, later Lord Chief Justice of England, whom Lord Coleridge called "the biggest advocate of the century"; Sir James Scarlett (Lord Abinger), one of England's greatest cross-examiners of all time; Sergeant Ballantine, Robert Emmet, Jeremiah Mason, Samuel Warren, Rufus Choate, probably the greatest jury lawyer America ever produced; William Fullerton, Charles O'Connor, Benjamin F. Butler, John K. Porter,—and the idol of all court lawyers of recent years, Joseph H. Choate.

In this third edition I am including examples of the skill of many present day successful practitioners such as John B. Stanchfield, who, at the time of his death, was the recognized leader of our bar among the lawyers engaged in court practice; Delancey Nicoll, who has spent a lifetime in great trials; Max D. Steuer, who probably, at the moment, tries as many important jury cases as any member of the American Bar; Martin W. Littleton, whose moral courage and fearless oratory in the trial of cases, as well as his intellectual attainments, rank him among the leaders of our court practitioners; Samuel Untermyer, whose unselfish and unrewarded public service in his efforts to bring about reforms in the Building Laws and in breaking up conspiracies against Trade and Commerce have given him a unique position among lawyers; William Rand, who has carried into his private practice the skill he developed as a cross-examiner during a brilliant career in the District Attorney's office, and last, but by no means least, my distinguished partner, Herbert C. Smyth.

One important feature of the book is the fact that the cases and illustrations are all *real,* and many of them heretofore unknown to the profession at large. They have not, at least intentionally, been either misrepresented or exaggerated.

My new edition is submitted with the hope that my readers may find as much of interest in its perusal as I have done in the researches necessary to its preparation.

NEW YORK,
  July 1, 1923.

Preface

IN OFFERING this book to the legal profession I do not intend to arrogate to myself any superior knowledge upon the subject, excepting in so far as it may have been gleaned from actual experience. Nor have I attempted to treat the subject in any scientific, elaborate, or exhaustive way; but merely to make some suggestions upon the art of cross-examination, which have been gathered as a result of twenty-five years' court practice, during which time I have examined and cross examined about fifteen thousand witnesses, drawn from all classes of the community.

If what is here written affords anything of instruction to the younger members of my profession, or of interest or entertainment to the public, it will amply justify the time taken from my summer vacation to put in readable form some points from my experience upon this most difficult subject.

BAR HARBOR, MAINE,
   September 1, 1903.

Foreword

PERHAPS I was among the earliest readers of Wellman's "Art of Cross-Examination." On its first appearance, over thirty years ago, it was thrust into my hands by my own father (who was himself a cross-examiner second to none that I ever knew), when he was trying to make a practicing lawyer out of his son. He, naturally, had a lively interest in my welfare and promised me pleasure and profit from the perusal of the book. I read it with interest then and have turned to it more than once since. If the resultant improvement was less than he had hoped, at least neither he nor the author were in any way to blame. I am still in debt to both of them. For the book is packed with wisdom and entertainment and its many new editions and the frequency of its reprinting are sufficient evidence of the high place it has won with lawyers and laymen. This last edition will be gladly welcomed.

Undoubtedly cross-examination is among the most difficult of all the arts of the advocate. It is also one of the most valuable. Every person familiar with the courts has seen cases won almost solely because of its skillful use; and also, sad to say, cases wholly lost by a bungling, an indiscreet, or an over-confident cross-examination. Just where the line lies between a cross-examination that is helpful and one that is harmful only experience can teach. Only experience can give the advocate that sixth sense which tells him when he has reached dangerous ground, when he may advance, when he must retreat, and when he can risk his case upon a single throw. There are, as Mr. Wellman points out, no set rules that will fit all situations, unless indeed it be the one which he reinforces with his quotation from Josh Billings: "When you strike 'ile,' stop boring; many a man has bored clean through and let the 'ile' run out of the bottom."

But to say that only practice can breed perfection in

any art is not to deny the value of precept and example. These Mr. Wellman gives in their most palatable form. Raw recruits at the Bar and veterans alike will profit by reading what he has laid before them—and prospective witnesses can learn much to their advantage, as Mr. Wellman speaks with the authority of a well-earned reputation among his contemporaries at the New York Bar.

JOHN W. DAVIS

Contents

PART ONE

THE PRINCIPLES OF CROSS-EXAMINATION

Chapter 1

Introductory

"THE ISSUE of a cause rarely depends upon a speech and is but seldom even affected by it. But there is never a cause contested, the result of which is not mainly dependent upon the skill with which the advocate conducts his cross-examination."

This is the conclusion arrived at by one of England's greatest advocates at the close of a long and eventful career at the Bar. It was written some seventy years ago and at a time when oratory in public trials was at its height. It is even more true at the present time, when what was once commonly reputed a "great speech" is seldom heard in our courts. The modern methods of practising our profession have had a tendency to discourage court oratory and the development of orators. The old fashioned orators who were wont to "grasp the thunderbolt" are now less in favor than formerly, though there will always be a high place in the profession for the man who speaks good English. With our modern jurymen the arts of oratory,— "law papers on fire," Lord Brougham's speeches used to be called,—though still enjoyed as impassioned literary efforts, have become almost useless as persuasive arguments or as a "summing up," to use the modern term.

Present day juries, especially in large cities, are composed of practical business men accustomed to think for themselves, experienced in the ways of life, capable of forming estimates and making nice distinctions, unmoved by the passions and prejudices to which court oratory is nearly always directed. Nowadays, jurymen, as a rule, are wont to bestow upon testimony the most intelligent and painstaking attention, and have a keen scent for truth. It is not intended to maintain that juries are no longer human, or that in certain cases they do not still go widely astray, led on by their prejudices if not by their passions. Nevertheless, in the vast majority of trials, the modern juryman, and especially the modern city juryman,—it is in our large cities that the greatest number of litigated cases is tried,—comes as near being the model arbiter of fact as the most optimistic champion of the institution of trial by jury could desire.

I am aware that many members of my profession still sneer at trial by jury. Such men, however,—when not among the unsuccessful and disgruntled,—will, with few exceptions, be found to have had but little practice themselves in court. They may also belong to that ever growing class in our profession who have relinquished their court practice and are building up fortunes such as were never dreamed of in the legal profession until this century, by becoming what may be styled business lawyers—men who are learned in the law as a profession, but who through opportunity, combined with rare commercial ability, have come to apply their learning, especially their knowledge of corporate law, to great commercial enterprises, combinations, organizations, and reorganizations, and have thus come to practise law as a business.

To such as these a book of this nature can have but little interest. It is to those who by choice or chance are, or intend to become, engaged in that most laborious of all forms of legal business, the trial of cases in court, that the suggestions and experiences which follow are especially addressed.

It is often truly said that many of our best lawyers —I am speaking now especially of New York City—are withdrawing from court practice because the nature of the litigation is changing. To such an extent is this change taking place in some localities that the more important commercial cases rarely reach a court decision. Our merchants prefer to compromise their difficulties, or to write off their losses, rather than enter into litigations that must remain dormant in the courts for upward of three years awaiting their turn for a hearing on the overcrowded court calendars. And yet fully ten thousand cases of one kind or another are tried or disposed of yearly in the Borough of Manhattan alone.

This congestion is not due to the fact that there are too few judges, or that they are not capable and industrious men; but is largely, it seems to me, the fault of the system in vogue in all our American courts of allowing any lawyer, duly enrolled as a member of the Bar, to practise in the highest courts. In the United States we recognize no distinction between barrister and solicitor; we are all barristers and solicitors by turn. One has but to frequent the courts to become convinced that, so long as the more than ten thousand members at the New York County Bar all avail themselves of their privilege to appear in court and try their own clients' cases, the great majority of the trials will be poorly conducted, and much valuable time will be wasted.

The conduct of a case in court is a peculiar art for which many men, however learned in the law, are not fitted; and where a lawyer has but one or even a dozen experiences in court in each year, he can never become a competent trial lawyer. I am not addressing myself to clients, who often assume that, because we are duly qualified as lawyers, we are therefore competent to try their cases; I am speaking in behalf of our courts, against the congestion of the calendars, and the consequent crowding out of weighty commercial litigations.

One *experienced* in the trial of causes will not require, at the utmost, more than a quarter of the time taken by the most learned inexperienced lawyer in developing his facts. His case will be thoroughly prepared and understood before the trial begins. His points of law and issues of fact will be clearly defined and presented to the court and jury in the fewest possible words. He will in this way avoid many of the erroneous rulings on questions of law and evidence which are now upsetting so many verdicts on appeal. He will not only complete his trial in shorter time, but he will be likely to bring about an equitable verdict in the case which may not be appealed from at all, or, if appealed, will be sustained by a higher court, instead of being sent back for a retrial and the consequent consumption of the time of another judge and jury in doing the work all over again.

These facts are being more and more appreciated each year, and in our local courts there is already an ever increasing coterie of trial lawyers, who are devoting the principal part of their time to court practice.

A few lawyers have gone so far as to refuse direct communication with clients excepting as they come represented by their own attorneys. We are thus beginning to appreciate in this country what the English courts have so long recognized: that the only way to insure speedy and intelligently conducted litigations is to *inaugurate a custom* of confining court practice to a comparatively limited number of trained trial lawyers.

The distinction between general practitioners and specialists is already established in the medical profession and largely accepted by the public. Who would think nowadays of submitting himself to a serious operation at the hands of his family physician, instead of calling in an experienced surgeon to handle the knife? And yet the family physician may have once been competent to play the part of surgeon, and doubtless has had, years ago, his quota of hospital experience. But he so infrequently enters the domain of surgery that he shrinks from undertaking it, except under circumstances where there is no alternative. There should be a similar distinction in the legal profession. The family lawyer may have once been competent to conduct the litigation; but he is out of practice—he is not "in training" for the competition.

There is no short cut, no royal road to proficiency, in the art of advocacy. It is experience, and one might almost say experience alone, that brings success. I am not speaking of that small minority of men in all walks of life who have been touched by the magic wand of genius, but of men of average endowments and even special aptitude for the calling of advocacy; with them it is a race of experience. The experienced advocate can look back upon those less advanced in years or experience, and rest content in the thought that they are just so many cases behind him; that if he keeps on, with equal opportunities in court, they can never overtake him. Some day the public will recognize this fact. But at present, what does the ordinary litigant know of the advantages of having counsel to conduct his case who is "at home" in the court room, and perhaps even acquainted with the very panel of jurors before whom his case is to be heard, through having already tried one or more cases for other clients before the same men? How little can the ordinary business man realize the value to himself of having a lawyer who understands the habits of thought and of looking at evidence—the bent of mind— of the very judge who is to preside at the trial of his case. Not that our judges are not eminently fair-minded in the conduct of trials; but they are men for all that, oftentimes very human men; and the trial lawyer who knows his judge starts with an advantage that the inexperienced practitioner little appreciates. How much, too, does experience count in the selection of the jury itself—one of the "fine arts" of the advocate! These are but a few of the many similar advantages one might enumerate, were they not apart from the subject we are now concerned with: the skill of the advocate in conducting the trial itself, once the jury has been chosen.

When the public realizes that a good trial lawyer is the outcome, one might say, of generations of witnesses, when clients fully appreciate the dangers they run in intrusting their litigations to so-called "office lawyers" with little or no experience in court, they will insist upon their briefs being intrusted to those who make a specialty of court practice, advised and assisted, if you will, by their own private attorneys. One of the chief disadvantages of our present system will be suddenly swept away; the court calendars will be cleared by speedily conducted trials; issues will be tried within a reasonable time after they are framed; the commercial cases, now disadvantageously settled out of court or abandoned altogether, will return to our courts to the satisfaction both of the legal profession and of the business community at large; causes will be more skilfully tried—the art of cross-examination more thoroughly understood.

Chapter 2

The Manner of Cross-Examination

IT NEEDS but the simple statement of the nature of cross-examination to demonstrate its indispensable character in all trials of questions of fact. No cause reaches the stage of litigation unless there are two sides to it. If the witnesses on one side deny or qualify the statements made by those on the other, which side is telling the truth? Not necessarily which side is offering perjured testimony,—there is far less intentional perjury in the courts than the inexperienced would believe. But which side is honestly mistaken, —for, on the other hand, evidence itself is far less trustworthy than the public usually realizes. The opinions of which side are warped by prejudice or blinded by ignorance? Which side has had the power or opportunity of correct observation? How shall we tell, how make it apparent to a jury of disinterested men who are to decide between the litigants? Obviously, by the means of cross-examination.

If all witnesses had the honesty and intelligence to come forward and scrupulously follow the letter as well as the spirit of the oath, "to tell the truth, the whole truth, and nothing but the truth," and if all advocates on either side had the necessary experience, combined with honesty and intelligence, and were similarly sworn to *develop* the whole truth and nothing but the truth, of course there would be no occasion for cross-examination, and the occupation of the cross-examiner would be gone. But as yet no substitute has ever been found for cross-examination as a means of separating truth from falsehood, and of reducing exaggerated statements to their true dimensions.

The system is as old as the history of nations. Indeed, to this day, the account given by Plato of Socrates's cross-examination of his accuser, Miletus, while defending himself against the capital charge of corrupting the youth of Athens, may be quoted as a masterpiece in the art of cross-questioning.

Cross-examination is generally considered to be the most difficult branch of the multifarious duties of the advocate. Success in the art, as some one has said, comes more often to the happy possessor of a genius for it. Great lawyers have often failed lamentably in it, while marvellous success has crowned the efforts of those who might otherwise have been regarded as of a mediocre grade in the profession. Yet personal experience and the emulation of others, trained in the art, are the surest means of obtaining proficiency in this all important prerequisite of a competent trial lawyer.

It requires the greatest ingenuity; a habit of logical thought; clearness of perception in general; infinite patience and self-control; power to read men's minds intuitively, to judge of their characters by their faces, to appreciate their motives; ability to act with force and precision; a masterful knowledge of the subject-matter itself; an extreme caution; and, above all, the *instinct to discover the weak point* in the witness under examination. One has to deal with a prodigious variety of witnesses testifying under an infinite number of differing circumstances. It involves all shades and complexions of human morals, human passions, and human intelligence. It is a mental duel between counsel and witness.

In discussing the methods to employ when cross-examining a witness, let us imagine ourselves at work in the trial of a cause, and at the close of the direct examination of a witness called by our adversary. The first inquiries would naturally be: Has the witness testified to anything that is material against us? Has his testimony injured our side of the case? Has he made an impression with the jury against us? Is it necessary for us to cross-examine him at all?

Before dismissing a witness, however, the possibility of being able to elicit some new facts in our own favor should be taken into consideration. If the witness is apparently truthful and candid, this can be readily done by asking plain, straightforward questions. If, however, there is any reason to doubt the willingness of the witness to help develop the truth, it may be necessary to proceed with more caution, and possibly to put the witness in a position where it will appear to the jury that he could tell a good deal if he wanted to, and then leave him. The jury will thus draw the inference that, had he spoken, it would have been in our favor.

But suppose the witness has testified to material facts against us, and it becomes necessary to break the force of his testimony, or else abandon all hope of a jury verdict. How shall we begin? How shall we tell whether the witness has made an honest mistake, or has committed perjury? The methods to be used in his cross-examination in the two alternatives would naturally be quite different. There is a marked distinction between discrediting the *testimony* and discrediting the *witness*. It is largely a matter of instinct on the part of the trained examiner. Some people call it the language of the eye, or the tone of the voice, or the countenance of the witness, or his "manner of testifying," or all combined, that betrays the wilful perjurer. It is difficult to say exactly what it is, excepting that constant practice seems to enable a trial lawyer to form a fairly accurate judgment on this point. A skilful cross-examiner seldom takes his eye from an important witness while he is being examined by his adversary. Every expression of his face, especially his mouth, even every movement of his hands, his manner of expressing himself, his whole bearing—all help the examiner to arrive at an accurate estimate of his integrity.

Let us assume, then, that we have been correct in our judgment of this particular witness, and that he is trying to describe honestly the occurrences to which he has testified, but has fallen into a serious mistake, through ignorance, blunder, or what not, which must be exposed to the minds of the jury. How shall we go about it? This brings us at once to the first important factor in our discussion, the *manner* of the cross-examiner.

It is absurd to suppose that any witness who has sworn, positively to a certain set of facts, even if he has inadvertently stretched the truth, is going to be readily induced by a lawyer to alter them and acknowledge his mistake. People as a rule do not reflect upon their meagre opportunities for observing facts, and rarely suspect the frailty of their own powers of observation. They come to court, when summoned as witnesses, prepared to tell what they think they know; and in the beginning they resent an attack upon their story as they would one upon their integrity.

If the cross-examiner allows the witness to suspect, from his manner toward him at the start, that he distrusts his integrity, he will straighten himself in the witness chair and mentally defy him at once. If, on the other hand, the counsel's manner is courteous and conciliatory, the witness will soon lose the fear all witnesses have of the cross-examiner, and can almost imperceptibly be induced to enter into a discussion of his testimony in a fair minded spirit, which, if the cross-examiner is clever, will soon disclose the weak points in the testimony. The sympathies of the jury are invariably on the side of the witness, and they are quick to resent any discourtesy toward him. They are willing to admit his *mistakes,* if you can make them apparent, but are slow to believe him *guilty of perjury.* Alas, how often this is lost sight of in our daily court experiences! One is constantly brought face to face with lawyers who act as if they thought that every one who testifies against their side of the case is committing wilful perjury. No wonder they accomplish so little with their *cross*-examination! By their shouting, browbeating style they often confuse the wits of the witness, it is true; but they fail to discredit him with the jury. On the contrary, they elicit sympathy for the witness they are attacking, and little realize that their "vigorous cross-examination," at the end of which they sit down with evident self-satisfaction, has only served to close effectually the mind of at least one fair minded juryman against their side of the case, and as likely as not it has brought to light some important fact favorable to the other side which had been over-looked in the examination-in-chief.

There is a story told of Reverdy Johnson, who once, in the trial of a case, twitted a brother lawyer with feeble-ness of memory, and received the prompt retort, "Yes, Mr. Johnson; but you will please remember that, unlike the lion in the play, I have something more to do than *roar*."

The only lawyer I ever heard employ this roaring method successfully was Benjamin F. Butler. With him politeness, or even humanity, was out of the question. And it has been said of him that "concealment and equivocation were scarcely possible to a witness under the operation of his methods." But Butler had a wonderful personality. He was aggressive and even pugnacious, but picturesque withal; witnesses were afraid of him. Butler was popular with the masses; he usually had the numerous "hangers-on" in the court room on his side of the case from the start, and each little point he would make with a witness met with their ready and audible approval. This greatly increased the embarrassment of the witness and gave Butler a decided advantage. It must be remembered also that Butler had a contempt for scruple which would hardly stand him in good stead at the present time. Once he was cross-questioning a witness in his characteristic manner. The judge interrupted to remind him that the witness was a Harvard professor. "I know it, your Honor," replied Butler; "we hanged one of them the other day." [1]

On the other hand, it has been said of Rufus Choate, whose art and graceful qualities of mind certainly entitle him to the foremost rank among American advocates, that in the cross-examination of witnesses, "He never aroused opposition on the part of the witness by attacking him, but disarmed him by the quiet and courteous manner in which he pursued his examination. He was quite sure, before giving him up, to expose the weak parts of his testimony or the bias, if any, which detracted from the confidence to be given it." [2] [One of Choate's *bon mots* was that "a

[1] "Life Sketches of Eminent Lawyers," G. J. Clark, Esq.
[2] "Memories of Rufus Choate," Neilson.

lawyer's vacation consisted of the space between the question put to a witness and his answer."]

Judah P. Benjamin, "the eminent lawyer of two continents," used to cross-examine with his eyes. "No witness could look into Benjamin's black, piercing eyes and maintain a lie."

Among the English barristers, Sir James Scarlett, Lord Abinger, had the reputation, as a cross-examiner, of having outstripped all advocates who, up to that time, had appeared at the British Bar. "The gentlemanly ease, the polished courtesy, and the Christian urbanity and affection, with which he proceeded to the task, did infinite mischief to the testimony of witnesses who were striving to deceive, or upon whom he found it expedient to fasten a suspicion."

Even so experienced an advocate as Sir James, however, sometimes loses his self-control in Court, and meets with the usual result.

At a trial between certain music publishing houses, as to an alleged piracy of a popular song, Tom Cooke, a well-known actor and musician, was subpoenaed as an expert witness by one of the parties. On his cross-examination by Sir James Scarlett, that learned gentleman rather flippantly questioned him in this wise:—

"Sir, you say that the two melodies are the same but different. Now, what do you mean by that?"

To this Cooke promptly answered, "I said that the notes in the two copies are alike, but with a different accent, the one being in a common time and the other in six-eighth time; and consequently the position of the accent of the notes was different."

Sir James. "What is a musical accent?"

Cooke. "My terms are nine guineas a quarter, sir." [A laugh].

Sir James (rather ruffled). "Never mind your terms here; I ask you, what is a musical accent? Can you *see* it?"

Cooke. "No, Sir James."

Sir James. "Can you *feel* it?"

Cooke. "A *musician* can." [Great laughter].

Sir James (very angry). "Now, pray, sir, don't beat about the bush, but explain to his Lordship, and the jury, who are expected to know nothing about music, the meaning of what you call accent."

Cooke. "Accent in music is a certain stress laid upon a particular *note* in the same manner as you would lay a stress upon a given word for the purpose of being better understood. Thus, if I were to say, 'You are an *ass,*' the accent rests on 'ass'; but if I were to say, '*You* are an ass,' it rests on *you,* Sir James."

Reiterated shouts of laughter by the whole court, in which the bench itself joined, followed this repartee.

A good advocate should be a good actor. The most cautious cross-examiner will often elicit a damaging answer. Now is the time for the greatest self-control. If you show by your face how the answer hurt, you may lose your case by that one point alone. How often one sees the cross-examiner fairly staggered by such an answer. He pauses, perhaps blushes, and after he has allowed the answer to have its full effect, finally regains his self-possession, but seldom his control of the witness. With the really experienced trial lawyer, such answers, instead of appearing to surprise or disconcert him, will seem to come as a matter of course, and will fall perfectly flat. He will proceed with the next question as if nothing had happened, or else perhaps give the witness an incredulous smile, as if to say, "Who do you suppose would believe that for a minute?"

An anecdote apropos of this point is told of Rufus Choate. "A witness for his antagonist let fall, with no particular emphasis, a statement of a most important fact from which he saw that inferences greatly damaging to his client's case might be drawn if skilfully used. He suffered the witness to go through his statement and then, as if he saw in it something of great value to himself, requested him to repeat it carefully that he might take it down correctly. He as carefully avoided cross-examining the witness, and in his argument made not the least allusion to his testimony. When the opposing counsel, in his close, came to that part of his case in his argument, he was so impressed with the idea that Mr. Choate had discovered that there was something in that testimony which made in his favor, although he could not see how, that he contented himself with merely remarking that though Mr. Choate had seemed to think that the testimony bore in favor of his client, it seemed to him that it went to sustain the opposite side and then went on with the other parts of his case." [1]

It is the love of combat which every man possesses that fastens the attention of the jury upon the progress of the trial. The counsel who has a pleasant personality; who speaks with apparent frankness; who appears to be an earnest searcher after truth; who is courteous to those who testify against him; who avoids delaying constantly the progress of the trial by innumerable objections and exceptions to perhaps incompetent but harmless evidence; who seems to know what he is about and sits down when he has accomplished it, exhibiting a spirit of fair play on all occasions—he it is who creates an atmosphere in favor of the side which he represents, a powerful though subconscious influence with the jury in arriving at their verdict. Even if, owing to the weight of testimony, the verdict is against him, yet the amount will be far less than the client has schooled himself to expect.

On the other hand, the lawyer who wearies the court and the jury with endless and pointless cross-examinations; who is constantly losing his temper and showing his teeth to the witnesses; who wears a sour, anxious expression; who possesses a monotonous, rasping, penetrating voice; who presents a slovenly, unkempt personal appearance; who is prone to take unfair advantage of witness or counsel, and seems determined to win at all hazards—soon prejudices a jury against himself and the client he represents, entirely irrespective of the sworn testimony in the case.

[1] "Memories of Rufus Choate," Neilson.

The evidence often *seems* to be going all one way, when in reality it is not so at all. The cleverness of the cross-examiner has a great deal to do with this; he can often create an atmosphere which will obscure much evidence that would otherwise tell against him. This is part of the "generalship of a case" in its progress to the argument, which is of such vast consequence.

There is eloquence to be displayed in the examination of witnesses as well as on the argument. "There is *matter* in *manner.*" I do not mean to advocate that exaggerated manner one often meets with, which divides the attention of your hearers between yourself and your question, which often diverts the attention of the jury from the point you are trying to make and centres it upon your own idiosyncrasies of manner and speech. As the man who was somewhat deaf, and could not get near enough to Henry Clay in one of his finest efforts, exclaimed, "I didn't hear a word he said, but, great Jehovah, didn't he make the motions!" The very intonations of voice and the expression of face of the cross-examiner can be made to produce a marked effect upon the jury, enabling them to appreciate fully a point they might otherwise lose altogether.

"Once, when cross-examining a witness by the name of Sampson, who was sued for libel as editor of the *Referee,* Russell asked the witness a question which he did not answer. 'Did you hear my question?' said Russell in a low voice. 'I did,' said Sampson. 'Did you understand it?' asked Russell, in a still lower voice. 'I did,' said Sampson. 'Then,' said Russell, raising his voice to its highest pitch, and looking as if he would spring from his place and seize the witness by the throat, 'why have you not answered it? Tell the jury why you have not answered it.' A thrill of excitement ran through the court room. Sampson was overwhelmed, and he never pulled himself together again." [1]

Speak distinctly yourself, and compel your witness to do so. Bring out your points so clearly that men of the

[1] "Life of Lord Russell," O'Brien.

most ordinary intelligence can understand them. Keep your audience, the jury, always interested and on the alert. Remember it is the minds of the jury you are addressing, even though your question is put to the witness. Suit the modulations of your voice to the subject under discussion. Rufus Choate's voice would seem to take hold of the witness, to exercise a certain sway over him, and to silence the court room into a hush. He allowed his rich voice to exhibit, in the examination of witnesses, much of its variety and all of its resonance. The contrast between his tone in examining and that of the counsel who followed him was very marked.

"Mr. Choate's appeal to the jury began long before his final argument; it began when he first took his seat before them and looked into their eyes. He generally contrived to get his seat as near them as was convenient, if possible having his table close to the Bar, in front of their seats, and separated from them only by a narrow space for passage. There he sat, calm, contemplative; in the midst of occasional noise and confusion solemnly unruffled; always making some little headway either with the jury, the court, or the witness; never doing a single thing which could by possibility lose him favor, ever doing some little thing to win it; smiling benignantly upon the counsel when a good thing was said; smiling sympathizingly upon the jury when any juryman laughed or made an inquiry; wooing them all the time with his magnetic glances as a lover might woo his mistress; seeming to preside over the whole scene with an air of easy superiority; exercising from the very first moment an indefinable sway and influence upon the minds of all before and around him. His manner to the jury was that of a *friend,* a friend solicitous to help them through their tedious investigation, never that of an expert combatant, intent on victory, and looking upon them as only instruments for its attainment." [1]

The genial, courteous attitude of the late John B. Stanch-

---

[1] "Reminiscences of Rufus Choate," Parker.

field toward everyone he came in contact with in the trial of his cases was one of the secrets of his success. Shortly before he died he told me of his experiences in Washington when he was retained by some of the leaders of the Washington Bar to conduct, with them, the defence of the president of the Riggs Bank. Immediately upon his arrival in Washington, Mr. Stanchfield was summoned to a meeting of all the lawyers in the case and was told that he had been selected to assume the burden of the trial. He was warned, however, that the feeling against the bank official was so intense, and the bias of the judge who was to preside at the trial was so marked that there was little hope of a successful defense, unless Mr. Stanchfield could so irritate the trial judge that he would not only display his prejudice to the jury and thus arouse their sympathy, but also make erroneous rulings that might upset the verdict upon appeal. It was apparent to Mr. Stanchfield that he had been called from New York to undertake a task none of the local attorneys was willing to assume. He promptly refused to depart from his usual method or conduct the trial upon any such lines as were laid down by the Washington lawyers. He would try the case in his own way or not at all.

Throughout the trial Mr. Stanchfield's attitude toward the court was one of extreme courtesy and respect. At the end of a week the issue had narrowed down practically to the single question of *reasonable doubt*. Was the defendant guilty "beyond all reasonable doubt?"—otherwise he should be acquitted. Mr. Stanchfield devoted practically his entire summing up to the jury to this question. He cited authorities and explained with great minuteness all the intricacies of this perplexing rule of law—to such good effect that when the judge came to charge the jury, he complimented the courteous gentleman from New York upon the clearness and accuracy with which he had stated the law to the jury and ended by saying he could think of nothing he could add to or subtract from Mr. Stanchfield's statement. The result was a prompt acquittal. When the jury had rendered their verdict, the judge invited Mr.

Stanchfield into his private chambers and then remarked: "Mr. Stanchfield, when I heard that you had been called from New York to try this case before me, I could almost see you arriving in the city and almost hear the instructions that were given you as to how to conduct yourself during the trial. I just want to say this one thing to you: *it pays to be a gentleman.*"

Chapter 3

The Matter of Cross-Examination

IF BY EXPERIENCE we have learned the first lesson of our art,—to control our *manner* toward the witness even under the most trying circumstances,—it then becomes important that we should turn our attention to the *matter* of our cross-examination. By our manner toward a witness we may have in a measure disarmed him, or at least thrown him off his guard, while his memory and conscience are being ransacked by subtle and searching questions, the scope of which will be hardly apparent to himself; but it is only with the matter of our cross-examination that we can hope to destroy him.

What shall be our first mode of attack? Shall we adopt the fatal method of those we see around us daily in the courts, and proceed to take the witness over the same story that he has already given our adversary, in the absurd hope that he is going to change it in the repetition, and not retell it with double effect upon the jury? Or shall we rather avoid carefully his original story, except in so far as is necessary to refer to it in order to point out its weak spots? Whatever we do, let us do it with quiet dignity, with absolute fairness to the witness; and let us frame our questions in such simple language that there can be no misunderstanding or confusion. Let us imagine ourselves in the jury box, so that we may see the evidence from their standpoint. We are not trying to make a reputation for ourselves with the audience as "smart" cross-examiners. We are thinking rather of our client and our employment by him to win the jury to his side of the case. Let us also avoid asking questions recklessly, without any definite purpose. Unskilful questions are worse than none at all, and only tend to uphold rather than to destroy the witness.

All through the direct testimony of our imaginary witness, it will be remembered, we were watching his every movement and expression. Did we find an opening for our cross-examination? Did we detect the weak spot in his narrative? If so, let us waste no time, but go direct to the point. It may be that the witness's situation in respect to the parties or the subject-matter of the suit should be disclosed to the jury, as one reason why his testimony has been shaded somewhat in favor of the side on which he testifies. It may be that he has a direct interest in the result of the litigation, or is to receive some indirect benefit therefrom. Or he may have some other tangible motive which he can gently be made to disclose. Perhaps the witness is only suffering from that partisanship, so fatal to fair evidence, of which oftentimes the witness himself is not conscious. It may even be that, if the jury only knew the scanty means the witness has had for obtaining a correct and certain knowledge of the very facts to which he has sworn so glibly, aided by the adroit questioning of the opposing counsel, this in itself would go far toward weakening the effect of his testimony. It may appear, on the other hand, that the witness had the best possible opportunity to observe the facts he speaks of, but had not the intelligence to observe these facts correctly. Two people may witness the same occurrence and yet take away with them an entirely different impression of it; but each, when called to the witness stand, may be willing to swear to that impression as a fact. Obviously, both accounts of the same transaction cannot be true; whose impressions were wrong? Which had the better opportunity to see? Which had the keener power of perception? All this we may very properly term the matter of our cross-examination.

It is one thing to have the opportunity of observation, or even the intelligence to observe correctly, but it is still another to be able to retain accurately, for any length of time, what we have once seen or heard, and what is perhaps more difficult still—to be able to describe it intelligibly. Many witnesses have seen one part of a transaction and heard about another part, and later on become confused in their own minds, or perhaps only in their modes of expression, as to what they have seen themselves and what they have heard from others. All witnesses are prone to exaggerate, to enlarge or minimize the facts to which they take oath.

A very common type of witness, met with almost daily, is the man who, having witnessed some event years ago, suddenly finds that he is to be called as a court witness. He immediately attempts to recall his original impressions; and gradually, as he talks with the attorney who is to examine him, he amplifies his story with new details which he leads himself, or is led, to believe are recollections and which he finally swears to as facts. Many people seem to fear that an "I don't know" answer will be attributed to ignorance on their part. Although perfectly honest in intention, they are apt, in consequence, to complete their story by recourse to their imagination. And few witnesses fail, at least in some part of their story, to entangle facts with their own beliefs and inferences. This subject is discussed in detail in a subsequent chapter on the "Fallacies of Testimony."

All these considerations should readily suggest a line of questions, varying with each witness examined, that will, if closely followed, be likely to separate appearance from reality and to reduce exaggerations to their proper proportions. It must further be borne in mind that the jury should not merely see the mistake; they should be made to appreciate at the time why and whence it arose. It is fresher then and scores a more lasting effect than if left until the summing up, and then drawn to the attention of the jury.

The experienced examiner can usually tell, after a few simple questions, what line to pursue. Picture the scene in your own mind; closely inquire into the sources of the witness's information, and draw your own conclusions as to how his mistake arose, and why he formed his erroneous impressions. Exhibit plainly your belief in his integrity and your desire to be fair with him, and try to beguile him into being candid with you. Then when the particular foible which has affected his testimony has once been discovered, he can easily be led to expose it to the jury. His mistakes should be drawn out often by inference rather than by direct question, because all witnesses have a dread of self-contradiction. If he sees the connection between your inquiries and his own story, he will draw upon his imagination for explanations, before you get the chance to point out to him the inconsistency between his later statement and his original one. It is often wise to break the effect of a witness's story by putting questions to him that will acquaint the jury at once with the fact that there is another more probable story to be told later on, to disclose to them something of the defence, as it were. Avoid the mistake, so common among the inexperienced, of making much of trifling discrepancies. It has been aptly said that "juries have no respect for small triumphs over a witness's self-possession or memory." Allow the loquacious witness to talk on; he will be sure to involve himself in difficulties from which he can never extricate himself. Some witnesses prove altogether too much; encourage them and lead them by degrees into exaggerations that will conflict with the common sense of the jury. Under no circumstances put a false construction on the words of a witness; there are few faults in an advocate more fatal with a jury.

If, perchance, you obtain a really favorable answer, leave it and pass quietly to some other inquiry. The inexperienced examiner in all probability will repeat the question with the idea of impressing the admission upon his hearers, instead of reserving it for the summing up, and will attribute it to bad luck that the witness corrects his answer or modifies it in some way, so that the point is lost. He is indeed a poor judge of human nature who supposes that if he exults over his success during the cross-examination, he will not quickly put the witness on his guard to avoid all future favorable disclosures.

David Graham, a prudent and successful cross-examiner, once said, perhaps more in jest than anything else,

"A lawyer should never ask a witness on cross-examination a question unless in the first place he knew what the answer would be, or in the second place he didn't care." This is somewhat on the principle of the lawyer who claimed that the result of most trials depended upon which side perpetrated the greater blunders in cross-examination. Certainly no lawyer should ask a *critical* question unless he is reasonably sure of the answer.

In a recent will contest tried in the Massachusetts courts, and conducted by one of the leaders of the New England bar, one of the witnesses to the will had been a stenographer in the office of the lawyer who drew the will. She testified, as is permitted under the law of that State, that in her opinion the testator, when he signed his will, was perfectly sane. The appearance of the witness was extremely youthful and inexperienced, and not calculated to have much, if any, weight with a court or jury.

Opposing counsel, however, forgetful of the useful maxim to let well enough alone, and concluding that, in view of the witness's apparent employment in a law office, she probably had never seen an insane person, nor had an opportunity to contrast the normal with the abnormal mind, chanced it by demanding of the witness:

Q. "Have you ever in your life seen any one who it was claimed was insane?"

The witness paused a moment, began to giggle, and replied:

A. "I guess I have—I have been employed in an insane asylum for the last two years as an attendant!"

Mr. Sergeant Ballantine, in his "Experiences," quotes an instance in the trial of a prisoner on the charge of homicide, where a once famous English barrister had been induced by the insistence of the prisoner's attorney, although against his own judgment, to ask a question on cross-examination, the answer to which convicted his client. Upon receiving the answer, he turned to the attorney who had advised him to ask it, and said, emphasizing each word, "Go home; cut your throat; and when you meet your client in hell, beg his pardon."

An advocate should always reserve the question he wants favorably answered, until his witness is in the right humor to answer it. Sometimes he can so frame his questions as to lay himself open to an obvious retort by the witness. If the latter takes the bait and gets a good laugh on the examiner, that is the time to put the important question. While the witness is still excited and exultant at getting the better of the examiner, then the important question should be put as if it were only a most casual inquiry; the truthful answer will come before the witness is aware of it.

Sometimes, again, it is useful not even to suggest the vital question until the witness has left the witness chair and has gone half-way to his seat. Then suddenly call him back, as if you had forgotten some detail,—and quickly get the answer wanted amidst his excitement in having to resume his testimony.

It is a safe rule never to reply to a witness or be led into a retort unless it is a crushing one. Curran with his jokes, in one way or another, always contrived to throw the witnesses he was examining off their composure, and he took care that they seldom recovered.

"My Lord, my Lord," vociferated a peasant witness, writhing under mental excruciation when being cross-examined by Curran, "I cannot answer yon little gentleman; he is putting me in such a doldrum."

"A doldrum, Mr. Curran? What does the witness mean by a doldrum?" exclaimed Lord Avonmere.

"Oh, my lord, it is a very common complaint with persons of this description; it is merely *a confusion of the head arising from a corruption of the heart.*"

A famous English barrister was once cross-examining a big *nouveau riche* jeweler in a money lending case, and began by looking him up and down in a sleepy, dismal way and then drawled out, "Well, Mr. Moselwein, and what are you?"

"A zhentlemans," replied the jeweler with emphasis.

"Just so, just so," ejaculated Holker with a dreary yawn, "but what were you before you were a gentleman?"

The famous reply of the artist Whistler to the Attorney General, who was cross-examining him in his celebrated suit for libel against John Ruskin, tried in England as long ago as 1878, still remains a warning to the uninitiated.

Ruskin, in describing a loan exhibition at the Grosvenor Gallery, where considerable prominence had been given to two of Whistler's "Nocturnes," spoke of the "ill educated conceit of the artist" (Whistler). The libel especially complained of was the concluding paragraph of the publication where Ruskin wrote: "I have seen and heard much of Cockney impudence before now; but never expected to hear a cockscomb ask 200 guineas for flinging a pot of paint in the public's face."

It is said that Whistler thoroughly enjoyed himself at the trial and was more than a match for the Attorney General, his famous reply to one of whose questions has passed into history:

"Can you tell me," asked Sir John Holker, "how long it took you to knock off that Nocturne?"

"Two days," replied Whistler.

"The labor of two days then is that for which you ask 200 guineas?"

"No. I ask it for the *knowledge of a life time.*"

The verdict of the jury after a prolonged trial, which was the talk of England at the time, was in favor of the plaintiff, Whistler, for one farthing; but Ruskin took the verdict so seriously that he resigned his art professorship at Oxford on the ground that "the result of the Whistler trial leaves me no further option." It is interesting to note, however, that the subsequent prices brought by some of Whistler's Nocturnes proved the futility of Ruskin's criticism, for the "Blue and Silver Nocturne," which was an exhibit at the trial, was ultimately purchased by the National Art Collection Fund for 2000 guineas, was presented to the Nation and now hangs in the National Gallery.

It is well, sometimes, in a case where you believe that the witness is reluctant to develop the whole truth, so to put questions that the answers you know will be elicited may come by way of a surprise and in the light of improbability to the jury. I remember a recent incident, illustrative of this point, which occurred in a suit brought to recover the insurance on a large warehouse full of goods that had been burnt to the ground. The insurance companies had been unable to find any stock-book which would show the amount of goods in stock at the time of the fire. One of the witnesses to the fire happened to be the plaintiff's bookkeeper, who on the direct examination testified to all the details of the fire, but nothing about the books. My cross-examination was confined to these few pointed questions.

"I suppose you had an iron safe in your office, in which you kept your books of account?" "Yes, sir."—"Did that burn up?" "Oh, no."—"Were you present when it was opened after the fire?" "Yes, sir."—"Then won't you be good enough to hand me the stock-book that we may show the jury exactly what stock you had on hand at the time of the fire on which you claim loss?" (This was the point of the case and the jury were not prepared for the answer which followed.) "I haven't it, sir."—"What, haven't the stock-book? You don't mean you have lost it?" "It wasn't in the safe, sir."—"Wasn't that the proper place for it?" "Yes, sir."—"How was it that the book wasn't there?" "It had evidently been left out the night before the fire by mistake." Some of the jury at once drew the inference that the all important stock-book was being suppressed, and refused to agree with their fellows against the insurance companies.

The average mind is much wiser than many suppose. Questions can be put to a witness under cross-examination, in argumentative form, often with far greater effect upon the minds of the jury than if the same line of reasoning were reserved for the summing up. The juryman sees the point for himself, as if it were his own discovery, and clings to it all the more tenaciously. During the cross-examination of Henry Ward Beecher, in the celebrated Tilton-Beecher case, and after Mr. Beecher had denied his alleged intimacy with Mr. Tilton's wife, Judge Fullerton read a passage from one of Mr. Beecher's sermons to the effect that if a person commits a great sin, the exposure of which would cause misery to others, such a person would not be justified in confessing it, merely to relieve his own conscience. Judge Fullerton then looked straight into Mr. Beecher's eyes and said, "Do you still consider that sound doctrine?" Mr. Beecher replied, "I do." The inference a juryman might draw from this question and answer would constitute a subtle argument upon that branch of the case.

The entire effect of the testimony of an adverse witness can sometimes be destroyed by a pleasant little passage-at-arms in which he is finally held up to ridicule before the jury, and all that he has previously said against you disappears in the laugh that accompanies him from the witness box. In a Metropolitan Street Railway case a witness whom I had badgered rather persistently on cross-examination, finally straightened himself up in the witness chair and said pertly, "I have not come here asking you to *play with me*. Do you take me for Anna Held?" [1] "I was not thinking of Anna Held," I replied quietly; "supposing you try *Ananias!*" The witness was enraged, the jury laughed, and I, who had really made nothing out of the witness up to this time, sat down.

These little triumphs are, however, by no means always one-sided. Often, if the counsel gives him an opening, a clever witness will counter on him in a most humiliating fashion, certain to meet with the hearty approval of jury and audience. At the Worcester Assizes, in England, a case was being tried which involved the soundness of a horse, and a clergyman had been called as a witness who succeeded only in giving a rather confused account of the transaction. A blustering counsel on the other side, after many attempts to get at the facts upon cross-examination, blurted out, "Pray, sir, do you know the difference between a horse and a cow?" "I acknowledge my ignorance," replied the clergyman: "I hardly do know the difference

[1] This occurrence was at the time when the late actress was singing her popular stage song, "Won't you come and play with me?"

between a horse and a cow, or between a bull and a bully —only a bull, I am told, has horns, and a bully (bowing respectfully to the counsel), *luckily for me,* has none." [1] Reference is made in a subsequent chapter to the cross-examination of Dr. —— in the Carlyle Harris case, where is related at length a striking example of success in this method of examination.

Some very amusing instances of resultant humiliation to inexperienced cross-examiners, who yield to the temptation of trying to humiliate a certain type of seemingly ignorant, but naturally clever foreign witness, have occurred recently in our local courts.

A Fire Insurance Company was being sued by a merchant for the loss of his stock of caviar. The merchant, the principal witness in his own behalf, was attempting to enhance the value and quality of his merchandise as much as possible without too close an approach to downright perjury. He gave testimony to the effect that practically all the caviar in the burned warehouse was Russian Astrakhan Beluga, a most excellent and expensive brand of sturgeon caviar. The cross-examiner thought he saw an opportunity to exhibit to the jury the ignorance of the witness, as well as his perjury.

Q. "Is it not a fact that all of your caviar in that warehouse was what is known as whitefish caviar, a poor and inferior type of the article—not even a true caviar?"

A. "No, sir, none of it."

Q. "How do you know it was not? Do you even know where whitefish caviar comes from?"

A. "Sure, I know."

Q. (Triumphantly, as if he were about to shatter the witness in the eyes of the jury on account of his general ignorance and lack of knowledge of his trade). "Where does it come from, then?"

A. (With a slight leer). "Why from whitefish, of course!"

[1] "Curiosities of Law and Lawyers."

In another recent case an Italian contractor was suing to recover for building a masonry wall for a garage which he alleged was in all respects built in a good workmanlike manner. The claim of the defense was that the wall was poorly built and not in accord with proper masonry standards. In support of this defense the cross-examiner was trying to show that the plaintiff's employees, Italian masons, were an inferior grade of workmen and knew little of the jobs required of them.

Q. "Was Domenico a good mason?"

A. "Oh, yes, verra fina mason."

Q. "And Giuseppi, was he a good mason?"

A. "Even better."

Q. "How about Giovanni?"

A. "Best of the three."

Q. (Slurringly). "I suppose then that you claim *all* masons are good masons?"

A. "No—no—justa lika lawyers—soma good—soma rotten."

J. W. Donovan, the author of "Modern Jury Trials," quotes the Brooklyn Eagle's account of a trial conducted by Charles Spencer against the late Edwin James as opposing counsel, involving a soldier's claim for $1,800, money loaned to a friend after the Civil War.

Defendant's counsel, Mr. James, cross-examining the plaintiff:—

Q. "You loaned him $1,800?"

A. "I did, sir."

Q. "When, sir?"

A. "In 1866."

Q. "Where did you get it?"

A. "I earned it, sir." (meekly).

Q. "When did you earn it?"

A. "During the war, sir." (meekly).

Q. "What was your occupation during the war?"

A. (modestly). "Fighting, sir."

Up to this time the issue had been much in doubt, but

now the jury plainly leaned to the side of the soldier. Col. Spencer, sensing this, closed the evidence as quickly as possible and summed up to the jury about the soldier, "who guarded our liberties, helped to save our nation, risked his life," etc., and won the verdict.

Commenting upon the case the same day, Mr. James said to Col. Spencer, "That war speech of yours did it, and it was all the fault of my cross-examination. Otherwise, you would have known nothing about his war record." "Ah," said Spencer, "the mistake that you made was that you didn't find out that my client was a *Confederate* soldier, or you could have changed the whole verdict yourself."

Oftentimes the main point in a litigation depends upon the correct version given of a conversation where only two persons are present, usually the opposing parties themselves. In a case of that kind the direct testimony of either is often of such a character that there is no hope of obtaining a contradiction out of the mouth of the witness himself. Here, the skilful cross-examiner would ignore the testimony given by the witness in chief and confine his efforts almost exclusively to destroying the witness, if possible, by attacking his integrity in connection with entirely collateral matters.

There is no one at the Eastern Bar who employs this method as frequently, or with greater skill, than Max D. Steuer. Something along this line of examination crops out in nearly every case he tries, but it would be difficult to find a more striking illustration of the complete annihilation of a witness by the above method—*i.e.,* by merely attacking his integrity on matters entirely collateral and which have nothing whatsoever to do with the pending issue,—than in the cross-examination conducted by him in the case of the People *vs.* Frank J. Gardner.

Gardner was indicted for attempted bribery. It was charged in the indictment that while on a train *en route* from Albany to New York, Gardner had offered to Hugo Foelker $3,000, in order to induce Foelker, who was then

Senator of the State of New York, to vote against an anti-racing bill then pending in the Legislature.

Senator Foelker appeared as the chief witness for the prosecution. He testified in brief that on a certain day when he and Gardner were riding on the same train from Albany to New York, Gardner, who knew Foelker because they had both been members of the Senate, came over to where Foelker was sitting with his secretary, and asked Foelker to step into his private drawing room, which Foelker did. Gardner closed the door, leaving the two absolutely alone; whereupon Gardner explained to Foelker that he had been put in charge of a fund for the purpose of "rounding up the boys," in order to get a sufficient number of votes to defeat the bill which Governor Hughes was urging for passage.

The witness testified that Gardner told him about a number of the members of the Senate who had accepted various sums, and that they had enough votes already to beat the bill, but that he, Gardner, was anxious to take care of some of the Brooklyn boys, and that Foelker might as well get in with them. Gardner then and there offered Foelker $3,000, which the witness had, of course, spurned.

Foelker had subsequently become ill, and had to undergo an operation, but nevertheless, on the day when the bill came up for vote, Foelker was carried into the Senate Chamber and there cast the vote which passed the bill. By this vote Foelker became quite a hero in political circles and in the ensuing autumn was elected to Congress and was a member of Congress at the time he gave the testimony referred to.

The trial aroused interest largely because of a well organized effort on the part of the prosecution to destroy Mayor Gaynor, then Mayor of New York City. The testimony was aimed principally against Charles H. Hyde, the City Chamberlain under the Gaynor administration, the claim being that Hyde himself had collected and supplied the funds used for the purpose of bribing a large number of the members of the Legislature.

Senator Foelker had recited the circumstances surrounding the alleged attempted bribery in a most graphic manner. There was no way of attacking his story. He very carefully placed himself alone with Gardner where no one else could hear the conversation, and he could be contradicted by no one but the defendant himself. And, as he had himself become quite famous in consequence of his deciding vote, and had since been elected to Congress and had even received public commendation from Governor Hughes, who had pronounced him the best and most worthy legislator that New York had had in many decades, he naturally assumed that his word would be believed as against the witness under indictment. This was particularly likely in view of the fact that the District Attorney had assured the Court that other Senators would be called to testify to offers made to them by the same defendant, and offered to prove that Gardner had hired a suite of rooms in Albany during the pendency of the bill, though his only business there was lobbying with relation to this bill.

The details of the cross-examination which followed would best be given in Mr. Steuer's own language.

"I first traced Foelker's life up to the time that he was testifying—of course, in a skeleton sort of way. He was born in Germany, came to this country when he was about fourteen, had reached the 'gymnasium,' and was very proficient in German. His parents settled in Brooklyn, and he always resided in Brooklyn. He always voted in Brooklyn. He was admitted to the Bar in the Second Department. He had obtained his education by attending night school. He never attended any university. To make himself eligible for admission to the Bar he had to pass the Regents' examinations. It was the knowledge that he acquired by attending at night school that enabled him to pass the Regents' examinations.

"He obtained the required points and was successful in the examination. The only language that he ever studied outside of English was German. Being proficient in German, he had found the examination in German very simple. He was sure that he took an examination in

German at the time that he passed his Regents' examinations. He could not remember where he took his Regents' examinations, he did not know what kind of a building it was, or where it was located, what floor of the building it was on. He could not remember the names of the examiners, nor, so far as he could recall, was there any one in the room with whom he had any acquaintance. He could not remember whether he took his Regents' examinations in Manhattan or in Brooklyn. He did not remember by what means it was that his Regents' certificate was delivered to him. He knew no other person by the same name as his—in fact, he had never heard of any person of that name.

"When informed, by means of questions, that his examination papers had disappeared from the place where they should be on file in Albany, he knew no reason for their disappearance, and was certain that he could not account for it in any way. He certainly had had nothing to do with their disappearance. He was sure that he had taken the examinations himself and had not engaged somebody else to pass them for him. He did not remember whether or not he signed a receipt for his Regents' certificate when it was delivered. On being shown the receipt that was on file for that certificate, he said that the letters which spelled the name 'Hugo Foelker' were not written by him. The address to which the certificate was delivered was at 215 Henry Street, in the Borough of Manhattan. He never had lived there, and he could assign no reason why his certificate should have been delivered at that address. He had no recollection of ever having authorized anybody to receipt for his certificate. He could not remember exactly what subjects he had passed his examinations in, but he supposed that it was English and German and arithmetic, reading, writing and spelling. He was sure that he never took a French examination. He never had studied French, or learned to read French or to translate French, or to speak French. When shown the card on file with the Board of Regents, indicating that 'Hugo Foelker' had passed his French examination with 100%, he could not account for it. When shown the French examination paper of that period, he admitted that he could not have answered a single question on that paper. He passed an examination in logarithms and advanced algebra with upwards of 95%. He admitted he had never studied logarithms nor advanced algebra. He could not explain how it was that the Board of Regents made such a terrible mistake as to give him these high percentages in subjects in which he did not pass an examination.

"Investigation made of Foelker's past had developed the following facts: Foelker had employed a young student, a very poor boy, who lived at 215 Henry Street, who attended the College of the City of New York, and was the best student in his class at that period. The only days upon which this boy was absent from the City College during that year were the days upon which 'Hugo Foelker' attended the Regents' examinations. The receipt for the Regents' certificate was signed 'Hugo Foelker' in the handwriting of this boy. At the very time when Foelker was testifying, this boy was an inmate of the Tombs, and had been brought to Court on a subpoena. He had pleaded guilty in the Court of Special Sessions to having passed Civil Service examinations for and on behalf of other persons, and when Foelker was asked whether he knew this boy he testified that he did not recall, but when the boy was asked to stand up, then his recollection improved, and he recognized the boy. Then everything came back to him about 215 Henry Street that he had theretofore forgotten, and he recalled that he had engaged this boy to give him instruction to enable him to pass his Regents' examinations, and that during that period he had actually resided for several days with that boy, and that was how it came about that the Regents' certificate was delivered at that boy's address. He could not account for the fact that, although all the examination papers for admission to the Bar of every applicant who was examined at the same time when Hugo Foelker was examined were still in Albany in their proper place, the examination papers of Hugo Foelker were not there. Even though he had taken lessons from this boy at 215 Henry Street, he still admitted that he had never learned French nor logarithms, although he was not so certain about advanced algebra. He could not tell anything that advanced algebra dealt with, nor had he any idea whether logarithms were part of the science of mathematics or whether they dealt with minerals.

"He admitted that he received $2,500 from a man who had a bill pending in the Legislature providing for the sprinkling of streets, and that he, Foelker, had voted in favor of the bill, in which this man was very much interested, and the man actually later received the contract for the sprinkling of the streets. Foelker's explanation of the receipt of that check was that the man sent it to him as a campaign contribution. It was of course true that the man did not live in Brooklyn, where Foelker was a candidate, nor could he distinctly remember that he had ever met the man, but he accepted campaign contributions, no matter from whom they came, without inquiry, because that was the custom among members of the Legislature. It was the fact that he had a bank balance at one time of upwards of $20,000, and that was just about the period when the racing bill was pending. He could not tell from what clients he had received that money, but he was positive that he had earned it in his practice, although he could not recall that he had tried a single case or that there was any transaction in which he was retained in which any fee was paid in excess of $250.

"When Foelker left the witness stand he was completely destroyed so far as his testimony was concerned, and during much of the time when he was under cross-examination the jury laughed at many of his answers. His discomfiture was so great that although it was cold without, he perspired so much that I personally loaned him two handkerchiefs during the time when he was on the witness stand.

"Although a member of Congress at the time when he was testifying, and less than one half of his term had been served, Foelker left the courtroom at the conclusion of his cross-examination, and has never been seen or heard from since. During the whole of his cross-examination he was asked nothing about the conversation on the train. As a matter of fact, I do not believe that the jury recalled that there was any conversation on the train. Gardner was acquitted after the jury had been out less than twenty minutes."

Henry E. Lazarus, a prominent merchant in this city, was indicted a few years ago by the Federal Grand Jury, charged with the offense of bribing a United States officer and violation of the Sabotage Act, but was honorably acquitted by a jury after a thirty minute deliberation. It was during the height of the war and Mr. Lazarus was a very large manufacturer of rubber coats and had manufactured hundreds of thousands for the Government under contract. The Government for its protection employed large numbers of inspectors, and in the heat and excitement of war times these inspectors occasionally tried to "make good." One of these efforts resulted in the indictment of Lazarus.

The chief witness against Lazarus was Charles L. Fuller, Supervising Inspector attached to the Depot Quartermaster's Office in New York City. Fuller testified that Lazarus gave money to him to influence him in regard to his general duties as an inspector, and to overlook the fact that Lazarus was manufacturing defective coats and thereby violating the Sabotage Act.

Martin W. Littleton acted as chief counsel for the defense and was fully appreciative of Mr. Lazarus's high character and of his conscientious discharge of his duties in the manufacture of material for the Government. He was also well informed as to the general character and history of Fuller. After Fuller testified in chief, he was first questioned closely as to the time when he became an employe of the Government, counsel knowing that he was *required to make and sign and swear to an application as to his prior experience.*

A messenger had been sent to the Government files to get the original of this application, signed by the witness, and came into court with the document in his hand just as counsel was putting the following question:

Q. "Did you sign such an application?"

A. "I did, sir."

Q. "Did you swear to it?"

A. "No, I did not swear to it."

Q. "I show you your name signed on the bottom of this blank, and ask you if you signed that?"

A. "Yes, sir."

Q. "Do you see it is sworn to?"

A. "I had forgotten it."

Q. "You see there is a seal on it?"

A. "I had forgotten that also."

Q. "This application appears to be subscribed on the 24th of May, 1918, by Charles Lawrence Fuller."

A. "It must be right if I have sworn to it on that date."

Q. "Do you remember in May, 1918, that you signed and swore to this application?"

A. "That is so, I must have sworn to it, sir."

Q. "Do you remember it?"

A. "Let me look at it and I can probably refresh my memory."

(Paper handed to witness)

Q. "Look at the signature. Does that help you?"

A. "That is my signature."

Q. "You said that. Do you remember in May, 1918, you signed and swore to this?"

A. "Well, the date is there."

Q. "Do you know that?"

A. "Yes, sir, I must have sworn to it. I don't remember the date."

Q. "Don't you remember you signed your name, Charles Lawrence Fuller, there?"

A. "I did, sir."

Q. "And you swore to this paper and signed it?"

A. "That date is correct there, yes, sir."

Q. "Don't you remember you swore to it the date you signed it?"

A. "I swore to it."

Q. "Was your name Fuller?"

A. "Yes, sir."

Q. "Has your name always been Fuller?"

A. "No, sir."

Q. "What was your name?"

The witness protested against any further inquiry along that line, but counsel was permitted to show that his name at one time was Finkler and that he changed his name, back and forth, from Finkler to Fuller.

Counsel then proceeded to bring the witness down to the actual oath he had taken in his application.

Q. "Now, Mr. Fuller, in your application you made to the Government, on which I showed you your signature and affidavit, you attached your picture, did you not?"

A. "Yes, sir."

Q. "And you stated in your application you were born in Atlanta, Georgia, did you not?"

A. "Yes, sir."

Q. "You were asked, when you sought this position, these questions: 'When employed, the years and the months,' and you wrote in, 'February, 1897 to August, 1917, number of years 20; Where employed—Brooklyn; Name of employer—Vulcan Proofing Company; Amount of salary,—$37.50 a week; also superintendent in the rubber and compound room.'

Q. "You wrote that, didn't you?"

A. "Yes, sir."

Q. "And swore to that, didn't you?"

A. "Yes, sir."

Q. "Now, were you employed from February, 1897, to August, 1917, twenty years, with the Vulcan Proofing Company?"

A. "No, sir."

Q. "That was not true, was it?"

A. "No, sir."

Q. "And had you been assistant superintendent of the rubber and compound room?"

A. "No, sir."

Q. "That was false, wasn't it?"

A. "Yes, sir."

Q. " 'And through my experience as chief inspector of the rubber and slicker division,' that was false, wasn't it?"

A. "Yes, sir."

Q. "You knew it was false, didn't you?"

A. "Yes, sir."

Q. "And you knew you were swearing to a falsehood when you swore to it?"

A. "Yes, sir."

Q. "And you swore to it intentionally?"

A. "Yes, sir."

Q. "And you knew you were committing perjury when you swore to it?"

A. "I did not look at it in that light."

Q. "Didn't you know you were committing perjury by swearing and pretending you had been twenty years in this business?"

A. "Yes, sir."

Q. "And you are swearing now, aren't you?"

A. "Yes, sir."

Q. "In a matter in which a man's liberty is involved?"

A. "Yes, sir."

Q. "And you know that the jury is to be called upon to consider whether you are worthy of belief or not, don't you?"

A. "Yes, sir."

Q. "When you swore to this falsehood deliberately, and wrote it in your handwriting, you knew it was false, you swore to it intentionally, and you knew that you were committing perjury, didn't you?"

A. "I did not look at it in that light."

Q. "Well, now, when you know you are possibly swearing away the liberty of a citizen of this community, do you look at it in the same light?"

A. "Yes, sir, I do."

Mr. Littleton then uncovered the fact that the witness, instead of having been twenty years superintendent of a rubber room with the Vulcan Proofing Company, as he had sworn in his own handwriting, was a stag entertainer in questionable houses, was a barker at a Coney Island show, was an advance agent of a cheap road show and had been published in the paper as having drawn checks that were worthless, the witness fully admitting all of the details of his twenty years of questionable transactions. The result was his utter collapse so far as his credibility was concerned, and the Government's case collapsed with him.

The point of the cross-examination and the design of the cross-examiner was to get the witness at the outset of his cross-examination in a position from which he could not possibly extricate himself, by confronting him with this document, written in his own handwriting in which he would be obliged to admit that he had sworn falsely. The witness having been thoroughly subjugated by this process would then, as he actually did, confess to twenty years of gadding about in questionable employment, under different names, and thus completely destroy himself as a reliable witness in the eyes of the jury.

To an absurd liar who burst out in a witness box, "My lord, you may believe me or not, but I have stated not a word that is false, for I have been wedded to truth from infancy." "Very likely," replied Mr. Justice Maule, who probably was the greatest wit on the English bench, "but the question is how long you have been a *widower!*"

This same judge, while examining a little girl who was about to give testimony as a witness, in order to determine whether or not she understood the nature of an oath before allowing her to be sworn, said:

Q. "Do you know what an oath is, my child?"

A. "Yes, sir; I am obliged to tell the truth."

Q. "And if you do always tell the truth, where will you go to when you die?"

A. "Up to Heaven, sir."

Q. "And what will become of you if you tell lies?"

A. "I shall go down to the naughty place, sir."

Q. "Are you quite *sure* of that?"

A. "Yes, sir; quite sure."

"Let her be sworn," said Justice Maule, "it is quite clear she knows a great deal more than I do." [1]

It may not be uninteresting to record in this connection one or two cases illustrative of matter that is valuable in cross-examination in personal damage suits where my sole object was to reduce the amount of the jury's verdict, and to puncture the pitiful tale of suffering told by the plaintiff in such cases.

A New York commission merchant, named Metts, sixty-six years of age, was riding in a Columbus Avenue open car. As the car neared the curve at Fifty-third Street and Seventh Avenue, and while he was in the act of closing an open window in the front of the car at the request of an old lady passenger, the car gave a sudden, violent lurch, and he was thrown into the street, receiving injuries from which, at the time of the trial, he had suffered for three years.

Counsel for the plaintiff went into his client's sufferings in great detail. Plaintiff had had concussion of the brain, loss of memory, bladder difficulties, a broken leg, nervous prostration, constant pain in his back. And the attempt to alleviate the pain attendant upon all these difficulties was gone into with great detail. To cap all, the attending physician had testified that the reasonable value of his professional services was the modest sum of $2,500.

Before beginning my cross-examination I had made a critical examination of the doctor's face and bearing in the witness chair, and had concluded that, if pleasantly handled, he could be made to testify pretty nearly to the truth, whatever it might me. I concluded to spar for an opening, and it came within the first half dozen questions:—

Counsel. "What medical name, doctor, would you give to the plaintiff's present ailment?"

Doctor. "He has what is known as 'traumatic neurosis.' "

Counsel. "*Neurosis,* doctor? That means, does it not,

[1] "What the Judge Thought," Barry.

the habit, or disease as you may call it, of making much of ailments that an ordinary healthy man would pass by as of no account?"

Doctor. "That is right, sir."

Counsel (smiling). "I hope you haven't got this disease, doctor, have you?"

Doctor. "Not that I am aware of, sir."

Counsel. "Then we ought to be able to get a very fair statement from you of this man's troubles, ought we not?"

Doctor. "I hope so, sir."

The opening had been found; witness was already flattered into agreeing with all suggestions, and warned against exaggeration.

Counsel. "Let us take up the bladder trouble first. Do not practically all men who have reached the age of sixty-six have troubles of one kind or another that result in more or less irritation of the bladder?"

Doctor. "Yes, that is very common with old men."

Counsel. "You said Mr. Metts was deaf in one ear. I noticed that he seemed to hear the questions asked him in court particularly well; did you notice it?"

Doctor. "I did."

Counsel. "At the age of sixty-six are not the majority of men gradually failing in their hearing?"

Doctor. "Yes, sir, frequently."

Counsel. "Frankly, doctor, don't you think this man hears remarkably well for his age, leaving out the deaf ear altogether?"

Doctor. "I think he does."

Counsel (keeping the ball rolling). "I don't think you have even the first symptoms of this 'traumatic neurosis,' doctor."

Doctor (pleased). "I haven't got it at all."

Counsel. "You said Mr. Metts had had concussion of the brain. Has not every boy who has fallen over backward, when skating on the ice, and struck his head, also had what you physicians would call 'concussion of the brain'?"

Doctor. "Yes, sir."

Counsel. "But I understood you to say that this plaintiff had had, in addition, hæmorrhages of the brain. Do you mean to tell us that he could have had hæmorrhages of the brain and be alive to-day?"

Doctor. "They were microscopic hæmorrhages."

Counsel. "That is to say, one would have to take a microscope to find them?"

Doctor. "That is right."

Counsel. "You do not mean us to understand, doctor, that you have not cured him of these microscopic hæmorrhages?"

Doctor. "I have cured him; that is right."

Counsel. "You certainly were competent to set his broken leg or you wouldn't have attempted it; did you get a good union?"

Doctor. "Yes, he has got a good, strong, healthy leg."

Counsel having elicited, by the "smiling method," all the required admissions, suddenly changed his whole bearing toward the witness, and continued pointedly:—

Counsel. "And you said that $2,500 would be a fair and reasonable charge for your services. It is three years since Mr. Metts was injured. Have you sent him no bill?"

Doctor. "Yes, sir, I have."

Counsel. "Let me see it. (Turning to plaintiff's counsel.) Will either of you let me have the bill?"

Doctor. "I haven't it, sir."

Counsel (astonished). "What was the amount of it?"

Doctor. "One thousand dollars."

Counsel (savagely). "Why do you charge the railroad company two and a half times as much as you charge the patient himself?"

Doctor (embarrassed at this sudden change on part of counsel). "You asked me what my services were worth."

Counsel. "Didn't you charge your patient the full worth of your services?"

Doctor (no answer).

Counsel (quickly). "How much have you been *paid* on your bill—on your oath?"

Doctor. "He paid me $100 at one time, that is, two years ago; and at two different times since he has paid me $30."

Counsel. "And he is a rich commission merchant down town!" (And with something between a sneer and a laugh counsel sat down.)

Another amusing incident, leading to the exposure of a manifest fraud, occurred in another of the many damage suits brought against the Metropolitan Street Railway and growing out of a collision between two of the company's electric cars.

The plaintiff, a laboring man, had been thrown to the street pavement from the platform of the car by the force of the collision, and had dislocated his shoulder. He had testified in his own behalf that he had been permanently injured in so far as he had not been able to follow his usual employment for the reason that he could not raise his arm above a point parallel with his shoulder. Upon cross-examination, while acting for the railroad, I asked the witness a few sympathetic questions about his sufferings, and upon getting on a friendly basis with him suggested that he be good enough to show the jury the extreme limit to which he could raise his arm since the accident. The plaintiff slowly and with considerable difficulty raised his arm to the parallel of his shoulder. "Now, using the same arm, show the jury how high you could get it up before the accident," was the next quiet suggestion; whereupon the witness extended his arm to its full height above his head, amid peals of laughter from the court and jury.

In a case of murder, to which the defence of insanity was set up, a medical witness called on behalf of the accused swore that in his opinion the accused, at the time he killed the deceased, was affected with a homicidal mania, and urged to the act by an *irresistible* impulse. The judge, not satisfied with this, first put the witness some questions on other subjects, and then asked, "Do you think the accused would have acted as he did if a police-man had been present?" to which the witness at once answered in the negative. Thereupon the judge remarked, "Your definition of an irresistible impulse must then be an impulse irresistible at all times except when a policeman is present."

Chapter 4

Cross-Examination of the Perjured Witness

IN THE preceding chapters it was attempted to offer a few suggestions, gathered from experience, for the proper handling of an honest witness who, through ignorance or partisanship, and more or less unintentionally, had testified to a mistaken state of facts injurious to our side of the litigation. In the present chapter it is proposed to discuss the far more difficult task of exposing, by the arts of cross-examination, the intentional fraud, the perjured witness. Here it is that the greatest ingenuity of the trial lawyer is called into play; here rules help but little as compared with years of actual experience. What can be conceived more difficult in advocacy than the task of proving a witness, whom you may neither have seen nor heard of before he gives his testimony against you, to be a wilful perjurer, as it were out of his own mouth?

It seldom happens that a witness's entire testimony is false from beginning to end. Perhaps the greater part of it is true, and only the crucial part—the point, however, on which the whole case may turn—is wilfully false. If, at the end of his direct testimony, we conclude that the witness we have to cross-examine—to continue the imaginary trial we were conducting in the previous chapter—comes under this class, what means are we to employ to expose him to the jury?

Let us first be certain we are right in our estimate of him—that he intends perjury. Embarrassment is one of the emblems of perjury, but by no means always so. The novelty and difficulty of the situation—being called upon to testify before a room full of people, with lawyers on all sides ready to ridicule or abuse, often occasion embarrassment in witnesses of the highest integrity. Then again some people are constitutionally nervous and could be nothing else when testifying in open court. Let us be sure our witness is not of this type before we subject him to the particular form of torture we have in store for the perjurer.

Witnesses of a low grade of intelligence, when they testify falsely, usually display it in various ways: in the voice, in a certain vacant expression of the eyes, in a nervous twisting about in the witness chair, in an apparent effort to recall to mind the exact wording of their story, and especially in the use of language not suited to their station in life. On the other hand, there is something about the manner of an honest but ignorant witness that makes it at once manifest to an experienced lawyer that he is narrating only the things that he has actually seen and heard. The expression of the face changes with the narrative as he recalls the scene to his mind; he looks the examiner full in the face; his eye brightens as he recalls to mind the various incidents; he uses gestures natural to a man in his station of life, and suits them to the part of the story he is narrating, and he tells his tale in his own accustomed language.

If, however, the manner of the witness and the wording of his testimony bear all the earmarks of fabrication, it is often useful, as your first question, to ask him to repeat his story. Usually he will repeat it in amost identically the same words as before, showing he has learned it by heart. Of course it is possible, though not probable, that he has done this and still is telling the truth. Try him by taking him to the midde of his story, and from there jump him quickly to the beginning and then to the end of it. If he is speaking by rote rather than from recollection, he will be sure to succumb to this method. He has no facts with which to associate the wording of his story; he can only call it to mind as a whole, and not in detachments. Draw his attention to other facts entirely disassociated with the main story as told by himself. He will be entirely unprepared for these new inquiries, and will draw upon his imagination for answers. Distract his thoughts again to some new part of his main story and then suddenly, when his mind is upon another subject, return to those matters to which you had first called his attention, and ask him the same questions a second time. He will again fall back upon his imagination and very likely will give a different answer from the first—and you have him in the net. He cannot invent answers as fast as you can invent questions, and at the same time remember his previous inventions correctly; he will not keep his answers all consistent with one another. He will soon become confused and, from that time on, will be at your mercy. Let him go as soon as you have made it apparent that he is not mistaken, but is lying.

An amusing account is given in the *Green Bag* for November, 1891, of one of Jeremiah Mason's cross-examinations of such a witness. "The witness had previously testified to having heard Mason's client make a certain statement, and it was upon the evidence of that statement that the adversary's case was based. Mr. Mason led the witness round to his statement, and again it was repeated verbatim. Then, without warning, he walked to the stand, and pointing straight at the witness said, in his high, impassioned voice, 'Let's see that paper you've got in your waistcoat pocket!' Taken completely by surprise, the witness mechanically drew a paper from the pocket indicated, and handed it to Mr. Mason. The lawyer slowly read the exact words of the witness in regard to the statement, and called attention to the fact that they were in the handwriting of the lawyer on the other side.

" 'Mr. Mason, how under the sun did you know that paper was there?' asked a brother lawyer. 'Well,' replied Mr. Mason, 'I thought he gave that part of his testimony just as if he'd heard it, and I noticed every time he repeated it he put his hand to his waistcoat pocket, and then let it fall again when he got through.' "

Daniel Webster considered Mason the greatest lawyer that ever practised at the New England Bar. He said of him, "I would rather, after my own experience, meet all the lawyers I have ever known combined in a case, than meet him alone and single-handed." Mason was always reputed to have possessed to a marked degree "the instinct for the weak point" in the witness he was cross-examining.

In a recent celebrated criminal case, known as the Triangle fire case, two proprietors of a ladies' shirtwaist factory were indicted on a charge of manslaughter. One hundred and seventy-five girls had lost their lives, because a door of a loft in the factory was kept locked during working hours, in violation of the Factory Law, it was charged. Max D. Steuer, while conducting the defense, developed a most striking illustration of the value, when the proper occasion arises, of compelling a witness to repeat on cross-examination every detail of the story given on direct. This is especially so where the story had been extremely helpful to the side for which it was given, and even calculated to create something of a sensation, but where a constant repetition of the story is apt to disclose evidences of a carefully prepared recital, rather than a spontaneous recollection of actual occurrences.

It was an essential part of the People's case to prove that the girl, Rose Schwartz, mentioned in the indictment, was in fact the same person who lost her life in the fire. One hundred witnesses had been sworn on behalf of the People, many weeks had been consumed in hearing the testimony, and not a word had been said about Rose Schwartz, named in the indictment, excepting that her name had been casually mentioned as on the list of employees.

The testimony, on the contrary, had all been to the effect that the bodies that had been discovered in the building were so charred that identification was impossible. At the very close of the People's case the court door was suddenly opened and one of the court attendants appeared with a very good looking young woman, who immediately attracted the attention of the jury on her way to the witness stand. The District Attorney became very solemn; a hushed air of expectancy was created in the court room;

the Judge himself proceeded to swear the witness, although all the other witnesses had been sworn in the ordinary way by the clerk of the court.

Having testified to many preliminary details,—such as that the witness had been employed at the factory and was there when the fire broke out and that she knew Rose Schwartz,—she was asked the question: "Now tell everything that you saw and did on the ninth floor of those premises from the time that the fire broke out." The witness then began to describe her first sight of the flames; how the girls scattered from one floor and ran to another; how many of them ran to the windows and began to jump out; how she herself had decided to follow their example. When she was at the window about ready to jump, she glanced around the room in a desperate effort to escape, and looking at the Washington Street door that was supposed to have been locked, she saw Rose Schwartz with both hands on the knob of the door desperately turning the knob in an attempt to open the door, both by pulling and pushing, but the door would not give. She stayed there transfixed, watching Rose, and saw the flames envelop her hands, saw her fall to the floor and then saw her once more struggle to her feet, again grab the knob of the door and turn it one way and then another, pull and then push, but the door would not give. Once more the flames enveloped Rose and again she had to withdraw her hands from the door knob and she fell to the floor; the flames were now coming very close to the witness; she turned once more toward the Washington Street door and there, for the third time, was Rose Schwartz, on her knees, screaming and praying, with both hands on the door knob, turning it first one way, then the other, and pulling and pushing, but the door would not give, and finally she was completely enveloped by the flames, and fell to the floor within a foot of the Washington Street door. There was not a dry eye in the jury box when she closed her testimony.

The first half hour of the cross-examination was confined to preliminaries, during which the witness told how she was rescued, first taken to a hospital and then home, how she had been brought to the District Attorney's office and had many interviews there with various assistants; how finally she had been moved to Philadelphia at the direction of the District Attorney so that she should be beyond the approach of the defendants, and was housed there at the expense of the People; how she was visited there a number of times by representatives of the District Attorney, etc., etc. At the end of the half hour she was asked: "Now, you remember just where you were seated at the time when you first saw the sign of a fire?" She answered "Yes." And then, in the exact words in which the District Attorney had put his question, the question was repeated to her, asking her to state all she did herself and all that she saw done on the ninth floor from that moment on. She began her narrative with exactly the same word that she had used when telling her story the first time, and continued in precisely the same words that she had used to the District Attorney in answering that question.

Thereupon the subject was once more changed, and nearly a half hour was used in examination upon various matters relating to the fire. At the end of this second half hour the question was for the third time put, and the witness started with the same word and continued to narrate the story in precisely the same words that she had used before, except that she omitted one word. She was asked whether it was not the fact that she had omitted a word, naming the word. Her lips began to move and start the narrative to herself all over again, and when she reached the position where that word belonged she said; "Yes, I made a mistake; I left that word out." *Q.* "But otherwise your answer was correct?" She again began to move her lips, obviously reciting to herself what she had previously said, and then said, "Yes, otherwise my answer is correct."

When the question was put to her for the third time the District Attorney vigorously objected, but was overruled. Another period of twenty minutes or more was used in examining her with relation to other matters, and then for the fourth time the question was put to her: "Will you please tell the jury what you saw and what you did after you first observed any sign of the flames?" She started with the same word, and continued her narrative, but again left out one word, this time a different word. Asked whether she had not now omitted a word, naming it, she went through the same lip performance and replied that she had, and upon being asked to place the word where it belonged, she proceeded to do so.

There was no further examination of that witness. There were no more tears in the jury box. The situation had entirely changed. The witness had not hurt, but had very materially helped, the defense; she had succeeded in casting grave suspicion on the testimony of many of the girls who had previously testified; her carefully prepared story had aroused the suspicion of the jury regarding the entire case of the prosecution.

If perjured testimony in our courts were confined to the ignorant classes, the work of cross-examining them would be a comparatively simple matter, but unfortunately for the cause of truth and justice this is far from the case. Perjury is decidedly on the increase, and at the present time in our local courts scarcely a trial is conducted in which it does not appear in a more or less flagrant form. Nothing in the trial of a cause is so difficult as to expose the perjury of a witness whose intelligence assists him to hide his lack of scruple. There are various methods of attempting it, but no uniform rule can be laid down as to the proper manner to be employed toward such a witness. It all depends upon the individual character you have to unmask. In a large majority of cases the chance of success will be greatly increased by not allowing the witness to see that you suspect him, before you have led him to commit himself as to various matters with which you have reason to believe you can confront him later on.

Two famous cross-examiners at the Irish Bar were Sergeant Sullivan, afterwards Master of the Rolls in Ireland, and Sergeant Armstrong. Barry O'Brien, in his "Life of Lord Russell," describes their methods. "Sullivan," he says, "approached the witness quite in a friendly way, seemed to be an impartial inquirer seeking information, looked surprised at what the witness said, appeared even grateful for the additional light thrown on the case. 'Ah, indeed! Well, as you have said so much, perhaps you can help us a little further. Well, really, my Lord, this is a very intelligent man.' So, playing the witness with caution and skill, drawing him stealthily on, keeping him completely in the dark about the real point of attack, the 'little sergeant' waited until the man was in the meshes, and then flew at him and shook him as a terrier would a rat.

"The 'big Sergeant' (Armstrong) had more humor and more power, but less dexterity and resource. His great weapon was ridicule. He laughed at the witness and made everybody else laugh. The witness got confused and lost his temper, and then Armstrong pounded him like a champion in the ring."

In some cases it is wise to confine yourself to one or two salient points on which you feel confident you can get the witness to contradict himself out of his own mouth. It is seldom useful to press him on matters with which he is familiar. It is the safer course to question him on circumstances connected with his story, but to which he has not already testified and for which he would not be likely to prepare himself.

A simple but perhaps instructive example of cross-examination, conducted along these lines, is quoted from Judge J. W. Donovan's "Tact in Court." It is mainly interesting in that it is reported to have occurred in Abraham Lincoln's first defence at a murder trial.

"Grayson was charged with shooting Lockwood at a camp-meeting, on the evening of August 9, 18—, and with running away from the scene of the killing, which was witnessed by Sovine. The proof was so strong that, even with an excellent previous character, Grayson came very near being lynched on two occasions soon after his indictment for murder.

"The mother of the accused, after failing to secure older counsel, finally engaged young Abraham Lincoln, as he was then called, and the trial came on to an early hearing. No objection was made to the jury, and no cross-examination of witnesses, save the last and only important one, who swore that he knew the parties, saw the shot fired by Grayson, saw him run away, and picked up the deceased, who died instantly.

"The evidence of guilt and identity was morally certain. The attendence was large, the interest intense. Grayson's mother began to wonder why 'Abraham remained silent so long and why he didn't do something!' The people finally rested. The tall lawyer (Lincoln) stood up and eyed the strong witness in silence, without books or notes, and slowly began his defence by these questions:

"Lincoln. 'And you were with Lockwood just before and saw the shooting?"'

"Witness. 'Yes.'

"Lincoln. 'And you stood very near to them?'

"Witness. 'No, about twenty feet away.'

"Lincoln. 'May it not have been *ten* feet?'

"Witness. 'No, it was twenty feet *or more.*'

"Lincoln. 'In the open field?'

"Witness. 'No, in the timber.'

"Lincoln. 'What kind of timber?'

"Witness. 'Beech timber.'

"Lincoln. 'Leaves on it are rather thick in August?'

"Witness. 'Rather.'

"Lincoln. 'And you think *this* pistol was the one used?'

"Witness. 'It looks like it.'

"Lincoln. 'You could see defendant shoot—see how the barrel hung, and all about it?'

"Witness. 'Yes.'

"Lincoln. 'How near was this to the meeting place?'

"Witness. 'Three-quarters of a mile away.'

"Lincoln. 'Where were the lights?'

"Witness. 'Up by the minister's stand.'

"Lincoln. 'Three-quarters of a mile away?'

"Witness. 'Yes,—I answered ye *twiste.'*

"Lincoln. 'Did you not see a candle there, with Lockwood or Grayson?'

"Witness. 'No! what would we want a candle for?'

"Lincoln. 'How, then, did you see the shooting?'

"Witness. 'By moonlight!' (defiantly).

"Lincoln. 'You saw this shooting at ten at night—in beech timber, three-quarters of a mile from the light— saw the pistol barrel—saw the man fire—saw it twenty feet away—saw it all by moonlight? Saw it nearly a mile from the camp lights?'

"Witness. 'Yes, I told you so before.'

"The interest was now so intense that men leaned forward to catch the smallest syllable. Then the lawyer drew out a blue covered almanac from his side coat pocket— —opened it slowly—offered it in evidence—showed it to the jury and the court—read from a page with careful deliberation that the moon on that night was unseen and only arose at *one* the next morning.

"Following this climax Mr. Lincoln moved the arrest of the perjured witness as the real murderer, saying: 'Nothing but *a motive to clear himself* could have induced him to swear away so falsely the life of one who never did him harm!' With such determined emphasis did Lincoln present his showing that the court ordered Sovine arrested, and under the strain of excitement he broke down and confessed to being the one who fired the fatal shot himself, but denied it was intentional."

I have quoted this occurrence verbatim as given by Judge Donovan. It affords a most striking illustration of the "fallacies of testimony." The occasion on which Lincoln acquitted his client of a charge of murder by confronting an eye witness with an almanac to refute the testimony given "by the light of the moon," instead of being the first criminal case tried by "young" Abraham Lincoln, was in reality one of the last and most important criminal cases he ever tried. The defendant's name instead of being Grayson was William Armstrong, who was tried

August 29, 1857, for the killing of one James Metzker, not Lockwood; and it was upon this occasion that Lincoln's talents as a trial lawyer saved the day for his client.

The story of this now famous case has often been recounted, and the distortions wrought by many versions of it, through many mouths and during many years, might well take a prominent place in the discussion of the unreliability of honest testimony, dealt with at some length in a subsequent chapter.

Frederick Trevor Hill, in his "Lincoln the Lawyer," has given a complete retelling of the facts, gathered directly from the records themselves and from the lawyer *who was associated with Lincoln in the trial,* and who was still living in Mason County at the time Mr. Hill wrote his book.

It appears that Lincoln, when working in a New Salem store, had won the respect and admiration of the rough element in that community by flooring one Jack Armstrong, the leader of a gang of boys, in a wrestling match, and the fallen champion instantly became his staunch friend and ally. Armstrong afterwards married, and Lincoln, who knew his wife, could not resist her appeal when she sought him out during the great debate with Douglas and begged him to come to the rescue of her son, who was charged with murder and about to be tried. Lincoln laid aside his pressing political engagements and plunged at once into the trial of the case. Popular indignation against Armstrong had become so violent in Mason County that his lawyers had obtained a change of venue upon the ground that a fair trial could not be had in the local courts. Mr. Hill goes on to say that not only were the facts against Lincoln's client, but the Illinois law of that day did not permit a defendant to testify in his own behalf; and Armstrong had no opportunity to deny the testimony of the accusing witnesses.

As most of the witnesses were young, Lincoln attempted to secure a jury of young men of the average age of not over twenty-five, and succeeded in handling the Government's witnesses, all of about the same age, so skilfully on cross-examination, that their testimony had but little weight against the accused. Almost all of them were from the neighborhood of New Salem, and when Lincoln heard a familiar name, he quickly took advantage of the opening to let the witness know he was familiar with his home, knew his family and wished to be his friend. These tactics succeeded so well that no very damaging testimony was elicited until a man by the name of Allen (not Sovine, as Judge Donovan has it) took the stand.

According to Mr. Hill, this witness swore that he actually saw the defendant strike the fatal blow with a slung shot or some such weapon (not a pistol) and Lincoln, pressing him closely, forced him to locate the hour of the assault as about eleven at night, and then demanded that he inform the jury how he managed to see so clearly at that time of night. "By the moonlight," answered the witness promptly. "Well, was there light enough to see everything that happened?" persisted the examiner. The witness responded that the moon was about in the same place that the sun would be at ten o'clock in the morning and was almost full, and the moment the words were out of his mouth the cross-examiner confronted him with a calendar showing that the moon afforded practically no light at eleven o'clock and had absolutely set at seven minutes after midnight. This was the turning point in the case, and from that moment Lincoln carried everything before him.[1]

The comparison of these two accounts of a very simple and familiar method of cross-examiners serves as a most striking illustration of the "fallibilities of testimony," for the *details* of the Armstrong case have been gossip at the Illinois bar almost to the present day, and the original story as given by Mr. Hill has evidently gradually reached the form in which it is given by Judge Donovan. The *main* feature of the examination was the same—the use of the calendar,—but the names of the defendant, and of

[1] "Lincoln the Lawyer," by Frederick Trevor Hill.

the witness, and all the details of the occurrence both before and after the trial are entirely different. It has even been frequently stated by members of the Illinois bar that Lincoln played a trick on the jury in this case by substituting an old calendar for the one of the year of the murder and virtually manufactured the testimony which carried the day. This rumor has been repeatedly exposed, but I am told it still persists on the Illinois circuit to this day.

In speaking of Lincoln as a cross-examiner, Mr. Hill points out that as there were no court stenographers during the twenty-three years that Lincoln practiced at the bar, it is impossible to secure a verbatim report of the questions and answers in Lincoln's cases illustrative of his methods of handling witnesses, but says that it was conceded by all his contemporaries that, as a cross-examiner, he had no equal at the bar, and "woe betide the unlucky individual who surpressed the truth or colored it." More than one man has described the effect of Lincoln's eyes by saying that they appeared to look directly *through* whatever he concentrated his gaze upon.

Incidentally, as Lincoln's biographers have devoted their attention almost entirely to his political career rather than to his career as a lawyer, it is interesting to note that in his twenty-three years at the bar he had no less than one hundred and seventy-two cases before the highest courts of Illinois, a record said to be unsurpassed by any of his contemporaries, and tried more cases than any other member of his local bar, being the attorney for the Illinois Central Railroad, the greatest corporation in the state at the time, as well as for the Rock Island Railroad, and many other important corporations and individuals.

He was a stickler for legal ethics, adopting the maxim "Better to make a life than a living," and on several occasions where he felt he was wrong, while he did not actually abandon the case, he ceased to coöperate with his associate counsel. "You speak to the jury," he once said to Leonard Swett, his associate counsel, "if I say a word, they will see from my face that the man is guilty and convict him." And Mr. Hill tells of another occasion when, as it developed that Lincoln's client had indulged in fraudulent practices, he walked out of the court room and refused to continue the case. The judge sent a messenger directing him to return, but he positively declined. "Tell the judge that my hands are dirty, and I have gone away to wash them," was his disgusted response.

A difficult but extremely effective method of exposing a certain kind of perjurer is to lead him gradually to a point in his story, where—in his answer to the final question, "Which?"—he will have to choose either one or the other of the only two explanations left to him, either of which would degrade if not entirely discredit him in the eyes of the jury.

The writer once heard the Hon. Joseph H. Choate make very telling use of this method of examination. A stockbroker was being sued by a married woman for the return of certain bonds and securities in the broker's possession, which she alleged belonged to her. Her husband took the witness stand and swore that he had deposited the securities with the stockbroker as collateral against his own market speculations, but that they did not belong to him, and that he was acting for himself and not as agent for his wife, and had taken her securities unknown to her.

It was the contention of Mr. Choate that, even if the bonds belonged to the wife, she had either consented to her husband's use of the bonds, or else was a partner with him in the transaction. Both of these contentions were denied under oath by the husband.

Mr. Choate. "When you ventured into the realm of speculations in Wall Street I presume you contemplated the possibility of the market going against you, did you not?"

Witness. "Well, no, Mr. Choate, I went into Wall Street to make money, not to lose it."

Mr. Choate. "Quite so, sir; but you will admit, will you not, that sometimes the stock market goes contrary to expectations?"

Witness. "Oh, yes, I suppose it does."

Mr. Choate. "You say the bonds were not your own property, but your wife's?"

Witness. "Yes, sir."

Mr. Choate. "And you say that she did not lend them to you for purposes of speculation, or even know you had possession of them?"

Witness. "Yes, sir."

Mr. Choate. "You even admit that when you deposited the bonds with your broker as collateral against your stock speculations, you did not acquaint him with the fact that they were not your own property?"

Witness. "I did not mention whose property they were, sir."

Mr. Choate (in his inimitable style). "Well, sir, in the event of the market going against you and your collateral being sold to meet your losses, *whom did you intend to cheat, your broker or your wife?*"

The witness could give no satisfactory answer, and for once a New York jury was found, willing to give a verdict against the customer and in favor of a Wall Street broker.

In the great majority of cases, however, the most skilful efforts of the cross-examiner will fail to lead the witness into such traps as these. If you have accomplished one such *coup,* be content with the point you have made; do not try to make another with the same witness; sit down and let the witness leave the stand. Remind yourself of Josh Billings' advice: "When you strike 'ile,' stop boring; many a man has bored clean through and let the 'ile' run out of the bottom."

A very prominent lawyer whose testimony, if accepted by the jury, would have ended an important litigation, was entirely discredited by a resourceful, watchful, young Hebrew lawyer (evidently having heard of the witness's desire to conceal the race of his birth), who saw his *chance* and pushed it to a victory with his first few questions.

Q. "Vat is your name, Mister Vitness?"

A. "Mr. Wiles."

Q. "Yes, I know your last name, but vat is your *full* name?"

A. "S. Coleman Wiles."

Q. "Yes, so you said, but vat does the 'S' stand for, Mister Viles?"

A. "I never use it—I am always addressed as 'Coleman Wiles.'

Q. "Vell, you have an 'S' in your name—vat does it stand for?"

A. "I tell you I never use it."

Counsel. "Judge, will you please tell the vitness to answer my question?"

Judge. "Certainly; Mr. Wiles, you will have to answer the question."

Witness. (Doggedly). " 'S' stands for Solomon."

Counsel (In great surprise). "Vy, Mr. Viles, vas you ashamed of the name?"

And no Jew in the jury box had any further use for either the witness or his testimony.

But let us suppose you are examining a witness with whom no such climax is possible. Here you will require infinite patience and industry. Try to show that his story is inconsistent with itself, or with other known facts in the case, or with the ordinary experience of mankind. There is a wonderful power in persistence. If you fail in one quarter, abandon it and try something else. There is surely a weak spot somewhere, if the story is perjured. Frame your questions skilfully. Ask them as if you wanted a certain answer, when in reality you desire just the opposite one. "Hold your own temper while you lead the witness to lose his" is a Golden Rule on all such occasions. If you allow the witness a chance to give his reasons or explanations you may be sure they will be damaging to you, not to him. If you can succeed in tiring out the witness or in driving him to the point of sullenness, you have produced the effect of lying.

However, it is not intended to advocate the practice of lengthy cross-examinations, because their effect, unless the witness is broken down, is to lead the jury to exaggerate the importance of evidence given by a witness who requires so much cross-examination in the attempt to upset him.

During the Tichborne trial for perjury, a remarkable man named Luie was called to testify. He was a shrewd witness and told his tale with wonderful precision and apparent accuracy. That it was untrue there could hardly be a question, but that it could be proved untrue was extremely doubtful and an almost hopeless task. It was an improbable story, but still was not an absolutely impossible one. If true, however, the claimant was the veritable Roger Tichborne, or at least the probabilities would be so immensely in favor of that supposition that no jury would agree in finding that he was Arthur Orton. His manner of giving his evidence was perfect. After the trial one of the jurors was asked what he thought of Luie's evidence, and if he ever attached any importance to his story. He replied that at the close of the evidence-in-chief he thought it so improbable that no credence could be given to it. "But after Mr. Hawkins had been at him for a day and could not shake him, I began to think, if such a cross-examiner as that cannot touch him, there must be something in what he says, and I began to waver. I could not understand how it was that, if it was all lies, it did not break down under such able counsel." [1]

The presiding judge, whose slightest word is weightier than the eloquence of counsel, will often interrupt an aimless and prolonged cross-examination with an abrupt, "Mr.———, I think we are wasting time," or "I shall not allow you to pursue that subject further," or "I cannot see the object of this examination." This is a setback from which only the most experienced advocate can readily recover. Before the judge spoke, the jury, perhaps, were already a little tired and inattentive and anxious to finish the case; they were just in the mood to agree with the remark of his Honor, and the "ATMOSPHERE of the case," as I have always termed it, was fast becoming unfavorable to the delinquent attorney's client. How important a part

[1] "Hints on Advocacy," Harris.

in the final outcome of every trial this atmosphere of the case usually plays! Many jurymen lose sight of the parties to the litigation—our clients—in their absorption over the conflict of wits going on between their respective lawyers.

It is in criminal prosecutions where local politics are involved that the jury system is perhaps put to its severest test. The ordinary juryman is so apt to be blinded by his political prejudices that, where the guilt or innocence of the prisoner at the Bar turns upon the question as to whether the prisoner did or did not perform some act, involving a supposed advantage to his political party, the jury is apt to be divided upon political lines.

Some time ago, when a wave of political reform was sweeping over New York City, the Good Government Clubs caused the arrest of about fifty inspectors of election for violations of the election laws. These men were all brought up for trial in the Supreme Court criminal term, before Mr. Justice Barrett. The prisoners were to be defended by various leading trial lawyers, and everything depended upon the result of the first few cases tried. If these trials resulted in acquittals, it was anticipated that there would be acquittals all along the line; if the first offenders put on trial were convicted and sentenced to severe terms in prison, the great majority of the others would plead guilty, and few would escape. All of these cases were assigned to me to prosecute.

At that time the county of New York was divided, for purposes of voting, into 1067 election districts, and on an average perhaps 250 votes were cast in each district. An inspector of one of the election districts was the first man called for trial. The charge against him was the failure to record correctly the vote cast in his district for the Republican candidate for alderman. In this particular election district there had been 167 ballots cast, and it was the duty of the inspectors to count them and return the result of their count to police headquarters.

At the trial twelve respectable citizens took the witness chair, one after another, and affirmed that they lived in the prisoner's election district, and had all cast their ballots on election day for the Republican candidate. The official count for that district, signed by the prisoner, was then put in evidence, which read: Democratic votes, 167; Republican, 0. There were a number of witnesses called by the defence who were Democrats. The case began to take on a political aspect, which was likely to result in a divided jury and no conviction, since it had been shown that the prisoner had a most excellent reputation and had never been suspected of wrong doing before. Finally the prisoner himself was sworn in his own behalf.

The object of my cross-examination was to leave the witness in such a position before the jury that no matter what their politics might be, they could not avoid convicting him. There were but five questions asked.

Counsel. "You have told us, sir, that you have a wife and seven children depending upon you for support. I presume your desire is not to be obliged to leave them; is it not?"

Prisoner. "Most assuredly, sir."

Counsel. "Apart from that consideration I presume you have no particular desire to spend a term of years in Sing Sing prison?"

Prisoner. "Certainly not, sir."

Counsel. "Well, you have heard twelve respectable citizens take the witness stand and swear they voted the Republican ticket in your district, have you not?"

Prisoner. "Yes, sir."

Counsel (pointing to the jury). "And you see these twelve respectable gentlemen sitting here ready to pass judgment upon the question of your liberty, do you not?"

Prisoner. "I do, sir."

Counsel (impressively, but quietly). "Well, now, Mr. ——, you will please explain to these twelve gentlemen (pointing to jury) how it was that the ballots cast by the other twelve gentlemen were not counted by you, and then you can take your hat and walk right out of the court room a free man."

The witness hesitated, cast down his eyes, but made no answer—and counsel sat down.

Of course a conviction followed. The prisoner was sentenced to five years in state prison. During the following few days nearly thirty defendants, indicted for similar offences, pleaded guilty, and the entire work of the court was completed within a few weeks. There was not a single acquittal or disagreement.

Occasionally, when sufficient knowledge of facts about the witness or about the details of the direct testimony can be correctly anticipated, a trap may be set into which even a clever witness, as in the illustration that follows, will be likely to fall.

During the lifetime of Dr. J. W. Ranney there were few physicians in this country who were so frequently seen on the witness stand as he, especially in damage suits. So expert a witness had he become that Chief Justice Van Brunt many years ago told me that "Any lawyer who attempts to cross-examine Dr. Ranney is a fool." A case occurred in my practice a few years before Dr. Ranney died, however, where a failure to cross-examine would have been tantamount to a confession of judgment, and, though fully aware of the dangers, I was left no alternative, and as so often happens where "fools rush in," I made one of those lucky "bull's-eyes" that is perhaps worth recording.

It was a damage case brought against the city by a lady who, on her way from church one spring morning, had tripped over an obscure encumbrance in the street, and had, in consequence, been practically bedridden for the three years leading up to the day of trial. She was brought into the court room in a chair and was placed in front of the jury, a pallid, pitiable object, surrounded by her women friends, who acted upon this occasion as nurses, constantly bathing her hands and face with ill-smelling ointments, and administering restoratives, with marked effect upon the jury. Her counsel, Ex-chief Justice Noah Davis, claimed that her spine had been permanently injured, and asked the jury for $50,000 damages.

It appeared that Dr. Ranney had been in constant attendance upon the patient ever since the day of her accident. He testified that he had visited her some three hundred times and had examined her minutely at least two hundred times in order to make up his mind as to the absolutely correct diagnosis of her case, which he was now thoroughly satisfied was one of genuine disease of the spinal marrow itself. Judge Davis asked him a few preliminary questions, and then gave the doctor his head and bade him "turn to the jury and tell them all about it." Dr. Ranney spoke uninterruptedly for nearly three quarters of an hour. He described in detail the sufferings of his patient since she had been under his care; his efforts to relieve her pain; the hopeless nature of her malady. He then proceeded in a most impressive way to picture to the jury the gradual and relentless progress of the disease as it assumed the form of creeping paralysis, involving the destruction of one organ after another until death became a blessed relief. At the close of this recital, without a question more, Judge Davis turned to me and said in a calm but triumphant tone, "Do you wish to cross-examine?"

Now the one point in dispute—there was no defence on the merits—was the nature of the patient's malady. The city's medical witnesses were unanimous that the lady had not, and could not have, contracted spinal disease from the slight injury she had received. They styled her complaint as "hysterical," existing in the patient's mind alone, and not indicating nor involving a single diseased organ; but the jury evidently all believed Dr. Ranney, and were anxious to render a verdict on his testimony. He must be cross-examined. Absolute failure could be no worse than silence, though it was evident that, along expected lines, questions relating to his direct evidence would be worse than useless. Counsel was well aware of the doctor's reputed fertility of resource, and quickly decided upon his tactics.

My first questions emphasized to the jury the fact that the witness had been the medical expert for the New York,

New Haven, and Hartford R. R. thirty-five years, for the New York Central R. R. forty years, for the New York and Harlem River R. R. twenty years, for the Erie R. R. fifteen years and so on until the doctor was forced to admit that he was so much in court as a witness in defence of these various railroads, and was so occupied with their affairs that he had but comparatively little time to devote to his reading and private practice.

Counsel (perfectly quietly). "Are you able to give us, doctor, the name of any medical authority that agrees with you when you say that the particular group of symptoms existing in this case points to one disease and one only?"

Doctor. "Oh, yes, Dr. Ericson agrees with me."

Counsel. "Who is Dr. Ericson, if you please?"

Doctor (with a patronizing smile). "Well, Mr. Wellman, Ericson was probably one of the most famous surgeons that England has ever produced." (There was a titter in the audience at the expense of counsel.)

Counsel. "What book has he written?"

Doctor (still smiling). "He has written a book called 'Ericson on the Spine,' which is altogether the best known work on the subject." (The titter among the audience grew louder.)

Counsel. "When was this book published?"

Doctor. "About ten years ago."

Counsel. "Well, how is it that a man, whose time is so much occupied as you have told us yours is, has leisure enough to look up medical authorities to see if they agree with him?"

Doctor (fairly beaming on counsel). "Well, Mr. Wellman, to tell you the truth, I have often heard of you, and I half suspected you would ask me some such foolish question; so this morning after my breakfast, and before starting for court, I took down from my library my copy of Ericson's book, and found that he agreed entirely with my diagnosis in this case." (Loud laughter at expense of counsel, in which the jury joined.)

Counsel (reaching under the counsel table and taking up his own copy of "Ericson on the Spine," and walking deliberately up to the witness). "Won't you be good enough to point out to me where Ericson adopts your view of this case?"

Doctor (embarrassed). "Oh, I can't do it now; it is a very thick book."

Counsel (still holding out the book to the witness). "But you forget, doctor, that thinking I might ask you some such foolish question, you examined your volume of Ericson this very morning after breakfast and before coming to court."

Doctor (becoming more embarrassed and still refusing to take the book). "I have not time to do it now."

Counsel. "*Time!*—why, there is all the time in the world."

Doctor. (no answer).

Counsel and witness eye each other closely.

Counsel (sitting down, still eyeing witness). "I am sure the court will allow me to suspend my examination until you shall have had time to turn to the place you read this morning in that book, and can reread it now aloud to the jury."

Doctor. (no answer).

The court room was in deathly silence for fully three minutes. The witness *wouldn't* say anything, counsel for plaintiff *didn't dare* to say anything, and counsel for the city *didn't want* to say anything; he saw that he had caught the witness in a manifest falsehood, and that the doctor's whole testimony was discredited with the jury unless he could open to the paragraph referred to which counsel well knew did not exist in the whole work of Ericson.

At the expiration of a few minutes, Mr. Justice Barrett, who was presiding at the trial, turned quietly to the witness and asked him if he desired to answer the question, and upon his replying that he did not intend to answer it any further than he had already done, he was excused from the witness stand amid almost breathless silence in the court room. As he passed from the witness chair to his seat, he stopped and whispered into my ear, "You are the ———est most impertinent man I have ever met."

After a ten days' trial the jury were unable to forget the collapse of the plaintiff's principal witness, and failed to agree upon a verdict.

Every now and then, it falls to the lot of every trial lawyer to experience one of those rare thrills that pay for many years of patient plodding. Especially is this the case when he succeeds in unmasking an over-prepared or over-schooled witness—giving testimony, though partly true, yet, in its essential features, usually false.

The Eno will case, tried in our Surrogate's Court within the last year, Max D. Steuer appearing for the contestants, afforded some interesting illustrations of the injury it is possible to do a case by calling an over-prepared or over-coached witness at a critical part of the trial, and subjecting such witness to the wiles of a skilful cross-examiner.

Columbia University had been made the residuary legatee in the will of Amos R. Eno. The will was contested by Mr. Eno's two nephews. The claim of the contestants was that the testator hated universities in general, and Columbia University and its president in particular. There was the further claim that he was very fond of two of his nephews, and that they had been discriminated against in the will.

The proponents, on the other hand, in answer, sought to show that the testator had a great contempt for these nephews, and that he was a great believer in educational institutions in general, and Columbia University in particular. They reserved for their last witness a most engaging lady, of gentle manners, and facility of speech, who really summed up the whole case for the proponents. In order to show that the testator favored universities in general, and Columbia in particular, she recalled three conversations. On one of these occasions she met the testator, who asked her to take a walk with him. As she told it, it seemed to her particularly pathetic, because he said: "Won't you walk with the blind old man?"—and of course she did!— and they happened to be in the vicinity of the University of the City of New York, which also became one of the legatees under the will. They walked by the University, and she asked the testator whether he had seen the University's new building, and he replied in the negative, but he was glad that this present building was still in the vicinity, and then said to her: "This University and Columbia College are soon going to be the Cambridge and Oxford of the United States," and spoke of both universities in terms of the highest praise. On another occasion, the testator happened to call at her home, and said: "I notice that your friend (naming him) died, and that he left a will naming Yale University as the residuary legatee." The testator proceeded to praise this will. He hardly knew the friend that died, but said he must have been a wonderful man in order to make a will of that kind, and extolled men who left their money to universities. Of course, the will that the friend left was in court, ready to be produced, and Yale University was made the residuary legatee in it, right enough. The witness recalled a third conversation in which the testator, in the presence also of the mother of this witness, lamented the fact that he was without people who were near and dear to him, and told the mother how fortunate she was to have such a devoted daughter, and pointed to his own situation as being a most unfortunate one, because none of his relatives paid the slightest attention to him. The mother said: "But you have a sister and brother and nephews," and made particular reference to his nephews. He spoke slightingly of his brother and sister. In reply to the question, "Was not one of your nephews named for you?" he answered: "Yes, but the trouble is that he thinks that I was named for him."

Thus the witness proceeded to overthrow the whole theory of the contestants, that the testator hated universities and that he had a strong affection for his nephews. The cross-examinaion of Mr. Steuer soon developed the inconsistencies of these alleged conversations. It was shown that the testator had made four wills *after* his alleged conversation when, the witness swore, Mr. Eno had stated that Columbia and the University of the City of New York would be the Oxford and Cambridge of the United States, and *had failed to mention either of these institutions* in any of those four wills. Another difficulty with her alleged conversation was that, after this friend of the family had died and named Yale University as the residuary legatee, Mr. Eno had made five wills, in none of which had he mentioned any university, either Columbia or any other, and yet in each he had disposed of a large residuary estate. And lastly, there was no nephew that was named for the testator, and the testator could never have been under any impression that there was a nephew that had been named for him unless his mind had become weak, and the very claim of the contestants was that the mind of the testator had become weak, so that the proponents had a choice of two evils: if the testator thought that he had a nephew that was named after him, it did not argue well for the proponents; if the testator did not think that he had a nephew named after him, it did not argue well for the veracity of the witness. The point was that while the summation through this witness was well prepared so as to influence the jury, it was not carefully prepared in view of the facts that were readily brought to light.

The testator being dead, and the mother of the witness also being dead, her story stood without contradiction, yet the facts which it covered were so inherently improbable and it was so apparent that this witness had been called last as a sort of climax in the case that, instead of helping the proponents, it proved a great detriment, and her cross-examination by Mr. Steuer was of the utmost value.

In this same case there was a further illustration of a practically similar situation. It should be borne in mind that the ground of the contest was that the testator was incompetent to make the will in question. A lawyer was called by the proponent, who testified that on the very day when the will was executed, entirely by accident, he met the testator on a train going from New York to Saratoga; that in the smoker, he also accidentally happened to sit next to the testator. He conversed with the testator in the smoking car all the way from New York to Albany. The conversation covered a great variety of subjects. The testator displayed a wonderful memory, a remarkable grasp of present day situations, and of all questions that were then current. He advised this lawyer with respect to investments, discussed with him decisions made by Appellate Courts, and clearly gave evidence of a mind in healthy condition. This conversation, of course, could not be contradicted. There was nobody alive other than this attorney who participated therein. The witness had a chair in the parlor car, had left his bag and other articles in the parlor car, and then had taken a seat in the smoker. The witness saw the deceased leaving the train at Albany, where they had to change cars. He saw nobody assist the deceased from the train, and the deceased got off in the same manner that other passengers did, and there was nothing unusual about his walk or gait, so that not only was the decedent in good mental condition, but he was in fine physical condition.

Here again Mr. Steuer's cross-examination exposed either the faulty memory or the perjury of the witness, although the witness could not be directly contradicted in his conversation with a deceased man. First, there was no parlor car on that train. The jury evidently found it very difficult for a man to leave his bag and things in the parlor car when there was no parlor car to leave them in. Second, the deceased never smoked and detested the odor of smoke. It annoyed him so much that, while he was a great entertainer, and gave numerous large dinner parties at his home, on each occasion when it came time for lighting cigars he withdrew from the men until the smoking period was over. At his country residence, when the cigars were passed he would go out on his porch and sit apart from the other guests so as not to be molested by the smoke. The day on which this trip was taken from New York to Saratoga was a very hot day, everybody agreed. The jury could not well reconcile the prior aversion of the deceased toward smoke with his affection for it on that particular day. All the witnesses on both sides had agreed that at that particular time the deceased was feeble. He had not been for years without an attendant. It was admitted that the attendant was with the deceased on his journey from New York to Saratoga. The witness had seen no attendant. Everybody except this witness agreed that the decedent had great difficulty in seeing steps, and that in passing from the curb he used his cane to tap, in order to gauge the distance that he would have to step down, and that his attendant always assisted him. The train step at Albany was rather high. The jury, knowing that the attendant was on the train, and the testimony all being to the effect that the man required assistance in going up or down stairs, found it difficult to reconcile the previous conduct of the deceased for a number of years with his supposed ability on that particular day when he signed his will and when he stepped from the train at Albany.

Chapter 5

Cross-Examination of Experts

IN THESE TIMES when it is impossible to know everything, but becomes necessary for success in any vocation to know something of everything and everything of something, the expert is more and more called upon as a witness both in civil and criminal cases. In these days of specialists their services are often needed to aid the jury in their investigations of questions of fact relating to subjects with which the ordinary man is not acquainted.

In our American courts, as they are now constituted, I think I am safe in saying that in half the cases presented to a jury the evidence of one or more expert witnesses becames a very important factor in a juror's effort to arrive at a just verdict. The proper handling of these witnesses, therefore, has become of greater importance at the present time than ever before. It is useless for our law writers to dismiss the subject of expert testimony, as is so often done, by quoting some authority like Lord Campbell, who gives it as his final judgment, after the experience of a lifetime at the bar and on the bench, that "skilled witnesses come with such a bias on their minds to support the cause in which they are embarked, that hardly any weight should be given to their evidence." Or, as Taylor even more emphatically puts it in the last edition of his treatise on the "Law of Evidence," "Expert witnesses become so warped in their judgment by regarding the subject in one point of view, that, even when conscientiously disposed, *they are incapable* of expressing a candid opinion." The fact still remains that the testimony of expert witnesses must be reckoned with in about sixty per cent of our more important litigated business, and the only possible way to enlighten our jurors and enable them to arrive at a just estimate of such testimony is by a thorough understanding of the art of cross-examination of such witnesses.

Although the cross-examination of various experts, whether medical, handwriting, real estate, or other specialists, is a subject of growing importance, yet it is not intended in this chapter to do more than to make some suggestions and to give a number of illustrations of certain methods that have been successfully adopted in the examination of this class of witnesses.

It has become a matter of common observation that not only can the honest opinions of different experts be obtained upon opposite sides of the same question, but also that dishonest opinions may be obtained upon different sides of the same question.

Attention is also called to the distinction between matters of scientific fact and mere matters of opinion. For example: medical experts may be called to establish certain medical facts which are not mere matters of opinion. On such facts the experts could hardly disagree; but in the province of mere opinion it is well known that the experts differ so widely among themselves that but little credit is given to mere expert opinion as such.

As a general thing, it is unwise for the cross-examiner to attempt to cope with a specialist in his own field of inquiry. Lengthy cross-examinations along the lines of the expert's theory are usually disastrous and should rarely be attempted.

Many lawyers, for example, undertake to cope with a medical or handwriting expert on his own ground, be it surgery, correct diagnosis, or the intricacies of penmanship. In some rare instances (more especially with poorly educated physicians) this method of cross-questioning is productive of results. More frequently, however, it only affords an opportunity for the doctor to enlarge upon the testimony he has already given, and to explain what might otherwise have been misunderstood or even entirely overlooked by the jury. Experience has led me to believe that a physician should rarely be cross-examined on his own specialty, unless the importance of the case has warranted so close a study by the counsel of the particular subject under discussion as to justify the experiment; and then only when the lawyer's research of the medical authorities, which he should have with him in court, convinces him that he can expose the doctor's erroneous conclusions, not only to himself, but to a jury who will not readily comprehend the abstract theories of the science upon which even the medical profession itself is divided.

A very amusing illustration on this point when "fools rush in where angels fear to tread" occurred in a rather recent case.

An inexperienced young attorney was defending his client on a charge of murder, claiming that the death was the result of suicide and not homicide. An elderly German physician had made the autopsy and had testified that, after a very careful examination of the course of the bullet as it entered and passed through the body, he was satisfied that it could not possibly have been self-inflicted. The witness offered diagrams illustrating his point, and if his opinion should be accepted by the jury, there could no longer be any question of suicide.

The young attorney started his cross-examination by addressing the witness in a rather flippant and disrespectful manner which, naturally, irritated the witness, somewhat along these lines:

Attorney. "Dr. ——, you seem very certain about your findings in this case. You do not give it as your opinion that the wound in this case could not have been self-inflicted, but you state it as a matter of fact—swear to it as a matter of fact. Now I'd like to ask you—by any chance is this the first autopsy you have ever made? I don't find your name anywhere in our local Medical Directory."

Doctor (sitting back in his seat and answering very quietly, holding up one of his hands and apparently counting his fingers). "No, I can say that I have made a previous autopsy."

Attorney (apparently encouraged by this answer). "Well, could you honestly say that you have made two autopsies, not counting this one?"

Doctor (again hesitating, and again counting his open

fingers, apparently reminiscing). "Yes, I think I can truthfully say I have made two prior autopsies."

Attorney (still more encouraged). "Well, can you go so far as to say that you have made five autopsies?"

Doctor (this time examining his outstretched hand very deliberately and apparently touching the tip of each finger as he counted up his cases before making a reply, and then looking up pleasantly at the attorney). "Yes—yes, I think I can say that I have made as many as five autopsies."

Attorney (exultant and with a scornful smile, walking toward the witness). "Well, sir, why beat about the bush? Let's put it this way: Can you say you have made ten thousand previous autopsies?"

Doctor (with a broad, rather amused smile on his face, but still in a low tone). "Well, I think I can truthfully say I probably have. *You see I was Coroner for forty years in the City of Berlin before I came to this country!!!*"

On the other hand, some careful and judicious questions, seeking to bring out separate facts and separate points from the knowledge and experience of the expert, which will tend to support the theory of the attorney's own side of the case, are usually productive of good results. In other words, the art of the cross-examiner should be directed to bring out such scientific facts from the knowledge of the expert as will help his own case, and thus tend to destroy the weight of the opinion of the expert given against him.

Another suggestion which should always be borne in mind is that no question should be put to an expert which is in any way so broad as to give the expert an opportunity to expatiate upon his own views, and thus afford him an opportunity in his answer to give his reasons, in his own way, for his opinions, which counsel calling him as an expert might not otherwise have fully brought out in his examination.

It was in the trial of Dr. Buchanan on the charge of murdering his wife, that a single, ill-advised question put upon cross-examination to the physician who had attended

Mrs. Buchanan upon her death-bed, and who had given
it as his opinion that her death was due to natural causes,
enabled the jury, after twenty-four hours of dispute among
themselves, finally to agree against the prisoner on a verdict of murder in the first degree, resulting in Buchanan's
execution.

The charge against Dr. Buchanan was that he had
poisoned his wife—a woman considerably older than himself, who had made a will in his favor—with morphine
and atropine, each drug being used in such proportion as
to effectually obliterate the group of symptoms attending
death when resulting from the use of either drug alone.

At Buchanan's trial District Attorney Nicoll and I found
ourselves in the extremely awkward position of trying to
persuade a jury to decide that Mrs. Buchanan's death was,
beyond all reasonable doubt, the result of an overdose of
morphine mixed with atropine administered by her husband, despite the fact that a respectable physician who
had attended her at her death-bed had given it as his
opinion that she died from natural causes, and had himself
made out a death certificate in which he attributed her
death to apoplexy.

It was only fair to the prisoner that he should be given
the benefit of the testimony of this physician. The District
Attorney, therefore, called the doctor to the witness stand
and questioned him concerning the symptoms he had
observed during his treatment of Mrs. Buchanan just prior
to her death, and developed the fact that the doctor had
made out a death certificate in which he had certified that
in his opinion apoplexy was the sole cause of death. The
doctor was then turned over to the lawyers for the defence
for cross-examination.

One of the prisoner's counsel, who had far more knowledge of medicine than of the art of cross-examination, was
assigned the important duty of cross-examining this witness. After badgering the doctor for an hour or so with
technical medical questions more or less remote from the
subject under discussion, and tending to show the erudi-
tion of the lawyer who was conducting the examination

rather than to throw light upon the inquiry uppermost in the minds of the jury, the cross-examiner finally produced the death certificate and put it in evidence, and calling the doctor's attention to the statement therein made— that death was the result of apoplexy—exclaimed, while flourishing the paper in the air:

"Now, doctor, you have told us what this lady's symptoms were, you have told us what you then believed was the cause of her death; I now ask you, has anything transpired since Mrs. Buchanan's death which would lead you to change your opinion as it is expressed in this paper?"

The doctor settled back in his chair and slowly repeated the question asked: "Has — anything — transpired — since — Mrs. Buchanan's — death — which — would — lead — me — to — change — my — opinion — as — it — is — expressed — in — this — paper?" The witness turned to the judge and inquired if in answer to such a question he would be allowed to speak of matters that had come to his knowledge since he wrote the certificate. The judge replied: "The question is a broad one. Counsel asks you if you know of *any reason* why you should change your former opinion?"

The witness leaned forward to the stenographer and requested him to read the question over again. This was done. The attention of everybody in court was by this time focussed upon the witness, intent upon his answer. It seemed to appear to the jury as if this must be the turning point of the case.

The doctor having heard the question read a second time, paused for a moment, and then straightening himself in his chair, turned to the cross-examiner and said, "I wish to ask *you* a question. Has the report of the chemist telling of his discovery of atropine and morphine in the contents of this woman's stomach been offered in evidence yet?" The court answered, "It has not."

"One more question," said the doctor, "Has the report of the pathologist *yet* been received in evidence?" The court replied, "No."

"Then," said the doctor, rising in his chair, "I can

answer your question truthfully, that *as yet,* in the absence of the pathological report and in the absence of the chemical report I know of no *legal evidence* which would cause me to alter the opinion expressed in my death certificate."

It is impossible to exaggerate the impression made upon the court and jury by these answers. All the advantage that the prisoner might have derived from the original death certificate was entirely swept away.

The trial lasted for fully two weeks after this episode. When the jury retired to their consultation room at the end of the trial, they found they were utterly unable to agree upon a verdict. They argued among themselves for twenty-four hours without coming to any conclusion. At the expiration of this time the jury returned to the court room and asked to have the testimony of this doctor reread to them by the stenographer. The stenographer, as he read from his notes, reproduced the entire scene which had been enacted two weeks before. The jury retired a second time and immediately agreed upon their verdict of death.

The cross-examinations of the medical witnesses in the Buchanan case conducted by this "Medico-legal Wonder" were the subject of very extended newspaper praise at the time, one daily paper devoting the entire front page of its Sunday edition to his portrait.

The whole effect of the testimony of an expert witness may sometimes effectually be destroyed by putting the witness to some unexpected and offhand test at the trial, as to his experience, his ability and discrimination as an expert, so that in case of his failure to meet the test he can be held up to ridicule before the jury, and thus the laughter at his expense will cause the jury to forget anything of weight that he has said against you.

I have always found this to be the most effective method to cross-examine a certain type of professional medical witness now so frequently seen in our courts. A striking instance of the efficacy of this style of cross-examination was experienced by the writer in a damage suit against the city of New York, tried in the Supreme Court some time in 1887.

A very prominent physician, president of one of our leading clubs at the time, but now dead, had advised a woman who had been his housekeeper for thirty years, and who had broken her ankle in consequence of stepping into an unprotected hole in the street pavement, to bring suit against the city to recover $40,000 damages. There was very little defence to the principal cause of action: the hole in the street *was* there, and the plaintiff *had* stepped into it. But her right to recover substantial damages was vigorously contested.

Her principal, in fact her only, medical witness was her employer, the famous physician. The doctor testified to the plaintiff's sufferings, described the fracture of her ankle, explained how he had himself set the broken bones and attended the patient, but affirmed that all his efforts were of no avail as he could bring about nothing but a most imperfect union of the bones, and that his housekeeper, a most respectable and estimable lady, would be lame for life. His manner on the witness stand was exceedingly dignified and frank, and evidently impressed the jury. A large verdict of fully $15,000 was certain to be the result unless this witness's hold upon the jury could be broken on his cross-examination. There was no reason known to counsel why this ankle should not have healed promptly as such fractures usually do; but how to make the jury *realize* the fact was the question. The intimate personal acquaintance between the cross-examiner and the witness was another embarrassment.

My cross-examination began by showing that the witness although a graduate of Harvard, had not immediately entered a medical school, but on the contrary had started in business in Wall Street, had later been manager of several business enterprises, and had not begun the study of medicine until he was forty years old. The examination then continued in the most amiable manner possible, each question being asked in a tone almost of apology.

Counsel. "We all know, doctor, that you have a large and lucrative family practice as a general practitioner; but is it not a fact that in this great city, where accidents are of such common occurrence, surgical cases are usually taken to the hospitals and cared for by experienced surgeons?"

Doctor. "Yes, sir, that is so."

Counsel. "You do not even claim to be an experienced surgeon?"

Doctor. "Oh, no, sir. I have the experience of any general practitioner."

Counsel. "What would be the surgical name for the particular form of fracture that this lady suffered?"

Doctor. "What is known as a 'Potts fracture of the ankle.'"

Counsel. "That is a well recognized form of fracture, is it not?"

Doctor. "Oh, yes."

Counsel (chancing it). "Would you mind telling the jury about when you had a fracture of this nature in your regular practice, the last before this one?"

Doctor (dodging). "I should not feel at liberty to disclose the names of my patients."

Counsel (encouraged). "I am not asking for names and secrets of patients—far from it. I am only asking for the date, doctor; but on your oath."

Doctor. "I couldn't possibly give you the date, sir."

Counsel (still feeling his way). "Was it within the year preceding this one?"

Doctor (hesitating). "I would not like to say, sir."

Counsel (still more encouraged). "I am sorry to press you, sir; but I am obliged to demand a positive answer from you whether or not you had had a similar case of 'Potts fracture of the ankle' the year preceding this one?"

Doctor. "Well, no, I cannot remember that I had."

Counsel. "Did you have one two years before?"

Doctor. "I cannot say."

Counsel (forcing the issue). "Did you have one within five years preceding the plaintiff's case?"

Doctor. "I am unable to say positively."

Counsel (appreciating the danger of pressing the inquiry further, but as a last resort). "Will you swear that you *ever* had a case of 'Potts fracture' within your own practice before this one? I tell you frankly, if you say you have, I shall ask you day and date, time, place, and circumstance."

Doctor (much embarrassed). "Your question is an embarrassing one. I should want time to search my memory."

Counsel. "I am only asking you for your best memory as a gentleman, and under oath."

Doctor. "If you put it that way, I will say I cannot now remember any case previous to the one in question, excepting as a student in the hospitals."

Counsel. "But does it not require a great deal of practice and experience to attend successfully so serious a fracture as that involving the ankle joint?"

Doctor. "Oh, yes."

Counsel. "Well, doctor, speaking frankly, won't you admit that 'Potts fractures' are daily being attended to in our hospitals by experienced men, and the use of the ankle fully restored in a few months' time?"

Doctor. "That may be, but much depends upon the age of the patient; and again, in some cases, nothing seems to make the bones unite."

Counsel (stooping under the table and taking up the two lower bones of the leg attached and approaching the witness). "Will you please take these, doctor, and tell the jury whether in life they constituted the bones of a woman's leg or a man's leg?"

Doctor. "It is difficult to tell, sir."

Counsel. "What, can't you tell the skeleton of a woman's leg from a man's, doctor?"

Doctor. "Oh, yes, I would say it was a woman's leg."

Counsel (smiling and looking pleased). "So in your opinion, doctor, this was a *woman's* leg?" [It *was* a woman's leg.]

Doctor (observing counsel's face and thinking he had

made a mistake). "Oh, I beg your pardon, it is a man's leg, of course. I had not examined it carefully."

By this time the jury were all sitting upright in their seats and evinced much amusement at the doctor's increasing embarrassment.

Counsel (still smiling). "Would you be good enough to tell the jury if it is the right leg or the left leg?"

Doctor (quietly, but hesitatingly). [It is very difficult for the inexperienced to distinguish right from left.] "This is the *right* leg."

Counsel (astonished). *"What* do you say, doctor?"

Doctor (much confused). "Pardon me, it is the *left* leg."

Counsel. "Were you not right the first time, doctor. Is it not in fact the *right* leg?"

Doctor. "I don't think so; no, it is the *left* leg."

Counsel (again stooping and bringing from under the table the bones of the foot attached together, and handing it to the doctor). "Please put the skeleton of the foot into the ankle joint of the bones you already have in your hand, and then tell me whether it is the right or left leg."

Doctor (confidently). "Yes, it is the left leg, as I said before."

Counsel (uproariously). "But, doctor, don't you see you have inserted the *foot* into the *knee joint*? Is that the way it is in life?"

The doctor, amid roars of laughter from the jury, in which the entire room joined, hastily readjusted the bones and sat blushing to the roots of his hair. Counsel waited until the laughter had subsided, and then said quietly, "I think I will not trouble you further, doctor."

This incident is not the least bit exaggerated; on the contrary, the impression made by the occurrence is difficult to present adequately on paper. Counsel on both sides proceeded to sum up the case, and upon the part of the defence no allusion whatsoever was made to the incident just described. The jury appreciated the fact, and returned a verdict for the plaintiff for $240. Next day the learned doctor wrote a four page letter of thanks and appreciation that the results of his "stage fright" had not been spread before the jury in the closing speech.

As distinguished from the lengthy, though doubtless scientific, cross-examination of experts in handwriting with which the profession has become familiar in many recent famous trials that have occurred in this city, the following incident cannot fail to serve as a forcible illustration of the suggestions laid down as to the cross-examination of specialists. It would almost be thought improbable in a romance, yet every word of it is true, which I can confidently assert as I tried the case myself.

Frank ("Biff") Ellison was accused of felonious assault upon one William Henriques, who had brought Mr. Ellison's attentions to his daughter, Mrs. Lila Noeme, to a sudden close by forbidding him his house. At the trial the authenticity of some letters, alleged to have been written by Mrs. Noeme to Mr. Ellison, was brought in question. The lady herself had strenuously denied that the alleged compromising documents had ever been written by her. Counsel for Ellison, the late Charles Brooks, had evidently framed his whole cross-examination of Mrs. Noeme upon these letters, and made a final effort to introduce them in evidence by calling Professor Ames, the well known expert in handwriting. He deposed to having closely studied the letters in question, in conjunction with an admittedly genuine specimen of the lady's handwriting, and gave it as his opinion that they were all written by the same hand. Mr. Brooks then offered the letters in evidence, and was about to read them to the jury when the assistant district attorney asked permission to put a few questions.

District Attorney. "Mr. Ames, as I understood you, you were given only one sample of the lady's genuine handwriting, and you base your opinion upon that single exhibit, is that correct?"

Witness. "Yes, sir, there was only one letter given me, but that was quite a long one, and afforded me great opportunity for comparison."

District Attorney. "Would it not assist you if you were

given a number of her letters with which to make a comparison?"

Witness. "Oh, yes, the more samples I had of genuine handwriting, the more valuable my conclusion would become."

District Attorney (taking from among a bundle of papers a letter, folding down the signature and handing it to the witness). "Would you mind taking this one and comparing it with the others, and then tell us if that is in the same handwriting?"

Witness (examining paper closely for a few minutes). "Yes, sir, I should say that was the same handwriting."

District Attorney. "Is it not a fact, sir, that the same individual may write a variety of hands upon different occasions and with different pens?"

Witness. "Oh, yes, sir; they might vary somewhat."

District Attorney (taking a second letter from his files, also folding over the signature and handing to the witness). "Won't you kindly take this letter, also, and compare it with the others you have?"

Witness (examining the letter). "Yes, sir, that is a variety of the same penmanship."

District Attorney. "Would you be willing to give it as your opinion that it was written by the same person?"

Witness. "I certainly would, sir."

District Attorney (taking a third letter from his files, again folding over the signature, and handing to the witness). "Be good enough to take just one more sample —I don't want to weary you—and say if this last one is also in the lady's handwriting."

Witness (appearing to examine it closely, leaving the witness chair and going to the window to complete his inspection). "Yes, sir; you understand I am not swearing to a fact, only an opinion."

District Attorney (goodnaturedly). "Of course I understand; but is it your honest opinion as an expert that these three letters are all in the same handwriting?"

Witness. "I say yes, it is my honest opinion."

District Attorney. "Now, sir, won't you please turn

down the edge where I folded over the signature to the first letter I handed you, and read aloud to the jury the signature?"

Witness (unfolding the letter and reading triumphantly). *"Lila Noeme."*

District Attorney. "Please unfold the second letter and read the signature."

Witness (reading). *"William Henriques."*

District Attorney. "Now the third, please."

Witness (hesitating and reading with much embarrassment). *"Frank Ellison!"* [1]

The alleged compromising letters were never read to the jury.

It will not be uninteresting, by way of contrast, I think, to record here another instance where the cross-examination of an expert in handwriting did more to convict a prisoner, probably, than any other one piece of evidence during the entire trial.

The examination referred to occurred in the famous trial of Munroe Edwards, who was indicted for forging two drafts upon Messrs. Brown Brothers & Company, who had offered a reward of $20,000 for his arrest.

Edwards had engaged Mr. Robert Emmet to defend him, and had associated with Emmet as his counsel Mr. William M. Evarts and several famous lawyers from outside the state. At that time the district attorney was Mr. James R. Whiting, who had four prominent lawyers, including Mr. Ogden Hoffman, associated with him upon the side of the government.

Recorder Vaux, of Philadelphia, was called to the witness stand as an expert in handwriting, and in his direct testimony had very clearly identified the prisoner with the commission of the particular forgery for which he was on trial. He was then turned over to Mr. Emmet for cross-examination.

[1] As a matter of fact, father and daughter wrote very much alike, and with surprising similarity to Mr. Ellison. It was this circumstance that led to the use of the three letters in the cross-examination.

Mr. Emmet (taking a letter from among his papers and handing it to the witness, after turning down the signature). "Would you be good enough to tell me, Mr. Vaux, who was the author of the letter which I now hand you?"

Mr. Vaux (answering promptly). "This letter is in the handwriting of Munroe Edwards."

Mr. Emmet. "Do you feel certain of that, Mr. Vaux?"

Mr. Vaux. "I do."

Mr. Emmet. "As certain as you are in relation to the handwriting of the letters which you have previously identified as having been written by the prisoner?"

Mr. Vaux. "Exactly the same."

Mr. Emmet. "You have no hesitation then in swearing positively that the letter you hold in your hand, in your opinion, was written by Munroe Edwards?"

Mr. Vaux. "Not the slightest."

Mr. Emmet (with a sneer). "That will do, sir."

District Attorney (rising quickly). "Let *me* see the letter."

Mr. Emmet (contemptuously). "That is your privilege, sir, but I doubt if it will be to your profit. The letter is directed to myself, and is written by the cashier of the Orleans bank, informing me of a sum of money deposited in that institution to the credit of the prisoner. Mr. Vaux's evidence in relation to it will test the value of his testimony in relation to other equally important points."

Mr. Vaux here left the witness chair and walked to the table of the prosecution, reëxamined the letter carefully, then reached to a tin box which was in the keeping of the prosecution and which contained New Orleans post office stamps. He then resumed his seat in the witness chair.

Mr. Vaux (smiling). "I may be willing, Mr. Emmet, to submit my testimony to your test."

Mr. Emmet made no reply, but the prosecuting attorney continued the examination as follows:—

District Attorney. "You have just testified, Mr. Vaux, that you believe the letter which you now hold in your hand was written by the same hand that wrote the Caldwell forgeries, and that such hand was Munroe Edwards's. Do you still retain that opinion?"

Mr. Vaux. "I do."

District Attorney. "Upon what grounds?"

Mr. Vaux. "Because it is a fellow of the same character as well in appearance as in device. It is a forgery, probably only intended to impose upon his counsel, but now by its unadvised introduction in evidence, made to impose upon himself and brand him as a forger."

The true New Orleans stamps were here shown to be at variance with the counterfeit postmark upon the forged letter, and the character of the writing was also proved by comparison with many letters which were in the forger's undoubted hand.

It turned out subsequently that the prisoner had informed his counsel, Mr. Emmet, that he was possessed of large amounts of property in Texas, some of which he had ordered to be sold to meet the contingent cost of his defence. He had drawn up a letter purporting to come from a cashier in a bank at New Orleans, directed to Mr. Emmet, informing him of the deposit on that day of $1500 to the credit of his client, which notification he, the cashier, thought proper to send to the counsel, as he had observed in the newspapers that Mr. Edwards was confined to the jail. Mr. Emmet was so entirely deceived by this letter that he had taken it to his client in prison, and had shown it to him as a sign of pleasant tidings.[1]

The manufacture or exaggeration of injuries in damage cases against surface railroads and other corporations had at one time, not many years ago, become almost a trade among a certain class of lawyers in the city of New York.

There are several medical books which detail the symptoms that may be expected to be exhibited in almost any form of railroad accidents. Any lawyer who is familiar with the pages of these books can readily detect indications

[1] "Pleasantries about Courts and Lawyers," Edwards.

of an equal familiarity with them on the part of the lawyer who is examining his client—the plaintiff in an accident case—as to the *symptoms* of his malady as set forth in these medical treatises, which have probably been put into his hands in order that he may become thoroughly posted upon the symptoms which he would be expected to manifest.

It becomes interesting to watch the history of some of these cases after the substantial amount of the verdict awarded by a jury has been paid over to the suffering plaintiff. Only recently a couple of medical gentlemen were called as witnesses in a case where a Mrs. Bogardus was suing the Metropolitan Street Railway Company for injuries she claimed to have sustained while a passenger on one of the defendant's cars. These expert physicians swore that Mrs. Bogardus had a lesion of the spine and was suffering from paralysis as a result of the accident. According to the testimony of the doctors, her malady was incurable and permanent. The records of the legal department of this railway company showed that these same medical gentlemen had, on a prior occasion in the case of one Hoyt against the railroad, testified to the same state of affairs in regard to Hoyt's physical condition. He, too, was alleged to be suffering from an incurable lesion of the spine and would be paralyzed and helpless for the balance of his life. The records of the company also showed that Hoyt had recovered his health promptly upon being paid the amount of his verdict. At the time of the Bogardus trial Hoyt had been employed by H. B. Claflin & Co. for three years. He was working from seven in the morning until six in the evening, lifting heavy boxes and loading trucks.

The moment the physicians had finished their testimony in the Bogardus case, this man Hoyt was subpœnaed by the railroad company. On cross-examination these physicians both recollected the Hoyt case and their attention was called to the stenographic minutes of the questions and answers they had given under oath in that case. They were then asked if Hoyt was still alive and where he could be found. They both replied that he must be dead by this time, that his case was a hopeless one, and if not dead, he would probably be found as an inmate of one of our public insane asylums.

At this stage of the proceedings Hoyt arrived in the court room. He was requested to step forward in front of the jury. The doctors were asked to identify him, which they both did. Hoyt then took the witness stand himself and admitted that he had never had a sick moment since the day the jury rendered a verdict in his favor; that he had gained thirty-five pounds in weight, and that he was then doing work which was harder than any he had ever done before in his life; that he worked from early morning till late at night; had never been in an insane asylum or under the care of any doctor since his trial; and ended up by making the astounding statement that out of the verdict rendered him by the jury and paid by the railroad company, *he had been obliged to forfeit upwards of $1,500 to the doctors who had treated him and testified in his behalf.*

This was a little too much enlightenment for the jury in Mrs. Bogardus's case, and this time they rendered their verdict promptly in favor of the railroad company.

I cannot forbear relating in this connection another most striking instance of the unreliability of expert testimony in personal injury cases. This is especially the case with certain New York physicians who openly confess it to be a part of their professional business to give expert medical testimony in court. Some of these men have taken a course at a law school in connection with their medical studies for the very purpose of fitting themselves for the witness stand as medical experts.

One of these gentlemen gave testimony in a recent case, which should forever brand him as a dangerous witness in any subsequent litigation in which he may appear. I have reference to the trial of Ellen McQuade against the Metropolitan Street Railway Company. This was a suit brought on behalf of the next of kin, to recover damages for the death of John McQuade who had fallen from a surface railway car and had broken his wrist so that the bone penetrated the skin. This wound was slow in healing and did not close entirely until some three months later. About six months after his accident McQuade was suddenly taken ill and died. An autopsy disclosed the fact that death resulted from inflammation of the brain, and the effort of the expert testimony in the case was to connect this abscess of the brain with the accident to the wrist, which had occurred six months previously.

This expert doctor had, of course, never seen McQuade in his lifetime, and knew nothing about the case except what was contained in the hypothetical question which he was called upon to answer. He gave it as his opinion that the broken wrist was the direct cause of the abscess in the brain, which was due to a pus germ that had traveled from the wound in the arm by means of the lymphatics up to the brain, where it had found lodgement and developed into an abscess of the brain, causing death.

The contention of the railway company was that the diseased condition of the brain was due to "middle-ear disease," which itself was the result of a cold or exposure, and in nowise connected with the accident; and that the presence of the large amount of fluid which was found in the brain after death could be accounted for only by this disease.

During the cross-examination of this medical expert, a young woman, wearing a veil, had come into court and was requested to step forward and lift her veil. The doctor was then asked to identify her as a Miss Zimmer, for whom he had testified some years previously in her damage suit against the same railway company.

At her own trial Miss Zimmer had been carried into the court room resting in a reclining chair, apparently unable to move her lower limbs, and this doctor had testified that she was suffering from chronic myelitis, an affection of the spine, which caused her to be paralyzed, and that she would never be able to move her lower limbs. His oracular words to the jury were, "Just as she is now, gentlemen, so she will always be." The witness's attention was called to these statements, and he was confronted with Miss Zimmer, now apparently in the full vigor of her health, and who had for many years been acting as a trained nurse. She afterward took the witness stand and admitted that the jury had found a verdict for her in the sum of $15,000, but that her paralysis had so much improved after the administration of this panacea by the railway company that she was able, after a few months, to get about with the aid of crutches, and shortly thereafter regained the normal use of her limbs, and had ever since earned her livelihood as an obstetrical nurse.

The sensation caused by the appearance of the Zimmer woman had hardly subsided when the witness's attention was drawn to another case, Kelly against the railway company, in which this doctor had also assisted the plaintiff. Kelly was really paralyzed, but claimed that his paralysis was due to a recent railroad accident. It appeared during the trial, however, that long before the alleged railroad accident, Kelly had lost the use of his limbs, and that his case had become so notorious as to be a subject for public lectures by many reputable city physicians. The doctor was obliged to admit being a witness in that case also, but disclaimed any intentional assistance in the fraud.

Sometimes a busy attorney finds himself confronted with a situation that compels him to cross-examine some very intimate professional friend who may be called as a witness against his client. It has happened to me so many times in the course of my practice, that I am tempted to relate an amusing incident which occurred some years ago in Chicago.

A very well known doctor had given important testimony in a case where his most intimate friend appeared as opposing counsel. These two men—doctor and lawyer —stood equally high in their respective professions, and had been close friends for many years and were frequent dinner companions at one another's homes, with their wives and children. In fact, they had practically grown up together. The lawyer knew that his friend had testified to his honest opinion, which no amount of cross-examination could weaken. He therefore confined himself to the following few interrogations; and, fearing that he could not keep a straight face while he put his questions, he avoided facing the witness at all, keeping his face turned toward a side window.

Q. "Doctor, you say you are a practicing physician. Have you practiced your profession in the City of Chicago for any length of time?"

A. "Yes, I have been in practice here in Chicago now for about forty years."

Q. "Well, doctor, during that time I presume you have had occasion to treat some of our most prominent citizens. Have you not?"

A. "Yes, I think I have."

Q. "By any chance, doctor, were you ever called as a family physician to prescribe for the elder Marshall Field?"

A. "Yes, I was his family physician for a number of years."

Q. "By the way, I haven't heard of him lately. Where is he now?" (Still looking out of the window.)

A. "He is dead."

Q. "Oh—I'm sorry. Were you ever the family physician to the elder Mr. McCormick?"

A. "Yes, also for many years."

Q. "Would you mind my asking where he is now?"

A. "He is dead."

Q. "Oh—I'm sorry."

Then he proceeded in the same vein to make inquiries about eight or ten of the leading Chicago citizens whom he knew his friend had attended, all of whom were dead, and having exhausted the list he sat down quietly amid the amused chuckles of the jurors with the comment: "I don't think it is necessary to ask you any more questions. Please step down."

An eminent X-ray specialist, sued for malpractice by his patient, faced the claim that, in treating her for cancer, he had negligently used the X-ray apparatus with the result that the plaintiff became permanently incapacitated and lost the use of one of her legs. The X-ray had admittedly caused a certain deterioration of the tissues, but the defence was that this was unavoidable.

Dr. Philip G. Hood was sworn as an expert for the plaintiff. On direct examination he testified that there had been excessive dosage—that the patient's condition had received "more X-ray than it could stand."

Mr. Lloyd P. Stryker cross-examined Dr. Hood as follows:

Q. "Doctor, are you admitted to practice in New York State?"

A. "Yes, sir."

Q. "You believe in X-ray, don't you?"

A. "With regard to therapy, you mean?"

Q. "You believe in X-ray as a proper therapeutic agency in the practice of medicine?"

A. "Yes, I do."

Q. "And it is a proper and approved method in assisting the treatment of disease, is it not?"

A. "It is."

Q. "And there are two types of X-ray therapy, one superficial and the other deep, is that not correct?"

A. "That is true."

Q. "Did I understand you to say, doctor, on your direct examination that you dealt in superficial X-ray therapy?"

A. "While I was connected with the Skin and Cancer Hospital."

Q. "So while you were there, you had to do only with the superficial variety of that specialty?"

A. "Yes, sir."

Q. "What is the difference between superficial and deep therapy?"

A. "Superficial therapy is the treatment of lesions on the skin and deep therapy of the deeper structures."

Q. "Have you treated the deeper structures as well?"

A. "Yes, sir."

Q. "You do that now?"

A. "I do it now."

Q. "Deep therapy is recognized, is it not, as a proper

and approved method of treating sarcomatous or malignant conditions?"

A. "It is."

Q. "In order to reach those conditions and have the X-ray affect them, it is necessary to have the electric X-rays or whatever rays they are, we don't know, do we, what they are—reach into the tissues through the outer skin, the fat and fascia, down to the place where the cancer is?"

A. "That is true."

Q. "In other words, the X-ray has to find this growth of the cancer in the same way as if it were done by surgery, that a knife would be used to find it? Do I make myself plain?"

A. "Yes."

Q. "In other words, it has to reach it in order to affect it?"

A. "Yes, of course."

Q. "How deep the X-rays extend into the body depends upon the particular condition that you are treating, does it not?"

A. "The depth of the X-rays depends upon the penetration of them."

Q. "The depth of the cancer you are treating or the sarcoma, whatever growth you are treating?"

A. "Yes, of course."

Q. "So that if you have a deepseated malignant growth, your rays have to go very deep, don't they?"

A. "Yes."

Q. "You don't criticize sending the rays as deep as the cancer is, do you?"

A. "No."

Q. "What effect do those X-rays have upon the growths when they reach them?"

A. "It causes a death of the new tumor cells."

Q. "Sarcoma is a disease of the cells, is it, or of the connecting tissues?"

A. "It is of the connective tissue."

Q. "And if the connective tissues between the cells are

affected, cancerous growths, the X-ray therapist must send his X-ray in as deep as those are, mustn't he?"

A. "Yes."

Q. "In order to perform X-ray therapy, it is necessary to resort to all the recognized methods of diagnosis available to the medical profession, is that correct?"

A. "Surely."

Q. "And it is proper and approved practice to resort to those methods?"

A. "Yes."

Q. "Is that not true?"

A. "Yes."

Q. "And among those methods are the taking of X-ray pictures?"

A. "True."

Q. "That is correct, isn't it?"

A. "Yes, it is."

Q. "You don't criticize the doctor here for taking X-ray pictures in connection with his diagnoses, do you?"

A. "I do not."

Q. "For instance, the deposition which you said you have read of the doctor who has been called as the plaintiff's witness, page 4: 'I made an X-ray examination and I confirmed that diagnosis,' that is proper and approved practice, isn't it?"

A. "Yes, sir."

Q. "When these X-rays from this machine reach into the deep tissues, to this cancerous or sarcomatous growth, they destroy the growth? That is the purpose of the rays?"

A. "They do, yes."

Q. "And sometimes do those rays, when they go very deep, have some effect upon the tissues between the sarcomatous growth and the external part of the body?"

A. "Yes."

Q. "Sometimes a greater effect than even an ordinary erythema?"

A. "On the deeper structures."

Q. "Well, on the superficial structures?"

A. "I suppose they might have an effect on the skin."

Q. "As a matter of fact, they do have, don't they?"

A. "Yes, I think I could say yes."

Q. "In other words, this heavy voltage of X-ray shot into a depth of the body to attack a cancer will have some effect *on that which it goes through,* to reach the cancer?"

A. "Yes."

Q. "In X-ray therapy, deep therapy, where you are after sarcoma, or a cancer, what you are looking for is to get at that cancer, isn't it?"

A. "True."

Q. "In the same way that a surgeon in going after a diseased condition, we will say in the abdomen, will make a slit in the body with his knife to go in for it, isn't that so?"

A. "That is true."

Q. "The theory is the same?"

A. "Yes."

Q. "The ultimate object of the doctor is to get at the seat of the disease and attack it and eliminate it? That is the purpose of it all, isn't it?"

A. "Yes, sir."

Q. "The same purpose in X-ray therapy as in surgery, am I right?"

A. "You are right."

Q. "Then, in order to do that, it is proper, isn't it, for the doctor to consider primarily the ultimate enemy that he is attacking, namely, the cancer, that is right, isn't it?"

A. "Yes."

Q. "And what intervenes between the enemy, the cancer, and the outside is an incident to the attacking of the real thing, isn't that correct?"

A. "Yes, sir."

Q. "Sometimes then, in order to make this attack, one of the incidents of the attack is some effect upon the fat and fascia through which you go to get at the cancer, isn't that true?"

A. "That is true."

Q. "Did you assume in this case, that this growth was deep or not deep?"

A. "From my own examination?"

Q. "No, no, not at all, from the facts in this case, the testimony of the doctor who has been called as the plaintiff's witness?"

A. "That it was just below the skin? *I understood it to be just below the skin.*"

Q. "And have you given your whole opinion upon that basis?"

A. "Yes."

Q. "If you are wrong in that assumption of fact, that would alter your whole opinion?"

A. "Yes."

Q. "In other words, if this particular mass were *not* just below the skin, but extended down to the bone, the criticism which you suggested, at least by your testimony, you would naturally take back, wouldn't you?"

A. "Yes, sir."

Q. "I call your attention to the testimony of the doctor in this case, called as the plaintiff's witness: '*Q.* Did you make a diagnosis independent of Dr. Schwartz? *A.* I made an X-ray examination and I confirmed that diagnosis. *The X-ray examination showed the mass to extend into the soft tissues down to the bone.*' Now assuming that to be a fact, you will withdraw your criticism, will you not?"

A. "Yes."

An appeal was taken and thereafter withdrawn.

One of the greatest vices of expert medical testimony is the *hypothetical* question and answer which have come to play so important a part in our trials nowadays. This is, perhaps, the most abominable form of evidence that was ever allowed to choke the mind of a juror or throttle his intelligence.

A hypothetical question is supposed to be an accurate synopsis of the testimony that has already been sworn to by the various witnesses who have preceded the appearance of the medical expert in the case. The doctor is then asked to assume the truth of every fact which counsel has included in his question, and to give the jury his opinion and conclusions as an expert from these supposed facts.

It frequently happens that the physician has never even seen, much less examined, the patient concerning whose condition he is giving sworn testimony. Nine times out of ten the jury take the answer of the witness as direct evidence of the existence of the fact itself. It is the duty of the cross-examiner to enlighten the jury in regard to such questions and make them realize that it is not usually the truth of the *answer,* but the truth and accuracy of the *question* which requires their consideration. These hypothetical questions are usually loosely and inaccurately framed and present a very different aspect of the case from that which the testimony of the witnesses would justify. If, however, the question is substantially correct, it is allowed to be put to the witness; the damaging answer follows, and the jury conclude that the plaintiff is certainly suffering from the dreadful or incurable malady the doctor has apparently sworn to.

A clever cross-examiner is frequently able to shatter the injurious effect of such hypothetical questions. One useful method is to rise and demand of the physician that he repeat, in substance, the question that had just been put to him and upon which he bases his answer. The stumbling effort of the witness to recall the various stages of the question (such questions are usually very long) opens the eyes of the jury at once to the dangers of such testimony. It is not always safe, however, to make this inquiry. It all depends upon the character of witness you are examining. Some doctors, before being sworn as witnesses, study carefully the typewritten hypothetical questions which they are to answer. A single inquiry will easily develop this phase of the matter, and if the witness answers that he has previously read the question, it is often useful to ask him which particular part of it he lays the most stress upon, and which parts he could throw out altogether. Thus one may gradually narrow him down to some particular factor in the hypothetical question, the truth of which the previous testimony in the case might have left in considerable doubt.

It will often turn out that a single sentence or *twist* in the question serves as a foundation for the entire answer of the witness. This is especially the case with conscientious physicians, who often suggest to counsel the addition of a few words which will enable them to answer the entire question as desired. The development of this fact alone will do much to destroy the witness with the jury. I discovered once, upon cross-examining one of our most eminent physicians, that he had added the words, "Can you say *with positiveness*," to a lawyer's hypothetical question, and then had taken the stand and answered the question in the negative, although had he been asked for his honest *opinion* on the subject, he would have been obliged to give a different answer.

Hypothetical questions put in behalf of a plaintiff would not of course include facts which might develop later for the defence. When cross-examining to such questions, therefore, it is often useful to inquire in what respect the witness would modify his answer if he were to assume the truth of these new factors in the case. "Supposing that in addition to the matters you have already considered, there were to be added the facts that I will now give you," etc., "what would your opinion be then?" etc.

Henry W. Taft has, of late years, frequently been called upon in our Surrogate's Court to establish the validity of will drawn in his office, which, like the majority of wills involving large sums of money, are attacked by disappointed relatives.

Mr. Taft has a method quite his own in his cross-examinations when dealing with expert witnesses who have given the stereotyped answer negativing the mental capacity of the testator to make a will, after listening to the reading of a long hypothetical question embodying most of the facts brought out by the opponents of the will, and omitting many of the important features of the proponent's evidence. Mr. Taft persuades the witness to forget the hypothetical question for the moment, and to try to imagine himself, not as an expert witness testifying to the mental capacity of a dead man, with whom he had never had any personal contact, but as being called into consultation before the will was executed, to pass upon the mental capacity of the man while still living.

Naturally, the witness admits that he would, first of all, wish to examine the individual himself and apply the various tests known to his profession to determine his exact mental condition. Having completed his own examination, his next step would be a questioning of the attending family physician. By easy stages Mr. Taft has the witness making inquiries of the attendant nurses, the inmates of the household and all persons in close and intimate contact with the testator, until, unwittingly, the doctor finds that he has admitted that he would have formulated his opinion upon the statements of the very witnesses who have already testified in court in favor of the will.

I quote from an article written by Mr. Taft and printed in the New York *Sun:*—

"Recently I tried a contested will case in which three of the most eminent alienists in the country testified that the testator, who had suffered from a stroke of apoplexy, indicating a lesion of the brain, and had committed suicide, was not competent to execute a will. The surrogate directed a verdict sustaining the will, thus ruling against the opinion of the experts, that the testator was competent. The decision was unanimously sustained by the Appellate Division and the Court of Appeals, thus in effect deciding that the uncontradicted testimony of three eminent alienists did not rise to the dignity of legal evidence.[1] And yet the time of the courts continues to be occupied by testimony of expert witnesses, the public is put to an enormous expense by protracted trials, and the litigants themselves pay enormous fees to medical experts."

Frequently hypothetical questions are so framed that

[1] 190 App. Div. 896 (aff'd, 229 N. Y. 567).

they answer themselves by begging the question. In the Guiteau case all the medical experts were asked in effect, though not in form, to assume that a man having an hereditary taint of insanity, exhibits his *insanity* in his youth, exhibits it in his manhood, and at a subsequent date, being under the *insane delusion* that he was authorized and commanded by God to kill the President of the United States, proceeded *without cause* to kill him; and upon these assumptions the experts were asked to give their opinion whether such a man was sane or insane.

To pick out the flaws in most hypothetical questions, to single out the particular sentence, adjective, or adverb upon which the physician is centering his attention as he takes his oath, requires no little experience and astuteness.

Mr. Henry W. Taft has written frequent articles touching on hypothetical questions. In one of his pamphlets—"Opinion Evidence of Medical Witnesses"—he concludes with this broad statement: "Where the mental condition of a person is under examination and opinion evidence is in hopeless conflict, it frequently happens that it has little weight attached to it. This is no more than saying that in vigorously contested law suits the tendency of human beings is to base their action on concrete facts rather than upon theories as to which scientists themselves do not agree. In my own State of New York it has been recently held that the uncontradicted evidence of medical experts does not alone constitute a scintilla of proof requiring even that a case should be submitted to a jury." And in the Tracy Peerage case Lord Campbell said of expert witnesses that, "Hardly any weight should be given to their evidence."

Few lawyers would contend that the present method in civil cases of investigating matters involving the science of medicine is efficient. Bar associations and bar reformers have for years sought to remedy its defects, but so long as there are specialists, lay juries will have to wrestle with disputed questions as best they may.

I quote from Stevens' "On Trial by Jury and the Evidence of Experts":—

"Few spectacles, it might be said, can be more absurd and incongruous than that of a jury composed of twelve persons who, without any previous scientific knowledge or training, are suddenly called upon to adjudicate in controversies in which the most eminent scientific men flatly contradict each other's assertions. How, it might be asked, can ordinary tradesmen and farmers, who have never been accustomed to give sustained attention to any subject whatever for an hour together, be expected to weigh evidence, the delivery of which occupies many days, and which bears upon subjects which can only be described in language altogether new and foreign to their understandings? . . . It is indeed a weighty and important reflection that men actually have at times to judge, and that in matters of life and death, upon scientific evidence, without sitting on juries. A man observes a small swelling on his thigh. He goes to a surgeon, who says: 'This is an aneurism, and if you do not allow me to cut down upon the artery, and tie it, you may fall down dead at any moment.' He shows it to another, who says: 'It is no aneurism at all, but a mere tumor on which I will operate; if I do not, you will be exposed to some dreadful consequence or other; but if I am wrong and it is an aneurism, as soon as I make the first cut you are a dead man.' Here a man is judge of life and death in his own case, nor can he escape the necessity of deciding. He would, if a man of sense, probably be able to come to a pretty clear conclusion as to whether he should trust the first surgeon or the second, although he might know very little of surgery."

Where opinion evidence is sought to be obtained on hypothetical questions concerning the mental condition of a deceased person at a given time, there is room for honest and often wide differences of opinion. But when enormous fees are to be paid to so-called expert witnesses and especially where, as frequently happens, their compensation is dependent upon the result of a trial, the best of them may be unconsciously influenced in their judgment, while the opinions of the less scrupulous may be purposely adjusted to the financial interest.

I would cover the subject very inadequately if I did not emphasize the absurdities introduced into legal procedure by the hypothetical question. This is particularly the case in that large class of probate litigation where the mental capacity of a testator is under examination. Mr. Taft says:

"Under the procedure in my own State, both the proponent of a will and the contestant call one or more medical experts whose testimony is elicited by hypothetical questions which assume the truth of facts which are summarized, however slight the evidence may be, to establish them. If a jury finds any of the assumed facts to be untrue or incredible, the elaborate structure of the question itself and the answer of the witness falls like a house of cards. It frequently happens that the testimony of the experts is practically ignored and the jury decides the case solely upon other evidence, but so long as answers to hypothetical questions are admitted, lawyers will not omit to adopt tactics to discredit them. To illustrate the lengths to which the hypothetical question has gone, I may mention a contested will case recently tried in New York, in which a hypothetical question was propounded to three experts on each side. The two questions together consisted of about 36,000 words, that is, about thirty-six columns of newspaper print, and occupied more than four hours in the reading. I believe that evidence elicited by such questions serves only to unnecessarily occupy the time of the court and to confuse the jury."

In a later chapter Mr. Taft's scientific cross-examination of two expert witnesses, who had testified positively against him but whose testimony—after the cross-examination was finished—was given no weight whatever by the presiding Surrogate, is given in some detail. In still another chapter a cross-examination of one of these same expert witnesses by Mr. George Z. Medalie is recorded.

A close study of these examples is highly recommended to students and trained lawyers, as well.

The professional witness is always partisan, ready and

eager to serve the party calling him. This fact should be ever present in the mind of the cross-examiner. Encourage the witness to betray his partisanship; encourage him to volunteer statements and opinions, and to give unresponsive answers. Jurors always look with suspicion upon such testimony. Assume that an expert witness called against you has come prepared to do you all the harm he can, and will avail himself of every opportunity to do so which you may inadvertently give him. Such witnesses are usually shrewd and cunning men, and come into court well prepared on the subject concerning which they are to testify.

Some experts, however, are mere shams and pretenders. I remember witnessing many years ago the utter collapse of one of these expert pretenders of the medical type. It was in a damage suit against the city, which I defended. The plaintiff's doctor was a loquacious gentleman of considerable personal presence. He testified to a serious head injury, and proceeded to "lecture" the jury on the subject in a sensational and oracular manner which evidently made a great impression upon them. Even the judge seemed to give more than the usual attention. The doctor talked glibly about "vasomotor nerves" and "reflexes" and expressed himself almost entirely in medical terms which the jury did not understand. He polished off his testimony with the prediction that the plaintiff could never recover, and if he lived at all, it would necessarily be within the precincts of an insane asylum. I saw at a glance that this was no ordinary type of witness. Any cross-examination on the medical side of the case would be sure to fail; for the witness, though evidently dishonest, was yet ingenious enough to cover his tracks by the cuttlefish expedient of befogging his answers in a cloud of medical terms. Dr. Allan McLane Hamilton, who was present as medical advisor in behalf of the city, suggested an expedient which I adopted as follows:

Counsel. "Doctor, I infer from the number of books that you have brought here to substantiate your position, and from your manner of testifying, that you are very familiar with the literature of your profession, and especially that part relating to head injury."

Doctor. "I pride myself that I am—I have not only a large private library, but have spent many months in the libraries of Vienna, Berlin, Paris, and London."

Counsel. "Then perhaps you are acquainted with Andrews's celebrated work 'On the Recent and Remote Effects of Head Injury'?"

Doctor (smiling superciliously). "Well, I should say I was. I had occasion to consult it only last week."

Counsel. "Have you ever come across 'Charvais on Cerebral Trauma'?"

Doctor. "Yes, I have read Dr. Charvais's book from cover to cover many times."

Counsel continued in much the same strain, putting to the witness similar questions relating to many other fictitious medical works, all of which the doctor had either "studied carefully" or "had in his library about to read," until finally, suspecting that the doctor was becoming conscious of the trap into which he was being led, counsel suddenly changed his tactics and demanded in a loud sneering tone if the doctor had ever read Page on "Injuries of the Spine and Spinal Cord" (a genuine and most learned treatise on the subject). To this inquiry the doctor laughingly replied, "I never heard of any such book and I guess you never did either!"

The climax had been reached. Dr. Hamilton was immediately sworn for the defence and explained to the jury his participation in preparing the list of bogus medical works with which the learned expert for the plaintiff had shown such familiarity.

On the other hand, when the cross-examiner has totally failed to shake the testimony of an able and honest expert, he should be very wary of attempting to discredit him by any slurring allusions to his professional ability, as is well illustrated by the following example of the danger of giving the expert a good chance for a retort.

Dr. Joseph Collins, a well known nerve specialist, was

giving testimony recently on the side of the Metropolitan Street Railway in a case where the plaintiff claimed to be suffering from a misplaced kidney which the railroad doctor's examination failed to disclose. Having made nothing out of the cross-examination of Dr. Collins, the plaintiff's lawyer threw this parting boomerang at the witness:

Counsel. "After all, doctor, isn't it a fact that nobody in your profession regards you as a surgeon?"

Doctor. "I never regarded myself as one."

Counsel. "You are a neurologist, aren't you, doctor?"

Doctor. "I am, sir."

Counsel. "A neurologist pure and simple?"

Doctor. "Well, I am moderately pure and altogether simple!"

In Los Angeles recently Milton Carlson, a well known handwriting expert, turned the tables upon Mr. Horace Appel, a noted local criminal lawyer, in a way that should serve as a warning to careless handling of expert witnesses accustomed to the witness chair.

This particular incident occurred during the trial of David Caplan, who was associated with the McNamara brothers in the dynamiting of the Times Building,—cases of international importance. The question of handwriting was one of the pivotal points at issue. Carlson was the sole expert relied upon by the prosecution in the Caplan case. Appel was defending the accused.

In the course of his testimony Carlson made the statement that *the opinion of handwriting experts is superior to another person's opinion, even of his own handwriting.*

Q. "Do you mean to say that you know more about my handwriting than I do?" asked Mr. Appel.

A. "I have said that the opinion of an expert is frequently of more weight than the opinion of the person who wrote the questioned writing."

Counsel waited for several minutes and then produced a paper on which there appeared a number of sentences in apparently different handwritings.

Q. "Can you tell me if one person wrote these, and if so, how many pens were used?"

The witness looked at the writing for a moment and asked for more time to examine it. The request was granted and the expert witness took the writing to his office.

After recess Carlson, who had imitated the questioned document during the noon hour, so that he could discuss it more intelligently, returned to court and inadvertently left the paper, which he had written in imitation of the other, on the table usually occupied by the cross-examining attorney. When Appel continued his cross-examination he picked up this paper, studied it and apparently recognizing it said:

Q. "Mr. expert witness, if you have sufficiently examined it, please now tell us how many people wrote this paper?"

Carlson reached for the paper, recognized it at once as his own imitation and answered politely—

A. "One person wrote this and he wrote it with one pen."

Q. "Are you sure?"

A. "Absolutely."

"I will prove that it was written with *two* pens for I wrote it myself in this very court room," shouted Appel, as he dashed across the court room to reach the two pens he had used.

Judge Willis then pointed out to the witness that he had made a very positive statement and not merely given his opinion, and Carlson again reiterated that he meant to be positive in his statement. Appel refused to cross-examine further.

Just as Carlson started to leave the stand, District Attorney Doran took the witness in hand.

Q. "How do you know one person wrote these statements, and that one pen was used?"

A. "Because," replied the witness, *"I wrote them myself with one pen in my office at the noon recess.* Mr. Appel evidently thought he recognized his own handwriting, and this incident may tend to prove what I said before, that sometimes handwriting experts know more about questioned writing, even than the person who wrote it."

The witness then explained that he had roughly imitated the writing given to him by the lawyer so that he could more readily explain his points to the jury.

That sometimes questioned writings may be convincingly proved without calling an expert, the following will serve as a startling illustration.

In a divorce action tried before a referee, part of the evidence introduced against the defendant wife, to show an adulterous disposition, was a series of exhibits consisting of love letters addressed to the co-respondent and apparently in the undisguised handwriting of the defendant.

The wife was sworn as a witness in her own defence and denied the writing of these letters. In one of them occurred the sentence: "Every one to-day was flattering me and it was so empty, the *touch* of your dear hand in mine, how it would rest me—when will you be down, dear, and when can we get married?"

Upon cross-examination Col. William Rand, who was conducting the case for the husband, asked the witness if she would be willing to write for the benefit of the referee. She readily complied with the suggestion and, after removing her glove and choosing pen and pencil to her liking, proceeded to write fifteen or more phrases dictated to her by the cross-examiner, first with pen and then with pencil, and in a handwriting indistinguishable from that of the exhibits. These contained words selected from the disputed letters, offered as evidence, but framed in somewhat different contexts. Among them was the sentence, "In the deep woods you and I are out of touch with the world."

Without hesitation, first with pen and then with pencil, the witness wrote:

"In the deep woods you and I are out of *touch* with the world."

Chapter 6

The Sequence of Cross-Examination

MUCH DEPENDS upon the *sequence* in which one conducts the cross-examination of a dishonest witness. You should never hazard the important question until you have laid the foundation for it in such a way that, when confronted with the fact, the witness can neither deny nor explain it. One often sees the most damaging documentary evidence, in the form of letters or affidavits, fall absolutely flat as betrayers of falsehood, merely because of the unskilful way in which they are handled. If you have in your possession a letter written by the witness, in which he takes an opposite position on some part of the case to the one he has just sworn to, avoid the common error of showing the witness the letter for identification, and then reading it to him with the inquiry, "What have you to say to that?" During the reading of his letter the witness will be collecting his thoughts and getting ready his explanations in anticipation of the question that is to follow, and the effect of the damaging letter will be lost.

The correct method of using such a letter is to lead the witness quietly into repeating the statements he has made in his direct testimony, and which his letter contradicts. "I have you down as saying so and so; will you please repeat it? I am apt to read my notes to the jury, and I want to be accurate." The witness will repeat his statement. Then write it down and read it off to him. "Is that correct? Is there any doubt about it? For if you have any explanation or qualification to make, I think you owe it to us, in justice, to make it before I leave the subject." The witness has none. He has stated the fact; there is nothing to qualify; the jury rather like his straightforwardness. Then let your whole manner toward him suddenly change, and

131

spring the letter upon him. "Do you recognize your own handwriting, sir? Let me read you from your own letter, in which you say,"—and afterward—"Now, what have you to say to that?" You will make your point in such fashion that the jury will not readily forget it. It is usually expedient, when you have once made your point, to drop it and go to something else, lest the witness wriggle out of it. But when you have a witness under oath, who is orally contradicting a statement he has previously made, when not under oath, but in his own handwriting, you then have him fast on the hook, and there is no danger of his getting away; now is the time to press your advantage. Put his self-contradictions to him in as many forms as you can invent:—

"Which statement is true?" "Had you forgotten this letter when you gave your testimony to-day?" "Did you tell your counsel about it?" "Were you intending to deceive him?" "What was your object in trying to mislead the jury?" [1]

"Some men," said a London barrister who often saw Sir Charles Russell in action, "get in a bit of the nail, and there they leave it hanging loosely about until the judge or some one else pulls it out. But when Russell got in a bit of the nail, he never stopped until he drove it home. No man ever pulled *that* nail out again."

It not infrequently happens that the plaintiff and defendant are themselves the only witnesses to some oral agreement which becomes the subject of their litigation. Such cases often afford the most striking opportunities for cross-examination, where the advocate is armed with letters written by the party examined.

In a case of this kind that I conducted some years ago the plaintiff swore that the defendant, the late James B. Haggin, owed him over a quarter of a million dollars as the result of an oral agreement made between them in the

[1] In Chapter XIII (*infra*) is given in detail the cross-examination of the witness Pigott by Sir Charles Russell, which affords a striking example of the most effective use that can be made of an incriminating letter.

presence of only one witness, who was *dead* at the time of the trial.

The first two hours of my cross-examination of the plaintiff were devoted to the effort to throw him off his guard. I exhibited to him, by my questions, an apparent want of appreciation of the case and of the surrounding circumstances allowed him to score on me over and over again, until he was in the best of humor and was evidently feeling very confident of himself, at least so far as any fear of me was concerned, but all the time he was making admissions and misleading statements of fact and even absolute fabrications which I knew would eventually be his undoing. I passed them all by as if they had aroused no suspicions in my mind whatsoever, although I was in a state of intense secret exultation. Finally he became so absolutely certain of himself that I was able to encourage him to hand me out big chunks of perjured testimony which I knew would fairly engulf him later on.

I had about a dozen of the plaintiff's letters which I was confident he had either forgotten having written or else felt assured were safe in a foreign country, and which I felt equally sure he would repudiate as forgeries if he recalled their contents, or had the faintest idea that they were in my possession; and if he denied them, it would be difficult to prove their genuineness and consequently be impossible to use them. I had no admittedly genuine specimens of his handwriting.

I was watching the clock all the time for the hour of adjournment, ever keeping the witness pleased and even smiling over the seeming weakness of my cross-examination. Just at four o'clock, the hour for adjournment, and as he began actually to feel that quarter of a million dollars already won and in his pocket, I handed up to him a bundle of his letters, in a manner from which he might readily infer that they were of no consequence or at least as if I had not had time to read them, and asked him if he would "please identify his handwriting before the court adjourned." He started to read the first one. Had he done so all would have been over, but I checked him by reminding him that it was four o'clock, and requested him to please not delay the adjournment by reading the letters, as all I wanted to know was if they were in his handwriting. In a moment or two he had identified them all and the court adjourned.

The following day I cross-examined him throughout the entire day about these letters. They contradicted in a hundred different ways the assertions he had made so glibly the afternoon before, and at the end of the court session his lawyer, the late John B. Stanchfield, actually withdrew from the case and a verdict was directed against him by the court, although neither side had called any witnesses other than the plaintiff himself.

It was one of those rare cases where the cross-examiner has the written proofs of a witness's perfidy, which become such deadly weapons in the hands of any experienced advocate.

Sometimes, on the other hand, it is advisable to deal the witness a stinging blow with your first few questions; this, of course, assumes that you have the material with which to do it. The advantage of putting your best point forward at the very start is twofold. First, the jury have been listening to his direct testimony and have been forming their own impressions of him, and when you rise to cross-examine, they are keen for your first questions. If you "land one" in the first bout, it makes far more impression on the jury than if it came later on when their attention has begun to lag, and when it might only appear as a chance shot. The second, and perhaps more important, effect of scoring on the witness with the first group of questions is that it makes him afraid of you and less hostile in his subsequent answers, not knowing when you will trip him again and give him another fall. This will often enable you to obtain from him truthful answers on subjects about which you are not prepared to contradict him.

I have seen the most determined witness completely lose his presence of mind after two or three well directed blows given at the very start of his cross-examination, and become as docile in the examiner's hands as if he were his own witness. This is the time to lead the witness back to his original story and give him the opportunity to tone it down or retint it, as it were; possibly even to switch him over until he finds himself supporting your side of the controversy.

This taming of a hostile witness, and forcing him to tell the truth against his will, is one of the triumphs of the cross-examiner's art. In a speech to the jury, Choate once said of such a witness, "I brand him a vagabond and a villain; they brought him to curse, and, behold, he hath blessed us altogether."

Some witnesses, under this style of examination, lose their tempers completely, and if the examiner only keeps his own and puts his questions rapidly enough, he will be sure to lead the witness into such a web of contradictions as entirely to discredit him with any fair minded jury. A witness, in anger, often forgets himself and speaks the truth. His passion benumbs his power to deceive. Still another sort of witness displays his temper on such occasions by becoming sullen, he begins by giving evasive answers, and ends by refusing to answer at all. He might as well go a little farther and admit his perjury at once, so far as the effect on the jury is concerned.

When, however, you have not the material at hand with which to frighten the witness into correcting his perjured narrative, and yet you have concluded that a cross-examination is necessary, as a general rule it is but a waste of time to put questions which will enable him to repeat his original testimony in the sequence in which he first gave it. You can accomplish nothing with him unless you abandon the train of ideas he followed in giving his main story. Select the weakest points of his testimony and the attendant circumstances he would be least likely to prepare for. Do not ask your questions in logical order, lest he invent conveniently as he goes along; but dodge him about in his story and pin him down to precise answers on all the accidental circumstances indirectly associated with his main narrative. As he begins to invent his answers, put your questions more rapidly, asking many unimportant ones to one important one, and all in the same voice. If he is not telling the truth, and answering from memory and associated ideas rather than from imagination, he will never be able to invent his answers as quickly as you can frame your questions, and at the same time correctly estimate the bearing his present answer may have upon those that have preceded it. If you have the requisite skill to pursue this method of questioning, you will be sure to land him in a maze of self-contradictions from which he will never be able to extricate himself.

One of the most thankless, but at the same time effective, uses of the opportunity to cross-examine opposing witnesses—a method which requires the greatest self-restraint and patience—is to content oneself with an apparently trifling admission from one witness, perhaps a further admission from the following witness, and thus gradually collect material which, when pieced into a mosaic, as it were, in the summing up, will surprise even your own client and compel a verdict in his favor. I have often employed this method myself, and have invariably had to meet at first the profound disappointment of my client, only to be congratulated by him at the finish of the case when he began to see the little bits of testimony gradually being fitted into one another in an unanswerable argument in his favor.

A real estate broker was suing to recover his commission on an alleged contract for the sale of a piece of real estate. The plaintiff claimed that the conversation between the parties comprising the purchase and sale had taken place on the 28th of December, the previous year, at the very premises that were the subject of the sale.

The janitress of the building took the witness stand and testified that on that day the plaintiff-broker, the defendant-owner and the proposed purchaser all appeared at the house at about noon. The owner directed her to show the proposed purchaser and the broker through the building. That gave her the opportunity to hear the conversation in question. But it took her away from her kitchen and therefore prevented her from preparing the noon day meal in time for her children, who were then about coming home from school. She remembered distinctly that when she came back from the trip through the building her two boys were home from school and complained that from the delay they would be late in returning. She, however, hurried through the preparations, serving them their meal, and got them off as soon as she could. Her elder son, a boy about twelve years of age, and a fine looking little chap, took the witness stand. He remembered the defendant and the plaintiff and the proposed purchaser being there. He recalled that his mother was delayed in coming down to serve them their meal, and he remembered that it got very late and that he was calling his mother's attention to the fact that he and his brother would be late at school. They ran all the way from home to the school, and when they got near the school there was one of the monitors in front of the school, ringing the bell, indicating that it was late. He rushed into his class room just at the last moment and was not late, but he remembered later that on his brother's report his brother was marked late for the afternoon session.

The cross-examination was unimportant and trivial— practically a repetition of what he had said on direct. The younger brother was then called, and he corroborated his mother and his brother, and added the fact that he did get in late and was marked late. His cross-examination was negligible.

The plaintiff and the proposed purchaser were then recalled by counsel and asked how it was that they fixed the date on which these incidents had occurred. The plaintiff produced an entry in his diary, and by other circumstances fixed the date with absolute certainty. It could not have been on any other day. The proposed purchaser fixed it by entirely different circumstances, but he, too, was positive that it could not have been any other day.

The elder of the two boys was then recalled to the witness box and asked whether he would mind explaining to the jury how it was that he went to school on the 28th of December, when every public school in the city happened to be closed between the 25th of December and the 1st of

January, both days inclusive. He looked all around the room in a most hopeless manner, said that he could not explain, and thus a perfect case was destroyed by an over-perfect story.

Some witnesses, though unwilling to perjure themselves, are yet determined not to tell the *whole* truth if they can help it, owing to some personal interest in, or relationship to, the party on whose behalf they are called to testify. If you are instructed that such a witness (generally a woman) is in possession of the fact you want and can help you if she chooses, it is your task to draw it out of her. This requires much patience and ingenuity. If you put the direct question to her at once, you will probably receive a "don't remember" answer, or she may even indulge her conscience in a mental reservation and pretend a willingness but inability to answer. You must approach the subject by slow stages. Begin with matters remotely connected with the important fact you are aiming at. She will relate these, not perhaps realizing on the spur of the moment exactly where they will lead her. Having admitted that much, you can lead her nearer and nearer by successive approaches to the gist of the matter, until you have her in such a dilemma that she must either tell you what she had intended to conceal or else openly commit perjury. When she leaves the witness chair, you can almost hear her whisper to her friends, "I never intended to tell it, but that man put me in such a position I simply had to tell or admit that I was lying."

One very skilful method of handling a witness, particularly when he is not only intelligent but shifty, is not to disclose your "trump card"—if you have one—until you have so completely committed the witness to the details of his story as to make it impossible to offer any plausible explanation of the damaging document with which you intend to destroy him.

In a recent case brought by the Standard Oil Company of New Jersey, in the name of the original assignee, against the Texas Company, which was tried in our State Supreme Court before Mr. Justice McAvoy, the issues, involving many millions of dollars, were decided in favor of the nominal plaintiff, George T. Rogers, largely because of an admission wrung from a co-defendant, Joseph H. Adams, while he was unaware of its importance.

This vital admission enabled the plaintiff to demonstrate that a long forgotten document, innocent enough in itself, which had been delivered to Rogers by Adams many years before, to inform him what the invention was in which he was buying an interest, described the very same mechanical features that the Texas Company claimed belonged to it alone.

The co-defendant Adams was an inventor of a valuable process for converting crude oil into gasoline, now in general use in the oil industry. Years before the suit, needing money for his early experiments, he transferred nearly half of his interest in the invention to Rogers for $5,000. At the time of the transfer, in 1907, fifteen years before the trial, Adams delivered to Rogers a sealed envelope supposed to contain a description of the invention, enjoining Rogers not to open the envelope until after his (Adams') death.

These early experiments proved unsuccessful, but later ones, dealing with the same general subject, resulted in the issuance of valuable patents and the acquisition of the entire invention by the Texas Company in 1919, to the complete exclusion of Rogers.

At the trial the Texas Company claimed that the invention as finally patented was not the invention assigned in part to Rogers, because, in the early experiments financed by Rogers, the inventor employed a vacuum feature, while in the valuable patented process, *pressure* was used and not *vacuum*. Whether Rogers, and through him the Standard Oil Company, had any interest in the pressure patents was the main issue involved.

It appeared that Adams had also assigned an interest in the same invention to the firm of Cary & Robinson by a contract which was subsequently cancelled. In this contract were references to a so-called "caveat," which mentioned the use of "pressure."

The cross-examination of Adams by Herbert C. Smyth had proceeded for nearly three days, committing the witness to a detailed narration of circumstances, during which time there had been no mention by the examiner of the apparently forgotten sealed document of 1907 until at the very close, when it was too late even to attempt to explain it away with any hope of plausibility:

Q. "Did you understand that Cary & Robinson, by their contract with you, were limited to the vacuum phase of your process?"

A. "No."

Q. "Did they have an interest in the pressure?"

A. "They might have had an interest for a time while their contract was in force."

The Court: Q. "The same interest as in the vacuum process?"

A. "They had an interest based upon the caveat which was in existence at that time, then filed in the early part of 1907."

Q. "That caveat was in respect to your possible internal heat and *pressure* process?"

A. "It did not state either one or the other, but it did mention both."

Q. "It was intended to refer to both processes?"

A. "It was intended to refer to either one or the other."

Q. "Did you intend it that way?"

A. "I drew the caveat. I mentioned that either was useful, either vacuum or pressure."

Mr. Smyth: Q. "Then it was based on the caveat that you made up your mind that this contract gave Cary & Robinson an interest in the pressure process as well as the vacuum process?"

A. "It covered both vacuum and pressure with relation to the use of the electric heater."

The Court: Q. "Was the agreement according to your understanding, giving them a right to the pressure process or an interest therein, because of what was described by you in the caveat?"

A. "That would apparently be so, because that was the only thing."

Mr. Smyth: Q. "I do not care about the because. Yes or no."

A. "That would apparently be so."

(The agreement with Cary & Robinson was then produced.)

Q. "Do you want to read it?"

A. "Yes, sir. (Reading) Yes, this is the agreement."

(The agreement was then marked in evidence and attention was called to its reference to the caveat.)

Q. "Is this the caveat, which has been handed to me by your counsel, that is referred to?"

A. "This is apparently a true copy of the caveat, if it is acknowledged by counsel." (Then some papers were produced written by the witness and filed in the Patent Office, which claimed the use of pressure as far back as 1907, the date of Adams' contract with the plaintiff.)

Q. "When you used the words in these papers 'dating back to 1907,' are you referring back to that caveat of January, 1907?"

A. "Presumably, since the caveat itself and the drawings attached were filed at that time."   .

Q. "I call your attention to the diagram which is attached to the caveat, and ask you, referring to defendants' exhibit F, which is labelled 'Internal heat and pressure,' whether that is not the same machine?"

A. "It is the same general type of heater, the two drawings being somewhat similar."

Q. "But they are shown in the caveat, being drawing B-116?"

A. "Yes, they are substantially the same."

Q. "Now, Mr. Adams, do you recollect that in your early negotiations with Mr. Rogers you gave him some papers that you sealed?"

A. "Yes, I believe I did."

Q. "Didn't you give him a copy of the caveat?"

A. *"I don't recollect at this time."*

Q. "You have no recollection of what you gave him?"

A. "I recollect I gave him some drawings and descriptions, but what they were I can't remember at this time."

Q. "Did not those drawings and descriptions refer to pressure as well as to vacuum?"

A. "I could not say."

Q. "Are you willing that the Court should see what you gave him?"

A. "I do not see why I should object."

Q. "Is this the envelope that you gave him?"

A. "It appears to be."

Q. "Is that your handwriting?"

A. "Yes."

Q. "Will you remove the contents and see if that is in your handwriting?"

A. "Yes, sir, that is a drawing that I made."

Q. "Is not that the original drawing of the caveat?"

A. "It appears to be a transfer from the original Patent Office drawing."

Q. "Now look at the description that is contained in the envelope that you have just removed; is not that the original form of the caveat in your own handwriting?"

A. "This is my own handwriting."

Q. "And is that what you gave Mr. Rogers, that and the drawing, fifteen years ago when the contract was made with him?"

A. "If this is the paper and the drawing that were in that envelope before it was opened, then I would say that. The envelope has been handed to me cut open with those papers within it."

Q. "I assure you that it is."

A. "I do not doubt your statement."

Q. "I can assure you that it is; that it was delivered to Mr. Rogers' attorneys intact; that the seal was broken by his attorneys, and that it is in the same condition now as when it was delivered."

Mr. Oeland: "Who authorized the opening of it?"

Mr. Smyth: "The Majesty of the Law."

Mr. Oeland: "Standard Oil, you mean."

Q. "Will you look at this end and see if it is the caveat, and I also call your attention to the legend at the top, in your own handwriting, and ask you to read it?"

A. (Witness reading.) *"Caveat, copy of original filed at Washington Patent Office, January 2, 1907."*

It was the successful use of this forgotten, fifteen year old written document, in Mr. Smyth's possession, which enabled him, in a few well directed blows, to shatter the entire stronghold of the defense, in a trial lasting many weeks, and involving questions of ownership in an invention that has been variously valued between ten and forty million dollars.

An English lady once asked the Lord Chief Justice what was necessary in order to win a case in court. He replied: "First, you need a good case, then you need good evidence, then you need good witnesses, then you need a good judge, then you need a good jury, and then you need *good luck.*"

The celebrated case of Reich *vs.* Cochran, which had been in the courts for thirty-two years and was only finally decided in favor of the defendant by the Court of Appeals a few months ago, affords a striking illustration, not only of the uncertainty of litigation, but of this *good luck* which is sometimes more important than skill on the part of the cross-examiner.

There had been three trials of this case and a dozen or more appeals to higher courts. The litigation concerned the old Cambridge Hotel at 33rd Street and Fifth Avenue, opposite the Waldorf Hotel. Reich had secured a long ground lease from the Astor Estate and wanted to rebuild the property. Cochran had been advancing him money for that purpose until the advances had aggregated several hundred thousand dollars. After numerous defaults on Reich's part, Cochran took over the lease and gave back to Reich a sub-lease for a term of years with the rentals so arranged that he (Cochran) would just about get back his money at the termination of the lease.

Reich defaulted in the payment of the rent and was dispossessed some time in 1902. Thereupon ensued a stream of litigation, beginning with an action by Reich, in which he claimed he was an illiterate Hungarian, unable to read or write English or any other language; that the assignment of the Astor lease to Cochran and the giving back of the sublease to him (Reich) were not absolute transfers, but were given as security for an usurious loan and that they were fraudulent.

The first trial was before Mr. Justice Giegerich, and the decision was in favor of Reich, whose long and intricate story of wrong-doing at the hands of Cochran was taken at its face value by the presiding judge, who denounced Cochran in unmeasured terms. The case was taken to the Appellate Division, where the judgment was reversed upon technical grounds, but the Court again took occasion to excoriate Cochran in an opinion in which Reich's story was upheld.

The next trial was before the late Justice Bischoff, and again lasted for six weeks. The plaintiff Reich had given his direct story and recited his wrongs during three or four days' session of the Court,—before being handed over for cross-examination to Mr. Samuel Untermyer, representing Cochran's executors, he having died.

After two days' cross-examination, the presiding judge called Mr. Untermyer to the bench and warned him to conclude his cross-examination, saying that it, in his judgment, had gone far enough, as Reich appeared to him to be telling the truth. Mr. Untermyer persuaded the Court to bear with him for another day, upon his agreement to finish the examination if by that time he had not succeeded in proving to the Court that the witness was a keen, clever business man, and merely posing as ignorant and illiterate.

Reich's entire story was predicated upon his claim of ignorance, illiteracy and want of understanding of the dozen or more documents that had been signed by him. He had also charged not only the defendant, Cochran, but the defendant's lawyers—prominent members of the Bar —with being parties to the conspiracy to defraud him of his rights.

Just at the close of the third day it occurred to Mr. Untermyer to make one last leap in the dark, and he turned sharply upon the witness with the question, "Were you not a Rabbi in the old country?"—to which the witness unguardedly replied: *"I don't remember."* Rabbis in the old country, as everybody knows, were men of deep learning, and from that time on Mr. Untermyer had very easy sailing in his cross-examination, which lasted for about ten days and which succeeded in completely demolishing the plaintiff's story.

Mr. Untermyer had no foundation for the question other than the general appearance of the man, which suggested that he might have been a Rabbi at one time in his life, and if so must, of necessity, be a highly educated man.

Judge Bischoff in deciding the case for Cochran denounced Reich and repudiated his entire story, and the Judge's findings went to the Court of Appeals, where the decision was unanimously affirmed.

It is not an uncommon practice among the younger lawyers, who have read of the triumphs of their more experienced seniors, to try to imitate them in their own practice. This is praiseworthy enough, but the proper occasion is not always selected.

The question: "Where were you on the 29th day of last October?" was put by one of these young advocates without the slightest motive on his part, but as a chance shot to see if he could develop something to his advantage— embarrassment, if nothing else.

Opposing Counsel. "I object to the question as immaterial, and as evidently intended to bring in some collateral matter that has nothing to do with the issue in this case."

By the Court. "How can I determine that, until I hear the answer?"

Cross-examining Counsel. "Oh, very well, if my opponent wants to conceal the facts from the jury, I am willing to withdraw the question."

Witness, to the Court. "Your Honor, I am perfectly willing to answer the question."

By the Court. "You see, gentlemen, the witness himself is willing to answer, so I presume all objections are withdrawn. Now, Mr. Witness, you may answer the question and tell the jury where you were on the 29th of last October."

Witness, promptly. "*I don't remember where I was,* your Honor."

In all your cross-examinations never lose control of the witness; confine his answers to the exact questions you ask. He will try to dodge direct answers, or if forced to answer directly, will attempt to add a qualification or an explanation which will rob his answer of the benefit it might otherwise be to you. And lastly, most important of all, let me repeat the injunction to be ever on the alert for a *good place to stop.* Nothing can be more important than to close your examination with a triumph. So many lawyers succeed in catching a witness in a serious contradiction; but, not satisfied with this, go on asking questons, and taper off their examination until the effect upon the jury of their former advantage is lost altogether. "Stop with a victory" is one of the maxims of cross-examination. If you have done nothing more than to expose an attempt to deceive on the part of the witness, you have gone a long way toward discrediting him with your jury. Jurymen are apt to regard a witness as a whole—either they believe him or they do not. If they distrust him, they are likely to disregard his testimony altogether, though much of it may have been true. The fact that remains uppermost in their minds is that he attempted to deceive them, or that he left the witness stand with a lie upon his lips, or after he had displayed his ignorance to such an extent that the entire audience laughed at him. Thereafter his evidence is dismissed from the case so far as they are concerned.

Erskine once wasted a whole day in trying to expose to a jury the lack of mental balance of a witness, until a physician who was assisting him suggested that Erskine ask the witness whether he did not believe himself to be Jesus Christ. This question was put by Erskine very cautiously and with studied humility, accompanied by a request for forgiveness for the indecency of the question. The witness, who was at once taken unawares, amid breathless silence and with great solemnity exclaimed, "I am the Christ"—which soon ended the case.

Chapter 7

Silent Cross-Examination

NOTHING could be more absurd or a greater waste of time than to cross-examine a witness who has testified to no material fact against you. And yet, strange as it may seem, the courts are full of young lawyers—and alas! not only young ones—who seem to feel it their duty to cross-examine every witness who is sworn. They seem afraid that their clients or the jury will suspect them of ignorance or inability to conduct a trial. It not infrequently happens that such unnecessary examinations result in the development of new theories of the case for the other side; and a witness who might have been disposed of as harmless by mere silence, develops into a formidable obstacle in the case.

The infinite variety of types of witnesses one meets with in court makes it impossible to lay down any set rules applicable to all cases. One seldom comes in contact with a witness who is in all respects like any one he has ever examined before; it is this that constitutes the fascination of the art. The particular method you use in any given case depends upon the degree of importance you attach to the testimony given by the witness, even if it is false. It may be that you have on your own side so many witnesses who will contradict the testimony, that it is not worth while to hazard the risks you will necessarily run by undertaking an elaborate cross-examination. In such cases by far the better course is to keep your seat and ask no questions at all. Much depends also, as will be readily appreciated, upon the age and sex of the witness. In fact, it may be said that the truly great trial lawyer is he who, while knowing perfectly well the established rules of his art, appreciates when they should be broken. If the witness happens to be a woman, and at the close of her testimony—

in-chief it seems that she will be more than a match for the cross-examiner, it often works like a charm with the jury to practise upon her what may be styled the silent cross-examination. Rise suddenly, as if you intended to cross-examine. The witness will turn a determined face toward you, preparatory to demolishing you with her first answer. This is the signal for you to hesitate a moment. Look her over good-naturedly and as if you were in doubt whether it would be worth while to question her—and sit down. It can be done by a good actor in such a manner as to be equivalent to saying to the jury, "What's the use? she is only a woman."

John Philpot Curran, known as the most popular advocate of his time, and second only to Erskine as a jury lawyer, once indulged himself in this silent mode of cross-examination, but made the mistake of speaking his thoughts aloud before he sat down. "There is no use asking you questions, for I see the villain in your face." "Do you, sir?" replied the witness with a smile. "I never knew before that my face was a looking-glass."

Since the sole object of cross-examination is to break the force of the adverse testimony, it must be remembered that a futile attempt only strengthens the witness with the jury. It cannot be too often repeated, therefore, that saying nothing will frequently have a better result than hours of questioning. It is experience alone that can teach us which method to adopt.

An amusing instance of this occurred in the trial of Alphonse Stephani, indicted for the murder of Clinton G. Reynolds, a prominent lawyer in New York, who had had the management and settlement of his father's estate. The defence was insanity; but the prisoner, though evidently suffering from the early stages of some serious brain disorder, was still not insane in the legal acceptation of the term. He was convicted of murder in the second degree and sentenced to a life imprisonment.

Stephani was defended by the late William F. Howe, who was certainly one of the most successful lawyers of his time in criminal cases. Howe was not a great lawyer, but the kind of witnesses ordinarily met with in such cases he often handled with a skill that was little short of positive genius.

Dr. Allan McLane Hamilton, the eminent alienist, had made a special study of Stephani's case, had visited him for weeks at the Tombs Prison, and had prepared himself for a most exhaustive exposition of his mental condition. Dr. Hamilton had been retained by Mr. Howe, and was to be put forward by the defence as their chief witness. Upon calling him to the witness chair, however, he did not question his witness so as to lay before the jury the extent of his experience in mental disorders and his familiarity with all forms of insanity, nor develop before them the doctor's peculiar opportunities for judging correctly of the prisoner's present condition. The wily advocate evidently looked upon District Attorney DeLancey Nicoll and myself who were opposed to him, as a couple of inexperienced youngsters, who would cross-examine at great length and allow the witness to make every answer tell with double effect when elicited by the state's attorney. It has always been supposed that it was a preconceived plan of action between the learned doctor and the advocate. In accordance therewith, and upon the examination-in-chief, Mr. Howe contented himself with this single inquiry:—

"Dr. Hamilton, you have examined the prisoner at the Bar, have you not?"

"I have, sir," replied Dr. Hamilton.

"Is he, in your opinion, sane or insane?" continued Mr. Howe.

"Insane," said Dr. Hamilton.

"You may cross-examine," thundered Howe, with one of his characteristic gestures. There was a hurried consultation between Mr. Nicoll and his associates.

"We have no questions," remarked Mr. Nicoll, quietly.

"What!" exclaimed Howe, "not ask the famous Dr. Hamilton a question? Well, *I* will," and turning to the witness began to ask him how close a study he had made of the prisoner's symptoms, etc.; when, upon our objection,

Chief Justice Van Brunt directed the witness to leave the witness box, as his testimony was concluded, and ruled that inasmuch as the direct examination had been finished, and there had been no cross-examination, there was no course open to Mr. Howe but to call his next witness!

Mr. Sergeant Ballantine in his autobiography, "Some Experiences of a Barrister's Life," gives an account of the trial for murder of a young woman of somewhat prepossessing appearance, who was charged with poisoning her husband. "They were people in a humble class of life, and it was suggested that she had committed the act to obtain possession of money from a burial fund, and also that she was on terms of improper intimacy with a young man in the neighborhood. A minute quantity of arsenic was discovered in the body of the deceased, which in the defence I accounted for by the suggestion that poison had been used carelessly for the destruction of rats. Mr. Baron Parke charged the jury not unfavorably to the prisoner, dwelling pointedly upon the small quantity of arsenic found in the body, and the jury without much hesitation acquitted her. Dr. Taylor, the professor of chemistry and an experienced witness, had proved the presence of arsenic, and, as I imagine, to the great disappointment of my solicitor, who desired a severe cross-examination, I did not ask him a single question. He was sitting on the bench and near the judge, who, after he had summed up and before the verdict was pronounced, remarked to him that he was surprised at the small amount of arsenic found; upon which Taylor said that if he had been asked the question, he should have proved that it indicated, under the circumstances detailed in evidence, that a very large quantity had been taken. The professor had learned never to volunteer evidence, and the counsel for the prosecution had omitted to put the necessary question. Mr. Baron Parke, having learned the circumstance by accidental means, did not feel warranted in using the information, and I had my first lesson in the art of 'silent cross-examination.' "

Another exceedingly interesting and useful lesson in the art of silent cross-examination will be found in the following story as told by Richard Harris, K. C., in the *London Law Journal* for 1902.

"A long time ago, in the East End of London, lived a manufacturer of the name of Waring. He was in a large way of business, had his country house, where his family lived, and his town establishment. He was a man of great parochial eminence and respectability.

"Among the many hands he employed was a girl of the name of Harriet Smith. She came from the country and had not quite lost the bloom of rusticity when the respectable Mr. Waring fell in love with her. Had Harriet known he was married, in all probability she would have rejected his respectable attentions. He induced her to marry him, but it was to be kept secret; her father was not to know of it until such time as suited Mr. Waring's circumstances.

"In the course of time there were two children; and then unfortunately came a crisis in Mr. Waring's affairs. He was bankrupt. The factory and warehouse were empty, and Harriet was deprived of her weekly allowance.

"One day when Waring was in his warehouse, wondering, probably, what would be his next step, old Mr. Smith, the father of Harriet, called to know what had become of his daughter. 'That,' said Mr. Waring, 'is exactly what I should like to know.' She had left him, it seemed, for over a year and, as he understood, was last seen in Paris. The old man was puzzled, and informed Waring that he would find her out, dead or alive; and so went away. It was a strange thing, said the woman in whose house Mrs. Waring had apartments, that she should have gone away and never inquired about her children, especially as she was so found of them.

"She had gone nearly a year, and in a few days Mr. Waring was to surrender the premises to his landlord. There never was a man who took things more easily than Mr. Waring; leaving his premises did not disturb him in the least, except that he had a couple of rather large parcels which he wanted to get away without anybody seeing him.

It might be thought that he had been concealing some of his property if he were to be seen taking them away.

"It happened that there had been a youth in his employ of the name of Davis—James Davis—a plain simple lad enough, and of kind obliging disposition. He had always liked his old master, and was himself a favorite. Since the bankruptcy he had been apprenticed to another firm in Whitechapel, and one Saturday night as he was strolling along toward the Minories to get a little fresh air, suddenly met his old master, who greeted him with his usual cordiality and asked him if he had an hour to spare, and, if so, would he oblige him by helping him to a cab with a couple of parcels which belonged to a commercial traveller and contained valuable samples? James consented willingly, and lighting each a cigar which Mr. Waring produced, they walked along, chatting about old times and old friends. When they got to the warehouse there were the two parcels, tied up in American cloth.

" 'Here they are,' said Mr. Waring, striking a light. 'You take one, and I'll take the other; they're pretty heavy and you must be careful how you handle them, or some of the things might break.'

"When they got to the curb of the pavement, Mr. Waring said, 'Stop here, and I'll fetch a four-wheeler.'

"While James was waiting, a strange curiosity to look into the parcels came over him; so strange that it was irresistible, and accordingly he undid the end of one of them. Imagine the youth's horror when he was confronted with a human head that had been chopped off at the shoulders!

" 'My hair stood on end,' said the witness, 'and my hat fell off.' But his presence of mind never forsook him. He covered the ghastly 'relic of mortality' up and stood like a statue, waiting Mr. Waring's return with his cab.

" 'Jump in, James,' said he, after they had put the 'samples' on the top of the cab. But James was not in the humor to get into the cab. He preferred running behind. So he ran behind all along Whitechapel road, over London bridge, and away down Old Kent road, shouting to every policeman he saw to stop the cab, but no policeman took any notice of him except to laugh at him for a lunatic. The 'force' does not disturb its serenity of mind for trifles.

"By and by the cab drew up in a back street in front of an empty house, which turned out to be in the possession of Mr. Waring's brother; a house built in a part of Old London with labyrinths of arches, vaults, and cellars in the occupation of rats and other vermin.

"James came up, panting, just as his old master had taken his first packet of samples into the house. He had managed somehow or other to get a policeman to listen to him.

"The policeman, when Mr. Waring was taking in the second parcel, boldly asked him what he'd got there.

" 'Nothing for you,' said Mr. Waring.

" 'I don't know about that,' replied the policeman; 'let's have a look.'

"Here Mr. Waring lost his presence of mind, and offered the policeman, and another member of the force who had strolled up, a hundred pounds not to look at the parcels.

"But the force was not to be tampered with. They pushed Mr. Waring inside the house, and there discovered the ghastly contents of the huge bundles. The policemen's suspicions were now aroused, and they proceeded to the police station, where the divisional surgeon pronounced the remains to be those of a young woman who had been dead for a considerable time and buried in chloride of lime.

"Of course this was no proof of murder, and the charge of murder against Waring was not made until a considerable time after—not until the old father had declared time after time that the remains were those of his daughter Harriet.

"At length the treasury became so impressed with the old man's statement that the officials began to think it might be a case of murder after all, especially as there were two bullet-wounds at the back of the woman's head, and her throat had been cut. There was also some proof that she had been buried under the floor of Mr. Waring's warehouse, some hair being found in the grave, and a button or two from the young woman's jacket.

"All these things tended to awaken the suspicion of the treasury officials. Of course there was a suggestion that it was a case of suicide, but the Lord Chief Justice disposed of that later on at the trial by asking how a woman could shoot herself twice in the back of the head, cut her throat, bury herself under the floor, and nail the boards down over her grave.

"Notwithstanding it was clear that no charge of murder could be proved without identification, the treasury boldly made a dash for the capital charge, in the hope that something might turn up. And now, driven to their wits' end, old Mr. Smith was examined by one of the best advocates of the day, and this is what he made of him:——

" 'You have seen the remains?'

" 'Yes.'

" 'Whose do you believe them to be?'

" 'My daughter's, to the best of my belief.'

" 'Why do you believe them to be your daughter's?'

" 'By the height, the color of the hair, and the smallness of the foot and leg.'

"That was all; and it was nothing.

"But there must needs be cross-examination if you are to satisfy your client. So the defendant's advocate asks:——

" 'Is there anything else upon which your belief is founded?'

" 'No,' hesitatingly answers the old man, turning his hat about as if there was some mystery about it.

"There is breathless anxiety in the crowded court, for the witness seemed to be revolving something in his mind that he did not like to bring out.

" 'Yes,' he said, after a dead silence of two or three minutes. 'My daughter had a scar on her leg.'

"There was sensation enough for the drop scene. More cross-examination was necessary now to get rid of the business of the scar, and some reëxamination, too.

"The mark, it appeared, was caused by Harriet's having fallen into the fireplace when she was a girl.

" 'Did you see the mark on the remains?' asked the prisoner's counsel.

" 'No; I did not examine for it. I hadn't seen it for ten years.'

"There was much penmanship on the part of the treasury, and as many interchanges of smiles between the officials as if the discovery had been due to their sagacity; and they went about saying, 'How about the scar? How will he get over the scar? What do you think of the scar?' Strange to say, the defendant's advisers thought it prudent to ask the magistrate to allow the doctors on both sides to examine the remains in order to ascertain whether there was a scar or not, and, stranger still, while giving his consent, the magistrate thought it was very immaterial.

"It proved to be so immaterial that when it was found on the leg, exactly as the old man and a sister had described it, the doctors cut it out and preserved it for production at the trial.

"After the discovery, of course the result of the trial was a foregone conclusion.

"It will be obvious to the sagacious reader that the blunder indicated was not the only one in the case. On the other side was one of equal gravity and more unpardonable, which needs no pointing out. Justice, baffled by want of tact on one side, was righted by an accident on the other."

Chapter 8

Cross-Examination to the "Fallacies of Testimony"

IT IS INTENDED in this chapter to analyze some of the elements of human nature and human understanding that combine to conceal the truth about any given subject under investigation, where the witnesses are themselves honest and unconscious of any bias, or partisanship, or motive for erroneous statement.

Rufus Choate once began one of his more abstruse arguments before Chief Justice Shaw in the following manner: "In coming into the presence of your Honor I experience the same feelings as the Hindoo when he bows before his idol. I realize that you are ugly, but I feel that you are great!"

I am conscious of something of the same feeling as I embark upon the following discussion. I realize the subject is dry, but I feel that its importance to all serious students of advocacy is great.

No one can frequent our courts of justice for any length of time without finding himself aghast at the daily spectacle presented by seemingly honest and intelligent men and women who array themselves upon opposite sides of a case and testify under oath to what appear to be absolutely contradictory statements of fact.

It will be my endeavor in what follows to deal with this subject from its psychological point of view and to trace some of the *causes* of these unconscious mistakes of witnesses, so far as it is possible. The inquiry is most germane to what has preceded, for unless the advocate comprehends something of the *sources* of the fallacies of testimony, it surely would become a hopeless task for him to try to illuminate them by his cross-examinations.

It has been aptly said that "Knowledge is only the impression of one's mind and *not the fact itself,* which may present itself to many minds in many different aspects." The *unconscious sense impressions*—sight, sound, or touch —would be the same to every human mind; but once you awaken the mind to consciousness, then the original impression takes on all the color of motive, past experience, and character of the individual mind that receives it. The *sensation* by itself will be always the same. The variance arises when the sensation is *interpreted* by the *individual* and becomes a *perception* of his own mind.

When a man on a hot day looks at a running stream and *sees* the delicious coolness, he is really adding something of himself, which he acquired by his past experience, to the *sense impression* which his eye gives him. A different individual might receive the impression of tepid insipidity instead of "delicious coolness," in accordance with his own past experiences. The material of sensation is acted on by the mind which clothes the sensation with the experiences of the individual.[1] Helmholtz distinctly calls the perception of *distance,* for example, an unconscious *inference,*— a mechanically performed act of judgment.

The *interpretation* of a sensation is, therefore, the act of the individual, and different individuals will naturally vary in their interpretations of the same sensation according to their previous experiences and various mental characteristics. This process is most instantaneous, automatic, and unconscious. "The artist immediately sees details where to other eyes there is a vague or confused mass; the naturalist sees an animal where the ordinary eye only sees a form." [2] An adult sees an infinite variety of things that are meaningless to the child.

Likewise the same impression may be differently interpreted by the same individual at different times, due in part to variations in his *state of attention* at the moment, and in the degree of the mind's readiness to look at the impression in the required way. A timid man will more readily fall into the illusion of ghost-seeing than a cool-headed

[1] "Illusions," Sully (in part).
[2] "Problems of life and Mind," G. H. Lewes, p. 107.

man, because he is less attentive to the actual impression of the moment.

Every mind is attentive to what it sees or hears, more or less, according to circumstances. It is in the region of hazy impressions that the imagination is wont to get in its most dangerous work. It often happens that, when the mind is either inactive, or is completely engrossed by some other subject of thought, the sensation may neither be perceived, nor interpreted, nor remembered, notwithstanding there may be evidence, derived from the respondent movements of the body, that it has been felt; as, for example, a person in a state of imperfect sleep may start at a loud sound, or turn away from a bright light, being conscious of the sensation and acting automatically upon it, but forming no kind of appreciation of its source and no memory of its occurrence.[1] Such is the effect of sensation upon *complete* inattention. It thus appears that it is partly owing to this variation in *intensity* of attention that different individuals get such contradictory ideas of the same occurrence or conversation. When we add to this variance in the degree of attention, the variance, just explained, in the individual *interpretation* or coloring of the physical sensation, we have still further explanation of why men so often differ in what they think they have seen and heard.

Desire often gives rise to still further fallacy. Desire prompts the will to fix the attention on a certain point, and this causes the emphasis of this particular point or proposition to the exclusion of others. The will has the power of keeping some considerations out of view, and thereby *diminishes* their force, while it fixes the attention upon others, and thereby *increases* their force.

Sir John Romilly, in an opinion reported in 16 Beavan, 105, says: "It must always be borne in mind how extremely prone persons are to believe what they wish. It is a matter of frequent observation that persons dwelling for a long time on facts which they believed must have oc-

[1] "Mental Philosophy," Carpenter (in part).

curred, and trying to remember whether they did so or not, come at last to persuade themselves that they do actually *recollect* the occurrences of circumstances which at first they only begin by *believing* must have happened. What was originally the result of imagination becomes in time the result of recollection. Without imputing anything like wilful and corrupt perjury to witnesses of this description, they often in truth *bona fide* believe that they have heard and remembered conversations and observations which in truth never existed, but are the mere offspring of their imaginations."

Still another most important factor and itself the course of an enormous number of "fallacies of testimony" is memory. We are accustomed to speak of memory as if it consisted of an *exact* reproduction of past states of consciousness, yet experience is continually showing us that this reproduction is very often *inexact*, through the modifications which the "trace" has undergone in the interval. Sometimes the trace has been partially obliterated; and what remains may serve to give a very erroneous (because imperfect) view of the occurrence. *When it is one in which our own feelings are interested, we are extremely apt to lose sight of what goes against them, so that the representation given by memory is altogether one-sided.* This is continually demonstrated by the entire dissimilarity of the accounts of the same occurrence or conversation which is often given by two or more parties concerned in it, even when the matter is fresh in their minds, and they are honestly desirous of telling the truth. This diversity will usually become still more pronounced with the lapse of time, the trace becoming gradually but unconsciously modified by the habitual course of thought and feeling, so that when it is so acted upon after a lengthened interval as to bring up a reminiscence of the original occurrence, that reminiscence really represents, *not* the original occurrence, but the modified trace of it.[1]

Mr. Sully says: "Just as when distant objects are seen

[1] Campbell's "Mental Physiology" (in part).

mistily our imaginations come into play, leading us to fancy that we see something completely and distinctly, so when the images of memory become dim, our present imagination helps to restore them, putting a new patch into the old garment. If only there is some relic even of the past preserved, a bare suggestion of the way in which it *may have* happened will often suffice to produce the conviction that it actually did happen in this way. The suggestions that naturally arise in our minds at such times will bear the stamp of our present modes of experience and habits of thought. Hence, in trying to reconstruct the remote past we are constantly in danger of importing our present selves into our past selves."

Senator George F. Hoar, in his recently published "Autobiography of Seventy Years," says:—

"The recollections of the actors in important political transactions are doubtless of great historic value. But I ought to say frankly that my experience has taught me that the memory of men, even of good and true men, as to matters in which they have been personal actors, is frequently most dangerous and misleading. I could recount many curious stories which have been told me by friends who have been writers of history and biography, of the contradictory statements they have received from the best men in regard to scenes in which they have been present."

Edgar James Swift, Professor of Psychology at Washington University, in his volume, "Psychology and the Day's Work," first published in 1918, some ten years subsequent to the suggestions on the subject, so far as it relates to the testimony of witnesses, offered by me in a previous edition, has devoted many pages to a most interesting and instructive discussion of this subject. It is a book with which every earnest student of cross-examination should be familiar.

Professor Swift relates some very interesting experiments in human observation that he has carried out with his psychology classes, from which he draws this conclusion: "My experiments have proved to me that, in general, when the average man reports events or conversations from memory and conscientiously believes that he is telling the truth, about one-fourth of his statements are incorrect, and this tendency to false memory is the greater the longer the time since the original experience."

Larguier des Bancels, in his "L'Année Psychologique," after reviewing various investigations of his own, expresses the opinion that in general about a tenth of the honest evidence given under oath is untrue. Mademoiselle Borst from her individual investigations concludes that a twelfth part of testimony is false; whereas Stern puts a lower value yet upon it. John Wigmore has written a very popular article on the subject in the Illinois Law Review.

Professor Swift states that upon one occasion when the regular work of one of his classes was in progress the following scene, which had been carefully rehearsed, was suddenly enacted before the eyes of the students who were seated in a semi-circle:

An altercation was heard in the corridor, then the door burst open and four students, two young men and two young women, dashed into the room. Miss R. immediately after entering dropped a brown paper package on the floor. This package contained a brick so that the occurrence might not be too inconspicuous. K. flourished a large yellow banana as though it were a pistol, and all struggled across the room to the side opposite the door where Professor Swift himself was seated among several members of the class. He stood up at once, protesting at the interruption, and as he arose he threw a small torpedo on the floor. H. fell back crying, "I am shot," and was caught by Miss R. All then hurried out through the open door, Miss T. picking up the brown paper package which had been dropped near the door by Miss R. The entire scene occupied less than thirty seconds, and it was startling to the class, all of whom jumped up and crowded back against the wall, believing that it was a real riot.

The twenty-nine students of the class were then told that the scene had been "made to order" and were asked to write in detail their memory and observation of what had occurred.

Three of the actors were actual members of the class, and Miss R., although not a member of the class, was a senior, prominent in college activities, and all of the class knew her.

Of the twenty-nine "witnesses" to the transaction, only three remembered that four persons had entered the room, and although no disguises were used, not a single person recognized all of the actors. Many described the occurrence as that of a "mob" or "crowd." Seven students recognized three, eleven recognized two, seven recognized one, and four recognized no one; yet all the actors were persons they met every day. Surprising as these figures may seem to those who think that even under excitement they could recognize an acquaintance whom they had seen at least three times a week for eight months, the results are nevertheless *too* favorable to observation and memory, for recognition by elimination of those present played an important rôle. Eight "saw" persons who not only took no part in the performance, but were not even present. Of these eight one "saw" a former member of the class who had withdrawn about three months earlier; and a young woman who had never been in the class and was not present was "seen" by two. The descriptions of clothing were so general as to be worthless for purposes of identification, and if details were given they were generally found to be inaccurate. Only one witness spoke of the brown paper parcel. No one saw Miss T. pick it up. Several students "saw" the flash of a pistol, and one young woman wrote that they were attempting to hold back a man with long black hair. This evidently referred to H., since the other young man, R., had light hair and followed H. into the room. H's. hair, however, was short, and the description was that of a young Italian who *had* been a member of the class early in the year but who withdrew several months before the experiment. Later this student in her deposition actually named that Italian as among the participants. *Five of the reports did not contain a single item of truth or fact.* Three witnesses saw nothing except a confusion and a mob bursting into the room. Six others were unable to testify to more than the identity of one of the participants. To these, all else was a blank.

Professor Swift draws this conclusion from his experiment: "Identification is always fundamental in criminal cases, and positive recognition by well intended uninterested persons is commonly accepted unless the alibi is convincing. In our drama experiment the observers were all well acquainted with the participants, yet they were surprisingly incompetent as witnesses. Their minds were prepared, had the event involved a real crime, to recognize one against whom there might appear to be corroborative evidence. The "witnesses" proved to have had little definite knowledge of what actually happened, and had a crime actually been committed, their testimony should have had slight value; *yet it would have been accepted because they were eye-witnesses*. Only a few identified actors, and in several instances these identifications were so uncertain as to be readily transferred to some one else under the influence of suggestion."

In estimating the accuracy of memory, Professor Swift gives some very illuminating additional experiments that he made with his classes, showing through how many mouths a story must pass before it loses its identity altogether.

A newspaper clipping was read to one member of the class, who in turn repeated it immediately to the next, and so on to the end. As soon as each student had heard it and had repeated it he immediately wrote in down. It originally read:

"Thomas McCarthy, who also used the names Burns and Hopkins, was arraigned yesterday on the charge of having conspired to forge and pass stolen money orders. His case was adjourned for a week. He was arrested on Monday night in a saloon. The Assistant District Attorney said yesterday that the score of money orders which the man was accused of passing at department stores were some of those stolen by yeggmen a month ago from the post office in St. Louis. The orders had been filled in for varying amounts, a number of which were more than $100.00. McCarthy was held in $10,000 bail."

The first paper, as quoted, shows how the story started down the line:

"Thomas McCarthy, who formerly gave the names of Burr and Buss, was arrested for forgery. The trial will come in a week. He was arrested last Monday night in a corner saloon. He tried to pass checks formerly used by Leighton in the departments stores. Since none of the amounts were over $100.00, he was let out on $1,000 bail before the district attorney."

Beginning with the second attempt at reproduction of the story, there were conditions and increasing omissions and additions with frequent changes in the aliases. The seventh report was so very reduced as to be worth quoting. It was as follows:

"There was a man named McCarthy, who went by the name of Burney. He forged a check of $100.00 and was arrested."

No. 11 lost the surname and changed the alias to Sussex. The story now becomes:

"There was man named Thomas. He went by the name of Sussex. He forged a check for $100.00 and escaped."

Here the story may be said to have lost all resemblance to that with which No. 1 began. These students were interested in the experiment. There was rivalry to see who could remember most accurately. They concentrated their attention to the limit of their ability, yet the results were chiefly remarkable for their omissions and additions.

From these experiments Professor Swift answers the following query:

"First, what are the chances for a truthful narration of that which has been seen or heard? Clearly the chances of even a reasonably accurate narration are small. We have found observation itself exceedingly defective and unreliable; and when to the inaccuracy of observation there is added the disturbing effect of reviewing them with the deflected influence of conversation about the events and the excitement of the imagination, the testimony of witnesses becomes extremely undependable. Imagination reconstructs evidence with many omissions and substitutions, and the final outcome is likely to be so different from the original as to be almost unrecognizable. Expectation of an act may cause it to be seen and an intention to do something translates the thought into deed. Suggestion is always operative—suggestion of actions when one is an observer and suggestion from questions even of fact in conversation or when on the witness stand."

In a previous chapter I drew attention to the discrepancies between the account of one of Abraham Lincoln's cross-examinations in the Armstrong case, and that given by the lawyers associated with Lincoln at the trial, which is quite as illuminating as any of Professor Swift's experiments.

Judge Edward Abbott Parry, in his remarkably entertaining volume, "What the Judge Thought," recently published in England, has a delightful chapter on "Psychology of Perjury." He says: "I trust that I have made it clear that the popular notion that Courts of Justice are constantly misled by wicked and abandoned perjurers and suborners conspiring to subvert the hands of Justice is a myth. . . . I am inclined, however, to hold the view that while the testimony given by the average citizens in the courts is singularly free from the taint of perjury, *yet if, on the other hand, you were to ask me whether, after a third of a century's experience of listening to sworn testimony in our courts, I was deeply impressed by the accuracy, reliability and truth of the daily round of evidence it has been my duty to consider, I should with sincere regret be bound to admit that the answer was in the negative.* . . . I am glad to know myself, and I hope I have convinced my fellow citizens, that most of the errors of testimony are due to defective observations, fase reminiscences, the deflecting influence of suggestion and the pleasure of the imagination. Very often, too, the *wish to believe* is a strong factor in bringing about false testimony. How many anxious citizens 'knew a friend' who had seen those splendid hordes of

Russians passing through the country with the snow on their boots in midnight trains at the beginning of the war! It would be harsh to call such legends perjuries.

"When mankind understands more fully and scientifically the real causes of error in human testimony, which the professors have only in recent years begun to study scientifically, we shall be able to set about amending our ways and checking our bias and imagination and shunning the perils of undue suggestion."

Professor Hugo Münsterberg, for many years Professor of Psychology at Harvard University, published a few years ago his book on this subject entitled "On the Witness Stand." I think I may fairly claim to have introduced this book to the local profession in a course of lectures delivered at the Columbia Law School, but my partner, Herbert C. Smyth, was the first New York lawyer to make practical use of its theories in one of his cases and thereby completely break down damaging testimony of a witness, of whose honesty of purpose there could be no question.

It was in a case tried some years ago before Mr. Justice Erlanger of our State Supreme Court. The suit was brought by the widow to recover a large sum in damages from Macy & Co., owners of a well known department store in New York, on account of the death of Professor John T. McNulty.

The plaintiff's intestate, a professor of philosophy in the College of the City of New York, met his death by falling through an open passenger elevator shaft at one of the upper floors of the building. The claim on behalf of the widow was that, as Professor McNulty approached the elevator, walking along the corridor on the sixth floor and intending to *enter* it, the waiting elevator suddenly shot up, before the barricading door was closed, and the professor, stepping into the unguarded shaft, was precipitated to the bottom.

On the other hand, the elevator operator, Macy & Co.'s only witness, insisted that Professor McNulty was *not* entering the elevated car at all, but, on the contrary, had ridden in the car up to the floor in question, that it was customary to stop the car at each landing, and that just as he, the operator, was starting it again and closing the collapsible door, the professor, suddenly realizing that he wished to get off, pushed back the partly closed door, stepped out, lost his balance and fell backwards into the shaft.

The case, therefore, directly turned on whether Professor McNulty fell while attempting to *enter* the car or while *leaving* it. If the former, Macy & Co. were liable for their employee's negligence; if the latter, it was the deceased's own fault.

The plaintiff called a Dr. Allison as her principal and only eye witness to the accident. He testified on direct examination that Professor McNulty walked past him on the sixth floor corridor toward the elevator shaft which was open, and he saw him disappear there, and heard the fall of his body.

Dr. Allison had originally told his version of the occurrence two days after the accident at the coroner's inquest, when he was asked by the lawyer for the deceased's family the following *leading* questions (there being no representative of Macy & Co. present):

Q. "As you were walking along this corridor on the sixth floor, you saw a man's form, which afterwards turned out to be Prof. McNulty, passing you going *toward* the elevator shaft?"

A. "Yes, sir."

Q. "And you saw this man disappear after he reached the shaft?"

A. "Yes, sir."

Q. "The entrance to the shaft was open at that time?"

A. "Yes, sir."

Q. "And you then heard the sound of the body striking the bottom?"

A. "Yes, sir."

It was these obviously *leading* questions which prompted Mr. Smyth to pursue the following line of cross-examination:

Q. "Dr. Allison, you were examined at the coroner's inquest about this accident, were you not?"

A. "Yes, sir."

Q. "That was only two days after Professor McNulty was killed, was it not?"

A. "I believe so."

Q. "Your testimony then and now are substantially the same, is that not so?"

A. "That is true, of course."

Q. "Was that the first time you had ever related the occurrence?"

A. "Yes, sir."

Q. "You have quite a large medical practice, have you not?"

A. "Fairly so, I believe."

Q. "Do you have many nervous and mental cases come under your notice and care?"

A. "Oh, yes; every physician does."

Q. "Has that led you to take any particular interest in psychology, generally?"

A. "Well, that is a subject which has always been of great interest to me."

Q. "Then you have read considerably about it?"

A. "Yes, a great deal."

Q. "I suppose, of course, then, you must be familiar with Professor Münsterberg's recent book, 'On the Witness Stand,' which has created so much comment?"

A. "Yes, indeed."

Q. "Do you remember the stress he laid on the power of suggestion, and the illusions of memory; and can you recall some of the curious examples he gave of these phenomena?"

A. "Yes; if you will call my attention to them, I am sure I will."

Q. "For instance (reading from the book): 'In the midst of a scholarly meeting, the doors open, a clown in highly colored costume rushes in in mad excitement, and a negro with a revolver in hand follows him. They both shout wild phrases; then one falls to the ground, the other jumps on him; then a shot, and suddenly both are out of the room. The whole affair, which was prearranged, took not more than twenty seconds. The scholars are asked immediately to write down a report of what they saw. Out of forty reports there were only six which did not contain positive wrong statements, only four noticed that the negro had nothing on his head; the others gave him a derby, or a high hat and so on; different colors and styles of clothing were invented for him, some said he had a coat on, others that he was in his shirt sleeves; and it was determined that a majority of the observers had omitted or falsified about half of the processes which occurred completely in their field of vision.' Do you remember that example of the frailty of memory?"

A. "Yes, sir, I remember it well."

Q. "Then do you remember this one (still referring to the book): 'A picture of a room in a farm house was shown to a class of picked students; then each was asked questions as to what he had seen. "Did you see where the stove was located?" Fifty-nine out of one hundred replied and gave the stove a definite place. "Did you see the farmer's wife winding the clock?" Thirty of the class described the clock, and so on. There was neither stove nor clock shown in the picture.' (To the witness) You remember that, do you not?"

A. "Yes, that was one of his examples, which quite forcibly impressed me."

Q. "I am going to burden you with the relation of one more incident from Münsterberg's book, and then I am going to ask you if you can see the relation of these cases to the one at bar. Do you remember this further example from 'On the Witness Stand' (turning to another portion of the book): 'A negro was being tried for murder committed on a highway at night. A disinterested witness, who claimed to have seen the whole occurrence, was asked these suggestive questions on cross-examination':

Q. "Did you see by the moonlight, the kind of trousers and coat the prisoner was wearing at the time?"

A. "Yes, I am sure they were brown or at least dark."

" 'As a matter of fact there was no moonlight; and all the other witnesses who had testified earlier said that the prisoner's attire consisted of blue trousers, white shirt and no coat.' (To the witness.) Do you remember this example of the remarkable power of suggestion, recorded by Prof. Münsterberg?"

A. "Yes, sir, I do."

Q. "Do you appreciate, Dr. Allison, that you are yourself easily subject to the power of suggestion?"

A. "No, sir, I do not."

Q. "Well, let us see. I now call your attention to your testimony given two days after the tragedy at the coroner's inquest which I will now read to you (counsel reads his testimony as quoted above). You recognize, do you not, that these questions, which for the first time brought out from you that you actually saw Prof. McNulty going toward the elevator, were exactly of the kind classed as suggestive, and exemplified in 'On the Witness Stand?' "

A. "That may be, but what of it? Do you mean to imply that I am testifying falsely?"

Q. "Not intentionally, no; but that you are what is known as a suggestible witness."

A. "Prove it!"

Q. "Very well. Would it surprise you to know that of the three instances I apparently read from Münsterberg's book, and all of which you said you remembered perfectly, only the first one was actually in the book, the second was only half true, and the third was an entire fabrication of my own? Here, take the book, and see for yourself (handing volume to witness).

A. (Hesitating, and his color rising.) "Mr. Smyth, I am afraid you are making a fool of me."

Q. "Not more so than any one of us are liable to be honestly mistaken; but now let me ask you, doctor, (and I would not put this question if I were not convinced of your fair-mindedness), in view of your answers, and looking back, and in the light of your scientific knowledge, can you really say you actually saw Prof. McNulty *approaching* the elevator shaft, or even saw him at all before the instant of his body disappearing down the shaft?"

A. (After much hesitation.) "I am afraid I cannot."

The witness with flushed countenance then hurriedly left the stand. The main prop to the plaintiff's case was gone, resulting in the jury finding a verdict in favor of Macy & Co.

It is obviously the province of the cross-examiner to detect the nature of any foreign element which may have been imported into a witness's memory of an event or transaction to which he testifies, and if possible to discover the source of the error; whether the memory has been warped by desire or imagination, or whether the error was one of original perception, and if so, whence it arose, whether from lack of attention or from wrong association of previous personal experience.

Not only does our idea of the past become inexact by the mere decay and disappearance of essential features; it becomes positively incorrect through the gradual incorporation of elements that do not properly belong to it. Sometimes it is easy to see how these extraneous ideas become imported into our mental representation of a past event. Suppose, for example, that a man has lost a valuable scarfpin. His wife suggests that a particular servant, whose reputation does not stand too high, has stolen it. When he afterwards recalls the loss, the chances are that he will confuse the fact with the conjecture attached to it, and say he remembers that this particular servant did steal the pin. Thus the past activity of imagination serves to corrupt and partially falsify recollections that have a genuine basis of fact.[1]

A very striking instance of the effect of *habit* on the memory, especially in relation to events happening in moments of intense excitement, was afforded by the trial of a man by the name of Twichell, who was justly convicted in Philadelphia some years ago, although by errone-

[1] "Illusions," p. 264 (in part).

ous testimony. In order to obtain possession of some of his wife's property which she always wore concealed in her clothing, Twichell, in great need of funds, murdered his wife by hitting her on the head with a slung shot. He then took her body to the yard of the house in which they were living, bent a poker, and covered it with his wife's blood, so that it would be accepted as the instrument that inflicted the blow, and having *unbolted the gate* leading to the street, left it ajar, and went to bed. In the morning, when the servant arose, she stumbled over the dead body of her mistress, and in great terror she rushed through the gate into the street, and summoned the police. The servant had always been *in the habit* of unbolting this gate the first thing each morning, and she swore on the trial that she had done the same thing upon the morning of the murder. There was no other way the house could have been entered from without excepting through this gate. The servant's testimony was, therefore, conclusive that the murder had been committed by some one from *within* the house, and Twichell was the only other person in the house.

After the conviction Twichell confessed his guilt to his lawyer and explained to him how careful he had been *to pull back the bolt and leave the gate ajar* for the very purpose of diverting suspicion from himself. The servant in her excitement had failed to notice both that the bolt was drawn and that the gate was open, and in recalling the circumstance later she had allowed her usual daily *experience* and *habit* of pulling back the bolt to become incorporated into her recollection of this particular morning. It was this piece of fallacious testimony that really convicted the prisoner.

As the day of the execution drew near, Twichell complained to the prison authorities that the print in the prison Bible was too fine for him to read, and requested that his friend, a druggist, be allowed to supply him with a Bible in larger type. This friend saturated some of the pages of the Bible with corrosive sublimate. Twichell rolled these pages up into balls, and, with the aid of water, swallowed them. Death was almost instantaneous.

Boswell, in his "Life of Dr. Johnson," [1] has related the particulars of his first meeting with Dr. Johnson, whom he had been long very desirous of seeing and conversing with. At last they accidentally met at the house of a Mr. Davies.

Mr. Arthur Murphy, in his "Essay on the Life and Genius of Dr. Johnson," likewise gives a description of Boswell's first meeting with Johnson. Concerning Mr. Murphy's account of the matter, Mr. Boswell says: "Mr. Murphy has given an account of my first meeting with Dr. Johnson considerably different from my own, and I am persuaded, without any consciousness of error, his memory at the end of near thirty years has undoubtedly deceived him, and he supposes himself to have been present at a scene which he has probably heard inaccurately described by others. In my own notes, *taken on the very day in which I am confident I marked everything material that passed,* no mention is made of this gentleman; and I am sure that I should not have omitted one so well-known in the literary world. It may easily be imagined that this, my first interview with Dr. Johnson, with all its circumstances, made a strong impression on my mind and would be registered with peculiar attention."

A writer in the *Quarterly Review,* [2] speaking of this same occurrence, says: "An erroneous account of Boswell's first introduction to Dr. Johnson was published by Arthur Murphy, *who asserted that he witnessed it.* Boswell's appeal to his own strong recollection of so memorable an occasion and to the narrative he entered in his Journal at the time show that Murphy's account was quite inaccurate, and that he *was not present* at the scene. This, Murphy did not later venture to contradict. As Boswell suggested, he had doubtless heard the circumstances repeated till at the end of thirty years he had come to fancy that he was an actor in them. His good faith was unquestionable, and that he should have been so deluded is a memorable example of the fallibility of testimony and of the extreme difficulty of arriving at the truth."

Every one appreciates how human is the tendency to enlarge upon a story, especially if we ourselves have participated in the events and are called upon to testify to them in open court. Professor James, in his "Principles of Psychology," says: "The most frequent source of false memory is the accounts we give to others of our experiences. Such acts we almost always make more simple and more interesting than the truth. We quote what we should have said or done rather than what we really said or did; and in the first telling we may be fully aware of the distinction, but ere long, the fiction expels the reality from memory and reigns in its stead alone. We think of what we wish had happened, of possible interpretation of acts, and soon we are unable to distinguish between things that actually happened and our own thoughts about what might have occurred. Our wishes, hopes, and sometimes fears are the controlling factor."

Professor Swift maintains that the undetected vagueness of memory details of witnesses furnishes a fertile soil for the growth of imaginary pictures. With a dim outline in mind, he claims there is always a strong tendency to fill in the outline, usually with what is in one's own mind; and he suggests as an illustration that you ask any group of persons to indicate the kind of a figure six which is upon their watch dial. They will be found to divide between VI and 6. A few whose "memory" is more accurate than the others, recalling that the figures take their line of direction from the center of the dial, will write the figures upside down. All, except those to whose attention the peculiarity has already been called, will "remember" seeing the figure. Yet, in watches with a hand denoting the seconds, there is no six.

Perhaps the most subtle and prolific of all of the "fallacies of testimony" arises out of *unconscious partisanship*. It is rare that one comes across a witness in court who is so candid and fair that he will testify as fully and favorably for the one side as the other.

It is extraordinary to mark this tendency we all have, when once we are identified with a "side" or cause, to accept all its demands as our own. To put on the uniform makes the policeman or soldier, even when himself corrupt, a guardian of law and order.

Witnesses in court are almost always favorable to the party who calls them, and this feeling induces them to conceal some facts and to color others which might, in their opinion, be injurious to the side for which they give their testimony. This partisanship in the witness box is most fatal to fair evidence; and when we add to the partisanship of the witness the similar leaning of the lawyer who is conducting the examination, it is easy to produce evidence that varies very widely from the exact truth. This is often done by overzealous practitioners by putting leading questions or by incorporating two questions into one, the second a simple one, misleading the witness into a "yes" for both, and thus creating an entirely false impression.

What is it in the human make-up which invariably leads men to take sides when they come into court? In the first place, witnesses usually feel more or less *complimented by the confidence* that is placed in them by the party calling them to prove a certain state of facts, and it is human nature to try to prove worthy of this confidence. This feeling is unconscious on the part of the witness and usually is not a strong enough motive to lead to actual perjury in its full extent, but it serves as a sufficient reason why the witness will almost unconsciously dilute or color the evidence to suit a particular purpose and perhaps add only a *bit* here, or suppress one there, but this bit will make all the difference in the meaning.

Many men in the witness box feel and enjoy a *sense of power* to direct the verdict toward the one side or the other, and cannot resist the temptation to indulge it and to be thought a "fine witness" for their side. I say their side; the side for which they testify always becomes their side the moment they take the witness chair, and they instinctively desire to see that side win, although they may be entirely devoid of any other interest in the case whatsoever.

It is a characteristic of the human race to be intensely interested in the success of some one party to a contest, whether it be a war, a boat race, a ball game, or a lawsuit. This desire *to win* seldom fails to color the testimony of a witness and to create fallacies and inferences dictated by the witness's *feelings,* rather than by his *intellect* or the dispassionate powers of observation.

Many witnesses take the stand with no well defined motive regarding what they are going to testify to, but upon discovering that they are being led into statements unfavorable to the side on which they are called, experience a sudden dread of being considered *disloyal,* or "going back on" the party who selected them, and immediately become unconscious partisans and allow this feeling to color or warp their testimony.

There is still another class of persons who would not become witnesses for either side unless they felt that some wrong or injustice had been done to one of the parties, and thus to become a witness for the injured party seems to them to be a vindication of the right. Such witnesses allow their feelings to become enlisted in what they believe to be the cause of righteousness, and this in turn enlists their sympathy and feelings and prompts them to color their testimony as in the case of those influenced by the other motives already spoken of.

One sees, perhaps, the most marked instances of partisanship in admiralty cases which arise out of a collision between two ships. Almost invariably all the crew on one ship will testify in unison against the opposing crew, and, what is more significant, such passengers as happen to be on either ship will almost invariably be found corroborating the stories of their respective crews.

Mr. Joseph H. Choate, Jr., had an amusing experience in one of his admiralty cases which illustrates the proper way to handle such a situation. The City of New York had sued the New Haven Railroad for damages growing out of a collision between boats owned by the respective parties. The City's fire-boat "New Yorker" had been run down, as it was backing out of its slip, by a car-float which one of the New Haven's tugs had been most improperly towing through the North River too close to the pier-ends. There was no possible denial of the tug's fault, and the defense had no evidence of any possible fault on the part of the fire-boat, though it was hard to see how the collision could have happened if she had been keeping a proper look-out. As usual, her crew were called as witnesses in succession. The first testified that he had been properly posted as look-out and had acted accordingly. This statement proving unshakable on cross-examination, the situation looked dark. With the next witness, however, the cross-examiner decided to see whether the well known tendency of crew witnesses to become advocates for their vessel might not be used to produce some proof in support of his belief that in spite of the first witness's testimony, there had been negligence in the keeping of the required look-out. He accordingly asked a number of questions as to just what the witness had been doing during the seconds preceding the impact. These questions were purposely framed so as to suggest that counsel thought that the witness had been asleep or otherwise negligent. Annoyed by this, the question, "Were you looking out for possible danger?" brought an immediate emphatic "Yes." A contemptuous "What business was that of yours?" led the witness to reply that he had been told to keep a look-out. A final question as to who had given him this order, established him as a second entirely regular look-out, who had been doing his duty.

The same tactics produced the same result with each succeeding member of the crew of nine. Each, jumping at the chance of defending his ship and his own vigilance at the same time, placed himself as an officially posted look-out. This left the vessel in the ridiculous position of starting its voyage with nine specially detailed look-outs. This was too much for the presiding Judge, who either concluded that he could not believe any of the look-outs or that divided responsibility had ruined the efficiency of all of them, and accordingly held the "New Yorker" also in fault and divided the damages.

It is the same, in a lesser degree, in an ordinary personal injury case against a surface railway. Upon the happening of an accident the casual passengers on board a street car are very apt to side with the employees in charge of the car, whereas the injured plaintiff and whatever friends or relatives happen to be with him at the time will invariably be found upon the witness stand testifying against the railway company.

The ordinary personal injury or "accident cases," which, owing to the congested traffic in our city streets some years ago, constituted about fifty per cent of the cases tried in the fourteen or more parts of our local Supreme Court, afford the most ordinary illustrations of auto-suggestion, or what is sometimes termed "attorney-suggestion." The New York City Railroad Company alone at one time had some four to five thousand of these cases on the calendar each year. It was amazing to hear how accurately the various witnesses remembered the minute details of occurrences of two or three years previous, giving the location and speed of colliding vehicles, the actions and relative positions and distances apart of the objects and persons, with assumed photographic accuracy. One soon formed the habit of leading these adverse witnesses along gently in their story until, quite unawares, they were led to admit that it was a "loud crash that first attracted their attention and made them take notice." Obviously everything that had preceded this moment was the result of someone's suggestion and not of the witness's personal observation. I have myself destroyed scores of witnesses by this simple method.

In cases where experts are used to bolster up the evidence of lay witnesses, they can sometimes be made to look ridiculous in the eyes of a jury by this same method of leading them into exaggerations. Joseph H. Choate, Jr., once made use of his own keen sense of humor to completely destroy such a witness.

One Crandall had built a ship railway for Robert Jacob's yacht-yard at City Island. In a year or two the teredo-worm had eaten into so many of the piles which supported it that the structure fell. The teredo was a recognized danger to structures in those waters, but could be foiled by sheathing, which Crandall's contract did not call for. In the ensuing litigation over the cause of collapse, Jacob's trial counsel—Mr. W. Benton Crisp, who must have weighed 300 pounds—contended that the railway fell, not because the worms ate it, but because its design, for which the builder was responsible, was faulty. In support of this he produced an expert who testified that the supporting piles were insufficient.

Cross-examining counsel had in court a piece of one of the piles, including the portion which had actually been severed by the worms. The structure, supported by piles many of which were in this state, had nevertheless sufficed to haul out one of the largest yachts just before the collapse. If it was true that the damaged piles had practically no bearing capacity, obviously the fact that the structure stood and worked without them showed that it was properly planned, with a large factor of safety. The cross-examiner's effort, therefore, was to obtain, and the experts' to avoid, an admission that the worm-eaten piles had no bearing capacity at all and thus added nothing to the structure's strength. The examination ran thus:

Q. "What is the bearing capacity of such a pile in good condition?"

A. "Ten tons."

Q. (Showing witness the worm-severed pile-end.)

"What was the bearing capacity of such a pile in the condition of the exhibit shown you?"

A. "Can't say."

Q. "Would it bear nine tons?"

A. "Probably not."

Q. "Seven tons?"

A. "I doubt it."

Q. "Five tons?"

A. "I don't know."

After a long series of similar questions as to whether it would bear particular weights, to all of which the witness had to make the same answer—that he did not know—

Q. "Would it bear five hundred pounds?"

A. (Witness obviously apprehensive over the effect of continued assertion of ignorance.) "I can't say."

Q. "Would you trust yourself on a pile like that with five hundred pounds?"

A. (Rattled.) "I don't weigh five hundred pounds."

Q. (Pointing to his well fed opponent.) "Would you trust Mr. Crisp on one?"

A. *"Not unless he could swim."*

Prompt verdict for the plaintiff.

It is difficult to point out the methods that should be employed by the cross-examiner in order to expose to a jury the particular source of the fallacy that has warped the judgment, choked the conscience, or blinded the intelligence of any individual witness. It must necessarily all depend upon the circumstances arising in each particular case. All I have attempted to do is to draw attention to the *usual* sources of these fallacies, and I must perforce leave it to the ingenuity of the trial lawyer to work out his own solution when the emergency arises. This he certainly would never be able to do successfully, unless he had given careful thought and study to this branch of his professional equipment.

The subject is a great one, and rarely, if ever, discussed by law writers, who usually pass it by with the bare suggestion that it is a topic worthy of deep investigation upon the proper occasion. I trust that my few suggestions may serve as a stimulus to some philosophic legal mind to elaborate and elucidate the reasons for the existence of this *flaw* in the human mechanism, which appears to be the chief stumbling block in our efforts to arrive at truth in courts of justice.

Chapter 9

Cross-Examination to Probabilities
—Personality of the Examiner, Etc.

IN DELIVERING one of his celebrated judgments Lord Mansfield said: "As mathematical and absolute certainty is seldom to be attained in human affairs, reason and public utility require that judges and all mankind in forming their opinion of the truth of facts should be regulated by the superior number of *probabilities* on the one side or the other."

Theoretically the goal we all strive for in litigation is the *probable* truth. It is therefore in this effort to develop the probabilities, in any given case, that a trial lawyer is called upon for the exercise of the most active imagination and profound knowledge of men and things.

It requires but little experience in court to arrive at the conclusion that the great majority of cases are composed of a few principal facts surrounded by a host of minor ones; and that the strength of either side of a case depends not so much upon the direct testimony relating to these principal facts alone, but, as one writer very tersely puts it, "upon the *support* given them by the probabilities created by establishing and developing the relation of the *minor* facts in the case."

One of the latest causes of any importance, tried in our New York courts this year, afforded an excellent illustration of the relative importance of the main facts in a case to the multitudinous *little* things which surrounded any given issue, and which when carefully gathered together and skilfully grouped, create the probabilities of a case. The suit was upon an oral agreement for the purchase and sale of a large block of mining stock with *an alleged guaranty against loss*. The plaintiff and defendant were both gentlemen holding prominent positions in the business world and of unquestioned integrity and veracity. The only issue in the case was the simple question, as to which one was correct in his memory of a conversation that had occurred five years before. The plaintiff swore there was an agreement by the defendant to repurchase the stock from him, at the price paid, at plaintiff's option. The defendant swore no such conversation ever took place. Where was the truth? The direct yea and nay of this proposition occupied about five minutes of the court's time. The surrounding circumstances, the countless straws pointing to the probabilities on the one side or the other, occupied three full days, and no time was wasted.

In almost every trial there are circumstances which at first may appear light, valueless, even disconnected, but which, if skilfully handled, become united together and at last form wedges which drive conviction into the mind. This is obviously the business of the cross-examiner, although it is true that the examination of one's own witnesses, as well, often plays an important part in the development of probabilities.

All men stamp as probable or improbable that which they themselves would, or would not, have said or done under similar circumstances. "As in water face answereth to face, so the heart of man to man." [1] Things inconsistent with human knowledge and experience are properly rated as improbable. It was Aristotle who first said, "Probability is never detected bearing false testimony."

Apart from experience in human affairs and the resultant knowledge of men, it is industry and diligent preparation for the trial which will enable an advocate to handle the circumstances surrounding the main facts in a case with the greatest effect upon a judge or jury.

One who has thought intently upon a subject which he is going to develop later on in court, and has sought diligently for "straws" to enable him to discover the true solution of a controversy, will, when the occasion arises upon

---

[1] Proverbs xxvii. 19.

the trial, catch and apply facts which a less thoughtful person would pass by almost unnoticed. Careful study of his case before he comes into court will usually open to an advocate avenues for successful cross-examination to the probabilities of a story, which will turn out to be his main arguments for a successful verdict in his favor.

"It is acute knowledge of human nature, thorough preliminary survey of the question and of the interests involved, and keen imagination which enable the questioner to see all the possibilities of a case. It is a cautious good judgment that prevents him from assuming that to be true which he only imagines may be true, and professional self-restraint that enables him to pass by all opportunities which may give a witness a chance for successful fencing." [1]

In the search for the probable it is often wise to use questions that serve for little more than a *suggestion* of the desired point. Sir James Scarlett used to allow the jurors and even the judges to discover for themselves the best parts of his case. It flattered their vanity. Scarlett went upon the theory, he tells us in the fragments of his autobiography which were written before his death, that whatever strikes the mind of a juror as the result of his own observation and discovery makes always the strongest impression upon him, and the juror holds on to his own discovery with the greatest tenacity and often, possibly, to the exclusion of every other fact in the case.

This search for probabilities, however, is a hazardous occupation for the inexperienced. There is very great danger of bringing out some incidental circumstance that serves only to confirm or corroborate the statements of a witness made before the cross-examination began. Thus one not only stumbles upon a new circumstance in favor of his opponent, but the fact that it came to light during the cross-examination instead of in the direct multiplies its importance in the eyes of a jury; for it has often been said, and it is a well recognized fact, that accidental testimony always makes a greater impression on a juror's mind than that deliberately and designedly given.

[1] Austin Abbott, in *The Daily Register*, December, 1886.

Another danger in this hazardous method of cross-examination is the development of such a mass of material that the minds of the jurors become choked and unable to follow intelligently. If one cannot make his points stand out clearly during his cross-examination, he had better keep his seat. It used to be said of Law, a famous English barrister, that "he wielded a huge two-handed sword to extract a fly from a spider's web."

There are occasions, however, where a cross-examiner can accomplish results only by a long drawn out, persistent questioning of a witness in an effort to bring the truth out of him after he has become brain weary. A striking example of this method can be found in the record of the trial in a suit brought by Miss Amanda Bird against her former employer, the National City Company, principal subsidiary of the National City Bank of New York, for false imprisonment and malicious prosecution. Miss Bird, without cause, had suddenly made a public announcement that the Bank which employed her, she had discovered, was systematically cheating the Government and also the Bank's clients. Her excitement became so pronounced that she was removed to the Psychopathic Ward of Bellevue Hospital for observation, where an investigation of the young woman developed that she had symptoms of paranoia. She was, however, a woman of very engaging personality and rather unusual intelligence, so that after an incarceration for a short period, the authorities voluntarily discharged her. She then took a trip to Washington in a Pullman train, visited the Senate office building, and there made similar charges against the Bank. Her career from that time on was a succession of incarcerations, but she always succeeded in persuading the authorities she was perfectly sane, and each time secured her discharge.

Finally she started her suit for $500,000 against the Bank. The case came on for trial in the New York Supreme Court. The burden obviously was upon the defendant to prove that her mental condition was that of a paranoiac with the usual delusions of persecution. Otherwise her incarceration would have been held to have been unjustified.

Her story on direct examination was succinct, straight-forward and very impressive. Mr. Herbert C. Smyth conducted the cross-examination and was confronted with the task of convincing a lay jury that she was mentally unbalanced. For two and one-half days he labored with her, trying to get her to exhibit some real symptoms of her delusions of persecution by the Bank, particularly after leaving Bellevue Hospital. She exhibited intimate knowledge of the symptoms of paranoia patients and was therefore constantly on her guard, frequently interrupting the questions by exclaiming, "Now, Mr. Smyth, are you trying to make me out a paranoiac?"

The long drawn out cross-examination was with the hope of making her so mentally weary that she might exhibit her true state of mind as regards her imagined persecutors. Nearing the end of the two and one-half days it seemed to be a question with the cross-examiner whether his mind could hold out as long as hers. His oft-reiterated question was, "Now, Miss Bird, will you please tell us the truth about your trip on the Pullman train to Washington?" The witness stood her ground hour after hour, until finally the cross-examiner asked her, "For the last time, why don't you tell us the truth about this trip?"—when, with a sudden flash in her eyes, she exclaimed: "Do you really mean, Mr. Smyth, that you are not trying to prove me a paranoiac?" This elicited the reply: "I am not trying to prove anything. I want the whole truth about that train trip. I have asked it of you over and over again and you have not yet told us."

The patiently awaited climax had been reached. The whole attitude of the witness changed as she replied: "Well, at last I believe you, Mr. Smyth. This is what happened. I sat in the Pullman car and on the opposite side of the aisle I noticed a representative of the National City Bank. In front of me was another representative, and farther along the aisle was a man who also represented the Bank, shielding his face with a newspaper. I noticed that he had several whispered conversations with the conductor. As we pulled out of Baltimore and had proceeded to a point where there were thick woods, the porter gave a signal and the conductor stopped the train, and there outside of my window I saw five thugs—all emissaries of the Bank—waiting to get me. I appealed to a passenger and he persuaded the conductor to proceed and *thus I was saved*."

One can imagine the relief of the cross-examiner that at last her real state of mind had been made apparent, if only by bearing down upon her until her resistance was gone. The case ended in a mistrial with the jury standing ten to two for the defendant. When the new trial opened it seemed best that some settlement should be made and a moderate amount was agreed to. Thereupon the Judge, thinking to close the incident permanently in the mind of the plaintiff, called her to the bench and tried to persuade her to forget the whole matter and not allow her mind to dwell upon the subject any longer. In a flash she exclaimed to the Judge: "So you, too, have joined the band of persecutors!"

Any one having ordinary contact with Miss Bird would have said that she was perfectly sane. It was only the persistent cross-examination urging her to disclose her hallucinations that finally broke her down and disclosed the weak spot in her mentality. This cross-examination would have been absolutely ineffectual if it had not been persisted in to the length that it was. In fact, the jurors after the trial was over admitted that their impression during the first two days of the examination was that she was a very much abused young woman and that if the interrogation had stopped before she broke down, there would have been a very substantial verdict.

At the end of a long but unsuccessful cross-examination of an opposing party, of the kind we have been discussing, an inexperienced trial lawyer once remarked rather testily, "Well, Mr. Whittemore, you have contrived to manage your case pretty well." "Thank you, counselor," replied the witness, with a twinkle in his eye, "perhaps I might return the compliment if I were not testifying under oath."

It so frequently happens that a lawyer who has made a failure of his cross-examination accentuates that failure by a careless side remark, instead of a dignified retreat, that I cannot refrain from relating another anecdote, in this connection, to illustrate the danger of these side remarks; for I am of the opinion that there is no surer way to avoid such occurrences than to have ever present in one's mind the mistakes of others.

One of the most distinguished practitioners in the criminal courts of the city of Philadelphia was prosecuting a case for the government. His witnesses had been subjected to a vehement cross-examination by the counsel for the prisoner, but with little effect upon the jury. Counsel for the prisoner bided his time, content to wait for another opportunity. After the testimony for the state had closed, the prosecuting attorney arose and foolishly remarked, "Now, Mr. Ingraham, I give you fair warning, after the way you have treated my witnesses, I intend to handle your witnesses *without gloves.*" "That is more than any one would care to do with yours, my friend," replied Mr. Ingraham; and the dirt seemed, somehow, to stick to the state witnesses throughout the trial.

An excellent example of effective cross-examination to the circumstances surrounding the main question in a case is found in Bigelow's "Bench and Bar." The issue was the forgery of a will; the proponent was a man of high respectability and good social standing, who had an indirect interest to a large amount, if the will, as offered, were allowed to be probated. Samuel Warren, the author of "Ten Thousand a Year," conducted the cross-examination.

Warren (*placing his thumb over the seal* and holding up the will). "I understand you to say you saw the testator sign this instrument?"

Witness. "I did."

Warren. "And did you sign it at his request, as subscribing witness?"

Witness. "I did."

Warren. "Was it sealed with red or black wax?"

Witness. "With red wax."

Warren. "Did you see him seal it with red wax?"

Witness. "I did."

Warren. "Where was the testator when he signed and sealed this will?"

Witness. "In his bed."

Warren. "Pray, how long a piece of red wax did he use?"

Witness. "About three inches long."

Warren. "And who gave the testator this piece of wax?"

Witness. "I did."

Warren. "Where did you get it?"

Witness. "From the drawer of his desk."

Warren. "How did he melt that piece of wax?"

Witness. "With a candle."

Warren. "Where did the candle come from?"

Witness. "I got it out of a cupboard in the room."

Warren. "How long should you say the candle was?"

Witness. "Perhaps four or five inches long."

Warren. "Do you remember who lit the candle?"

Witness. "I lit it."

Warren. "What did you light it with?"

Witness. "Why, with a match."

Warren. "Where did you get the match?"

Witness. "On the mantel shelf in the room."

Here Mr. Warren paused, and fixing his eye upon the witness, he again held up the will, his thumb still resting upon the seal, and said in a solemn, measured tone:

Warren. "Now, sir, upon your solemn oath, you saw the testator sign this will—he signed it in his bed—at his request you signed it as a subscribing witness—you saw him seal it—it was with red wax he sealed it—a piece of wax about three inches long—he lit the wax with a piece of candle which you procured from a cupboard—you lit the candle with a match which you found on a mantel-shelf?"

Witness. "I did."

Warren. "Once more, sir—upon your solemn oath, you did?"

Witness. "I did."

Warren. "My lord, *you will observe this will is sealed with a wafer!*"

In "Irish Wit and Humor" there is given an illustration of the dexterity of Daniel O'Connell in bringing about his client's acquittal by a very simple ruse of cross-examination. O'Connell was employed in defending a prisoner who was tried for a murder committed in the vicinity of Cork. The principal witness swore strongly against the prisoner. One corroborative circumstance was that the prisoner's hat was found near the place where the murder was committed. The witness swore positively that the hat produced was the one found, and that it belonged to the prisoner, whose first name was James.

O'Connell. "By virtue of your oath, are you positive that this is the same hat?"

Witness. "I am."

O'Connell. "Did you examine it carefully before you swore in your information that it was the property of the prisoner?"

Witness. "I did."

O'Connell (taking up the hat and examining the inside carefully). "Now let me see—J-A-M-E-S—do you mean those letters were in the hat when *you* found it?"

Witness. "I do."

O'Connell. "Did you see them there?"

Witness. "I did."

O'Connell. "And you are sure this is the same hat?"

Witness. "I am sure."

O'Connell (holding up the hat to the Bench). "Now, my lord, I submit this is an end of this case. There is no name whatever inscribed in this hat!"

Akin to the effect produced upon a jury by the probabilities in a case is the *personal conviction* of the lawyer who is conducting it. A man who genuinely and thoroughly believes in his own case will make others agree with him, often though he may be in the wrong.

Rufus Choate once said, "I care not how hard the case

is—it may bristle with difficulties—if I *feel* I am on the right side, that case I win."

It is this personal consciousness of right that has a strong moral and mental effect upon one's hearers. In no way can a lawyer more readily communicate to the minds of the jury his personal belief in his case than in his method and manner of developing, throughout his examinations, the probability or improbability of the tale which is being unfolded to them. In fact, it is only through his examination of the witnesses and general conduct of the trial, and his own personal deportment, that a lawyer is justified in impressing upon the jury his individual belief regarding the issues in the case. The expression in words of a lawyer's opinion is not only considered unprofessional, but produces an entirely different effect upon a juror from the influence which springs from earnestness and a profound conviction of the righteousness of the cause advocated.

Writing upon this branch of the subject, Senator Hoar says:[1] "It is not a lawyer's duty or his right to express his individual opinion. On him the responsibility of the decision does not rest. He not only has no right to accompany the statement of his argument with any assertion as to his individual belief, but I think the most experienced observers will agree that such expressions, if habitual, tend to diminish and not to increase the just influence of the lawyer. . . . There never was a weightier advocate before New England juries than Daniel Webster. Yet it is on record that he always carefully abstained from any positiveness of assertion. He introduced his weightiest arguments with such phrases as, 'It will be for the jury to consider,' 'It may, perhaps, be worth thinking of, gentlemen,' or some equivalent phrase, by which he kept scrupulously off the ground which belonged to the tribunal he was addressing."

However, an advocate is justified in arousing in the minds of a jury all the enthusiasm which he feels about

[1] "Autobiography of Seventy Years," Hoar.

the case himself. If he feels he is in the right, he can show it in a hundred different ways which cannot fail to have their effect upon his hearers. It was Gladstone's profound seriousness that most impressed itself upon everything that he said. He always made the impression upon his hearers that the matter he was discussing was that upon which the foundations of heaven and earth rested. Rufus Choate's *heart* was always in the court house. "No gambler ever hankered for the feverish delight of the gaming table as Choate did for the absorbing game, half chance, half skill, where twelve human dice must all turn up together one way, or there is no victory. . . . It was a curious sight to see on a jury twelve hard headed and intelligent countrymen—farmers, town officers, trustees, men chosen by their neighbors to transact their important affairs—after an argument by some clear headed lawyer for the defence about some apparently not very doubtful transaction, who had brought them all to his way of thinking, and had warned them against the wiles of the charmer, when Choate rose to reply for the plaintiff—to see their look of confidence and disdain—'You needn't try your wiles upon me.' The shoulder turned a little against the speaker—the averted eye—and then the change; first, the changed posture of the body; the slight opening of the mouth; then the look, first, of curiosity, and then of doubt, then of respect; the surrender of the eye to the eye of the great advocate; then the spell, the charm, the great enchantment—till at last, jury and audience were all swept away, and followed the conqueror captive in his triumphal march." [1]

Sir James Scarlett, England's greatest verdict getter, always had an appearance of confidence in himself and his cause which begot a feeling of confidence in all who listened to him. He used to "wind himself into a case like a great serpent." He always had about him "a happy mixture of sparkling intelligence and good nature, which told amazingly with juries." A writer in the *Britannia* gives the following graphic description of Scarlett's appear-

[1] *Ibid.*

ance in court: "A spectator unacquainted with the courts might have supposed that anybody rather than the portly, full faced, florid man, who was taking his ease on the comfortable cushions of the front row, was the counsel engaged in the cause. Or if he saw him rise and cross-examine a witness, he would be apt to think him certainly too indolent to attend properly to his business, so cool, indifferent, and apparently unconcerned was the way in which the facts which his questions elicited were left to their fate, as though it were of no consequence whether they were attended to or not. Ten to one with him that the plaintiff's counsel would get the verdict, so clear seemed the case and so slight the opposition. But in the course of time the defendant's turn would come; and then the large-headed, ruddy-faced, easy-going advocate would rise slowly from his seat, not quite upright, but resting on his left hand placed upon the bar, and turning sideways to the jury to commence the defence of his client. Still the same unpretending *nonchalant* air was continued; it almost seemed too great an exertion to speak; the chin of that ample face rested upon the still more ample chest as though the motion of the lips alone would be enough for all that might have to be said. So much for the first impression. A few moments' reflection sufficed to dispel the idea that indolence had anything to do with the previous quiescence of the speaker. Now it became clear that all the while he seemed to have been taking his ease bodily, he had been using his powers of observation and his understanding. That keen gray eye had not stolen glances at the jury, nor at the witnesses either, for nothing. Nor had those abandoned facts, drawn out in cross-examination, been unfruitful seeds or cast in barren places. Low as the tone of voice was, it was clear and distinct. It was not a mere organ of sound, but a medium of communication between the mind of the advocate and the minds of the jury. Sir James Scarlett did not attempt, like Denman or Brougham, to carry the feelings of a jury by storm before a torrent of invective or of eloquence; nor was there any obvious sophistry, such as occupied too large a space in the speeches of Campbell or Wilde; it was with facts—admitted, omitted or slurred over, as best suited his purpose—and with inferences made obvious in spite of prepossessions created by the other side, that this remarkable advocate achieved his triumphs."

Personal magnetism is, perhaps, the most important of all the attributes of a good trial lawyer. Those who possess it never fully realize it themselves and only partially, perhaps, when under the influence of a large audience. There is nothing like an audience as a stimulant to every faculty. The cross-examiner's questions seem to become vitalized with his knowledge of the topic of inquiry and his own shrewd discernment of the situation of the witness and the relation which the witness's interest and feelings bear to the topic. His force becomes almost irresistible, but it is a force in questions, a force aroused in the mind of the witness, not in the voice of the questioner. He seems to be able to concentrate all the attention of his hearers upon the vital points in the case; he imparts weight and solidity to all he touches; he unconsciously elevates the merits of his case; he comes almost intuitively to perceive the elements of truth or falsehood in the face itself of the narrative, without any regard to the narrator, and new and un-dreamed-of avenues of attacking the testimony seem to spring into being almost with the force of inspiration.

Such is the life and such the experiences of the trial lawyer. But I cannot leave this branch of the subject without voicing one sentiment in behalf of the witness, as distinguished from the lawyer, by quoting the following amusing lamentation, which has found its way into public print:—

"Of all unfortunate people in this world, none are more entitled to sympathy and commiseration than those whom circumstances oblige to appear upon the witness stand in court. You are called to the stand and place your hand upon a copy of the Scriptures in sheepskin binding, with a cross on the one side and none on the other, to accommodate either variety of the Christian faith. You are then arraigned before two legal gentlemen, one of whom smiles at you blandly because you are on his side, the other eying you savagely for the opposite reason. The gentleman who smiles, proceeds to pump you of all you know; and having squeezed all he wants out of you, hands you over to the other, who proceeds to show you that you are entirely mistaken in all your supposition; that you never saw anything you have sworn to; that you never saw the defendant in your life; in short, that you have committed direct perjury. He wants to know if you have ever been in state prison, and takes your denial with the air of a man who thinks you ought to have been there, asking all the questions over again in different ways; and tells you with an awe inspiring severity, to be very careful what you say. He wants to know if he understood you to say so and so, and also wants to know whether you meant something else. Having bullied and scared you out of your wits, and convicted you in the eye of the jury of prevarication, he lets you go. By and by everybody you have fallen out with is put on the stand to swear that you are the biggest scoundrel they ever knew, and not to be believed under oath. Then the opposing counsel, in summing up, paints your moral photograph to the jury as a character fit to be handed down to time as the typification of infamy—as a man who has conspired against innocence and virtue, and stands convicted of the attempt. The judge in his charge tells the jury if they believe your testimony, etc., indicating that there is even a *judicial* doubt of your veracity; and you go home to your wife and family, neighbors and acquaintances, a suspected man—all because of your accidental presence on an unfortunate occasion!"

Chapter 10

Cross-Examination to Credit, and its Abuses

THE PRECEDING CHAPTERS have been devoted to the legitimate uses of cross-examination—the development of truth and exposure of fraud.

Cross-examination as to credit has also its legitimate use to accomplish the same end; but this powerful weapon for good has almost equal possibilities for evil. It is proposed in the present chapter to demonstrate that cross-examination as to credit should be exercised with great care and caution, and also to discuss some of the abuses of cross-examination by attorneys, under the guise and plea of cross-examination as to credit.

Questions which throw no light upon the real issues in the case, nor upon the integrity or credit of the witness under examination, but which expose misdeeds, perhaps long since repented of and lived down, are often put for the sole purpose of causing humiliation and disgrace. Such inquiries into private life, private affairs, or domestic infelicities, perhaps involving innocent persons who have nothing to do with the particular litigation and who have no opportunity for explanation nor means of redress, form no legitimate part of the cross-examiner's art. The lawyer who allows himself to become the mouthpiece of the spite or revenge of his client may inflict untold suffering and unwarranted torture. Such questions may be within the legal rights of counsel in certain instances, but the lawyer who allows himself to be led astray by his zeal or by the solicitations of his client, at his elbow, ready to make any sacrifice to humiliate his adversary, thereby debauches his profession and surrenders his self-respect, for which an occasional verdict, won from an impressionable jury by such methods, is a poor recompense.

To warrant an investigation into matters irrelevant to the main issues in the case, and calculated to disgrace the witness or prejudice him in the eyes of the jury, they must at least be such as tend to impeach his general moral character and his credibility as a witness. There can be no sanction for questions which tend simply to degrade the witness personally, and which can have no possible bearing upon his veracity.

In all that has preceded we have gone upon the presumption that the cross-examiner's art would be used to further his client's cause by all fair and legitimate means, not by misrepresentation, insinuation, or by knowingly putting a witness in a false light before a jury. These methods doubtless succeed at times, but he who practises them acquires the reputation, with astounding rapidity, of being "smart," and finds himself discredited not only with the court, but in some almost unaccountable way with the very juries before whom he appears. Let him once get the reputation of being "unfair" among the habitués of the court house, and his usefulness to clients as a trial lawyer is gone forever. Honesty is the best policy quite as much with the advocate as in any other walk of life.

Counsel may have in his possession material for injuring the witness, but the propriety of using it often becomes a serious question even in cases where its use is otherwise perfectly legitimate. An outrage to the feelings of a witness may be quickly resented by a jury, and sympathy take the place of disgust. Then, too, one has to reckon with the judge, and the indignation of a strong judge is not wisely provoked. Nothing could be more unprofessional than for counsel to ask questions which disgrace not only the witness, but a host of innocent persons, for the mere reason that the client wishes them to be asked.

There could be no better example of the folly of yielding to a client's hatred or desire for revenge than the outcome of the famous case in which Mrs. Edwin Forrest was granted a divorce against her husband, the distinguished tragedian. Mrs. Forrest, a lady of culture and refinement, demanded her divorce upon the ground of adultery, and her husband had made counter charges against her. At the trial, in 1851, Charles O'Conor, counsel for Mrs. Forrest, called as his first witness the husband himself, and asked him concerning his infidelities in connection with a certain actress. John Van Buren, who appeared for Edwin Forrest, objected to the question on the ground that it required his client to testify to matters that might incriminate him. The question was not allowed, and the husband left the witness stand. After calling a few unimportant witnesses, O'Conor rested the case for plaintiff without having elicited any tangible proof against the husband. Had a motion to take the case from the jury been made at this time, it would of necessity have been granted, and the wife's suit would have failed. It is said that when Mr. Van Buren was about to make such a motion and end the case, Mr. Forrest directed him to proceed with the testimony for the defence, and develop the nauseating evidence he had accumulated against his wife. Van Buren yielded to his client's wishes, and for days and weeks continued to call witness after witness to the disgusting details of Mrs. Forrest's alleged debauchery. The case attracted great public attention and was widely reported by the newspapers. The public, as so often happens, took the opposite view of the evidence from the one the husband had anticipated. Its very revolting character aroused universal sympathy on the wife's behalf. Mr. O'Conor soon found himself flooded with offers of evidence, anonymous and otherwise, against the husband, and when Van Buren finally closed his attack upon the wife, O'Conor was enabled, in rebuttal, to bring such an avalanche of convincing testimony against the defendant that the jury promptly exonerated Mrs. Forrest and granted her the divorce. At the end of the first day's trial the case could have been decided in favor of the husband, had a simple motion to that effect been made; but, yielding to his client's hatred of his wife, and after a hard fought trial of thirty-three days, Van Buren found both himself and his client ignominiously defeated. This error of Van Buren's was widely commented on by the profession at the time. He had but lately resigned his office at

Albany as attorney general, and up to the time of this trial had acquired no little prestige in his practice in the city of New York, which, however, he never seemed to regain after his fatal blunder in the Forrest divorce case.[1]

An instructive example of the use of cross-examination solely for the purpose of minimizing the damages in a case is to be found in one of DeLancey Nicoll's cross-examinations where a well known impresario, and owner of opera houses, had brought an action for libel against one of our morning newspapers, demanding two hundred and fifty thousand dollars. The article, which was the subject of the suit, and which appeared on the front page, was as follows:

"My opinion of you is that you are the sort of man who would steal his mother's bones from the grave and sell them to buy flowers for a harlot."

The plaintiff testified in his own behalf. On cross-examination by Mr. Nicoll it developed that the plaintiff had written the editor who had composed the article an offensive note almost as violent as the one sued upon; that while manager of a trade journal he, himself, had been sued for libel, where the verdict was four thousand five hundred dollars against him; and that he was put upon the jail limits for failure to pay the judgment. It also appeared that he had been convicted of assault upon the opposing lawyer, a most respectable member of the bar; that he had been twice bankrupt; that his sister had recovered a judgment against him for money borrowed; and that his wife had been persuaded to help him in his business affairs and had been driven into bankruptcy on his account. During seven of the twenty years of his married life he kept a mistress, and even occupied, with her, on many occasions, a box in his own opera house directly over his wife's box. He also wrote her impassioned letters, and allowed her to use his wife's horses and carriages. The object of the cross-examiner was, of course, to show that the reputation of such a man could not be injured by anything a newspaper

[1] "Extraordinary Cases," H. L. Clinton.

might say about him. The jury agreed with counsel that one thousand dollars out of the two hundred and fifty sued for was balm enough for his injured feelings.

In actions for defamation such as the one just described, it is always legitimate to attack the character of the plaintiff, whether or not he becomes a witness in his own behalf. The question in such cases is one of sound tactics rather than of professional ethics. The plaintiff's character is directly material on the issue as to how much he has been damaged by what the defendant has said or written of him. Hence, the manner in which he may be handled by opposing counsel is to be clearly distinguished from pure cross-examination to credit.

The abuse of cross-examination to credit has been widely discussed in England in recent years, partly in consequence of the cross-examination of a Mrs. Bravo, whose husband had died by poison. He had lived unhappily with her on account of the attentions of a certain physician. During the inquiry into the circumstances of her husband's death, the story of the wife's intrigue was made public through her cross-examination. Sir Charles Russell, who was then regarded as standing at the head of the bar, both in the extent of his business and in his success in court, and Sir Edward Clark, one of Her Majesty's law officers, with a high reputation for ability in jury trials, were severely criticised as "forensic bullies," and complained of as "lending the authority of their example to the abuse of cross-examination to credit which was quickly followed by barristers of inferior positions, among whom the practice was spreading of assailing witnesses with what was not unfairly called a system of innuendoes, suggestions, and bullying from which sensitive persons recoil." And Mr. Charles Gill, one of the many imitators of Russell's domineering style, was criticised as "bettering the instructions of his elders."

The complaint against Russell was that by his practices as displayed in the Osborne case—robbery of jewels—not only may a man's, or a woman's, whole past be laid bare to malignant comment and public curiosity, but there is no means afforded by the courts of showing how the facts really stood or of producing evidence to repel the damaging charges.

Lord Bramwell, in an article published originally in *Nineteenth Century* for February, 1892, and republished in legal periodicals all over the world, strongly defends the methods of Sir Charles Russell and his imitators. Lord Bramwell claimed to speak after an experience of forty-seven years' practice at the Bar and on the Bench, and long acquaintance with the legal profession.

"A judge's sentence for a crime, however much repented of, is not the only punishment; there is the consequent loss of character in addition, which should confront such a person whenever called to the witness stand." "Women who carry on illicit intercourse, and whose husbands die of poison, must not complain at having the veil that ordinarily screens a woman's life from public inquiry rudely torn aside." "It is well for the sake of truth that there should be a wholesome dread of cross-examination." "It should not be understood to be a trivial matter, but rather looked upon as a trying ordeal." "None but the sore feel the probe." Such were some of the many arguments of the various upholders of broad license in examinations to credit.

Lord Chief Justice Cockburn took the opposite view of the question. "I deeply deplore that members of the Bar so frequently unnecessarily put questions affecting the private life of witnesses, which are only justifiable when they challenge the credibility of a witness. I have watched closely the administration of justice in France, Germany, Holland, Belgium, Italy, and a little in Spain, as well as in the United States, in Canada, and in Ireland, and in no place have I seen witnesses so badgered, brow-beaten, and in every way so brutally maltreated as in England. The way in which we treat our witnesses is a national disgrace and a serious obstacle, instead of aiding the ends of justice. In England the most honorable and conscientious men loathe the witness box. Men and women of all ranks shrink with terror from subjecting themselves to the wanton insult and bullying misnamed cross-examination in our English courts. Watch the tremor that passes the frames of many persons as they enter the witness box. I remember to have seen so distinguished a man as the late Sir Benjamin Brodie shiver as he entered the witness box. I daresay his apprehension amounted to exquisite torture. Witnesses are just as necessary for the administration of justice as judges or jurymen, and are entitled to be treated with the same consideration, and their affairs and private lives ought to be held as sacred from the gaze of the public as those of the judges or the jurymen. I venture to think that it is the duty of a judge to allow no questions to be put to a witness, unless such as are clearly pertinent to the issue before the court, except where the credibility of the witness is deliberately challenged by counsel and that the credibility of a witness should not be wantonly challenged on slight grounds." [1]

The propriety or impropriety of questions to credit is of course largely addressed to the discretion of the court. Such questions are generally held to be fair when, if the imputation they convey be true, the opinion of the court would be seriously affected as to the credibility of the witness on the matter to which he testifies; they are unfair when the imputation refers to matters so remote in time, or of such character that their truth would not affect the opinion of the court, or if there be a great disproportion between the importance of the imputation and the importance of the witness's evidence. [2]

A judge, however, to whose discretion such questions are addressed in the first instance, can have but an imperfect knowledge of either side of the case before him. He cannot always be sure, without hearing all the facts, whether the questions asked would or would not tend to develop the truth rather than simply degrade the witness. Then, again, the mischief is often done by the mere asking of the question, even if the judge directs the witness not

[1] "Irish Law Times," 1874.
[2] Sir James Stephen's Evidence Act.

to answer. The insinuation has been made publicly—the dirt has been thrown. The discretion must therefore, after all, be largely left to the lawyer himself. He is bound in honor, and out of respect to his profession, to consider whether the question ought in conscience to be asked—whether in his own honest judgment it renders the witness unworthy of belief under oath—before he allows himself to ask it. It is much safer, for example, to proceed upon the principle that the relation between the sexes has no bearing whatever upon the probability of the witness telling the truth, unless in the extreme case of an abandoned woman.

In criminal prosecutions the district attorney is usually regarded by the jury much in the light of a judicial officer and, as such, unprejudiced and impartial. Any slur or suggestion adverse to a prisoner's witness coming from this source, therefore, has an added power for evil, and is calculated to do injustice to the defendant. There have been many flagrant abuses of this character in the criminal courts of our own city and elsewhere. "Is it not a fact that you were not there at all?" "Has all this been written out for you?" "Is it not a fact that you and your husband have concocted this whole story?" "You have been a witness for your husband in every lawsuit he has had, have you not?" —were all questions that were recently criticised by the court, on appeal, as "innuendo," and calculated to prejudice the defendant—by the Michigan Supreme Court in the People *vs.* Cahoon—and held sufficient, in connection with other similar errors, to set a conviction aside.

Assuming that the material with which you propose to assail the credibility of a witness fully justifies the attack, the question then arises, as to how to use this material to the best advantage. The sympathies of juries are keen toward those obliged to confess their crimes on the witness stand. The same matters may be handled to the advantage or positive disadvantage of the cross-examiner. If you hold in your possession the evidence of the witness's conviction, for example, but allow him to understand that you know his history, he will surely get the better of you. Conceal it from him, and he will likely try to conceal it from you, or lie about it if necessary. "I don't suppose you have ever been in trouble, have you?" will bring a quick reply, "What trouble?"—"Oh, I don't refer to any particular trouble. I mean generally, have you ever been in jail?" The witness will believe you know nothing about him and deny it, or if he has been many times convicted, will admit some small offence and attempt to conceal everything but what he suspects you know already about him. This very attempt to deceive, if exposed, will destroy him with the jury far more effectually than the knowledge of the offences he has committed. On the other hand, suppose you taunt him with his crime in the first instance; ten to one he will admit his wrong-doing in such a way as to arouse toward himself the sympathy of the jury and their resentment toward the lawyer who was unchristian enough to uncover to public view offences long since lived down.

Chief Baron Pollock once presided at a case where a witness was asked about a conviction years gone by, though his (the witness's) honesty was not doubted. The baron burst into tears at the answer of the witness.

In the Bellevue Hospital case (the details of which are fully described in a subsequent chapter), and during the cross-examination of the witness Chambers, who was confined in the Pavilion for the Insane at the time, the writer was imprudent enough to ask the witness to explain to the jury how he came to be confined on Ward's Island, only to receive the pathetic reply: "I was sent there because I was insane. You see my wife was very ill with locomotor ataxia. She had been ill a year; I was her only nurse. I tended her day and night. We loved each other dearly. I was greatly worried over her long illness and frightful suffering. The result was, I worried too deeply; she had been very good to me. I overstrained myself, my mind gave way; but I am better now, thank you."

Chapter 11

Two "Lurking, if Not Great, Dangers" That Confront a Cross-Examiner, by Max D. Steuer

A.

CROSS-EXAMINATION is usually regarded as the means by which adverse witnesses are discredited, and it is for that purpose that it is usually employed by the Bar. The importance of it in that regard is self-evident. If through the instrumentality of the cross-examination the integrity of the witness is destroyed, even though it be not with respect to the particular testimony given at the trial, if his general reputation for truth and veracity is shown to be bad by his own utterances, clearly the examiner has very greatly helped his case. In this effort, however, there are two lurking, if not great, dangers. One is to cross-examine when it is quite unnecessary and the other to overdo the cross-examination. A recent experience will perhaps tend to illustrate the point.

A defendant in a criminal case was charged with having bribed a government inspector. Witnesses were called to establish the good reputation for truth and veracity of the defendant. There was a time when such testimony was of real and substantial value. At the present time, particularly in the federal court, under the rules there in vogue, that character of testimony has become of very slight importance. In this particular case, a number of witnesses took the stand to testify that the defendant bore an excellent reputation for truth and veracity. In each instance, the prosecutor undertook to cross-examine the reputation witness. What I am endeavoring to demonstrate is the ill effect of cross-examining when it really is not necessary or of overdoing it. The judge had several times stated that the direct examination was limited to the inquiry as to whether or not the witness knew the reputation for truth and veracity of the defendant by the speech of the people in his vicinity, and if he indicated that he did, to state whether that reputation was good or bad. He made it quite obvious that he did not consider testimony of that kind very significant in a case where a man was charged with bribing a government official, and particularly where it was conceded that money had passed from the defendant to the official after the latter had made known to the United States Attorney that it had been proffered and arrangement had been made so that the defendant should be caught in the act. Nevertheless, as has been stated, several witnesses were called to testify and in each instance they were asked, and this particular witness had put to him, the question:

Q. "When you came to know him and knew people who knew him, from the way that they have spoken of him, do you know what his reputation is in the community?"

The Prosecutor. "I object to the question as immaterial."

The Court. "Isn't it in the same form you expressed with the previous witness, by knowing the speech of those who know him?"

Defendant's Counsel. "Yes. I think very frequently you gather what a man's reputation is by the way people talk."

The Court. "There is a stereotyped form that you know well. Just ask him about it. You have asked that question many, many times."

Q. "By the speech of the people, have you come to know the reputation of the defendant for truth and veracity?"

A. "I have."

CROSS-EXAMINATION:

Q. "Mr. Witness, you are not giving us hearsay statements of others, you are giving us your own opinion?"

A. "I do."

The Prosecutor. "I move to strike it out as incompetent."

The Court. "Strike it out."

The Witness. "The opinion of others that I have heard—"

The Court. "Let us boil it down. You were asked by defendant's counsel if you know by the speech of those who knew him what his reputation was. You say you do?"

The Witness. "Yes."

The Court. "Tell us in a few words what that reputation is, not what you thought, but what you have heard."

The Witness. "I have heard that he is a very fine family man, he is a good father to his children, he is a good husband to his wife, that he lives in a very noble way in his neighborhood."

The Prosecutor. "I object and move to strike out the answer."

The Court. "It only has a bearing on his reputation for veracity and honesty. What is his reputation for veracity and honesty?"

The Witness. "Very good, first class."

The Court. "That is all that is necessary."

If there had not been a word of cross-examination, the usual humdrum of the witness being permitted to be asked one question on direct examination—to which the answer would be "very good, excellent, or even the best," practically no attention would be given to the testimony and nothing of importance would be elicited. Here, by reason of an attempted cross-examination, the witness was permitted to say that the defendant "is a very fine family man, he is a good father to his children, he is a good husband to his wife, that he lives in a very noble way in his neighborhood." How much that testimony had to do with the disagreement of the jury in that particular case, nobody will ever know. But there may have been several men who reached the conclusion that if a man is "a very fine family man," is "a good father to his children," is "a good husband to his wife," and does "live in a very noble way in his neighborhood," it is difficult to believe that a person of that type would stoop to bribing a public official. At any rate, the testimony was made much more important and impressive after the cross-examination than could possibly have been at the conclusion of the direct. Instances of that kind, of course, can be multiplied. They occur with the ut-

most frequency, and it is important for a lawyer who prepares himself for the trial of causes to bear that in mind.

B.

Only in rare instances does the lawyer who is in the trial
of a case give serious thought to the cross-examination before he is confronted with the necessity of proceeding with
it, and particularly in few instances is it that the lawyer
gives serious consideration to the law applicable to the
particular situation with relation to which he is about to
cross-examine.

In the same case to which I previously referred, the inspector who it was claimed had been bribed by the defendant was under cross-examination. It is of the utmost
importance to bear in mind that where a defendant is
charged with bribery, if in fact the person bribed originates
the suggestion, and thus sows the seed, so that the idea of
bribery came to the defendant first through something that
the government official said, by reason of which the defendant starts to plan the bribe, the defendant may not be
convicted. The inspector was interrogated on cross-examination as follows:

The Witness. "He (defendant) said, 'Can you wait a
few days on the report until I can secure the names of the
people who have licenses?' And I told him, 'No, I could
not wait.'"

Q. "You said you could not?"
A. "I could not."
Q. "Was it then that you started to go to the elevator?"
A. "At the time he began explaining how important it
was, over and over again, and how he was scared. He had
mentioned over and over that he was afraid he was going
to lose his license, and could I remain. It was about that
time that I went to the elevator."
Q. "He asked you whether you could remain for a few
days?"
A. "Yes."

Q. "Did you give him a reason why you could not?"

A. "Yes."

Q. "What reason did you give him as to why you could not?"

A. "I said I had to return, to get back to my work."

Q. "Is that the only reason that you gave him?"

A. "Yes."

Q. "Nothing said about the expenses involved in your staying there?"

A. "The only time that expenses was mentioned, he asked me where I was staying and I said the Hotel New Yorker. He made a gesture with his hands like it was a pretty high class hotel."

Q. "He made a gesture with his hands like it was a pretty high class hotel? Do you really mean that?"

A. "Yes."

Q. "You understood from his hand that he was gesturing or talking about the fact of the New Yorker being a high priced hotel?"

A. "At the time I said that the Hotel New Yorker is rather expensive. That is the only time expenses were referred to, and after that he never mentioned expenses in any way whatsoever."

Q. "You said that from the time you referred to the hotel being rather expensive he never referred to expensive or expenses again?"

A. "No."

Q. "Did you refer to expensive or expenses again?"

A. "No."

Q. "After that one utterance by you about expensive, that ended your reference to expensive or expenses, is that right?"

A. "That is correct."

Q. "When you went to the elevator there was nothing said about expenses?"

A. "I told you what was said about expenses."

Q. "I understood you. I just want to make sure. Was there or was there not anything said?"

A. "The only mention of expenses was when he asked

me where I was staying, and I said the Hotel New Yorker, and he made a gesture, and I said, 'Yes, it is rather expensive.' "

The Court. "Do you recall whether that was in the office or in the elevator?"

The Witness. "That was in the elevator."

Juror No. 12. "Will you have him speak clearer, please."

The Court. "A little louder."

Q. "That having been at the elevator, was there anything said about money or expenses or expensive at any other time or at any other place while you were in the defendant's premises?"

A. "Yes, sir, that was the only time any mention was made of expenses or expensive.

Q. "Is it entirely clear that there was no suggestion by you or by him with respect to money, paying you anything or making good your expenses, or anything of that sort?"

A. "There was no statement whatsoever."

Q. "But you asked him to call you up?"

A. "I did not ask him. He asked me could he call me up."

Q. "What did you say to that?"

A. "I said yes."

Q. "Did you fix a time when he should call you up?"

A. "He asked me if he could call me at six o'clock."

Q. "You told him he could call you at six o'clock?"

A. "Yes."

Q. "Did you intimate to him that you might stay over?"

A. "No, sir. Only I told him when he asked me could he call me at six o'clock, and I said he could, he took that as an indication to grab my hand and said, 'I will seal our secrecy with death.' "

Q. " 'Seal our secrecy with death?' "

A. "Yes, I know the word 'death' was in there. I got a little chill at the time."

Q. "What?"

A. "I know the word death was in there."

Q. "What did you add?"

A. "When he mentioned 'death' I got a little chill up my spine."

Q. "Got a chill up your spine?"

A. "Yes."

Q. "When he was coming up after you concluded your telephone message did you then understand that he was bringing the money?"

A. "No, sir."

Q. "Had it occurred to you that he might bring money?"

A. "Yes, it did, because he said he was going to make it worth my while."

Q. "Did you ask him how?"

A. "No, I strictly stayed away from asking him anything about that."

Q. "When he took out the money, were you surprised?"

A. "No, sir, I was not surprised."

Q. "Did you ask him how much it was?"

A. "Yes, sir."

Q. "When did you ask him how much it was?"

A. "When he took the money and placed it on the dresser."

Q. "Were you right by the dresser at the time?"

A. "Yes, sir."

Q. "In a position to put your hand on it and count it?"

A. "Yes, sir."

Q. "It was free there, was it not?"

A. "Yes, sir."

Q. "But before you touched it you asked him how much it was?"

A. "Yes, sir."

Q. "Did he tell you how much it was?"

A. "Yes, sir."

Q. "Did he say anything else?"

A. "No, sir."

Q. "Did you reach for the money?"

A. "Yes, sir, and counted it."

Q. "What did you then do with it?"

A. "Put it in my pocket."

Bearing in mind that the authorities are to the effect that where the offense originated in the mind of a government agent or officer and would not otherwise have been committed, entrapment is a defense to the accused (a very comprehensive note upon this subject is to be found in 66 A. L. R. 478, 483, in which most of the authorities are reviewed, and in addition thereto one might examine *DeMarco* v. *U. S.,* 296 Fed. 667; *Brown* v. *U. S.,* 290 Fed. 870; *U. S.* v. *Lynch,* 256 Fed. 983), the court was asked to charge: "Even if you believe beyond a reasonable doubt that the defendant paid the money to the government inspector to induce him to alter his report of his investigation, by omitting the inspector's own list and substituting the defendant's list, still if you are satisfied that the suggestion originated with the inspector and was first made by him, and that the defendant would not otherwise have done it, the defendant may not be convicted and the verdict must be not guilty; and if you have a reasonable doubt as to whether the suggestion of a payment of a bribe originated with the defendant or with the inspector, your verdict must be not guilty."

The elicitation from the inspector of the suggestion that he had said something about the New Yorker Hotel, where he was stopping, being very expensive may have been the means of creating a doubt in the minds of some of the jurors as to whether or not the idea originated with the inspector or the defendant. If an examination of the law had not been made prior to the trial, that charge might not have been made and the cross-examination along that line might not have been pursued.

Perhaps a much more striking illustration of the necessity for having in mind the law applicable to the particular subject matter of cross-examination is another recent case in the New York Supreme Court. The plaintiff brought suit against the defendant to recover an amount paid by the plaintiff for certificates of stock which the plaintiff alleged he purchased from the defendant, and as part of the inducement for the purchase the defendant promised to repurchase upon the demand of the plaintiff. The plaintiff alleged that he had tendered the stock to the defendant and had asked the defendant to repurchase it and pay him the amount that had been paid therefor. Such an agreement is not within the Statute of Frauds, the authorities holding that the agreement to repurchase is part of the original contract of sale and hence constitutes an original obligation, no writing being required to evidence the obligation. The amount sued for was a large amount. If the stock in fact was not purchased from the defendant but was treasury stock purchased from a corporation which was organized by the defendant and which the defendant did urge people to buy, and the defendant then made a promise that he would purchase the stock from the plaintiff at any time upon the plaintiff's demand, at the price which the plaintiff paid for it, then the contract of purchase on the part of the defendant from the plaintiff was a contract for the purchase and sale of goods or choses in action of the value of $50 or upwards and is not enforceable unless the buyer shall accept part of the goods or choses in action so contracted for, and actually receive the same, or give something in earnest to bind the contract, or unless some note or memorandum of the contract or sale be signed by the party to be charged or his agent in that behalf. That is the Statute of Frauds (section 85 of the Personal Property Law).

The plaintiff in this case took the stand and testified, as alleged in the complaint, that he bought the stock from the defendant, paid by check to the order of the defendant, and that the defendant made the promise to repurchase.

Fortunately, the plaintiff was not well informed on the law. His attention apparently had not been called to the decisions in *Morse* v. *Douglas,* 112 App. Div. 798 and *Gainsburg* v. *Bachrack,* 241 App. Div. 28, aff'd 266 N. Y. 468. So, on cross-examination, the plaintiff testified that he was told by he defendant that this was a new corporation that was about to be organized; that the defendant said that he would be an important member of the executive force of the corporation; that his brother would be a very important member in the administrative force of the corporation and that he, the plaintiff, was going to be let in on the ground floor; that the defendant thought the plaintiff would make a great deal of money on the purchase of the stock. A very important admission that the plaintiff made was that the defendant had said to him that he would notify the plaintiff when the corporation would be ready to receive subscriptions for the stock and he, the plaintiff, expected to get treasury stock and that he actually received treasury stock; and that when the defendant asked him to sign a subscription, he did sign one; and when the stock was delivered, he signed a receipt acknowledging that he received it from the corporation. He also testified that the defendant had told him that he expected that the corporation was going to do a very profitable business and that everybody concerned in it would make a great deal of money on that stock; and that he knew that the corporation had started to do business. He admitted that on account of the purchase contract which he alleged, with the defendant, the defendant had made no part payment, had not accepted delivery of any part of the stock and that there was no memorandum signed by the defendant in which he had agreed to purchase the stock, nor by his agent in that behalf. After the plaintiff had put a considerable number of witnesses on the stand, all of whom testified to the oral agreement made by the defendant, the plaintiff rested and, on the defendant's motion, the complaint was dismissed because it fell within the Statute of Frauds.

The only lesson to be deduced from this and any number of illustrations that may be added is that the law applicable to the situation which it is proposed to develop on cross-examination should be thoroughly known to the person who is trying the case, to the end that there may be developed, as the result of the cross-examination, a legal bar to recovery by the side that is being cross-examined.

It is to be emphasized that in these instances the cross-examination is not at all conducted for the purpose of impeaching the veracity or integrity of the witness nor is it to show the improbability or impossibility of the story told. The certainty exists that many cases have resulted in recovery where on cross-examination a bar to the right of recovery might readily have been created if the examiner had been apprised of the law applicable to the situation then confronting him.

MAX D. STEUER.

Chapter 12

Comments on the "Uses and Abuses" of Cross-Examination, by Emory R. Buckner

MORE CROSS-EXAMINATIONS are suicidal than homicidal. There are two reasons for this: a mistaken conception as to the function of cross-examination, and faulty technique.

The purpose of cross-examination should be to catch truth, ever an elusive fugitive. If the testimony of a witness is wholly false, cross-examination is the first step toward its destruction. If the testimony of a witness is partly true and partly false, cross-examination is the first step in an effort to destroy that which is false. One should willingly accept that which he believes to be true whether or not it damages his case. If the testimony of a witness is false only in the sense that it exaggerates, distorts, garbles, or creates a wrong sense of proportion, then the function of cross-examination is to whittle down the story to its proper size and its proper relation to other facts. A composite photograph of a man's face with its ears ten times enlarged is not a true photograph of the man. If the cross-examiner believes the story told to be true and not exaggerated, and if the story changes counsel's appraisal of his client's case, then what is indicated is not a "vigorous" cross-examination but a negotiation for adjustment during the luncheon hour. If this fails, counsel should accept the story and get his settlement by the judgment of the court or verdict of the jury. No client is entitled to have his lawyer score a triumph by superior wits over a witness who the lawyer believes is telling the truth. Lawyers can do more for the improvement of the administration of justice in their daily practice than by serving on committees or making speeches at bar associations, however helpful that may be.

As to technique. The worst cross-examiners belong to the major school. They take careful notes of the witness's testimony, thus dividing their attention and sacrificing careful listening and study of the character and personality of the witness. When they rise they begin at the beginning and stoutly march through to the end. The court or jury always listens more attentively to cross-examination that direct examination. The direct examiner frequently puts too much of himself and too little of the witness in the direct testimony. Cross-examination is a combat and therefore always interesting. The lawyer who begins at the beginning and shouts his way to the end generally achieves the result of underscoring the important parts of the testimony, thus emphasizing by repetition the damage he may have suffered. He is a Micawber, always hoping that something will "turn up." Sometimes, though rarely, it does. A deliberately and wisely enforced repetition of the whole story from beginning to end sometimes is indicated to bring out the phonograph record quality of a coached witness.

A cross-examiner should limit himself to the vital points of the story he is seeking to discredit or to reduce to its proper proportions. A witness makes an unimportant error,—the train he took, the floor on which he got off, the route he drove in his car. The truth, if developed, will neither help nor hurt either side. Time is consumed, the evidence marshaled, the admission of error finally triumphantly wrung from the witness, all to no purpose. In the meantime, the cross-examiner has lost momentum, the high spots of his case are forgotten. In cross-examination as well as in direct examination, opening, and summation, the best advocate is he who never leaves the turnpike of his case, who is never lured into attractive country roads, who never stops to buy frankfurters or cider on the way. The *motif* of the case, whether plaintiff's or defendant's, must ever recur. Cross-examination can frequently be skillfully and legitimately used as a sounding-board for the plaintiff's case or the defendant's defense.

Except where the circumstances make it wholly natural,

there should be no place in cross-examination for indignation, shouting, belligerent hostility. A kindly voice and courtesy dig a better trap than high blood pressure. A jury regards the combat as unequal because of the skill and experience of the lawyer. Their sympathies are naturally with the underdog. They do not like to see him shouted at and brow-beaten. Generally speaking, the adroit cross-examiner will endeavor to have the witness destroy himself and waive his personal triumph, keeping his co-operation in the destruction well in the background.

In many cases there is a fruitful field for preparation of cross-examination. Every letter or other document the anticipated witness may have signed, which has a bearing upon the case, should be secured if possible and carefully studied. The life history of every expected witness should be ascertained, if possible. Diligent search should be made for conversations about the case in which the witness may have indulged. Many cases are won solely by cross-examination prepared in advance. Notwithstanding this fact, immediate improvisation is what is most frequently needed.

When the cross-examiner rises and does not know exactly what to ask or where to begin, he should say "No cross-examination!"

EMORY R. BUCKNER

Chapter 13

Some Famous Cross-Examiners and Their Methods

ONE of the best ways to acquire the art of cross-examination is to study the methods of the great cross-examiners who serve as models for the legal profession. Indeed, nearly every great cross-examiner attributes his success to the fact of having had the opportunity to study the art of some great advocate in actual practice. In view of the fact also that a keen interest is always taken in the personality and life sketches of great cross-examiners, it has seemed fitting to introduce some brief sketches of great cross-examiners, and to give some illustrations of their methods.

Sir Charles Russell, Lord Russell of Killowen, who died in February, 1901, while he was Lord Chief Justice of England, was altogether the most successful cross-examiner of modern times. Lord Coleridge said of him while he was still practising at the bar, and on one side or the other in nearly every important case tried, "Russell is the biggest advocate of the century."

It has been said that his success in cross-examination, like his success in everything, was due to his force of character. It was his striking personality, added to his skill and adroitness, which seemed to give him his overwhelming influence with the witnesses whom he cross-examined. Russell is said to have had a wonderful faculty for using the brain and knowledge of other men. Others might possess a knowledge of the subject far in excess of Russell, but he had the reputation of being able to make that knowledge valuable and to use it in his examination of a witness in a way altogether unexpected and unique.

Unlike Rufus Choate, "The Ruler of the Twelve," and by far the greatest advocate of the last century on this side of the water, Russell read but little. He belonged to the category of famous men who "neither found nor pretended to find any real solace in books." With Choate, his library of some eight thousand volumes was his home, and "his authors were the loves of his life." Choate used to read at his meals and while walking in the streets, for books were his only pastime. Neither was Russell a great orator, while Choate was ranked as "the first orator of his time in any quarter of the globe where the English language was spoken, or who was ever seen standing before a jury panel."

Both Russell and Choate were consummate actors; they were both men of genius in their advocacy. Each knew the precise points upon which to seize; each watched every mood of the jury, knew at a glance what was telling with them, knew how to use to the best advantage every accident that might arise in the progress of the case.

"One day a junior was taking a note in the orthodox fashion. Russell was taking no note, but he was thoroughly on the alert, glancing about the court, sometimes at the judge, sometimes at the jury, sometimes at the witness or the counsel on the other side. Suddenly he turned to the junior and said, 'What are you doing?' 'Taking a note,' was the answer. 'What the devil do you mean by saying you are taking a note? Why don't you watch the case?' he burst out. *He* had been 'watching' the case. Something happened to make a change of front necessary, and he wheeled his colleagues around almost before they had time to grasp the new situation." [1]

Russell's maxim for cross-examination was, "Go straight at the witness and at the point; throw your cards on the table; mere *finesse* English juries do not appreciate." [2]

Speaking of Russell's success as a cross-examiner, his biographer, Barry O'Brien, says: "It was a fine sight to see him rise to cross-examine. His very appearance must

---

[1] "Life of Lord Russell," Barry O'Brien.
[2] From this it would seem that Russell's method might require some adaptation in order to achieve full success before a sophisticated New York jury of to-day.

have been a shock to the witness,—the manly, defiant bearing, the noble brow, the haughty look, the remorseless mouth, those deep-set eyes, widely opened, and that searching glance which pierced the very soul. 'Russell,' said a member of the Northern Circuit, 'produced the same effect on a witness that a cobra produces on a rabbit.' In a certain case he appeared on the wrong side. Thirty-two witnesses were called, thirty-one on the wrong side, and one on the right side. Not one of the thirty-one was broken down in cross-examination; but the one on the right side was utterly annihilated by Russell.

" 'How is Russell getting on?' a friend asked one of the judges of the Parnell Commission during the days of Pigott's cross-examination. 'Master Charlie is bowling very straight,' was the answer. 'Master Charlie' always bowled 'very straight,' and the man at the wicket generally came quickly to grief. I have myself seen him approach a witness with great gentleness—the gentleness of a lion reconnoitring his prey. I have also seen him fly at a witness with the fierceness of a tiger. But, gentle or fierce, he must have always looked a very ugly object to the man who had gone into the box to lie.' "

Rufus Choate had little of Russell's natural force with which to command his witnesses; his effort was to magnetize; he was called "the wizard of the court room." He employed an entirely different method in his cross-examinations. He never assaulted a witness as if determined to browbeat him. "Commenting once on the cross-examination of a certain eminent counsellor at the Boston Bar with decided disapprobation, Choate said, 'This man goes at a witness in such a way that he inevitably gets the jury all on the side of the witness. I do not,' he added, 'think that is a good plan.' His own plan was far more wary, intelligent, and circumspect. He had a profound knowledge of human nature, of the springs of human action, of the thoughts of human hearts. To get at these and make them patent to the jury, he would ask only a few telling questions—a very few questions, but generally, every one of them was fired point blank and hit the mark.

His motto was: 'Never cross-examine any more than is absolutely necessary. If you don't break your witness, he breaks you.' He treated every man who appeared like a fair and honest person on the stand, as if upon the presumption that he was a gentleman; and if a man appeared badly, he demolished him, but with the air of a surgeon performing a disagreeable amputation—as if he was profoundly sorry for the necessity. Few men, good or bad, ever cherished any resentment against Choate for his cross-examination of them. His whole style of address to the occupants of the witness stand was soothing, kind, and reassuring. When he came down heavily to crush a witness, it was with a calm, resolute decision, but no asperity—nothing curt, nothing tart." [1]

Choate's idea of the proper length of an address to a jury was that "a speaker makes his impression, if he ever makes it, in the first *hour,* sometimes in the first fifteen minutes; for if he has a proper and firm grasp of his case, he then puts forth the outline of his grounds of argument. He plays the *overture,* which hints at or announces all the airs of the coming opera. All the rest is mere filling up: answering objections, giving one juryman little arguments with which to answer the objections of his fellows, etc. Indeed, this may be taken as a fixed rule, that the popular mind can never be vigorously addressed, deeply moved, and stirred and fixed more than *one hour* in any single address."

It used to be said of Choate that "he did not argue very many great cases, but he made many little ones great." To a favorite junior, who was specializing in domestic cases, he once remarked, "Let me give you my dying advice—never cross-examine a woman. It is of no use. They cannot disintegrate the story they have once told. They cannot eliminate the part that is for you from that which is against you. They can neither combine nor shade nor qualify. They go for the whole thing; and the moment you begin to cross-examine one of them, instead of being bitten

[1] "Reminiscences of Rufus Choate," Parker.

by a single rattlesnake, you are bitten by a whole barrelful. I never, except in a case absolutely desperate, dare to cross-examine a woman."

What Choate was to America, and Erskine, and later Russell, to England, John Philpot Curran was to Ireland. He ranked as a jury lawyer next to Erskine. The son of a peasant, he became Master of Rolls for Ireland in 1806. He had a small, slim body, a stuttering, harsh, shrill voice, originally of such a diffident nature that in the midst of his first case he became speechless and dropped his brief to the floor, and yet by perseverance and experience he became one of the most eloquent and powerful forensic advocates of the world. As a cross-examiner it was said of Curran that "he could unravel the most ingenious web which perjury ever spun, he could seize on every fault and inconsistency, and build on them a denunciation terrible in its earnestness." [1]

It was said of Scarlett, Lord Abinger, that he won his cases because there were twelve Sir James Scarletts in the jury box. He became one of the leading jury lawyers of his time, so far as winning verdicts was concerned. Scarlett used to wheedle the juries over the weak places in his case. Choate would rush them right over with that enthusiasm which he put into everything, "with fire in his eye and fury on his tongue." Scarlett would level himself right down to each juryman, while he flattered and won them. In his cross-examinations "he would take those he had to examine, as it were by the hand, made them his friends, entered into familiar conversation with them, encouraged them to tell him what would best answer his purpose, and thus secured a victory without appearing to commence a conflict."

A story is told about Scarlett by Justice Wightman, who was leaving his court one day and found himself walking in a crowd alongside a countryman, whom he had seen, day by day, serving as a juryman, and to whom he could not help speaking. Liking the look of the man, and finding that this was the first occasion on which he had been at the

[1] "Life Sketches of Eminent Lawyers," Gilbert J. Clark.

court, Judge Wightman asked him what he thought of the leading counsel. "Well," said the countryman, "that lawyer Brougham be a wonderful man, he can talk, he can, but I don't think nowt of lawyer Scarlett."—"Indeed!" exclaimed the judge, "you surprise me, for you have given him all the verdicts."—"Oh, there's nowt in that," was the reply, "he be so lucky, you see, he be always on the right side." [1]

Choate also had a way of getting himself "into the jury box," and has been known to address a single juryman, who he feared was against him, for an hour at a time. After he had piled up proof and persuasion all together, one of his favorite expressions was, "But this is only *half* my case, gentlemen, I go now to the main body of my proofs."

Like Scarlett, Erskine was of medium height and slender, but he was handsome and magnetic, quick and nervous, "his motions resembled those of a blood horse—as light, as limber, as much betokening strength and speed." He, too, lacked the advantage of a college education and was at first painfully unready of speech. In his maiden effort he would have abandoned his case, had he not felt, as he said, that his children were tugging at his gown. "In later years," Choate once said of him, "he spoke the best English ever spoken by an advocate." Once, when the presiding judge threatened to commit him for contempt, he replied, "Your Lordship may proceed in what manner you think fit; I know my duty as well as your Lordship knows yours." His simple grace of diction, quiet and natural passion, was in marked contrast to Rufus Choate, whose delivery has been described as "a musical flow of rhythm and cadence, more like a long, rising, and swelling song than a *talk* or an argument." To one of his clients who was dissatisfied with Erskine's efforts in his behalf, and who had written his counsel on a slip of paper, "I'll be hanged if I don't plead my own cause," Erskine quietly replied, "You'll be hanged if you do." Erskine boasted that in twenty years he had never been kept a day from court by

[1] "Curiosities of Law and Lawyers."

ill health. And it is said of Curran that he has been known to rise before a jury, after a session of sixteen hours with only twenty minutes' intermission, and make one of the most memorable arguments of his life.

Among the more modern advocates of the English Bar, Sir Henry Hawkins stands out conspicuously. He is reputed to have taken more money away with him from the Bar than any man of his generation. His leading characteristic when at the Bar was his marvellous skill in cross-examination. He was associated with Lord Coleridge in the first Tichborne trial, and in his cross-examination of the witnesses, Baignet and Carter, he made his reputation as "the foremost cross-examiner in the world." [1] Sir Richard Webster was another great cross-examiner. He is said to have received $100,000 for his services in the trial before the Parnell Special Commission, in which he was opposed to Sir Charles Russell.

One of the most picturesque lawyers at the Irish Bar was Daniel O'Connell, known to his friends and neighbors as the "counselor." He was famous for his ability to "stand up to the Crown Prosecutor and bandy words with the judge and bully the witnesses of the prosecution into truth or shame." One of O'Connell's last and greatest triumphs was in defence of the Doneraile conspirators, for the details of which I am beholden to Justice Edward A. Parry.

A murder had taken place, and the authorities proceeded to round up all and sundry into the dock, and a special commission was sent down to try them at Cork. The first batch of five prisoners was found guilty on most unsatisfactory evidence and sentenced to be hanged in six days. One of these was a responsible old farmer of nearly seventy who rented a farm for $200 a year. He was firmly believed to be innocent, and these convictions struck terror and dismay through the countryside. There was but one thought in every mind: O'Connell must be sent for. He was then at Kerry, ninety miles away. The conviction took place on Saturday afternoon, and another lot of prisoners was to be tried on Monday morning at nine o'clock.

[1] "Life Sketches of Eminent Lawyers," Clark.

William Burke, of Bally-Hea, was the messenger, and on Sunday morning he was at Darrynane in the counselor's presence. Said he:

"I left Cork yesterday evening at five o'clock and rode all night, ninety long miles, to see your honor. The friends of the poor boys who are in the dock for the Doneraile conspiracy sent me to you, and unless you are in Cork before the court opens every man of them will be hanged, though as innocent as the child unborn."

O'Connell was fifty-six years old at this time, but he was vigorous and strong, and a fast gig took him over the mountains in the black of night. Burke had gone ahead, and great was the excitement when it was heard that the counselor was on his way. The judges were asked to postpone the hearing, which was refused, Barren Pennefather declaring "the trial should proceed without delay."

Scouts were placed along Killarney Road, but no news came. The jury was sworn, and the Solicitor General had begun to address the jury when a loud, increasing volume of cheers arose and swept towards the court house. It was not possible to hear anything but the shouts of the people. *"The counselor is coming!"*

How he took his seat at the bar in his traveling robes; how he munched sandwiches and supped a bowl of milk whilst he corrected the Solicitor General's law between each mouthful; how he bantered and bullied the crown witnesses; and how Nowlan, the most infamous of them, broke down in his lies and howled in his agony: "Wisha the God knows, 'tis little I thought I would meet you here to-day, Counselor O'Connell. May the Lord save me from you!"—these things are all faithfully recorded in the chronicles of the trial.

The jury, though kept without food for a day and a half, disagreed, and a further batch of prisoners was acquitted, and then the Crown abandoned the prosecution and reprieved those already convicted. Small wonder the counselor was loved throughout the land.[1]

---

[1] "What the Judge Thought," E. A. Parry.

Rufus Choate said of Daniel Webster that he considered him the grandest lawyer in the world. And on his death-bed Webster called Choate the most brilliant man in America. Parker relates an episode characteristic of the clashing of swords between these two idols of the American Bar. "We heard Webster once, in a sentence and a look, crush an hour's argument of Choate's curious workmanship; it was most intellectually wire-drawn and hair-splitting, with Grecian sophistry, and a subtlety the Leontine Gorgias might have envied. It was about two car-wheels, which to common eyes looked as like as two eggs; but Mr. Choate, by a fine line of argument between tweedle-dum and tweedle-dee, and a discourse on 'the fixation of points' so deep and fine as to lose itself in obscurity, showed the jury there was a heaven-wide difference between them. 'But,' said Mr. Webster, and his great eyes opened wide and black, as he stared at the big twin wheels before him, 'gentlemen of the jury, there they are—look at 'em'; and as he pronounced this answer, in tones of vast volume, the distorted wheels seemed to shrink back again into their original similarity, and the long argument on the 'fixation of points' died a natural death. It was an example of the ascendency of mere *character* over mere *intellectuality;* but so much greater, nevertheless, the *intellectuality.*" [1]

Jeremiah Mason was quite on a par with either Choate or Webster before a jury. His style was conversational and plain. He was no orator. He would go close up to the jury box, and in the plainest possible logic force conviction upon his hearers. Webster said he "owed his own success to the close attention he was compelled to pay for nine successive years, day by day, to Mason's efforts at the same Bar." As a cross-examiner he had no peer at the New England Bar.

In the history of our own New York Bar there have been, probably, but few equals of Judge William Fullerton as a cross-examiner. He was famous for his calmness and mildness of manner, his rapidly repeated questions, his

[1] "Reminiscences of Rufus Choate," Parker.

sallies of wit interwoven with his questions, and an ingenuity of method quite his own.

Fullerton's cross-examinations in the celebrated Tilton *vs.* Henry Ward Beecher case gave him an international reputation, and were considered the best ever heard in this country. And yet these very examinations, laborious and brilliant, were singularly unproductive of results owing probably to the unusual intelligence and shrewdness of the witnesses themselves. The trial as a whole was by far the most celebrated of its kind the New York courts have ever witnessed. One of the most eminent of Christian preachers was charged with using the persuasive powers of his eloquence, strengthened by his religious influence, to alienate the affections and destroy the probity of a member of his church—a devout and theretofore pure souled woman, the wife of a long loved friend. He was charged with continuing the guilty relation during the period of a year and a half, and of cloaking the offence to his own conscience and to hers under specious words of piety, of invoking first divine blessing on it, and then divine guidance out of it; and finally of adding perjury to seduction in order to escape the consequences. His accusers, moreover, Mr. Tilton and Mr. Moulton, were persons of public reputation and honorable station in life.

The length and complexity of Fullerton's cross-examinations preclude any minute mention of them here. Once when he found fault with Mr. Beecher for not answering his questions more freely and directly, the reply was frankly made, *"I am afraid of you!"*

While cross-examining Beecher about the celebrated "ragged letter," Fullerton asked why he had not made an explanation to the church, if he was innocent. Beecher answered that he was keeping his part of the compact of silence, and added that he did not believe the others were keeping theirs. There was audible laughter throughout the court room at this remark, and Judge Neilson ordered the court officer to remove from the court room any person found offending—"Except the counsel," spoke up Mr. Fullerton. Later the cross-examiner exclaimed impatiently to Mr. Beecher that he was bound to find out all about these things before he got through, to which Beecher retorted, "I don't think you are succeeding very well."

Mr. Fullerton (in a voice like thunder). "Why did you not rise up and deny the charge?"

Mr. Beecher (putting into his voice all that marvellous magnetic force, which so distinguished him from other men of his time). "Mr. Fullerton, that is not my habit of mind, nor my manner of dealing with men and things."

Mr. Fullerton. "So I observe. You say that Theodore Tilton's charge of intimacy with his wife, and the charges made by your church and by the committee of your church, made no impression on you?"

Mr. Beecher (shortly). "Not the slightest."

At this juncture Mr. Thomas G. Sherman, Beecher's personal counsel, jumped to his client's aid, and remarked that it was a singular coincidence that when counsel had not the record before him, he never quoted correctly.

Mr. Fullerton (addressing the court impressively). "When Mr. Sherman is not impertinent, he is nothing in this case."

Judge Neilson (to the rescue). "Probably counsel thought—"

Mr. Fullerton (interrupting). "What Mr. Sherman *thinks,* your Honor, cannot possibly be of sufficient importance to take up the time either of the court or opposing counsel."

"Are you in the habit of having your sermons published?" continued Mr. Fullerton. Mr. Beecher acknowledged that he was, and also that he had preached a sermon on "The Nobility of Confession."

Mr. Sherman (sarcastically). "I hope Mr. Fullerton is not going to preach *us* a sermon."

Mr. Fullerton. "I would do so if I thought I could convert brother Sherman."

Mr. Beecher (quietly). "I will be happy to give you the use of my pulpit."

Mr. Fullerton (laughing). "Brother Sherman is the only audience I shall want."

Mr. Beecher (sarcastically). "Perhaps he is the only audience you can get."

Mr. Fullerton. "If I succeed in converting brother Sherman, I will consider my work as a Christian minister complete."

Mr. Fullerton then read a passage from the sermon, the effect of which was that if a person commits a great sin, and the exposure of it would cause misery, such a person would not be justified in confessing it, merely to relieve his own conscience. Mr. Beecher admitted that he still considered that "sound doctrine."

At this point Mr. Fullerton turned to the court, and pointing to the clock, said, "Nothing comes after the sermon, I believe, but the benediction." His Honor took the hint, and the proceedings adjourned.[1]

In this same trial Hon. William M. Evarts, as leading counsel for Mr. Beecher, heightened his already international reputation as an advocate. It was Mr. Evarts's versatility in the Beecher case that occasioned so much comment. Whether he was examining in chief or on cross, in the discussion of points of evidence, or in the summing up, he displayed equally his masterly talents. His cross-examination of Theodore Tilton was a masterpiece. His speeches in court were clear, calm, and logical. Mr. Evarts was not only a great lawyer, but an orator and statesman of the highest distinction. He has been called "the Prince of the American Bar." He was a gentleman of high scholarship and fine literary tastes. His manner in the trial of a case has been described by some one as "all head, nose, voice, and forefinger." He was five feet seven inches tall, thin and slender, "with a face like parchment."

Mr. Joseph H. Choate once told me he considered that he owed his own success in court to the nine years during which he acted as Mr. Evarts's junior in the trial of cases. No one but Mr. Choate himself would have said this. His

[1] Extracts from the daily press accounts of the proceedings of one of the thirty days of the trial, as reported in "Modern Jury Trials," Donovan.

transcendent genius as an advocate could not have been acquired from any tutelage under Mr. Evarts. He was not only easily the leading trial lawyer of the New York Bar, but was by many thought to be the representative lawyer of the American Bar. Surely no man of his time was more successful in winning juries. His career was one uninterrupted success. Not that he shone especially in any particular one of the duties of the trial lawyer, but he was preëminent in the quality of his humor and the keenness of his satire. His whole conduct of a case, his treatment of witnesses, of the court, of opposing counsel, and especially of the jury, were so irresistibly fascinating and winning that he carried everything before him. One would emerge from a three weeks' contest with Choate in a state almost of mental exhilaration, despite the jury's verdict.

It was not so with the late Edward C. James; a contest with him meant great mental and physical fatigue for his opponent. James was ponderous and indefatigable. His cross-examinations were labored in the extreme. His manner as an examiner was dignified and forceful, his mind always alert and centered on the subject before him; but he had none of Mr. Choate's fascination or brilliancy. He was dogged, determined, heavy. He would pound at you incessantly, but seldom reached the mark. He literally wore out his opponent, and could never realize that he was on the wrong side of a case until the foreman of the jury told him so. Even then he would want the jury polled to see if there was not some mistake. James never smiled except in triumph and when his opponent frowned. When Mr. Choate smiled, you could not help smiling with him. During the last ten years of his life James was found on one side or the other of most of the important cases that were tried. He owed his success to his industrious and indefatigable qualities as a fighter; not, I think, to his art.

James T. Brady was called "the Curran of the New York Bar." His success was almost entirely due to his courtesy and the unusual skill of his cross-examinations. He had a serene, captivating manner in court, and was one of the foremost orators of his time. He had the proud record of having defended fifty men on trial for their lives, and of saving every one of them from execution.

On the other hand, William A. Beach, "the Hamlet of the American Bar," was a poor cross-examiner. He treated all his witnesses alike. He was methodical, but of a domineering manner. He was slow to attune himself to an unexpected turn in a case he might be conducting. He lost many cases and was not fitted to conduct a desperate one. It was as a court orator that he was preëminent. His speech in the Beecher case alone would have made him a reputation as a consummate orator. His vocabulary was surprisingly rich and his voice wonderfully winning.

It is said of James W. Gerard, the elder, that "he obtained the greatest number of verdicts against evidence of any one who ever practised at the New York Bar. He was full of expedients and possessed extraordinary tact. In his profound knowledge of human nature and his ready adaptation, in the conduct of trials, to the peculiarities, caprices, and whims of the different juries before whom he appeared he was almost without a rival. . . . Any one who witnessed the telling hits made by Mr. Gerard on cross-examination, and the sensational incidents sprung by him upon his opponents, the court, and the jury, would have thought that he acted upon the inspiration of the moment—that all he did and all he said was *impromptu*. In fact, Mr. Gerard made thorough preparation for trial. Generally his hits in cross-examination were the result of previous preparation. He made briefs for cross-examination. To a large extent his flashes of wit and his extraordinary and grotesque humor were well pondered over and studied up beforehand." [1]

Justice Miller said of Roscoe Conkling that "he was one of the greatest men intellectually of his time." He was more than fifty years of age when he abandoned his arduous public service at Washington, and opened an office in New York City. During his six years at the New York Bar, such was his success, that he is reputed to have

[1] "Extraordinary Cases," Henry Lauran Clinton.

accumulated, for a lawyer, a very large fortune. He constituted himself a barrister and adopted the plan of acting only as counsel. He was fluent and eloquent of speech, most thorough in the preparation of his cases, and an accomplished cross-examiner. Despite his public career, he said of himself, "My proper place is to be before twelve men in the box." Conkling used to study for his cross-examinations, in important cases, with the most painstaking minuteness. In the trial of the Rev. Henry Burge for murder, Conkling saw that the case was likely to turn upon the cross-examination of Dr. Swinburne, who had performed the autopsy. The charge of the prosecution was that Mrs. Burge had been strangled by her husband, who had then cut her throat. In order to disprove this on cross-examination, Mr. Conkling procured a body for dissection and had dissected, in his presence, the parts of the body that he wished to study. As the result of Dr. Swinburne's cross-examination at the trial, the presiding judge felt compelled to declare the evidence so entirely untrustworthy that he would decline to submit it to the jury and directed that the prisoner be set at liberty.

This studious preparation for cross-examination was one of the secrets of the success of Benjamin F. Butler. He was once known to have spent days in examining all parts of a steam engine, and even learning to drive one himself, in order to cross-examine some witnesses in an important case in which he had been retained. At another time Butler spent a week in the repair shop of a railroad, part of the time with coat off and hammer in hand, ascertaining the capabilities of iron to resist pressure—a point on which his case turned. To use his own language: "A lawyer who sits in his office and prepares his cases only by the statements of those who are brought to him, will be very likely to be beaten. A lawyer in full practice, who carefully prepares his cases, must study almost every variety of business and many of the sciences." A pleasant humor and a lively wit, coupled with wonderful thoroughness and acuteness, were Butler's leading characteristics. He was not a great lawyer, nor even a great advocate like Rufus Choate, and yet he would frequently defeat Choate. His cross-examination was his chief weapon. Here he was fertile in resource and stratagem to a degree attained by few others. Choate had mastered all the little tricks of the trial lawyer, but he attained also to the grander conceptions and the forensic powers of the really great advocate. Butler's success depended upon zeal, combined with shrewdness and not overconscientious trickery.

In his autobiography, Butler gives several examples of what he was pleased to call his legerdemain, and to believe were illustrations of his skill as a cross-examiner. They are quoted from "Butler's Book," but are not cited as illustrations of the subtler forms of cross-examination, but rather as indicative of the tricks to which Butler owed much of his success before country juries.

"When I was quite a young man I was called upon to defend a man for homicide. He and his associate had been engaged in a quarrel which proceeded to blows and at last to stones. My client, with a sharp stone, struck the deceased in the head on that part usually called the temple. The man went and sat down on the curbstone, the blood streaming from his face, and shortly afterward fell over dead.

"The theory of the government was that he died from the wound in the temporal artery. My theory was that the man died of apoplexy, and that if he had bled more from the temporal artery, he might have been saved—a wide enough difference in the theories of the cause of death.

"Of course, to be enabled to carry out my proposition I must know all about the temporal artery,—its location, its functions, its capabilities to allow the blood to pass through it, and in how short a time a man could bleed to death through the temporal artery; also, how far excitement in a body stirred almost to frenzy in an embittered conflict, and largely under the influence of liquor on a hot day, would tend to produce apoplexy. I was relieved on these two points in my subject, but relied wholly upon the testimony of a surgeon that the man bled to death from the cut on the temporal artery from a stone in the hand of

my client. That surgeon was one of those whom we sometimes see on the stand, who think that what they don't
know on the subject of their profession is not worth knowing. He testified positively and distinctly that there was
and could be no other cause for death except the bleeding
from the temporal artery, and he described the action of
the bleeding and the amount of blood discharged.

"Upon all these questions I had thoroughly prepared
myself.

"*Mr. Butler.* 'Doctor, you have talked a great deal about
the temporal artery; now will you please describe it and
its functions? I suppose the temporal artery is so called
because it supplies the flesh on the outside of the skull,
especially that part we call the temples, with blood.'

"*Witness.* 'Yes; that is so.'

"*Mr. Butler.* 'Very well. Where does the temporal artery
takes its rise in the system? Is it at the heart?'

"*Witness.* 'No, the aorta is the only artery leaving the
heart which carries blood toward the head. Branches from
it carry the blood up through the opening into the skull at
the neck, and the temporal artery branches from one of
these.'

"*Mr. Butler.* 'Doctor, where does it branch off from it?
on the inside or the outside of the skull?'

"*Witness.* 'On the inside.'

"*Mr. Butler.* 'Does it have anything to do inside with
supplying the brain?'

"*Witness.* 'No.'

"*Mr. Butler.* 'Well, doctor, how does it get outside to
supply the head and temples?'

"*Witness.* 'Oh, it passes out through its appropriate
opening in the skull.'

"*Mr. Butler.* 'Is that through the eyes?'

"*Witness.* 'No.'

"*Mr. Butler.* 'The ears?'"

"*Witness.* 'No.'

"*Mr. Butler.* 'It would be inconvenient to go through
the mouth, would it not, doctor?'

"Here I produced from my green bag a skull. 'I cannot

find any opening on this skull which I think is appropriate to the temporal artery. Will you please point out the appropriate opening through which the temporal artery passes from the inside to the outside of the skull?'

"He was utterly unable so to do.

"Mr. Butler. 'Doctor, I don't think I will trouble you any further; you can step down.' He did so, and my client's life was saved on that point.

"The temporal artery doesn't go inside the skull at all.

"I had a young client who was on a railroad car when it was derailed by a broken switch. The car ran at considerable speed over the cross-ties for some distance, and my client was thrown up and down with great violence on his seat. After the accident, when he recovered from the bruising, it was found that his nervous system had been wholly shattered, and that he could not control his nerves in the slightest degree by any act of his will. When the case came to trial, the production of the pin by which the position of the switch was controlled, two-thirds worn away and broken off, settled the liability of the road for any damages that occurred from that cause, and the case resolved itself into a question of the amount of damages only. My claim was that my client's condition was an incurable one, arising from the injury to the spinal cord. The claim put forward on behalf of the railroad was that it was simply nervousness, which probably would disappear in a short time. The surgeon who appeared for the road claimed the privilege of examining my client personally before he should testify. I did not care to object to that, and the doctor who was my witness and the railroad surgeon went into the consultation room together and had a full examination in which I took no part, having looked into that matter before.

"After some substantially immaterial matters on the part of the defence, the surgeon was called and was qualified as a witness. He testified that he was a man of great position in his profession. Of course in that I was not interested, for I knew he could qualify himself as an expert. In his direct examination he spent a good deal of the time in giving a very learned and somewhat technical description of the condition of my client. He admitted that my client's nervous system was very much shattered, but he also stated that it would probably be only temporary. Of all this I took little notice; for, to tell the truth, I had been up quite late the night before and in the warm court room felt a little sleepy. But the counsel for the road put this question to him:—

" 'Doctor, to what do you attribute this condition of the plaintiff which you describe?'

" 'Hysteria, sir; he is hysterical.'

"That waked me up. I said, 'Doctor, did I understand—I was not paying proper attention—to what did you attribute this nervous condition of my client?'

" 'Hysteria, sir.'

"I subsided, and the examination went on until it came my turn to cross-examine.

"Mr. Butler. 'Do I understand that you think this condition of my client wholly hysterical?'

"Witness. 'Yes, sir; undoubtedly.'

"Mr. Butler. 'And therefore won't last long?'

"Witness. 'No, sir; not likely to.'

"Mr. Butler. 'Well, doctor, let us see; is not the disease called hysteria and its effects hysterics; and isn't it true that hysteria, hysterics, hysterical, all come from the Greek word νστερα?'

"Witness. 'It may be.'

"Mr. Butler. 'Don't say it may, doctor; isn't it? Isn't an exact translation of the Greek word νστερα the English word "womb"?'

"Witness. 'You are right, sir.'

"Mr. Butler. 'Well, doctor, this morning when you examined this young man here,' pointing to my client, 'did you find that he had a womb? I was not aware of it before, but I will have him examined over again and see if I can find it. That is all, doctor; you may step down.' "

John R. Fellows, for many years District Attorney in this county, was in many respects one of the most remarkable lawyers of our time. He had that rare gift—a self-recording mind—to a more marked degree than any one I have ever come in contact with in or out of court. He was a *genius* in the strictest sense of the word. A man who read little, and studied less, but who could marshal the facts in a case and present them to a jury with a clearness and eloquence that could be equalled by no man of his time.

I well remember when he and DeLancey Nicoll were together conducting the famous trial of the People *vs.* Jacob Sharp, who was charged with the crime of having bribed the entire Board of Aldermen of the City of New York in order to obtain a franchise on Broadway for his surface railroad. The trial lasted about seven weeks. The labor of examining and cross-examining the witnesses fell to the lot of Mr. Nicoll. Colonel Fellows was to sum up the case to the jury.

During the entire trial he was uniformly late in his attendance at court; upon arrival he would at once call for pen and ink and begin writing notes to his friends, paying, apparently, little if any attention to what was going on in the court room. But, as District Attorney, none of his associates could question his right to present the case to the jury, though all were apprehensive of the result. No one who heard his summing up in that case will ever forget it; not a single important item of evidence had escaped what I have styled his self-recording mind. Of course, Sharp was promptly convicted. That same evening, before the jury had rendered their verdict, I happened to dine with one of Sharp's lawyers, the late Albert B. Stickney, one of the recognized leaders of our Bar. Mr. Stickney, naturally, could talk of nothing but the trial *and* Colonel Fellows. He told me he had always heard of Fellows, though he had never met him or even seen him, and that he had anticipated listening to a great speech; but that he never *dreamed* that there existed any lawyer at the American Bar who was capable of such surpassing flights of oratory.

Almost the next court appearance of Colonel Fellows was in the celebrated prosecution of Sheriff Flack, who was defended by a great array of prominent lawyers who were, however, unfamiliar with the criminal courts and therefore unacquainted with the talents of our District Attorney. Here, again, Colonel Fellows would walk into court, with his high silk hat and tiny bamboo cane, and sit at the counsel table and write letters and occasionally fall asleep. Upon one of these occasions—I was an eyewitness of the occurrence—a most objectionable question was put to a witness. Immediately one of his assistants nudged the Colonel and woke him up, and almost involuntarily he exclaimed, "I object, your honor!" Whereupon one of the prisoner's lawyers smiled at the jury and turning to the District Attorney, exclaimed contemptuously, "What possible ground for objecting can you have, Colonel Fellows? —you were fast asleep." No one who heard it will ever forget the way in which Colonel Fellows arose, with marked deliberation, his diminutive stature of five feet three gradually assuming the dimensions of full seven feet, and in those wonderfully deep, modulated tones of his, said, *"I was not asleep, but if perchance I should slumber, it were well for your client not to awaken me!"* The effect was electrifying. There was complete silence in the court room for fully thirty seconds, and Flack never had a chance with the jury after that.

On account of my intimate knowledge and appreciation of the characteristics and talents of most of the present day advocates, especially in the East, the temptation to contrast their various methods and applaud their successes is almost overwhelming, but, for obvious reasons, I have limited the discussion to those whose labors have ceased. No record of the successful advocates of our time, however, would be complete that did not include my beloved friend John B. Stanchfield—Chesterfield of our Bar. His talents as a trial lawyer are too fresh in the memory of all who knew him to warrant any minute discussion of them. He was thoroughly trained and experienced in all branches of the profession; his learning was not superficial, but profound and comprehensive. He had the advantage which comes from a long acquaintance with corporate and governmental affairs. When his advice was sought in difficult and perplexing situations, he displayed such soundness of judgment that his clients were uniformly inspired with confidence in the outcome. In council he was wise, resourceful and courageous, and he was ready and able to carry out in court the plan and policy of the consultation room.

Mr. Stanchfield combined qualities which make a great advocate. Tall in stature and very erect, with great depth of chest and breadth of shoulder, a large and shapely head and a handsome countenance,—his presence was commanding and impressive. His voice was strong, resonant and magnetic, and his speech evinced an unusual command of pure and simple English, perhaps the result of his fondness for reading the classics. He had the power of clear and concise statement, whether of fact or law, a fine imagination, a keen sense of humor, a master of irony. And when the occasion required he was capable of eloquence of a high order. In the trial of cases he was alert and resourceful and never became disturbed or confused, even when the unexpected suddenly took place. Indeed, his composure under all circumstances and his courage in the most desperate crises were the chief weapons at his command. He was a past master of the art of cross-examination, always respectful to the court, and so fair in presenting his own case and in attacking the case of his opponents that it is not surprising that juries gave him verdicts which a man less gifted and accomplished would have found it impossible to obtain.

His ability, industry, and loyalty to his clients goes without saying and was universally recognized; but the memory of his overwhelming courtesy and politeness to every one he associated with in and out of court—clients, judges, jurors, witnesses, and adversaries as well—will long remain in the minds of every one who knew and loved him. His devotion to his profession was the one absorbing thought of his life. And on his deathbed, when informed of the gravity of his illness, and that he could never with safety practice in the courts again, almost his last words were, "Then let me die."

I know of no better example of Mr. Stanchfield's resourcefulness during the trial of a losing case than his master stroke toward the end of his defense of two officers of the Riggs Bank in Washington which is referred to in some detail at the close of the chapter on "The Manner of Cross-Examination."

When the time came, during the Riggs Bank trial, to introduce character witnesses on behalf of the two young men whose conduct of the affairs of the Riggs Bank was the cause of the indictment, Mr. Stanchfield—who knew Col. Theodore Roosevelt, at that time Vice-President— arranged for breakfast with him and told him that he wanted him as a character witness, incidentally asking him if he happened by any chance to have a deposit in the Riggs Bank.

Later in the day he called Mr. Roosevelt to the witness stand. It was hardly necessary to frame any preliminary questions to introduce Mr. Roosevelt, so he started right in by asking him whether by any chance he was a depositor in the Riggs Bank at the time the indictment was found. This question was immediately objected to, and the Judge peremptorily ruled it out. Mr. Stanchfield was thus forced to fall back upon the simple, narrow questions allowed to be put to character witnesses under the strict rules of evidence.

When he came to the vital question regarding Mr. Roosevelt's opinion of the two defendants, based on their general reputation in the community—to which the answer ordinarily would have been "good" or "excellent"—Mr. Roosevelt sat up straight in his chair and said: "I have known these two young men ever since they were boys, and watched their careers. What I think of them can best be shown by the fact that not only I but all the members of my family have deposited their savings in the Riggs Bank." Then he triumphantly turned to the Judge with one of those tooth-revealing smiles of his—as much as to say, "Wipe that out if you can!"

He immediately jumped up, left the witness stand, shook hands with the Judge and then with each one of the jurors individually, and rushed out of the court room.

This incident probably had more to do with the verdict of acquittal than any other phase of the case.

Robert Ingersoll took part in numerous noted law-suits in all parts of the country. But he was almost helpless in court without a competent junior. He was a born orator if ever there was one. Henry Ward Beecher regarded him as "the most brilliant speaker of the English tongue in any land on the globe." He was not a profound lawyer, however, and hardly the equal of the most mediocre trial lawyer in the examination of witnesses. Of the art of cross-examining witnesses he knew practically nothing. His definition of a lawyer, to use his own words, was "a sort of intellectual strumpet." "My ideal of a great lawyer," he once wrote, "is that great English attorney who accumulated a fortune of a million pounds, and left it all in his will to make a home for idiots, declaring that he wanted to give it back to the people from whom he took it."

Judge Walter H. Sanborn relates a conversation he had with Judge Miller of the United States Court about Ingersoll. "Just after Colonel Ingersoll had concluded an argument before Mr. Justice Miller, while on Circuit, I came into the court and remarked to Judge Miller that I wished I had got there a little sooner, as I had never heard Colonel Ingersoll make a legal argument.—'Well,' said Judge Miller, 'you never will.' " [1]

Ingersoll's genius lay in other directions. Who but Ingersoll could have written the following?

"A little while ago I stood by the grave of the old Napoleon—a magnificent tomb of gilt and gold, fit almost for a dead deity, and gazed upon the sarcophagus of black marble, where rest at last the ashes of that restless man. I leaned over the balustrade, and thought about the career of the greatest soldier of the modern world. I saw him walking upon the banks of the Seine, contemplating suicide; I saw him at Toulon; I saw him putting down the mob in the streets of Paris; I saw him at the head of the army in Italy; I saw him crossing the bridge of Lodi, with the tricolor in his hand; I saw him in Egypt, in the shadows

[1] "Life Sketches of Eminent Lawyers," Gilbert J. Clark.

of the Pyramids; I saw him conquer the Alps, and mingle the eagles of France with the eagles of the crags; I saw him at Marengo, at Ulm, and at Austerlitz; I saw him in Russia, where the infantry of the snow and the cavalry of the wild blast scattered his legion like winter's withered leaves. I saw him at Leipsic, in defeat and disaster; driven by a million bayonets back upon Paris; clutched like a wild beast; banished to Elba. I saw him escape and retake an empire by the force of his genius. I saw him upon the frightful field of Waterloo, where chance and fate combined to wreck the fortunes of their former king. And I saw him at St. Helena, with his hands crossed behind him, gazing out upon the sad and solemn sea. I thought of the orphans and widows he had made, of the tears that had been shed for his glory, and of the only woman who had ever loved him, pushed from his heart by the cold hand of ambition. And I said I would rather have been a French peasant, and worn wooden shoes; I would rather have lived in a hut, with a vine growing over the door, and the grapes growing purple in the kisses of the autumn sun. I would rather have been that poor peasant, with my loving wife by my side, knitting as the day died out of the sky, with my children upon my knees, and their arms about me. I would rather have been that man, and gone down to the tongueless silence of the dreamless dust, than to have been that imperial impersonation of force and murder, known as Napoleon the Great."

PART TWO

SOME FAMOUS EXAMPLES
OF CROSS-EXAMINATION

Chapter 14

The Cross-Examination of Mrs. Reginald Vanderbilt

by Herbert C. Smyth, in the celebrated Habeas Corpus Proceeding brought by Mrs. Vanderbilt against Mrs. Harry Payne Whitney, to recover the custody of her child.

SELDOM in recent years has any case been tried in the civil branch of our local courts that occasioned so much publicity, discussion, criticism and even notoriety as the suit brought by Mrs. Gloria Vanderbilt, through *habeas corpus* proceedings, to recover the possession of her eleven-year-old daughter who she claimed had been technically kidnaped by her paternal aunt, Mrs. Harry Payne Whitney, with whom the child had been living at her Long Island country estate for about two years before the inception of this suit.

During the first few days of the trial the court room was packed to the doors, and hundreds of a sensation-loving public were daily refused admission. Then out of a clear sky an ill-advised question put to one of the servant witnesses in cross-examination by Mrs. Vanderbilt's counsel—apparently forgetful of the precept about "where angels fear to tread"—provoked such a scandalous answer that the presiding justice thereafter peremptorily excluded every one from the court room excepting counsel and interested parties and their witnesses and proceeded to conduct the subsequent four weeks of the trial, as it were, *in camera*. Not even the newspaper reporters were allowed to be present, and the parties to this litigation, as well as their attorneys and such witnesses as were present from time to time, were not only put on their honor not to disclose anything that transpired in the court room, but were threatened with contempt proceedings in case the court order was not strictly obeyed.

Mr. Nathan Burkan brought the proceeding on behalf of Mrs. Vanderbilt, and Mr. Herbert C. Smyth acted as trial counsel for Mrs. Whitney and personally conducted the proceedings throughout the litigation.

The presumption in favor of a mother's right to the possession and custody of her own daughter is so powerful that, in order to succeed, it was incumbent upon Mrs. Whitney and her lawyer to produce indisputable evidence of the mother's inexcusable neglect of her child during the nine years which followed the death of the father, Mr. Reginald Vanderbilt.

Many witnesses were called *pro* and *con,* but the task of convincing the Court, out of the mouth of the mother herself, that Mrs. Vanderbilt had forfeited the right to the custody of her child, rested on the shoulders of Mr. Smyth, fortified as he was with the all-powerful weapon of cross-examination.

It had been testified by witnesses that the mother, a young and beautiful woman, had paid scant attention to her child's welfare for many years preceding the trial. She had herself traveled most of the time, sometimes taking her young daughter along with her, from New York to London —Paris—Biarritz—Cannes—as suited her fancy, so that the child was never allowed to remain in any one place long enough to form the friendship or enjoy the companionship of other children. It had also been claimed she had neglected the child to such a degree that she had lost her daughter's affection; so much so that the daughter had threatened that if she were compelled to go back to her mother now that she was in Mrs. Whitney's care, she would throw herself out of the window. The child was submitted to a long examination by the Judge himself in his private chambers, but nothing could shake her in this dread of her mother and determination to end her own life if she had to resume her experiences of the past.

At this stage the trial had literally become the talk of the town. It was the prevailing topic of discussion at nearly every social gathering—dinner parties, clubs and, it may almost be said, in every household, even the humblest. Prince Hohenlohe, Lady Furness, Mrs. Vanderbilt's twin sister, and her brother had all hastily taken passage from abroad to be present at the trial and to testify in Mrs. Vanderbilt's behalf. Other names of people prominent in London society had been brought into the testimony, Mrs. Vanderbilt herself being widely known socially throughout the principal cities of Europe, so that the trial had come to assume an international aspect.

The popular sympathy was naturally all in favor of the mother who was trying to regain possession of her child, but the more conservative judgment waited to hear what the mother had to say in her own behalf.

When Mrs. Vanderbilt took the stand as her own last witness, she assumed the attitude of an hysterical, much abused young mother. She was frequently unable to continue her story coherently, to a degree that prompted the court to order a succession of short recesses so that the witness might regain her self-possession, and the court attendants were called upon to administer to her wants on frequent occasions. I am told that at the end of Mrs. Vanderbilt's direct examination everybody in the court room, perhaps with the exception of the opposing lawyers, felt that the lady had been inexcusably abused.

Possibly once in the career of every prominent attorney who has lived his life, so to speak, in a court room, there arises a situation such as confronted Mr. Smyth at this stage of the litigation. There was no jury, no audience, no public, no daily newspapers to win over to his side. His one task was to unmask the witness's habits of life, during her widowhood, and to exhibit her to the presiding Judge as a young, pleasure-loving woman,—a mother who always made her undoubted affection for her offspring subservient to her own enjoyment of her youth, freedom to travel and opportunity to enjoy the attentions and allurements that foreigners are wont to shower upon any beautiful American woman who will entertain them at her sumptuous apartments in Paris and elsewhere, attended as she was by a retinue of servants and all the luxuries that go with such surroundings.

This could only be done by a patient, lengthy, painstaking, persistent cross-examination, and few know how to conduct that kind of examination better than does Mr. Smyth.

At this stage of the case the odds were undoubtedly in favor of the mother. True, her maid and her child's governess had given very damaging testimony against her; and even her own mother had corroborated much of their evidence. But the statements of discharged domestic servants are never regarded as very convincing evidence, while the surprising conduct of Mrs. Vanderbilt's mother in voluntarily testifying against her—however estimable a woman Mrs. Morgan might be—was bound to detract from the weight given to whatever she might say.

Altogether, the success or failure of this cross-examination might very well prove to be the turning point in the case. Mr. Smyth knew he had some valuable material with which to confront the witness, but could it be used with sufficient telling effect to counteract the favorable impression she had made during her direct testimony?

The cross-examination occupied three days, so that it would be impossible to include here more than a few excerpts from it. In any event the measure of Mr. Smyth's success is best evidenced by the court decision overwhelmingly in his client's favor.

His first unusual move was to take a position at such a point in the court room that the witness would be obliged to look at him across the bench, thereby allowing the Judge to observe every expression of her face which accompanied her spoken words. Few lawyers would have thought to avail themselves of this advantage.

Throughout his examination Mr. Smyth treated the witness with the utmost courtesy, even deference at times, and never confronted her with her obvious contradictions, as would have been done were there a jury present. Instead, he left it to the sagacity of the ever alert, attentive Judge to form his own opinion whether the witness was frank and willing to tell the whole story, or prone to suppress or distort important portions of it.

The cross-examination had proceeded only a few minutes before the weeping mother began to exhibit a fighting mood. Her tears promptly disappeared, and she was ever on the alert, many times with caustic comments and replies which proved, at least to Mr. Smyth, that it was obviously stage play which she had indulged in during her direct examination and had now suddenly forgotten.

The object of the cross-examination, as has already been said, was to lead the witness throughout the history of her life during the preceding nine years, and thereby to demonstrate by his questions and her answers how little attention she had paid to her daughter while she was consorting with people who could have no sympathy with the child's welfare, and further to demonstrate, if he could, the thoughtless if not flagrant neglect of the mother, right up to the time when she was suddenly faced with the horrible possibility of losing all claim to the custody of her only child—and incidentally, the allowance of $4,000 a month paid out of the child's property.

There had been much evidence previously sworn to regarding the intimate relations existing between Mrs. Vanderbilt and Prince Hohenlohe. But any adverse effect of this testimony was largely mitigated by the undisputed fact that the couple were for two years engaged to be married. The marriage had been abandoned because, as the mother said, she wished to have her child brought up in America rather than abroad, and also for the reason that neither of them had sufficient means of their own outside of the allowance for the support of the daughter. And that allowance might possibly be revoked or much reduced if the daughter took up her permanent residence outside of the United States.

However, there was still another suggestion of impropriety introduced by Mrs. Whitney's witnesses in relation to an intimacy between Mrs. Vanderbilt and a married man named Blumenthal, who enjoyed the nickname of "Blumie." Mrs. Vanderbilt had insisted that her acquaintance with Mr. Blumenthal was purely casual and, in this one connection, Mr. Smyth apparently could not resist the temptation to lead his witness into a trap, in order to demonstrate her lack of sincerity as a witness. This maneuver, judging from the wording of his opinion, evidently made a profound impression on the Court. Mr. Smyth had in his possession what he considered an important telegram which he had succeeded in quietly marking for identification during Mrs. Vanderbilt's direct examination, reserving the right to disclose its contents and to use it at the psychological moment.

It appeared that shortly before one of the mother's numerous trips to Europe, Mrs. Whitney had sent her a telegram suggesting that they meet on a certain day for luncheon at Mrs. Whitney's home, when they could discuss the welfare of the child for the coming winter. It was the reply, signed "Blumie," that Mr. Smyth used with an effect that only a dyed-in-the-wool cross-examiner knows how to achieve. He first casually asked Mrs. Vanderbilt if she had any acquaintance by the name of "Blumie," to which she replied with an emphatic *"no."* She was asked about the invitation to lunch with Mrs. Whitney, which she remembered but could not recall whether she had telephoned or telegraphed her acquiescence. Here was the opportunity Mr. Smyth had been waiting for. He very quietly confronted her with the telltale telegram which he proceeded to read aloud: *"We are very happy to see you Thursday noon, love—Blumie."*

This message produced a stunning effect upon her and she began to flounder about in an effort to find any plausible explanation. First she rather helplessly insisted it must have been a mistake of some kind, but when pressed further she had to admit that the telegram bearing the initials "A. H."—those of the Ambassador Hotel— must have come from that hotel, where Mr. Blumenthal lived and also had an office. She still insisted, however, that it must have been sent by mistake as she could not imagine how "love—Blumie" could have been signed to a telegram sent by her. She tried to argue that the mistake must have been made by Mr. Blumenthal's secretary, but as the telegram showed that it had been sent after secretarial hours, the most natural inference that could be drawn from the occurrence was that she was at least on that occasion definitely in Mr. Blumenthal's apartment and under circumstances which, for whatever reason, precluded both of them from realizing their embarrassing error.

Mr. Smyth backed up this incident by drawing Mrs. Vanderbilt's attention to the fact that she had sailed without her child on the *Europa,* but in company with this same Mr. Blumenthal. She first expressed doubt that he was on board but thought "possibly he was." She was then shown the printed passenger list which did not disclose either his or her name—a fact that elicited a triumphant smile from her. But later, when confronted with photographs that were taken of her and Mr. Blumenthal just before the sailing of the ship and were published in the New York newspapers the following day, the smile suddenly vanished.

Mr. Smyth. "I now show you the list headed 'No Publicity' and ask if you find your name as well as Mr. Blumenthal's on *that* list."

A. "I do, and I also find Mr. Rockefeller's."

Q. "He had nothing to do with you, had he?"

A. "Neither had Mr. Blumenthal."

Q. "Are you sure about that?"

A. "I am quite sure about it."

Q. "You have never seen Mr. Rockefeller, have you?"

A. "I don't know him."

Q. "So there is no reason you can think of to put him in the same category with yourself, excepting as one other passenger who might wish to conceal his sailing date?"

(No answer.)

Q. "Let us see. You notice there are only five names under the heading of 'No Publicity'?"

A. "I suppose all these gentlemen sailed with me."

Q. "No indeed. It appears here that the only single man is Mr. Blumenthal. Look at it. He was not even single, but he was there without his wife."

A. "I am sure I don't know what that means."

Q. "How far away from his stateroom was yours?"

A. "I can't remember that. It must have been—I don't know whether it was on the same side, or not."

Q. "You see that your number is 94?"

A. "I can't remember the number. You must show me a plan of the boat."

Q. "I have got it here for you (handing to witness); you were both on the same deck, were you not?"

A. "Yes, I believe we were."

Q. "You believe you were?"

A. "Yes."

Q. "Didn't you have cocktails in your room when Mr. Blumenthal came in there?"

A. "No. I didn't have a suite and Mr. Blumenthal was not in my stateroom."

Q. "You are sure about that?"

A. "I am quite sure of it."

Q. "What deck were you on?"

A. "I do not remember."

Q. "It is marked here somewhere. You know ship plans pretty well, do you not?"

A. "Yes."

Q. "You know that those that are colored blue mean the very good ones and the large rooms?"

A. "Suites."

Q. "Now, you were in 94?"

A. "Show me the plan, please."

Q. "I will show it to you. I want to find it so that you will not have to look at too much. This is on Deck A. Those are the quarters which you had (indicating)."

A. "Yes, the white. It is not a suite."

Q. "True enough. Now, look at Mr. Blumenthal's."

A. "I suppose it is the marked one."

Q. "138. You see that?"

A. "138, yes."

Q. "You see this little stateroom that is right back of Mr. Blumenthal's (indicating)?"

A. "Yes."

Q. "That was your maid's room, was it not?"

A. "It was."

Q. "How did it happen that your maid had a stateroom right adjoining and connecting with Mr. Blumenthal's."

A. "That is purely an accident, Mr. Smyth."

Q. "I see."

A. "You don't think for one single moment—I know the insinuation you are trying to make—considering my friendship with Mr. Blumenthal that I would park my maid in the cabin next door so that she could listen to everything that went on?"

Q. "No, but it did give access to Mr. Blumenthal's room?"

A. "You mean to insinuate that I went through my maid's room into Mr. Blumenthal's room. Really you are Machiavellian in thinking things up."

Q. "Mr. Blumenthal had 138. That was a suite?"

A. "Yes, it was."

Q. "And part of the suite was your maid's room?"

A. "My maid had a room. I don't know whose suite it was. I understood it was next to Mr. Blumenthal's drawing room."

Q. "Were you ever in Mr. Blumenthal's drawing room?"

A. "I was."

After some other questions which showed the witness that the cross-examiner knew more of the facts than she originally had thought, she admitted that she and Mr. Blumenthal with some other passengers dined together every night the vessel was at sea. Although she had tried to say that Mr. Blumenthal's being on the vessel was quite a coincidence, she admitted the authenticity of the photographs, and finally in relation to purchasing her transportation the following was brought out:

Q. "When you got the transportation on the *Europa,* from what agent did you get it?"

A. "Well, that is a long story."

Q. "I can shorten it for you. It was Mr. Benjamin, was it not?"

A. "Yes, it was Mr. Benjamin."

Q. "Mr. Benjamin is the agent from whom Mr. Blumenthal got his transportation?"

A. "Yes, I introduced him."

The trial justice showed plainly the impression this Blumenthal episode was making upon him, and in his written opinion he criticized Mrs. Vanderbilt for subjecting herself to the notoriety that must necessarily follow the disclosure of her friendship with a married man, especially one so well known to New York's "night life."

The trial was unique in many other respects, not the least of which was that Mrs. Vanderbilt's mother had steeled herself to take the witness stand against her, in spite of the fact that she had for years been living on her daughter's bounty. Mrs. Morgan even produced many letters which she had received from her grandchild expressing distrust and fear of her mother.

Mrs. Vanderbilt's father had died a year or so before this trial, but during her cross-examination she was obliged to admit that she had received a letter from him enclosing a petition which he intended to use in the Surrogate's Court in this city, severely criticizing his daughter's conduct and her extravagant mode of living in her luxurious Paris apartment.

Mr. Smyth's sole effort was to create a situation which would entirely justify his client, Mrs. Whitney, in her claim that the child's best welfare depended upon her being allowed to remain in Mrs. Whitney's custody and to live a healthful, outdoor, childish existence at her country estate on Long Island, where she could also have proper medical care and schooling. To this end he pressed Mrs. Vanderbilt to give him some motive for her mother and father taking the attitude that they did against her, other than a conviction that it was for the best interests of the child. And he especially demanded some explanation as to what had caused her father to assume the position he had taken in his attempt to lay the whole matter before the New York Surrogate who had awarded the $48,000 yearly allowance to Mrs. Vanderbilt as custodian of her child. Mrs. Vanderbilt's only explanation was that her mother was motivated by money and hinted that Mrs. Whitney was probably back of the whole thing.

Mr. Smyth. "Let me read you a paragraph from this document which you say your father sent you with the information that he was proposing to use it in the Surrogate's Court. Please try to concentrate your attention on this:

(Reading) "That in the City of Paris the said Gloria M. Vanderbilt has maintained a large apartment consisting of fifteen to sixteen rooms, has had from twelve to fifteen servants and has been living in the most extravagant and most luxurious manner and has been entertaining her friends, many of bad reputation, and improperly and irregularly spending almost all the moneys which had been dispensed and directed by this Court to be used for the maintenance, education and support of the above-named infant." [1]

Q. "Of course, you don't agree with that, do you?"

A. "Well, as the infant was living with me in all this luxury that my father writes about in that document, I really cannot see how she did not benefit by it. You say fifteen servants for fifteen rooms—one servant for every room—lavish entertainment and so on, I should say my child would benefit by that." (It is the French custom to have most of a large staff of servants live at their own homes.)

Q. "How did your child benefit by this lavish entertainment?"

---

[1] This paper was not admitted in evidence as proof of the truth of its statements—the father not being a witness—but the Court allowed it to be used as contradicting Mrs. Vanderbilt's assertion in her direct testimony that her father was fully aware of and approved the life she lived abroad and her care of her daughter.

A. "She may have entertained herself and her friends."

Q. "At four years of age?"

A. "She had little friends come in. You know Mrs. Whitney has children."

Q. "The remark you made a moment ago was that your child benefited by this lavish entertainment, was that right?"

A. "No, I said by that whole paragraph that you read just now."

Q. "How could the child possibly benefit?"

A. "She might have given parties. No, I might have given them for her."

Q. "You didn't keep her up late at night, did you?"

A. "I didn't say at night."

Q. "Your entertainments were usually at night?"

A. "Were they? Luncheon, is that an entertainment at night? Tea, is that at night?"

Q. "Didn't you have dinner parties?"

A. "I had dinner parties."

Q. "Was the child there?"

A. "No."

Q. "Well, did the child benefit by that?"

A. "She might have from the friends I made for her."

Q. "This four-year-old child?"

A. "Yes."

Q. "Are you sincere about that?"

A. "Yes."

Q. "Were you then creating friendships for the benefit of your child which she could benefit by when she grew up?"

A. "When she went to Paris, yes."

Q. "Were any of them titled people in Europe?"

A. "Some were people living in Paris, there were French, there were some English, there were some Scotch, some German, some Swiss. Maybe Italians. I don't know."

Q. "Did you expect that that was going to be for the benefit of your child later on in life?"

A. "Why certainly, why not?"

Q. "How much of your allowance did you spend in entertaining Prince Hohenlohe?"

A. "That is an insulting question. I did not entertain Prince Hohenlohe. I gave dinner parties, but it was not for the Prince especially, although he may have been there with others."

Mr. Smyth. "I read further from the document which you admit your father sent to you:

(Reading) "That during the time that the aforesaid infant was living in Biarritz in a château or villa at that place her mother indulged in the same extravagance and consorted with and brought to said infant's home persons of evil repute and bad moral character and both in Paris and Biarritz failed to extend the care, kindness and solicitude to the above named infant which motherly instincts and duty should prompt."

Q. "Now you read that, didn't you?"

A. "Yes, I did, but my father later retracted it."

Q. "I thought you said a little while ago that your father fully approved of the way you brought up your child and your mode of living in Paris."

A. "Well, I can only repeat that my father retracted, in my presence and in my sister's presence, the statements made in that document and, in any event, I am sure it was done upon the instigation of my mother, and I will add that Mrs. Whitney knew all about this document because I told her about it and I told her that my mother, Mrs. Morgan, was trying to take my child away from me. I told her that in July, 1934. Yes, I told Mrs. Whitney that and I can look her straight in the face when I say it now. One of the last words my father said was that his only regret in life was this document, and my sister was present at the time."

Q. "What was the occasion for your having this conversation with Mrs. Whitney?"

A. "Well, I just thought I could speak to her. I trusted Mrs. Whitney, but I misplaced my trust and that is all I can say. I told Mrs. Whitney that my father, through the instigation of my mother, had written me a document, but that I had seen my father many times after that document was written. I was at the head of his bed when he died and that document was never mentioned once." (This contradicts her previous statement about her father's dying words.)

Q. "Did you tell Mrs. Whitney that your father had retracted it?"

A. "I do not remember. I believe I must have."

Q. "You knew that your mother was very fond of her grandchild, your daughter, did you not?"

A. "I would say my mother is unnaturally fond of that child."

Q. "What do you mean by that?"

A. "I think she is hysterically fond of that child. I think she exaggerates things."

Q. "Can you imagine any motive that your mother could have for saying anything against you except the welfare of the child?"

A. "Yes, I can."

Q. "I am willing you should state it. What motive can your mother have?"

A. "I am sorry to say that the only motive that my mother can have is money."

Q. "Why should money come into this as the motive on the part of your mother to take sides against you?"

A. "You better ask Mrs. Whitney that."

Q. "Is that your only answer?"

A. "It is a very hard thing for me to say, but I must say it, even though it is against my mother, since you are forcing me to say this. She wants the guardianship of the child so she can have the $48,000 a year allowance."

Q. "Then you think that Mrs. Morgan's motive in trying to take the child away from you is so that she can have the expenditure of $4,000 a month, is that right?"

A. "Yes, that is right."

Q. "Do you really mean that?"

A. "I certainly do. My mother is money-mad."

Mrs. Whitney was shown to be a woman of very considerable wealth who, in addition to her own three children, had eight grandchildren for whom she had provided separate, private homes surrounding her country place. At the very end of the cross-examination the following colloquy occurred:

Mr. Smyth. "Let me ask you this question and it is an important one. You know that Mrs. Whitney is the grandmother of eight grandchildren, do you not?"

A. "Yes, I do."

Q. "You know also that she has undertaken the care of a large family ever since her own three children were born?"

A. "No, I don't know that. What do you mean that she has undertaken the care of a large family?"

Q. "Well, she has, hasn't she?"

A. "What large family?"

Q. "Three children and eight grandchildren. Isn't that a pretty good sized family nowadays?"

A. "Does she bring them all up? Don't they live with their own mothers?"

Q. "You know, don't you, that Mrs. Whitney in the country, close to her own house, has erected three private houses for her three children in addition to her central home down there where her eight grandchildren are being raised? Don't you know that?"

A. "No, I don't. I have never been in that house and I don't know a thing about them."

Q. "You know she has eight grandchildren, don't you?"

A. "I suppose she has if you say so."

Q. "Don't you know that she is interested in the welfare of all these children?"

A. "I don't know. What is she doing, conducting an orphan asylum? Don't their own mothers look after their own children?"

Q. "You are not listening to my question."

A. "I cannot answer such a stupid question."

Q. "You don't know what my question is going to be."

A. "I have answered what you said so far."

Q. "Now, bearing in mind the multiple responsibilities

that Mrs. Whitney has outside her own family circle, her own private art museum on West 8th Street, her own activities as a sculptress, and in view of all these activities can you now or will you now tell this court any motive that Mrs. Whitney can have in her effort to keep the custody of her brother's child, excepting to care for its welfare?"

A. "That is very difficult for me to answer."

Q. "I should say so."

A. "But wait a minute. I want to say this. That if Mrs. Whitney insists upon bringing up her eight grandchildren and my child as well, she can only have a mania for rearing children."

Q. "Then your response is this—that as to your mother you think she is money-mad and as to Mrs. Whitney that she has an obsession to bring up children, is that it?"

A. "No, it is not right, it is what you say."

Q. "Haven't you said it?"

A. "No, I see no reason why Mrs. Whitney should want to bring up my child. I cannot give any reason because I do not know what her motives are. I do not pretend to be behind that brain of hers."

Q. "You know about Mrs. Whitney's philanthropies, don't you?"

A. "Yes."

Q. "Can you imagine how any philanthropic woman can be actuated by any ulterior motive to have the custody of her brother's child excepting the welfare of that child?"

A. "There is a certain little child here in New York that needs Mrs. Whitney's looking after more than mine does."

Q. "Are you trying now to bring something else into this picture that we do not know about?"

A. "You are opening many doors to me to say many things."

Q. "You can open any door and at your risk say anything you choose, but I am *now* asking you this question— can you imagine what motive Mrs. Whitney has to take care of her brother's child excepting the welfare of that child, unless you charge her, as you apparently do, with having a mania for bringing up children?"

A. "No, Mrs. Whitney has told me herself repeatedly and as she has testified on the witness stand, she has never seen me drunk or unladylike, that her mother liked me and respected me, and I really do not see why Mrs. Whitney wants my child.

"It is still a mystery to me. I can only say that if my child, after spending two years with Mrs. Whitney, is in a state of mind where she shrinks at the thought of me, then it is high time that the child should be taken away from Mrs. Whitney."

Chapter 15

The Cross-Examination, by
Lee Parsons Davis

of Leonard Kip Rhinelander, in his notorious annulment action against his colored wife, Alice Jones Rhinelander

THE CROSS-EXAMINATION of the plaintiff, conducted by Lee Parsons Davis, former Westchester County District Attorney, in one of the most widely publicized cases of recent years—the notorious annulment action brought by Leonard Kip Rhinelander against his colored wife, Alice Jones Rhinelander—was considered by his Westchester County colleagues as the outstanding example of his unusual skill as a cross-examiner.

Rhinelander, scion of an old, socially prominent and wealthy New York family, had, at the age of twenty-two, secretly married Alice Jones, twenty-five, daughter of a white mother and a colored father, with whom he had carried on a scandalous liaison for some months before coming of age. In the marriage license, Alice Jones was designated as "white."

They lived happily for a time until the reporters learned of the secret alliance. Then headlines blared forth from every front page: "Rhinelander Marries Mulatto"; "Society Man Weds Colored Woman"; etc.

For a week after this dénouement, Rhinelander continued to live with his bride at the home of her parents, but then he was spirited away by representatives of his family. A few days after his disappearance, a suit was brought for annulment of the marriage on the ground of fraud.

Taking advantage of the fact that the wife was of light color, with no pronounced negroid features, the young husband contended that prior to the marriage the wife had represented that she was of pure white extraction.

At the trial the defense admitted the wife to be of colored blood but denied that she had made any such representation; further, the defense contended, though not conceding, that regardless of any representations on her part, the plaintiff knew the real truth, having lived on terms of intimacy with her in a prominent New York hotel prior to the marriage, and could not have believed such a representation.

To substantiate his contention, counsel for the plaintiff (the late New York Supreme Court Justice Isaac N. Mills) took the ground that his client was suffering from a nervous disorder and was mentally unsound.

Mr. Davis had peculiar situations to cope with in the trial of the case, of which two were outstanding: First, racial prejudice. Second, Rhinelander's impediment in his speech which caused him to stammer when excited, at times so much so as to interrupt his testimony.

Rhinelander's very appearance on direct examination excited the sympathy of the jury and gave the impression that the plaintiff's counsel sought from the start to convey, viz.: that here was a society youth, both weak-minded and innocent, who had been trapped by an unscrupulous colored girl, his senior in age and in worldly experience.

Mr. Davis began his cross-examination cautiously, treating Rhinelander with the utmost kindness and consideration, patiently asking his questions until he felt convinced that the sympathy in the jury box toward the witness had been gradually overcome.

From then on Mr. Davis changed his tactics, and the tone of his questioning indicates that he felt he had reached a point where it was safe to adopt an emphatic and sometimes a harsh tone toward the witness.

To demonstrate to the jury that Rhinelander's mind was functioning clearly, even under the stress of being on a witness stand in a crowded courtroom where photographers and reporters bustled about, Mr. Davis deliberately, though not apparently, misquoted his testimony, which was promptly corrected by the witness, forgetting that he had been branded as mentally unsound by his own lawyer.

Gradually, and by continually harping on the point, leaving it for a moment only to return to it again, Mr. Davis forced admissions from Rhinelander that he was not acting on his own convictions—that he did not himself believe the truth of several allegations he had sworn to in his complaint.

With this picture of the asserted mentally deficient witness in the box, the jury visibly in sympathy with him and his family, the cross-examination began:

Mr. Davis. "Mr. Rhinelander, because of your affliction of speech I want to be just as gentle as I possibly can with you. Do you understand that?"

A. "I do."

Q. "And will you keep carefully in mind that if I ask you any question that you don't understand, you are at liberty to tell me so?"

A. "Yes."

Q. "I will try and make my questions clear to you. Your mind is all right, isn't it?"

A. "I believe it is."

Q. "Your trouble is that you stammer? Is that right?"

A. "It is."

Q. "As you sit there, Mr. Rhinelander, your mind's all right, isn't it?"

A. "It is."

Q. (Sympathetically.) "You don't want Judge Mills and this jury to gather the impression that you are an imbecile?"

A. "No."

Q. "You don't want this jury to have any impression that you are not mentally sound?"

A. "No."

Q. "Your only difficulty is that you have this unfortunate impediment in your speech?"

A. "Yes."

Q. "In 1921 was your mind all right?" (This was the year he met the defendant.)

A. "Yes."

Q. (Slightly more emphatic.) "You knew what you were doing every minute of that year, didn't you?"

A. "Yes."

Q. (Still more emphatically.) "You don't want this jury to get any impression from anything that Judge Mills said that you didn't know what you were doing in 1921, do you?"

A. "No."

Q. "Your only trouble back in 1921 was the fact that you stuttered? Is that right?"

A. "It is, yes."

Q. "You stutter more at one time than you you do at others?"

A. "Yes."

Q. "How do you feel now—that you can talk fairly clearly?"

A. "Maybe, yes."

Q. (Patronizingly.) "It is when you get excited, is it, that you stutter a little more than ever?"

A. "It is, yes."

Q. "This (indicating the defendant) is your wife, isn't it, sitting here?"

A. "It is, yes."

Q. "Well, Mr. Rhinelander, you left your wife on November 20th of 1924, did you not?"

A. "I did."

Q. "And who went with you?"

A. "My attorney, Mr. Jacobs."

Q. "You both got into an automobile that was closely curtained?"

A. "Yes."

Q. "And Mr. Jacobs hurried you into that automobile, didn't he?" (Deliberately putting words into the witness's mouth.)

A. "I went there of my own initiative."

Q. (Sharply.) "Did I ask you that question, Mr. Rhinelander?"

A. "You asked me who hurried me."

Q. "I will repeat my question. (Forcefully.) He hurried you into that automobile, did he not?"

A. "No."

Q. (Quickly.) "What? The answer is 'yes' isn't it?"

A. "I hurried into the automobile."

Q. "You hurried?"

A. "Yes."

Q. "So you are able to make that distinction as you sit there on the stand, aren't you?"

A. "Yes."

Q. "Your mind is working very clearly now, isn't it?"

A. "Yes."

Q. "Well, where did you hurry to after you got into the automobile?"

A. "I went to Jamaica, Long Island. Mowack Avenue."

Q. "What kind of a place is it?"

A. "That is a high-class boarding house."

Q. "Had you ever been there before?"

A. "No."

Q. "Who took you there?"

A. "My attorney."

Q. "That is Mr. Jacobs, who is sitting here with his back turned?"

A. "It is."

Q. "How long did you stay at this high-class boarding house?"

A. "One night."

Q. (In a tone indicating an important discovery.) "So, you went out of the state, did you?"

A. "Yes."

Q. "Did you make any stops between the time that you left your wife and getting out of the State of New York?"

A. "That evening I did, yes."

Q. "What time did you leave your wife, Alice?"

A. "Around four in the afternoon."

Q. "What stop did you make on your way from going from where you left her until you got in this high-class boarding house in Jersey?" (Deliberately misquoting the witness.)

A. (Promptly.) "It isn't in Jersey. It is in Jamaica."

Q. (With a glance toward the jury indicating that here is a witness who certainly has a keen mind.) "Oh, yes, I am wrong. You are right. You corrected me, didn't you?"

A. "Yes, I did."

It was contended by the defence that Rhinelander was happy with his wife until his family forced him to abandon her and bring the action for annulment. So the cross-examination continued:

Q. "Then where did you go?"

A. "I went to Washington."

Q. "Who went with you to Washington?"

A. "Mr. Jacobs went with me."

Q. "You came back from Washington to the Robert Treat in Newark?"

A. "That is right."

Q. "And from the Robert Treat you went right on through to Melrose, L. I.?"

A. "That is right."

Q. "How did you go there?"

A. "I went by train."

Q. "Did you stop over anywhere on the way to Melrose?"

A. "Yes."

Q. "Where?"

A. "In the subway tube."

Q. "What subway tube?"

A. "Ninth Avenue, I believe."

Q. "And then you went down to Melrose?"

A. "Then I went back to the hotel."

Q. (With emphasis.) "You just thought of Strong's testimony, haven't you?"

A. "Yes, sir."

Q. "Did that just come to your mind?"

A. "Yes."

Q. "You didn't go on through to Melrose, L. I.?"

A. "No, I did not."

Q. "Well, you said you did a moment ago, didn't you?"

A. "Yes."

Q. "And then you changed because you remembered Strong's testimony?"

A. "Yes."

Q. "Well, I might just as well ask you what you did in the subway station."

A. "I signed the complaint."

Q. "You signed the complaint. You were keeping out of the way of the public, weren't you?"

A. "Yes, I was."

Q. "You didn't like this notoriety? What?"

A. "No, I didn't."

Q. "You were a little timid about the public after this story had come out in the press?"

A. "Yes."

Q. "Who picked out the subway station, of all the places in New York, to sign a document of this importance?"

A. "I followed orders."

Q. (In an apparently surprised tone.) "You followed orders?"

A. "Yes."

Q. "That is what we have been trying to get at. Whose orders did you follow?"

A. "Mr. Jacobs'."

Q. "Where did he give you those orders?"

A. "At the Robert Treat."

Q. "He told you to go with Mr. Strong to New York?"

A. "Yes."

Q. "Told you to go to a subway station and sign this annulment action?"

A. "Yes."

Q. "And you followed his orders?"

A. "I did."

Q. "And you signed it and knew what you were signing?"

A. "I did, yes."

Q. "You understood it, didn't you?"

A. "I did."

Q. "And when you swore to it you meant every word of it?"

A. "I did."

Q. "Why, you didn't want to sign this paper, did you?"

A. "I did."

Q. "What date did you first desire to sign this annulment action?"

A. "I don't remember."

Q. "How long after you left your wife? Or was it before? Was it after or before that you first desired to sign this complaint?"

A. "It was after."

Q. "How long after?"

A. "Two days."

Q. "Two days. Where were you when you first desired to sign a complaint against your wife?"

A. "In Washington."

Q. "And you had had some talks with Mr. Jacobs before that?"

A. "Yes."

Q. "So when you left this girl you didn't want to sign a complaint in an annulment action against her, did you? Did you? Just yes or no."

A. "I can't answer that, your Honor."

Q. "You can't answer it?"

A. "Not yes or no."

Q. "Did you want to sign a complaint?"

A. "Yes."

Q. "So you could answer that question yes or no, couldn't you?"

A. "Not the way you asked it at first I couldn't, no."

Q. "Well, you left your wife on the 20th of November, didn't you?"

A. "Yes."

Q. "Did you want to sign a complaint in an annulment action on the 19th of November? Just yes or no."

A. "I can't answer that, your Honor, yes or no."

Q. "You can't answer it. *Did you have any thoughts on the subject of signing a complaint on November 19th?*"

A. "No."

Q. "Mr. Jacobs was at the house on the 18th of November, was he not?"

A. "He was, yes."

Q. "And he was there on the 20th?"

A. "Yes."

Q. "And the 20th was the first day that you wanted to sign a complaint against your wife? Right?"

A. "On the—"

Q. (Forcefully and slowly, emphasizing each word.) "The 20th is the first day, according to your testimony. That is right, isn't it?"

A. "On the 19th there was sufficient doubt in my mind."

Q. "What?"

A. "On the 19th there was a suspicion."

Q. "Well, you were never really sure that your wife had colored blood in her veins until some time in May, 1924?"

A. "About March."

Q. "March, 1924?"

A. "Yes."

Q. "So that you had doubts up to March, 1924?"

A. "1925."

Q. "1925. Thank you for the correction. Your mind's working clearly, isn't it?"

A. "Yes."

Q. "So that that is a correct answer. Up to March, 1925, you had doubts as to whether or not your wife had colored blood in her veins?"

A. "Yes."

Q. "And *you swore to this original complaint on November 24, 1924, didn't you?* Look at it."

A. "*I did, yes.*"

Q. "And you knew the contents of it?"

A. "Yes."

Q. "And you knew the meaning of the English language?"

A. "Yes."

Q. "Do you remember swearing to this Paragraph 3 of your complaint: 'That the consent of the said plaintiff to said marriage was obtained by fraud. That prior to said marriage the defendant represented to and told the plaintiff that she was white and not colored and had no colored blood, which representation the plaintiff believed to be true and was induced thereby to consent to said marriage, and entered into said marriage relying upon such representations, which representations plaintiff, after said marriage, discovered to be wholly untrue.' Did you swear to that?"

A. "I did, yes."

Q. "Was it true or was it not true—that which you swore to?"

A. "It was true."

Q. "So that you swore on November 24th that you knew that her representation that she had no colored blood was wholly untrue, didn't you? Take your time."

A. "I can't answer that, your Honor."

Q. "You can't answer it? Just take your time. Read paragraph—

A. "I must qualify."

Q. (Handing the witness a copy of the complaint.) "Now, you just take Paragraph 3 and read it over to yourself. Have you read it over?"

A. "Yes."

Q. "You told this jury that you doubted she had colored blood in her veins up to *March, 1925,* didn't you?"

A. "Yes."

Q. "And in that complaint, verified in November, '24, you swore, did you not, that when she stated that she was of white blood that that statement was wholly untrue, to your knowledge?"

A. "Yes."

Q. "Which is true—that you did not know or were not satisfied that she had colored blood until March of 1925 or that you knew that she had colored blood on November 24, four days after you left her. Which is true?"

A. "I wasn't—

Q. "Oh, just a moment. Won't you answer my question directly? You know both can't be true, don't you? In plain English, on November 24 you swore that she was lying to you, didn't you?"

A. "Yes."

Q. (With emphasis.) "And lying in that she claimed that she had nothing but white blood?"

A. "Yes."

Q. "And you have told this jury that you had doubts as to whether or not she had colored blood down to March of 1925. That is true?"

A. "Yes."

Q. "Now, which is true—that you knew she had colored blood on the 24th of November, '24, or that you had doubts down until March, 1925? Which is the truth?"

A. "I had doubts until March."

Q. "That wasn't correct, was it? Take your time. Just yes or no. You swore there that on November 24th, when she said she was all of white blood, that that was wholly untrue, didn't you?"

A. "Yes."

Q. "And you have told this jury—I repeat again—that you had doubts that she had colored blood away down to March of 1925? Correct?"

A. "Yes."

Q. "Do you recognize that those two statements are opposed?"

A. "Yes."

Q. "And you recognize that both can't be true, don't you?"

A. "Yes."

Q. "Now, which is true? Take your time, because I want to be kind to you."

A. "I had definite—

Q. "No. Which one of the two statements is true—the one about March, 1925, or the one in that complaint? You have said they both can't be true."

A. *"The one in March."*

Q. "The one in March is true. So you swore to something that was untrue in your original complaint down in this telephone booth? That is a fact, isn't it?"

A. "No, because there was enough doubt in my mind at that—

Q. "There was enough doubt in your mind so that you could swear emphatically that she was a liar, in ordinary everyday English? Is that it? Is that your explanation?"

A. "From the newspapers."

Q. (With sarcasm.) "Did anybody ask you anything about newspapers?"

A. "No."

Q. "Well, answer the question, please."

A. "Yes."

Q. "Don't you know that you never read that complaint at all until it was signed?"

A. "I did read it."

* * * * *

Q. "You had a little apartment fixed up for Alice Rhinelander, didn't you?"

A. "Yes."

Q. "You had the furniture in there, didn't you?"

A. "Yes."

Q. "Did you give that to her?"

A. "I did, yes."

Q. "And you gave this Mr. Jacobs the note to take that away from her?"

A. "I did not."

Q. "Then if he did any such thing as that he did it without any instructions from you?"

A. "Yes."

Q. "Has he ever told you that he took your wife's furniture—it didn't amount to much—took it out of this apartment and put it in storage where she couldn't touch it?"

A. "Yes."

Q. "He told you that?"

A. "Afterwards."

Q. "How long afterwards?"

A. "About a month afterwards. I don't remember. Some time in there."

Q. "Did you give instructions to him to give it back to her? Just yes or no."

A. "No."

Q. "So Mr. Jacobs took it into his own hands to take your wife's furniture away from her?"

A. "Yes."

Q. "He is sort of generaling this case, isn't he—doing things without your orders?"

A. "Not always."

Q. "How many times has he done things without instructions from you?"

A. "I don't know how many times."

Q. "Do you know in whose office he is working?"

A. "My father's office."

Q. "And how long has Mr. Jacobs been working in your father's office?"

A. "Eleven years."

Q. "You have released a lot of very confidential letters of your wife's in this case, haven't you?"

A. "Yes."

(Judge Mills had read at great length into the record letters of the most intimate nature written by the wife.)

Q. "You didn't do it, did you?"

A. "I did not."

Q. "Where were these letters when you last saw them?"

A. "In my room in 48th Street."

Q. "And what were they in?"

A. "In the trunk."

Q. "Locked up?"

A. "I believe so, yes."

Q. "And they disappeared, did they?"

A. "Yes."

Q. "Without your knowledge?"

A. "Yes."

Q. "You were doing this all of your own volition? You said that when you left your wife, Alice, you left of your own volition, did you not?"

A. "I did, yes."

Q. "You signed this complaint of your own volition?"

A. "I did."

Q. "No pressure brought to bear?"

A. "No."

Q. "But it was Mr. Jacobs, who worked in your father's office, that took the furniture away from her without your orders?"

A. "Yes."

Q. "Who took the letters out of your trunk?"

A. "Mr. Jacobs did."

Q. "Without your knowledge?"

A. "Yes."

Q. "And without your authority?"

A. "Yes."

Q. "That is your father's home, isn't it, where your room was?"

A. "Yes."

Q. "Did you object to his taking them out of your trunk?"

A. "Not after I signed the complaint."

Q. "Did you? Yes or no. Did you object to his taking your wife's private, confidential letters out of your trunk without your consent or authority?"

A. "In a way I did, yes."

Q. "Was this after you had signed the original complaint in this case or before?"

A. "After."

Q. "How long after?"

A. "Several months after."

Q. "How many months."

A. "I don't remember how many months."

Q. "When did you last see these letters before Mr. Jacobs got hold of them without your authority?"

A. "Around the first part of November."

Q. "The first part of November was the last you saw of them?"

A. "Yes. Not the last. I saw them in Melrose."

Q. "Who brought them down there?"

A. "Mr. Jacobs did."

Q. "When did he bring them to Melrose?"

A. "Around December."

Q. "Did you read any of them?"

A. "Yes."

Q. "Did you read them all?"

A. "No."

Q. "Which ones did you read down in Melrose after Mr. Jacobs had—withdrawn? Well, he stole them out of your trunk, didn't he, to be frank?"

A. "No."

Q. "He took them without your consent?"

A. "He had a right to."

Q. "Oh, he had a right to?"

A. "Yes."

Q. "He had a right to go into your effects and take anything he wanted?"

A. "Yes."

Q. "That is it, is it? That is what you believed?"

A. "Yes."

Q. "No authority from you to go and take your personal letters from your wife before you were married? What? No authority from you?"

A. "He was my attorney."

Q. "What authority did you give him to go into your trunk or into your bureau drawer and take these exceedingly confidential letters?"

A. "In that particular case, it was his own initiative."

Q. "Oh, his own initiative?"

A. "Yes."

Q. "So, that is twice that he acted on his own initiative? Once he took your wife's furniture away from her without your order, and the next thing he did was to take all of these confidential letters that have been spread on this record for days? That is correct, isn't it?"

A. "Yes."

Q. "He was still working in your father's office at this time?"

A. "Yes."

Q. "Did you object to the letters being used in this trial? Just yes or no. Take your time."

A. "I did, yes."

Q. "When did you object to their being used in this trial?"

A. "In September some time."

Q. "This year?"

A. "Yes."

Q. "Was that the first time you were told they were going to be used in this trial?"

A. "Yes."

Q. "Did you object after that?"

A. "It was for my own benefit. I had to permit them."

Q. (With great emphasis.) "You were TOLD for your own benefit that you HAD to submit them to the jury in open court, were you?"

A. "Yes."

Q. "In September of this year?"

A. "I believe so, yes."

Q. "Then you didn't object any more, did you?"

A. "No."

Q. "Then you were willing to have them used? You didn't object any more, you say. You were willing to have them used?"

A. "Yes, after that."

Q. "Willing to have these letters read about somebody crawling over your stomach, as long as it was for your benefit?"

A. "Yes."

Q. "And you had promised this girl that you would keep them safely, hadn't you?"

A. "Yes."

Q. "But as long as it was for your benefit to put this stuff on the record in Court, you were willing to forget that promise to her, were you? You were, weren't you?"

A. "I followed the advice of my counsel."

Q. "You are a man, aren't you?"

A. "Yes."

Q. "And a gentleman?"

A. "I try to be one."

Q. "And, as a man and a gentleman, as long as they could be used for your benefit, you were willing to break the promise to this girl that you would keep them safely? That is right, isn't it?"

A. "Yes."

Q. "And you still consider yourself a man, do you? Just yes or no. Do you?"

A. "Yes."

Q. "You made that promise many times to your wife, didn't you, while you were corresponding with her—that you would keep all her letters sacred?"

A. "Yes."

Q. "And by sacred you mean secret?"

A. "Yes."

Q. "And that you would take good care of them?"

A. "Yes."

Q. "And not let any others see them? What?"

A. "Yes."

Q. "Did you mean it when you said it?"

A. "I did, yes."

Q. "Well, you did break your promise, didn't you, when you used them?"

A. "I did not—"

G. "You told this jury that you were willing to have your lawyers use them when you learned that it would be for your benefit. You told this jury that a moment ago, didn't you? Take your time. Isn't that what you told these twelve men?"

A. "My attorney used them."

Q. "But didn't you tell his Honor and these twelve men that when your lawyers advised you it was for your benefit to use them, you were willing to have them used then in open court?"

A. "It wasn't in my power to prevent it."

Q. "It wasn't in your power to control your own lawsuit? Is that your answer?"

A. "Yes."

Q. "Did you hear counsel for the defense open to this jury?"

A. "Yes."

Q. "So you were powerless to prevent it, were you, in your own lawsuit?"

A. "Yes."

Q. "A moment ago did you tell this jury that when they advised you it was for your benefit that then you were willing to have the letters used?"

A. "Yes."

Q. "Did you mean that statement?"

A. "Yes, I meant it."

Q. "So you were both willing to have them used and powerless to prevent it?"

A. "Yes."

* * * * *

Q. "When did you first make any inquiry or did you make any inquiry of her as to what her color was?"

A. "I did not make any."

Q. "Did you ever make an inquiry of anyone as to her color before you married her?"

A. "No. I did not."

Q. "That you are sure of?"

A. "Yes."

Q. "You never introduced this subject of color to her, did you?"

A. "No."

Q. "And you are sure of that answer?"

A. "Yes."

Q. "Did you swear to this: 'Plaintiff had become informed of the fact that Emily, a sister of the defendant, had married a colored man and was residing with him as his wife in said City of New Rochelle or its immediate neighborhood and this fact led him in some way to introduce to the defendant the subject of her parentage and blood.' Did you swear to that?"

A. "I did."

Q. "Which is true, your statement in this courtroom, that you never introduced the subject to her or as you have sworn in your bill of particulars, that you did tell her, which is true? Take your choice. Which one?"

A. "They introduced the subject to me."

Q. "They introduced it to you?"

A. "Yes, sir."

Q. "Then when you swore in your bill of particulars that you introduced the subject because you had heard that Emily had married a colored man that was not true? Just yes or no. Take your time, no hurry about this, it is too important."

A. "They presented it to me."

Q. "When you made the statement in this sworn bill of particuars that you introduced the subject because you had heard that Emily married a colored man, that statement was not true, was it?"

A. "No. I did not introduce it."

Q. "It was not true, then, when you swore to it? Now, that becomes a simple inquiry for you to answer. Frankly, Mr. Rhinelander, that was not true. It was not, was it?"

A. "I followed the advice of my attorney when I signed it."

Q. "So you followed the advice of your lawyer when you swore to a lie. That is your explanation, is it?"

A. "No. It is not."

Q. "That statement is not true, is it, that you introduced the subject. Just yes or no?"

A. "No. It is not."

Q. "And your explanation is that you followed the advice of your attorney?"

A. "Yes."

Q. "Well, that certainly was not Judge Mills. It was Mr. Jacobs, wasn't it?"

A. "Yes."

Q. "So you followed the advice of Mr. Jacobs in swearing against your wife, to a statement that you knew was not true. That is so, isn't it?"

A. "I went on his advice."

Q. "His advice. You told him it was not true, didn't you? You told him that you did not introduce the subject of her blood, frankly, Mr. Rhinelander. You did, didn't you? Be frank with me."

A. "I believe not."

Q. (Surprised.) "You believe not? Well, you did not tell him that you had introduced the subject of blood, did you?"

A. "No."

Q. "And you do not know where he got that from? He did not get it from you, did he?"

A. "I believe not."

Q. "And you do not know where he got an untruthful statement to put in a legal document?"

A. "No."

Q. "He has been building this case up for you, hasn't he?"

A. "He has advised me; yes."

Q. "You recognize the importance in this statement, in part of the pleadings, as to who introduced the subject of blood, don't you?"

A. "Yes."

Q. "You never told him that you introduced it?"

A. "I think not; no."

Q. "And you were the only one that knew, outside of your wife's family, who introduced it, if anyone did?"

A. "Yes."

Q. "And he didn't get that from you to put in a paper —this member of the bar—did he?"

A. "No, he did not."

Q. "So now we have this fact, have we—that Mr. Jacobs put an untrue statement in part of the pleadings in this case, which you never told him about?"

A. "Yes."

Q. "You swore to this bill of particulars before the same notary who took your verification of your original complaint, Mr. Strong?"

A. "Yes."

Q. "You read this over?"

A. "I did, yes."

Q. "And you understood it when you read it?"

A. "Yes."

Q. "Now, when you came to that important part which was not true, you most assuredly called it to the attention of Mr. Jacobs, didn't you?"

A. "No, I did not."

Q. "Just signed and swore to a lie because he had prepared the paper for your signature? That is right, is it?"

A. "I was advised."

Q. "He advised you to sign it after you had read it?"

A. "Yes."

*   *   *   *   *

Judge Mills in his opening and during the trial had strenuously contended that his client was an innocent young man who had been pursued by a woman of the world. After the plaintiff had been forced to admit that practically his entire bill of particulars was false the examination continued:

Q. "Now, you voluntarily, you say, shortly after you met her, fell in love with her. How long might that be?"

A. "Several weeks."

Q. "A couple of weeks?"

A. "Yes."

Q. "And you fell in love with her on your own volition?"

A. "Yes."

Q. "That wasn't a very long time for a girl to pursue you, was it?"

A. "No."

Q. "You pursued Alice, as a matter of fact, didn't you, frankly?"

A. "At that time, I did, yes."

Q. "You were trying to get her love in return for yours?"

A. "Yes."

Q. "And when you started making love to Alice Rhinelander, two weeks after you met her, you were a man about it, weren't you?"

A. "Yes."

Q. "And you weren't making love to a girl and seeking her love in return without honest marriage in view, were you?"

A. "No."

Q. "Now, when did Alice return this love that you extended to her?"

A. "About the same time."

Q. "So within two weeks of meeting her you confessed to her that you loved her?"

A. "I believe I did, yes."

Q. "And she confessed her love to you?"

A. "Yes."

Q. "And then the courtship began?"

A. "Yes."

Q. "With marriage in view?"

A. "Not exactly; no."

Q. "Well, what were you making love to each other for? Were you making love to her to pass the time away?"

A. "No."

Q. "What were you making love to her for?"

A. "Because I liked her."

Q. "What did you have in view in making love to her? You didn't just want to pass the time away. What did you have in view?"

(There was no answer.)

Q. "Mr. Rhinelander, so we may get it perfectly straight and you can follow the sequence, did you hear Judge Mills paint you as a very innocent individual?"

A. "Yes."

Q. "Lacking brains?"

A. "Yes."

Q. "You heard him do that?"

A. "Yes."

Q. "We have disposed of those two things, haven't we, frankly? We have disposed of those two branches of the case, haven't we? You don't lack brains, do you?"

A. "Maybe we have."

Q. "Haven't you admitted it?"

A. "Yes."

Q. "You, as plaintiff in this case, and myself, being counsel for the defense, have eliminated this theory of Mr. Jacobs that you lacked brains? We have, haven't we? Between us we have eliminated that from the case, haven't we?"

A. "Yes."

Q. "And you, as the plaintiff in this action, want that eliminated, don't you?"

A. "Yes."

Q. "Did you hear the defense open in this case?"

A. "I did."

Q. "Did you hear the defense contend that you were under the control of someone else?"

A. "Yes."

Q. "You have admitted that, too, haven't you?"

A. "In what way?"

Q. "Well, Mr. Jacobs put all these things in the bill of particulars?"

A. "Yes."

Q. "Without your telling them?"

(There was no answer.)

Q. "And you swore to it because Mr. Jacobs told you to do it?"

A. "Yes."

Q. "And Mr. Jacobs stole letters without your consent, didn't he?"

A. "Yes."

Q. "And you put them into this case because Mr. Jacobs told you to do it? Is that right?"

A. "Yes."

Q. "Now, the next classification we come to of the

plaintiff's case is innocence. You were not so awfully innocent when you met Alice, were you, frankly?"

A. "I was."

Q. "You were, eh?"

A. "Yes."

Q. "You knew how to play stud poker and straight
poker?"

A. "Yes."

Q. "For money?"

A. "Yes."

Q. "You had had a drink before you met Alice, hadn't
you?"

A. "I might have had; yes."

Q. "You made love to Alice?"

A. "Yes."

Q. "You knew how to do that?"

A. "Yes."

Q. "You were not innocent about that, were you?"

A. "It was—"

Q. "You see, we have been running right through on
the cross-examination on the different titles that the plaintiff's case has presented to the jury. We are down to the
third one now. You were not innocent so far as being able
to make love to a girl is concerned?"

A. "I was, yes."

Q. "You didn't know how to go about it?"

A. "No."

Q. "Let me see. Did you know how to hold the hand
of a girl?"

A. "Yes."

Q. "Did you know how to put your arm around her?"

A. "Yes."

Q. "Did you know how to kiss a girl?"

A. "Yes."

Q. "I don't know as there is much else to do. You knew
all those things. I am talking about decent love."

A. "Yes."

Q. "Nothing much to it, is there?"

A. "No."

Q. "So you knew those things when you met Alice?"

A. "Yes."

Q. "So, so far as your case was concerned, you were not innocent on those subjects, were you? Do you hesitate because you feel your case slipping out from under you or just that you want to think?"

A. "No. I knew that."

Q. "How did you go about making love to Alice? You see, I want to see just how innocent you were."

A. "We rode around in the automobile."

Q. "Now, if everybody who rode around in an automobile is made love to, we would have a lot of it. What did you do to make love to her? That is what I am after. You see why I have to ask you these questions, don't you, Mr. Rhinelander?"

A. "Yes."

Q. "Well, you rode around in an automobile. Now, how did you start making love to her?"

A. "I put my arm around her."

Q. "In the automobile?"

A. "Yes."

Q. "So your first move to make love to Alice Rhinelander was to put your arm around her? Is that right?"

A. "I believe it was, yes."

Q. "What did you say to her when you put your arm around her?"

A. "I don't remember."

Q. "Could one forget?"

A. "Yes."

Q. "You have forgotten then?"

A. "Yes."

Q. "Did you say anything to her?"

A. "I have no recollection of it."

Q. "What?"

A. "I haven't any recollection of it."

Q. "What was your next move in making love to Alice Rhinelander, the one whom they claim snared you, or tried to?"

A. "I believe I kissed her."

Q. "Oh, you kissed her?"

A. "Yes."

Q. "The same evening?"

A. "I believe so; yes."

Q. "Did you tell her you loved her?"

A. "I don't think I did."

Q. "Now, you were not putting your arm around a girl and kissing her without being in love with her, were you?"

A. "I liked her. I was attracted."

Q. "Oh, you liked her?"

A. "Yes."

Q. "But you didn't have any thought then of real love?"

A. "No."

Q. "It amused you then, it pleased you to put your arm around a girl and kiss her?"

A. "Yes."

Q. "You got a thrill from it, did you?"

A. "Yes."

Q. "What inside of you induced you to put your arm around her?"

A. "Human instinct."

Q. "Well, that same human instinct prompted you, when you were just about to put your arm around her, that it would give you sort of a thrill—someone of the opposite sex?"

A. "Yes."

Q. "So inside of you you knew what you were doing, didn't you?"

A. "Yes."

Q. "And the same way with kissing her—the same thing, wasn't it?"

A. "Yes."

Q. "You knew, before you kissed her, that something inside of you dictated it was going to please you?"

A. "Yes."

Q. "When did you first tell her you loved her?"

A. "Several weeks after that."

Q. "Well, did she return your love when you told her that you loved her?"

A. "Yes."

Q. "You were the first one to mention that, weren't you—that you loved her?"

A. "I believe I was, yes."

Q. "You were taking the initiative, weren't you?"

A. "Yes."

Q. "Did you love her?"

A. "I did, yes."

* * * * *

The jury's verdict in the case was in favor of the defendant. Young Rhinelander almost immediately hid himself in some western city. A year or so later he started a suit for divorce in Reno. The wife simultaneously brought suit for a separation, but later withdrew it and allowed her husband to get his divorce, upon making a trust fund which would yield her $400 a month for life, whether she married again or not.

Chapter 16

The Cross-Examination of
Mr. and Mrs. Cecil Barret

*by Lloyd Paul Stryker, in the suit brought
against him by Mrs. Marie S. Livingston*

THIS CASE involved the application to a new state of facts
of an old and settled principle of law. So far as the author
has been able to find, it was the first of its kind decided by
the courts of this state. The inquiries received from
many lawyers both in this state and others (addressed not
only to the attorney who conducted the trial, but to the
Supreme Court Justice who presided) were so numerous,
it is apparent that both the legal profession and the financial world were deeply interested in the application of
well-settled principles of law to a state of facts such as
recorded here.

The author particularly wishes to emphasize the fact
that throughout the litigation there was no question of the
good faith of Mr. Barret involved in his stock transactions
with Mrs. Livingston, but the cross-examinations are offered as striking examples of how perfectly honest witnesses can lose the confidence of Judge or jury by ill-
advised answers to the inquiries of a skilled cross-examiner.

The defendant and his fellow partners compose the
well-known firm of Spencer Trask & Co., brokers and
dealers in securities. Mr. Barret became acquainted with
the plaintiff at Bar Harbor, where the Barrets and Livingstons were social friends. In the course of time financial
matters and the stocks in which the firm of Spencer Trask
& Co. were interested came under discussion.

Mrs. Livingston was the mother of five children. Her
youngest son was born in February, 1925. Mr. Livingston

died on April 12, 1925. Three weeks before Mr. Livingston's death Mr. Barret became the godfather of the plaintiff's youngest son. After Mr. Livingston's death Mr. Barret called on Mrs. Livingston "to condole with her." He told her that "it was a terrible thing for her to have lost her husband and be left as she was with five children." He told her that he would be glad to do anything he could for her. On May 15, 1925, a little more than a month after Mr. Livingston's death, Mr. Barret wrote Mrs. Livingston:

"I hate to intrude upon you with any question of business, but I remember that you spoke to me about the likelihood of your having some money to invest for Denise" (Mrs. Livingston's oldest daughter).

He then recommended Purity Bakeries 7% preferred stock, which he said "would be entirely safe and satisfactory."

Time went on and in the fall of 1925 Mrs. Livingston decided to go abroad to live with her five children. Before doing so she called on Mr. Barret and executed "a general uncontrolled power of attorney." She turned over to him at that time securities worth upwards of $70,000, including such stock as Standard Oil of Indiana. Mr. Barret then proceeded to sell the securities turned over to him and to invest for Mrs. Livingston in various other securities. It developed that the securities in which he invested were securities which were owned by the firm of Spencer Trask & Co. and he, therefore, sold to her stocks which he and his partners owned. Profits were derived by the firm on the sales of these stocks. Concerning this Mr. Barret was asked:

Q. "Did you ever tell Mrs. Livingston that you and your partners had made profits on those stocks? Yes or No?"

A. "No."

In writing to Mrs. Livingston about these sales he made no direct statement of any kind to the effect that the stocks had been the property of his firm. At the trial Mrs.

Livingston testified that she did not know that the stocks thus sold were the property of Spencer Trask & Co.

The defendants contended that the information which the defendant Barret sent to the plaintiff by way of circulars describing the issues of stock and the statements in his letters to the effect that the firm was either financing or bringing out an issue were sufficient to apprise Mrs. Livingston that the stocks purchased were stocks owned by the defendants.

Mrs. Livingston was a woman of no business experience. The court found that "she was not versed in the methods of corporate financing and the marketing of securities," nor did she have any knowledge of the financial practices of Wall Street, and that she did not possess the type of mind that would be aroused to inquiry by the information which the defendants sent to her. Such information, the court found, was to her "equivocal, ambiguous and indefinite."

The plaintiff's case rested upon the proposition of law enunciated in *Wendt v. Fischer,* 243 N. Y. 439, 443 and the cases therein cited to the effect that

"If dual interests are to be served, the disclosure to be effective must lay bare the truth, without ambiguity or reservation, in all its stark significance."

The plaintiff further rested upon the proposition enunciated by the English Court in *Dunne v. English,* L. R. 18 Eq. Cas. 524, where the court said:

"It is not enough for an agent to tell the principal that he is going to have an interest in the purchase, or to have a part in the purchase. He must tell him all the material facts. He must make a full disclosure."

The court found that in his dealings with Mrs. Livingston, Mr. Barret had acted throughout in good faith. The court rendered a judgment in favor of Mrs. Livingston accepting the proposition laid down in *Wendt v. Fischer,* 243 N. Y. 439, p. 443, where Judge Cardozo said:

"Finally we are told that the brokers acted in good faith, that the terms procured were the best obtainable at the moment, and that the wrong, if any, was unaccompanied by damage. *This is no sufficient answer by a trustee forgetful of his duty. The law 'does not stop to inquire whether the contract or transaction was fair or unfair. . . .'* "

Judge Cardozo further said:

"Only by this uncompromising rigidity has the rule of undivided loyalty been maintained against disintegrating erosion."

A judgment was rendered in favor of the plaintiff setting aside all of the sales made by the defendant and his partners to the plaintiff of stocks of which the defendants were the owners. The judgment was affirmed on appeal to the effect that

"If dual interests are to be served, the disclosure *to be effective must lay bare the truth, without ambiguity or reservation, in all its stark significance.*"

At the trial the defendants conceded that for a trustee of an ordinary personal trust, to sell or purchase from his beneficiary, would be a most unusual transaction and any honest trustee would feel that he ought very carefully to explain the fact that he was selling his own property. It was important, therefore, for the plaintiff to show that the defendant was not only under the duty imposed by the rule in *Wendt v. Fischer,* but was, in the highest sense, under a trust obligation to the plaintiff. On this point, the defendant Barret was cross-examined by Mr. Stryker as follows:

Q. "Well, you have no doubt that this stock was bought as a result of your praise and boosting of the stock?"

A. "None whatever."

Q. "Now, Mr. Barret, you felt, did you not, a great sense of responsibility to this lady whose general power of attorney you had?"

A. "Yes."

Q. "With unrestricted and unlimited power?"

A. "Yes."

Q. "Is there any doubt about that?"

A. "No."

Q. "You felt, and your conscience was impressed with the fact, that the widow of your friend, with five children, living abroad, having given you a general uncontrolled power of attorney, that the trust and confidence reposed in you was very great?"

A. "Yes."

Q. "And that you owed her a very great obligation of good faith? Didn't you feel that?"

A. "No. Owed her an obligation of good faith."

Q. "What?"

A. "Why should I owe her such a thing?"

Q. "You didn't feel that you owed her any good faith in the handling of her affairs?"

A. "Oh, yes, of course. I thought you meant that I was under an obligation to her to do certain things."

Q. "Well, I will make it quite clear."

A. "All right."

Q. "You knew that you were under a strong and powerful obligation to exercise the highest degree of good faith in the handling of the affairs of this woman, didn't you, Mr. Barret?"

A. "Certainly."

Q. "And I think you have told us in your direct examination that hers was an exceptional case, and that there were only five other instances in your whole experience where you did anything like this."

A. "One."

Q. "One. So that, in a career beginning in 1905 as a partner, this was the second time you had accepted such a weighty obligation and charge; is that right?"

A. "The second time I had a complete power of attorney."

Q. "You understand, don't you, Mr. Barret, by an obligation of good faith, an obligation to be fair and frank, and to tell your customer the truth?"

A. "Yes, sir."

Q. "And all the truth?"

A. "Certainly."

Q. "In clear, unambiguous, unequivocal language?"
A. "Yes."

As a result of this cross-examination, no doubt was left in the case as to the obligation which the defendants owed to the plaintiff.

In this case, the question of trust and confidence was a vital issue. The purchases of the stock in question took place while the plaintiff was abroad with her five children.

In his letters to her the defendant Barret devoted much time to personal matters, discussed his affection for his godson, and frequently wrote about his wife's health and sent plaintiff many letters conveying friendly messages from his wife. All of these expressions tended to substantiate and emphasize the relationship of trust and confidence.

Mrs. Barret, the defendant's wife, took the stand and testified, in effect, that she was present at many conversations between her husband, Mr. Barret, and the Livingstons, and that the stocks generally discussed were what were called "the specialties" and things Spencer Trask & Company dealt in.

In an effort to minimize the trust relationship, Mrs. Barret testified on direct:

"Well, I would like to say that I felt decidedly that the friendship that the Livingstons had for us—or so-called friendship—was based on the possibility or probability of my husband being able to do something for them in a money way. I thought we were being rushed, as one might call it, a little bit."

The purpose of the cross-examination of Mrs. Barret was to establish that the feeling thus expressed by her was an after-thought and that there were, as far as Mr. Barret was concerned, representations of warm friendship that emphasized and established his relation of trust and confidence. The further purpose of the cross-examination was to establish that if there was any "rushing," the rushing came from the Barrets and not from the Livingstons.

Cross-Examination by Mr. Stryker:

Q. "Mrs. Barret, I gather from your testimony that you felt the Livingstons were rather rushing you?"

A. "Quite."

Q. "How often did you see Mrs. Livingston during the summer of 1924?"

A. "Well, on various occasions."

Q. "Very often, didn't you?"

A. "Oh, not very often. Perhaps three times in one week, maybe twice in the next week."

Q. "They had a house of their own up there in Bar Harbor, didn't they?"

A. "Yes, a lovely house."

Q. "And you were living in a hotel cottage?"

A. "Yes."

Q. "And each time they invited you to their house, you felt that their motive in inviting you and welcoming you there was ulterior?"

A. "Well, because—"

Q. "Did you feel that that was the motive? Yes or no?"

A. "I can't answer that yes or no."

Q. "Then answer it your own way."

A. "Because the business end would be brought up."

Q. "I see. Then the fact is that you did feel that each invitation had an ulterior motive?"

A. "Well, I think you would too."

Q. "I am asking you now if that is what *you* felt?"

A. "Well, I think you would and I would, and we all would."

Q. "Please, don't let us debate what I would do, because that really is not germane."

A. "No, I suppose not."

Q. "So would you mind answering my question?"

A. "Yes, certainly."

Q. "That is what you felt, isn't it?"

A. "Certainly."

Q. "There never was an occasion when you met socially but what immediately the Livingstons would crash in with a business discussion? Is that what you are telling us?"

A. "Oh, no, there were lots of occasions when business was not discussed."

Q. "I see; but always, when business was discussed, the Spencer Trask specialties were always brought up; is that right?"

A. "Those were the only ones I ever heard spoken of."

Q. "And they seemed very much interested in Spencer Trask's specialties?"

A. "They didn't seem to be; they were. They wanted my husband to tell them what he was interested in, and when he told them, it was those things."

Q. "And the next time that you would meet the Livingstons after that, the same questions would be asked?"

A. "Oh, no, not the same questions every time; of course not."

Q. "Well, every other time or something like that?"

A. "I couldn't say whether it was every other time, but whenever business was discussed the Spencer Trask specialties were what were spoken of. It was quite clear that that was what they were after."

Q. "Then you were being invited simply to provide the Livingstons with business opportunities?"

A. "Not in the beginning, I don't think so, until they found out we were doing pretty well in business. Then the thing began."

Q. "Didn't it occur to you, Mrs. Barret, that if Mr. Livingston had wanted to find out about these wonderful opportunities, that he could have called on Mr. Barret in his office and said, 'Now, what are the specially fine things you have to sell?' Did you think there was some peculiarly secret and confidential information that Mr. Barret was giving the Livingstons?"

A. "Well, he may have telephoned; I don't know."

Q. "Did your husband tell them anything particularly confidential, in your presence?"

A. "About his business?"

Q. "Yes."

A. "I should say not, no. Mr. Livingston would ask

what he had to suggest, and my husband would tell him what he knew about, which were those specialties."

Q. "It must have been very hard for you to go about with Mrs. Livingston, feeling as you did that her motives were ulterior?"

A. "Well, it wasn't any harder than anything else. As my husband said to me, 'I think you may be imagining this thing.'"

Q. "I see; what thing did he refer to?"

A. "That they were trying to do business out of us."

Q. "Well, you were trying to prevent your husband from seeing them?"

A. "No, not from seeing them."

Q. "But you didn't like him to see them, because you felt they were rushing you for their own financial benefit?"

A. "Yes."

Q. "Now, after you felt that way did you keep on seeing them?"

A. "Only during the summer, in the usual course of things, there in Bar Harbor."

Q. "Well, Bar Harbor is quite a large place, isn't it?"

A. "Very large."

Q. "Were they the only people you knew there in Bar Harbor?"

A. "Oh, no."

Q. ". . . Did you know that your husband was asked to act as Mrs. Livingston's son's godfather?"

A. "Yes, I knew that."

Q. "You felt that was ulterior, too?"

A. "I was amazed."

Q. "Did you feel that was ulterior?"

A. "Absolutely."

Mrs. Barret testified that the first time she saw Mrs. Livingston after Mr. Livingston's death, was at Bar Harbor.

Q. "Then you saw her at Bar Harbor, I take it?"

A. "Yes."

Q. "That was the first time you saw her after her husband's death?"

A. "Yes, after she was a widow."

Q. "Did you call on her there?"

A. "Yes."

Q. "Express your condolence?"

A. "Yes."

Q. "Was that sincere?"

A. "Certainly. I was very fond of her husband."

Q. "And yet you felt that his motives were ulterior?"

A. "No, not so much his as his wife's."

Q. "I see; it was only his wife whose motives were ulterior?"

A. "I felt that his were and hers were."

Q. "You were fond of him?"

A. "Yes, he was a cousin of mine."

Q. "But you thought his motives were ulterior?"

A. "I felt that both of them together had ulterior motives."

Q. "Well, then he had ulterior motives, too?"

A. "Much less so than his wife, however."

Q. "Well, did you think he had them?"

A. "No, I should think if he had, it was a good deal less than his wife had."

Q. "Then you absolve Mr. Livingston, and you say the ulterior motives were largely Mrs. Livingston's?"

A. "Largely, yes."

While she was abroad, Mr. Barret wrote Mrs. Livingston:

"I am wondering if you are still planning to come home for the summer, because if not, it would be such fun for *us* all to be at some watering place *together*."

". . . *Gladys* (Mrs. Barret) *joins me* in sending you our best love to you all from us all.

"Affectionately yours."

And in another letter:

"I have no further news. I hope that *you and Gladys* (Mrs. Barret) *may have come together* in the flesh before I join her, but if not let's hope that we shall *all get together* somewhere at least for a short time during the summer."

In another letter:

"Gladys and the children join me in fondest love to you all until we meet."

And another letter:

"I see that *Gladys has just been writing you* so I am sure that she has given you all her news."

And another:

"With much love to you all *in which I know Gladys would join did she know I were writing,* and best wishes for a complete recovery from your illnesses . . ."

The cross-examination of Mrs. Barret left Mr. Barret in this dilemma: Either the expressions of his warm friendship were sincere and true, or were insincere and false. If they were sincere and true, there would be no question of the trust relationship. If they were false, then that would tend to affect the question of whether he was looking after Mrs. Livingston's interests, or was beguiling her into a sense of security by the false expressions of friendship.

There was a decision for the plaintiff, which was unanimously affirmed by the Appellate Division and by the Court of Appeals as recently as January of this year.

Chapter 17

The Cross-Examination of Ada and Phoebe Brush

by George W. Whiteside, in their suit against two prominent Huntington, L. I., physicians, to recover damages for their ten-year incarceration in Kings Park State Hospital as insane patients

THE DEFENDANTS in this case were two well-known physicians of Huntington, Long Island, who were sued by two sisters for the sum of $250,000 as damages, the claim being that the doctors had signed false certificates of lunacy which resulted in confining both plaintiffs in the Kings Park State Hospital for a period of ten years, at which time they were released under *habeas corpus* proceedings as perfectly sane.

The case was tried before four different juries. The first trial was dismissed upon the plaintiffs' opening. In the second trial, a year and a half later, the jury returned a verdict of $10,000, which was in due course set aside by the appellate court. In the third trial, lasting five days, the jury disagreed. The fourth trial, which occurred two and a half years after the original trial, and again a five-day session in court, resulted in a verdict of $1.00, and even that amount was set aside by the presiding justice.

At the time of the last trial one of the sisters was sixty years of age and the other seventy-three. They had lived in Huntington nearly all their lives. They were descended from an old family, prominent in Long Island before the Revolutionary War, and had been bountifully provided for by their father.

The form of insanity which the plaintiffs were alleged to be suffering from is commonly known as paranoia, the principal symptoms of which are marked delusions of persecution.

It was the claim of the defendants' lawyer, Mr. George W. Whiteside, that there was no ulterior motive connected with the incarceration, but that these two sisters were and had been for a long time suffering from delusions of persecution and that a Mr. Smith, who was then Overseer of the Poor, regarded it for the best interests of the community that they should be confined to some institution. He only arrived at this conclusion after many complaints had been made to him by prominent citizens in Huntington.

Paranoiacs as a rule make notoriously good witnesses in court unless the cross-examiner is able to expose their pet delusions. There was a famous case once where, after days of cross-examination, the witness had maintained his apparent rationality until he was asked if he believed in Christ, whereupon the witness straightened himself, and in a very impressive tone of voice shouted, "I am the Christ."

Mr. Whiteside's cross-examination in this particular case is cited for the simple and very clever way in which he disclosed to the court and jury the particular delusions under which these two witnesses were suffering and which would entirely justify their incarceration in an insane asylum.

All through their direct examination their testimony was apparently that of perfectly tranquil minds until their life at the Kings Park State Hospital was inquired into. Then they began to get excited, telling how they were forcibly grabbed by the hair, pushed into a chair while screaming and calling for help, and how the more they protested the more their arms were wrung and their hair pulled until finally some strange man came in and threw them on the floor with his knee on their necks, choking them to death, while a doctor produced a bottle and a needle which was jabbed into their arms.

Mr. Whiteside began his cross-examination by showing that although the doctors lived in Huntington not more than two blocks away from the plaintiffs' home, neither of the sisters had even spoken to the doctors for more than fifteen years prior to their incarceration in Kings Park Hospital.

Someone who was in the courtroom during Mr. Whiteside's examination described it as "like turning a key in a door which suddenly flew open, apparently of its own accord, as if by some powerful spring, thereby disclosing a mass of material which could only be described as the groping about and stumblings of a demented mind."

Mr. Whiteside:

Q. "As to Dr. Lindsay to whom you had not spoken in twenty-four years—please give us the basis for your claim that he had a wilful and malicious motive for swearing out a warrant against you."

A. "Why, he had a daughter in the matrimonial market who was continually entertaining Mr. Seem, and the doctor seemed very angry that Mr. Seem was so intimate with me, so I thought they would like to get me out of the way."

Q. "Who was this Mr. Seem?"

A. "Why, he was a young minister—rather he was the preacher in the Presbyterian Church in Huntington."

Q. "Was he married?"

A. "No, unmarried."

Q. "You say the basis of your claim that the doctor acted maliciously toward you was that he had a daughter of marriageable age who you believed was chasing after Mr. Seem, an unmarried, eligible clergyman in your town, and that the doctor's whole family resented the fact that this young minister seemed to be very attentive to you."

A. "Well, that is the way I looked at it."

Q. "Was Mr. Seem in reality attentive to you or did he ever propose marriage to you?"

A. "Why, he had a list of the marriageable young ladies at the time and told me that when he got married he wanted the money thrown in and I told him there was nothing doing along that line with me."

Q. "Did he propose marriage to you?"

A. "Not exactly in those words."

Q. "Did he ever call upon you at your house?"

A. "I never asked him."

Q. "I repeat the question—did he call upon you at your house?"

A. "No."

Q. "So that this Mr. Seem never really called upon you and never really proposed marriage to you?"

A. "No."

Q. "Still you believe he was sufficiently interested in you with a view to matrimony and is that what would have caused the Lindsay family, whom you had not seen for twenty-four years, to have feelings of hatred against you for fear that you were going to grab their clergyman away, was that right?"

A. "Well, that is the way it looked to me."

Q. "Do you think that was the reason they had you incarcerated in an insane asylum?"

A. "Yes."

Q. "Supposing you tell the jury when this Mr. Seem came to Huntington, L. I."

A. "1898."

Q. "Did it look to you that way down to the time Dr. Lindsay signed his certificate 12 years later?"

A. "Why, I cannot see any other reason for doing such a wicked thing."

Q. "Now as regards the other doctor—Dr. Gibson— I understand that you had not seen him for fifteen years prior to the time of your incarceration, is that right?"

A. "That is as I remember it."

Q. "Will you kindly state any fact upon which you base your opinion that he had a wicked motive in certifying to your mental condition?"

A. "Well, I will tell you this—Dr. Gibson was the health officer and there was a man by the name of Rogers who lived back of us who maintained a cesspool that emptied in our well. This was in 1901. We went to Dr.

Gibson and made our complaint and he refused to do anything about it and he claimed that it was empty, but it was measured with a stick and there was three or four inches in it and Dr. Gibson never would do anything about it."

Q. "And the reason you say he had this wicked motive toward you then was in relation to this cesspool back nine years before you were committed to Kings Park?"

A. "Yes."

Q. "Was there anything else?"

A. "Well, I want to add, he failed to do his duty as a health officer and he knew we could put the law on him any time and therefore he wanted to get us out of the way."

Q. "In other words, you say that Dr. Gibson realized you could put the law on him?"

A. "Why, anyone would realize that if they had allowed a nuisance to exist and they were sensible enough to know that I could do this if I chose."

Q. "So you say they were in constant fear of you these nine years lest you put the law on them?"

A. "Why, I cannot see any other reason."

Here Mr. Whiteside produced a "black-red face list" of men whom these two ladies had listed as people who were particularly offensive to them and asked the witness whether the Rev. C. Herbert Carter, pastor of her church, annoyed her, and she replied that Dr. Carter had gone past her house while she was sitting on the lawn.

Q. "How did his face look at that time?"

A. "It was very angry and unsmiling."

Q. "Why, what color was it?"

A. "I do not remember the color just now."

Q. "I call your attention to what you said at the previous trial in answer to this question. Do you remember saying, 'I would like to explain so that the jury can understand why I call Mr. Carter a nuisance. Before we were taken to Kings Park he rode by my house in his automobile with his children and as he approached my house in his auto, I being on the lawn, he stuck his head out of the machine with his face black-red and yelled and yelled with his head stuck up in the air enough to raise the canopy of Heaven. I call that disorderly conduct, for I was not doing anything. If I had been acting in such a way I think he would have been justified in calling me insane and whereas they did it to me and nothing was thought of it'?"

A. "I remember it now."

When later shown the list of the names of people in their town that the sisters had special objections to, the witness admitted that the list was in her own handwriting.

Q. "Now, this list contains the names, does it not, of people who were residents of Huntington?"

A. "Yes."

Q. "And it is headed 'Torments and Nuisances,' is it not?"

A. "Yes."

Mr. Whiteside proceeded to use this list to elicit all kinds of fantastic reasons why the witness had included these names on her list.

Finding the names of Ed and Zabina Carl, Mr. Whiteside asked if they were residents of Huntington and what experience, if any, the witness had which justified their names heading the list of "Torments and Nuisances," which developed the complaint that these people had been riding around in automobiles on a Sunday morning when the witness was ready to go to church and when she came out they "turned around and laughed and turned black-red in their faces." Mr. Whiteside then proceeded to take up, *seriatim,* each of the names that were on the "Torments and Nuisances" list.

Q. "Take for instance F. Sammis. He was one of the Elders of the Church, wasn't he?"

A. "Yes."

Q. "What was your grievance against him?"

A. "Why, he would stop in front of our house with strange men, point at our house and commence to laugh and talk, and he charged us $25 for taking us to Kings Park Hospital when other automobiles only charge $5."

To each inquiry about the different men on the list the reply would be very much the same. One man would "ride by in his automobile and laugh with his face black-red," another would "put his camera on the lawn and take a picture of our lawn which he hadn't any right to do," and another man when passing the house would "jump up and down in his automobile and laugh with a black-red face." Still another would "stand on the corner and point at the house." The editor of one of the local newspapers in Huntington would do the same thing. The ex-police commissioner would talk so loudly when he passed the house that he could be heard a block away. And finally the attention of the witness was drawn to some Italian laborers who were working with steam rollers in front of her house and the witness replied, "They were there Sundays and all times, talking to each other, saying that they were getting seven days' pay a week, and they came and stood on our walk and they evidently were paid for standing there, and *spying* on us and we felt they were going to throw vitriol in our faces."

Q. "In other words, Dr. Gibson and J. Abner Smith and all the others were in a plot to injure you, is that right?"

A. "They were in the cesspool frameup."

Q. "And what other frameups were there besides the cesspool one?"

A. "Why, there didn't need to be any other, that was enough."

Verdict for plaintiffs in the sum of $1.00.

Chapter 18

The Cross-Examination of
Miss Martinez

by Hon. Joseph H. Choate in the celebrated breach of promise case, Martinez *v.* Del Valle

THE MODERN METHOD of studying any subject, or acquiring any art, is the inductive method. This is illustrated in our law schools, where to a large extent actual cases are studied in order to get at the principles of law, instead of acquiring those principles solely through the study of textbooks.

As already indicated, this method is also the only way to become a master of the art of cross-examination. In addition to actual personal experience, however, it is important to study the methods of great cross-examiners, or those whose extended experience makes them safe guides to follow.

Hence, the writer believes, it would be decidedly helpful to the students of the art of cross-examination to have placed before them in a convenient and somewhat condensed form, some good illustrations of the methods of well known cross-examiners, as exhibited in actual practice, in the cross-examination of important witnesses in famous trials.

For these reasons, and the further one that such examples are interesting as a study of human nature, I have in the following pages introduced the cross-examinations of some important witnesses in several remarkable trials.

Often when it is necessary to demonstrate the fact that a witness has given colored or false testimony, it is not some effective point that is the true test of a great cross-examination, but the general effect which is produced upon a jury by a review of all the witness has said, bringing out inconsistencies, contradictions, and improbable situations which result finally in the breakdown of the witness's story. The brief extracts from the cross-examinations that have already been given do not fully illustrate this branch of the cross-examiner's work.

Really great triumphs in the art of cross-examination are but seldom achieved. They occur far less frequently than great speeches. All of us who attend the courts are now and then delighted with a burst of eloquence, but we may haunt them for months and never hear anything even faintly approaching a great cross-examination; yet few pleasures exceed that afforded by its successful application in the detection of fraud or the vindication of innocence.

Some of the greatest cross-examinations in the history of the courts become almost unintelligible in print. The reader nowadays must fancy in vain such triumphs as those attained by Lord Brougham in his cross-examination of the Italian witness Majocchi, in the trial of Queen Caroline. To a long succession of questions respecting matters of which he quite obviously had a lively recollection, the only answers to be obtained on cross-examination from this witness was *"Non mi recordo"* (I do not remember).

Ninety years ago this cross-examination was reputed "the greatest masterpiece of forensic skill in the history of the world," and *Non mi recordo* became household words in England for denoting *mendacity*. Almost equally famous was the cross-examination of Louise Demont by Williams, in the same trial. And yet nothing could be less interesting or less instructive, perhaps, than the perusal in print of these two examinations, robbed as they now are of all the stirring interest they possessed at the time when England's queen was on trial charged with adulterous relations with her Italian *courier de place*.

Much that goes to make up an oration dies with its author and the event that called it into being. Likewise the manner of the cross-examiner, the attitude of the witness, and the dramatic quality of the scene, cannot be reproduced in print. In order to appreciate thoroughly the examples of successful cross-examinations which here follow, the reader must give full vent to his imagination. He must try to picture to himself the crowded court room, the excitement, the hush, the expectancy, the eager faces, the silence and dignity of the court, if he wishes to realize even faintly the real spirit of the occasion.

MARTINEZ *v.* DEL VALLE

One of the most brilliant trials in the annals of the New York courts was the celebrated action for breach of promise of marriage brought by Miss Eugénie Martinez against Juan del Valle. The cross-examination of the plaintiff in this case was conducted by the Hon. Joseph H. Choate, and is considered by lawyers who heard it as perhaps the most brilliant piece of work of the kind Mr. Choate ever did.[1]

The case was called for trial in the Supreme Court, New York County, before Mr. Justice Donohue, in January, 1877. The plaintiff was represented by Mr. William A. Beach, and Mr. Choate appeared for the defendant, Mr. del Valle. The trial lasted for a week and was the occasion of great excitement among the habitués of the court house. To quote from the daily press, "All those who cannot find seats within the court room, remain standing throughout the entire day in the halls, with the faint hope of catching a sight of the famous plaintiff, whose beauty and grace have attracted admirers by the score, from every stage of society, who haunt the place regardless of inconvenience or decency."

[1] When Mr. Choate retired from practice his court records had become so voluminous that many of them were destroyed, including all record of this trial. Both of the court stenographers who reported the trial have since died. Mr. Beach's recollection of the case had died with him and all his notes had likewise been destroyed. It was by the merest accident that a full transcript of the stenographic minutes of the trial was discovered in the possession of a former friend and legal representative of the defendant.

There is no more popular occasion in a court room than the trial of a breach of promise case, and none more interesting to a jury. Such cases always afford the greatest satisfaction to an eager public who come to witness the conflict between the lawyers and to listen to the cross-examinations and speeches. With Mr. Beach, fresh from his nine days' oration in the Henry Ward Beecher case, pitted against Mr. Choate, who told the jury that this was his first venture in this region of the law; and with a really beautiful Spanish woman just twenty-one years of age, "with raven black hair and melting eyes shadowed by long, graceful lashes, the complexion of a peach, and a form ravishing to contemplate," suing a rich middle aged Cuban banker for $50,000 damages for seduction and breach of promise of marriage, the intensity of the public interest on this particular occasion can be readily imagined. It must have served as a stimulus to both counsel to put forth their grandest efforts.

The plaintiff and defendant were strangers until the day when she had slipped on the ice, and had fallen in front of the Gilsey House on the corner of 29th Street and Broadway. Mr. del Valle had rushed to her assistance, had lifted her to her feet, conducted her to her room, received the permission of her mother to become her friend, and six months later had become the defendant in this notorious suit which he had tried to avoid by offering the plaintiff $20,000 not to bring it into court.

Mr. Choate spoke of it to the jury as an excellent illustration of the folly, in these modern times, of attempting to raise a fallen woman! To quote his exact words:—

"Now I want to speak a word of warning to all Good Samaritans, if there are any in the jury box, against this practice of going to the rescue of fallen women on the sidewalks. I do not think my client will ever do it again. I do not think anybody connected with the administration of justice in this case will ever again go to the relief of one of our fair fallen sisters under such circumstances. I know the parable of the Good Samaritan is held up as an example for Christian conduct and action to all good people, but, gentlemen, it does not apply in this case, because it was 'a certain man' who went down to Jericho and fell among thieves, and not a woman, and the Good Samaritan himself was of the same sex, and there is not a word of injunction upon any of us to go to the rescue of a person of the other sex if she slips upon the ice. Why, gentlemen, that is an historical trick of the 'nymphs of the pave.' Hundreds of times has it been practised upon the verdant and inexperienced stranger in our great city."

Mr. Choate felt that he had a good case, a perfectly clear case, but that there was one obstacle in it which he could not overcome. There was a beautiful woman in the case against him, "a combination of beauty and eloquence which would outweigh any facts that might be brought before a jury."

Very early in the trial Mr. Choate warned the jury against the seductive eloquence and power of the learned counsel whom the plaintiff had enlisted in her behalf,— "one of the veterans of our Bar, of whose talents and achievements the whole profession is proud. In that branch of jurisprudence which I may call *sexual* litigation he is without a peer or a rival, from his long experience! You can no more help being swayed by his eloquence than could the rocks and the trees help following the lyre of Orpheus!"

When it came Mr. Beach's turn to address the jury he replied to this sally of Choate's:—

"During the progress of this trial, counsel has seen fit to make some personal allusions to myself. (Here Mr. Choate faced around.) It seemed to me not conceived in an entirely courteous spirit. He belabored me with compliments so extravagant and fulsome that they assumed the character of irony and satire. It is a common trick of the forum to excite expectations which the speaker knows will not be gratified, and blunt even the force of plain and simple arguments which may be addressed to the jury. The courtesy of the learned counsel requires a fitting acknowledgment, and yet I confess my utter inability to do it. I lack the language to delineate in proper colors the brilliant faculties of the learned gentleman, and I am perforce driven to borrow from others the words which describe him properly. I know no other source more likely to do the gentleman justice than the learned and accomplished friends among us taking notes. I noticed a description of my learned friend so appropriate and just that I adopt the language of it. (Here counsel read.) 'The eloquent and witty Choate sat with his classic head erect, while over his Cupid features his blue eyes shed a mild light.' (Great laughter.) Allow me to tender it to you, sir. (Mr. Choate smilingly accepted the newspaper clipping.)

"And how completely does my learned friend fulfil this description! How like a god he is! What beauty! The gloss of fashion and the mould of form! [*Laughter.*] The observed of all observers! Why, how can I undertake to contend with such a heaven-descended god! [*Laughter.*] He chooses to attribute to me something of Orpheonic enchantments, but should I attempt to imitate the fabled musician, sure I am I could not touch his heart of stone! But *he* strikes the Orpheonic lyre which he brings with him from the celestial habitation. How can you resist him? What hope have I with like weapons or efforts? If the case of this poor and crushed girl depends on any contest of wit or words between the counsel and myself, how hopeless it is; and yet I have some homely words, some practical facts and considerations to address to your understandings, which I hope and believe will reach your conviction."

Miss Martinez took the witness stand in her own behalf and told her story:—

"I became acquainted with Juan del Valle under the following circumstances: On or about the fourteenth of January, 1875, when passing through 29th Street, near Broadway, I slipped on a piece of ice and fell on the sidewalk, badly spraining my ankle. Recovering from my bewilderment, I found myself being raised by a gentleman, who called a carriage and took me home. He assisted me into the house, and asked whether he might call again and see how I was getting on. I asked my mother, and she gave him permission. He called the next day, and passed half or three quarters of an hour with me, and told me he was a gentleman of character and position, a widower, and lived at 55 West 28th Street, that he was very much pleased with and impressed by me, and that he desired to become better acquainted. He then asked whether he might call in the evening and take me to the theatre. I told him that my stepfather was very particular with me, and would not permit gentlemen to take me out in the evening, but that, as mother had given her consent, I had no objections to his calling in the afternoon. He called three of four times a week, sometimes with his two younger children, and sometimes taking me to drive in the Park.

"About three weeks after the beginning of our acquaintance he told me he had become very fond of me, and would like to marry me; that his wife had been dead for three years, and that he was alone in the world with four children who had no mother to care for them, and that if I could sacrifice my young life for an old man like him, he would marry me and give me a pleasant home; that he was a gentleman of wealth, able to provide for my every want, and that if I would accept him I should no longer be compelled, either to endure the strict discipline of my stepfather, or to struggle for simple existence by teaching. He gave me the names of several residents of New York, some of whom my stepfather knew personally, of whom I might make inquiries as to his character and position.

"I asked Mr. del Valle whether he was in earnest, saying that I was comparatively poor, and since my stepfather's embarrassment in business had not mingled in society, and wondered that he should select me when there were so many other ladies who would seem more eligible to a gentleman of his wealth and position. He replied that he was in earnest and that he had once married for wealth, but should not do so again. He told me to talk with mother and give him an answer as soon as possible. He said that he loved me from the first moment he saw me, and could not do without me. My mother gave consent and I promised to marry him. Mr. del Valle then took me to Delmonico's and after we had dined we went to a jewellery store in 6th Avenue, and he selected an amethyst ring for an engagement ring, as he said. The ring was too large and was left to be made smaller. Two or three days afterward he called on me at my house, placed the ring on my finger, and said, 'Keep that ring on that finger until I replace it with another.'

"At the third interview after the presentation of the ring, Mr. del Valle said that owing to some difficulties in his domestic affairs, which he called a 'compromise,' he did not think it best to be married publicly, as he feared that the publication of his marriage might cause trouble. So he urged me to marry him immediately and privately. I was greatly surprised, and said: 'If there is any trouble, why marry at all? I hope there is nothing wrong. What is the nature of the "compromise"?' and he replied: 'Oh, there is nothing wrong, but I have a "compromise" in Cuba, and it is not convenient for you or me to marry publicly, as the person concerned might make you trouble.'

"I told Mr. del Valle that I would not marry him privately, and that I would release him from his engagement. A day or two afterward he took me to a restaurant to dine with him, and I then gave him a letter in which I enclosed the engagement ring, and told him I would not marry him privately. This letter I sealed, asking him not to open it until after we had separated. Five or six days afterward he called again, and seemed ill. He said that my letter had made him sick, and he asked, 'What could induce you to write such a letter, Eugénie? You could not have loved me if you thought so much about the nonsense I told you about a compromise. The compromise is all arranged, and I want you to take back the ring, and say when and where we shall be married.' I said I still loved him, and if the 'compromise' had been arranged, I would accept the ring, but would not marry him secretly. He then put the ring on my finger, and said, 'Now I want you to tell when and where we shall get married.' It was finally agreed that we should be married in the fall.

"From the date of this conversation, which was early in March, 1875, until the twenty-eighth of April, 1875, Mr. del Valle called almost daily and took me to theatres and other places, and was received at home by all my family, except my stepfather, as my accepted suitor. He frequently complained that he could not call in the evening, and wished me to live in his house in Twenty-eighth Street, and take charge of his children. I refused, and he then proposed to take a place in the country, where the children could have plenty of air and exercise, if I would go and take charge of them, and as we were to be married so soon, he wished me to get well acquainted with his children, adding that if I really loved him, I need have no doubt about his honorable intentions.

"I laughed at the idea, but finally consented to leave my home and go into the country with his family. As I was losing all my pupils he insisted upon giving me $100 a month. He persuaded me there was no impropriety in his suggestion, as we were to be married, and that I should never return home excepting as his wife. I had told him that my stepfather had threatened to shoot me and any man whom I might marry. He persuaded me to leave my home at once, and as he had not yet secured a country house for the summer, I was to go to the Hotel Royal for a few days and live under an assumed name, which I did. He kept me at the hotel for five weeks, persuading me not to return home, and by the first of June he had secured a country place at Poughkeepsie, and I went there to live with himself and his four children.

"His conduct toward me up to this time had always been everything that could be desired,—always kind and considerate and anxious for my every comfort,—neither by word nor act did he indicate to me that his intention was any other than to make me his wife. He had engaged a very fine mansion at Poughkeepsie, overlooking the

Hudson, fine grounds, and everything one could desire in a country house. Mr. del Valle gave me the keys to the house and told me the entire establishment was under my charge.

"Six days after I arrived at Poughkeepsie he forced his way into my bedroom. I insisted upon an immediate marriage as my right. He told me he had not been able to arrange the compromise in Cuba, and begged me to be reasonable and he would be my life friend; that I could not return home under the circumstances, and that anything I might at any time want he would always do for me. He tried to persuade me that I would best accept the situation as it was, and that it was a very common occurrence. I had no home to go to and did not dare to record the circumstances to my mother; I would have died first. Three months later, or at the end of the summer, his manner entirely changed toward me. I repeatedly asked him for some explanation. He persuaded me that his coldness was assumed to prevent the servants from talking, that he was going to Cuba to try to fix up the compromise, and prevailed upon me to go back to my home and parents and wait. This I did on the sixth of September. After I returned to New York I wrote to him but received no reply, and have never seen him since."

Nothing could be more witty or brilliant than Mr. Choate's own description to the jury of "the appearance of this fair and beautiful woman while she was giving her evidence on the witness stand." It was a part of the exhibition, he said, which no reporter had been adequate to describe.

"Gentlemen, have you seen since the opening of this trial one blush, one symptom of distress upon her sharp and intelligent features? Not one. There was in a critical point of her examination a breaking down or a breaking up, as I should prefer to call it. Her handkerchief was applied to her eyes; there was a loud cry for 'Water, water,' from my learned friend, echoed by his worthy and amiable junior, as though the very Bench itself were about to be wrapped in flames! [*Laughter.*] But when the crisis was over, then it appeared that there had only been a momentary eclipse of the handkerchief,—that she had been shedding *dry* tears all the while! Not a muscle was disturbed; she advanced in the progress of her story with sparkling eyes and radiant smile and tripping tongue, and thus continued to the end of the case!

"The great masters of English fiction have loved nothing better than to depict the appearance in court of these wounded and bleeding victims of seduction when they come to be arrayed before the gaze of the world.

"You cannot have forgotten how Walter Scott and George Eliot have portrayed them sitting through the ordeal of their trials,—the very pictures of crushed and bleeding innocence, withering under the blight that had fallen upon them from Heaven, or risen upon them from Hell. Never able so much as to raise their eyes to the radiant dignity of the Bench [*Laughter*], seeming to bear mere existence as a burden and a sorrow. But, gentlemen, our future novelist, if he will listen and learn from what has been exhibited here, will have a wholly different picture to paint. He will not omit the bright and fascinating smile, the sparkling eye, the undisturbed composure from the beginning to the end of the terrible ordeal. With what zest and relish and keen enjoyment she detailed her story! What must be the condition of mind and heart of the woman who can detail such stories to such an audience as was gathered together here!"

Speaking of the whole case, Mr. Choate said: "Never did a privateer upon the Spanish main give chase to and board a homeward bound Indiaman with more avidity and vigor than this family proposed to board this rich Cuban and make a capture of him. It was a 'big bonanza' thrown to them in their distress."

It will be seen that the one great question of fact to be disposed of in the case was whether there was a breach of any promise of marriage on the part of the defendant to the plaintiff; that being decided in the negative, everything else would disappear from the case. All other matters were simply incidental to that. The conflicting evidence could not be reconciled. One side was wholly true, the other side wholly false, and the jury were to be called upon to say where the truth was. Was there a promise of marriage three weeks after the plaintiff and defendant met on the corner of 29th Street and Broadway?

The plaintiff had stated in substance that after three weeks the defendant proposed marriage and she accepted him; that he took her in a carriage to Delmonico's to lunch and took her to a jeweller's store in Sixth Avenue and there purchased a ring as a binding token of the promise of marriage. That was her case. If the jury believed that, she would succeed. If they did not, her case would fail. That ring was a clincher, according to her statement of the story, given on the heels of the promise of marriage. What else could it mean but to bind that bargain? This was the way the case stood when Mr. Choate rose to cross-examine Miss Martinez.

There could be no better evidence of the success of the particular method of examination that Mr. Choate chose to adopt on this occasion than the comment in the *New York Sun:* "A vigorous cross-examination by Mr. Joseph Choate did not shake the plaintiff's testimony. Miss Martinez told her story over again, only more in detail!" How poor a judge of the art of cross-examination this newspaper scribe proved himself to be! He had entirely failed to penetrate the subtlety of Mr. Choate's methods or to realize that, in the light of the testimony that was to follow for the defence, Miss Martinez, during her ordeal, which she appeared to stand so well, had been wheedled into a complete annihilation of her case, unconsciously to herself and apparently to most of those who heard her.

In sharp contrast to Mr. Choate's style of cross-examination is that adopted by Sir Charles Russell in the cross-examination of the witness Pigott,—which is given in the following chapter,—and where the general verdict of the audience as Pigott left the witness box was, *"smashed."* And yet, though the audience did not realize it, Miss Martinez left the witness stand so effectually "smashed" that there never afterwards could be any doubt in Mr. Choate's mind as to the final outcome of the case. In his summing up Mr. Choate made this modest reference to his cross-examination: "I briefly ask your attention to her picture as painted by herself,—to her evidence, and her letters, giving us her history and her career." And then he proceeded to tear her whole case to pieces, bit by bit, in consequence of the admissions she had unsuspectingly made during her cross-examination.

"And now, gentlemen, with pain and sorrow I say it, has not this lady by her own showing, by her own written and spoken evidence and the corroborating testimony of her sister, *established* her character in such a way that it will live as long as the memory of this trial survives?"

In starting his cross-examination Mr. Choate proceeded to introduce the plaintiff to the jury by interrogating her with a series of short, simple questions, the answers to which elicited from the lady a detailed account of her life in New York since the year of her birth.

She said she was twenty-one years old; was born in New York City; her parents were French; her own father was a wine merchant; he died when she was seven years old; two years later her mother married a Mr. Henriques, with whom she had lived as her stepfather for the fourteen years preceding the trial. She had been educated in a boarding school, since graduation had been employing herself as a teacher of languages, etc., etc.

Mr. Choate had in his possession a letter written by the plaintiff to Mr. del Valle during the first few weeks of their acquaintance. In this letter Miss Martinez had complained of the wretchedness of her home life in consequence of the amorous advances made to her by her stepfather. Mr. Choate was evidently of the opinion that this letter was a hoax and had been written by Miss Martinez for the sole purpose of eliciting Mr. del Valle's sympathy, and of inducing him to allow her to come and live in his family as the governess of his children with the idea that a proposal of marriage would naturally result from such propinquity. Suspecting that the contents of this letter[1] were false, and judging from statements made in the plaintiff's testimony-in-chief that she had either forgotten all about this letter or concluded that it had been destroyed, Mr. Choate set the first trap for the plaintiff in the following simple and extremely clever manner.

Mr. Choate. "By what name did you pass after you returned home from boarding school and found your mother married to Mr. Henriques?"

Miss Martinez. "Eugénie Henriques, invariably."

Mr. Choate. "And when did you first resume the name of Martinez?"

Miss Martinez. "When I left the roof of Mr. Henriques."

Mr. Choate. "Always until that time were you called by his name?"

Miss Martinez. "Always."

Mr. Choate. "Did your father exercise any very rigid discipline over yourself and your sister that you remember?"

Miss Martinez. "He did."

---

[1] DEAR FRIEND: I believe I promised to write and tell you my secret. I will now do so. When I was nine years of age my father died. My mother married my uncle, who is not my father. To make a long story short, papa loves me, and has done everything in his power to rob me of what is dearer to me than my life,— my honor. And ever since I was a little child he has annoyed me with infamous propositions and does so still. You can easily imagine how unhappy and miserable he made me, for I don't love him the way he wishes me to, and I cannot give him what he wants, for I would sooner part with my life. I have only God to thank for my unsullied honor. He has watched over me in all my troubles, for oh, my dear friend, I have had so many, many trials! But it is God's will and I always tried to be a good girl, and now you know my secret, my heart feels light. I now leave you, wishing you all my sincere good wishes, and with many kisses to the dear little girls, I remain your friend.

"Eugénie.

"N.B. I will meet you on Saturday at 1 o'clock, corner of Twenty-eighth Street and Broadway."

Mr. Choate. "When did that rigid discipline begin?"

Miss Martinez. "It commenced when I first knew him."

Mr. Choate. "And it was very rigid, wasn't it?"

Miss Martinez. "It was, very."

Mr. Choate. "Both over yourself and over your younger sister?"

Miss Martinez. "Yes."

Mr. Choate. "Taking very strict observation and care as to your morals and your manners?"

Miss Martinez. "Exceedingly so."

Mr. Choate. "How did this manifest itself?"

Miss Martinez. "Well, in preventing my having any other associates. He thought there was no one good enough to associate with us."

Mr. Choate. "Then he was always very strict in keeping you in the path of duty, was he not?"

Miss Martinez. "Most undeniably so."

Mr. Choate. "Was this a united family of which you were a member? Were they united in feeling?"

Miss Martinez. "Very much so indeed. There are very few families that are more united than we were."

Mr. Choate. "All fond of each other?"

Miss Martinez. "Always."

One can readily picture to himself Mr. Choate and the fair plaintiff smiling upon each other as these friendly questions were put and answered. And the plaintiff, entirely off her guard, is then asked, probably in a cooing tone of gentleness and courtesy that can be easily imagined by any one who has ever heard Mr. Choate in court, the *important* question:—

Mr. Choate. "As to your *stepfather,* you were all fond of him and he of you?"

Miss Martinez. "Very fond of him indeed, and he very fond of us."

Mr. Choate. "And except this matter of his rigid discipline, was he kind to you?"

Miss Martinez. "Very."

Mr. Choate. "And gentle?"

Miss Martinez. "Very gentle and very kind."

Mr. Choate. "Considerate?"

Miss Martinez. "Very considerate always of our happiness, but he did not wish us to associate with the people by whom we were surrounded, as we were not in circumstances to live amongst our class."

Mr. Choate. "When was it that he first introduced the subject of marriage, or forbidding you to marry, or thinking of marrying?"

Miss Martinez. "Well, when I was about sixteen or seventeen."

Mr. Choate. "And was it then that he said that if you married, he would shoot you and shoot any man that you married?"

Miss Martinez. "He did."

Mr. Choate. "That was the one exception to his ordinary gentleness and kindness, wasn't it?"

Miss Martinez. "Yes."

Mr. Choate. "And the only one?"

Miss Martinez. "And the only one."

Mr. Choate. "Your stepfather is no longer living, is he?"

Miss Martinez. He is not. He died last October."

It will be observed that Mr. Choate did not confront the witness at this point with the letter that she had written, complaining of her father's brutal advances to her, and implying the necessity of her leaving her home in consequence. Many cross-examiners would have produced the letter and would have confronted the witness on the spot with the contradiction it contained, instead of saving it for the summing up. It is interesting to study the effect of such a procedure. By a production of this letter, the witness would have been immediately discredited in the eyes of the jury; the full force of the contradictory letter would have been borne in upon the jury as perhaps it could not have been at any other time in the proceeding, and the *Sun* reporter could not have said the plaintiff had not been "shaken." On the other hand, it would have put the witness upon her guard at the very start of her cross-examination, and she would have avoided many of the pitfalls which she confidingly stepped into later in her testimony. All through the examination Mr. Choate had frequent opportunities to put the witness on her guard, but at the same time *off her balance*. It is a mooted question which method is the better one to employ. It all depends upon the nature of the case and the personality of the witness.

Richard Harris, K. C., an English barrister who has written several clever books on advocacy, says: "From a careful observation, I have reluctantly come to the conclusion that in five cases out of six, I would back the advocate and not the case." This is especially true when the suit is for breach of promise of marriage, but when owing to the unwise conduct of the defendant's lawyer at the trial in unnecessarily attacking the woman plaintiff, the verdict of the jury in her favor is really for *slander*. It may have been some such consideration as this which determined Mr. Choate to save his "points" for his summing up.

It is perhaps the *safer* course of the two in cases of this kind, but I doubt very much if, in the great majority of cases, it is the wiser one; for it must be remembered that there are few lawyers at the Bar who can make such use of their "points" in their summations as did Mr. Choate.

Had Miss Martinez been confronted with her own letter in which she had written of her stepfather, "He loves me and had done everything in his power to rob me of what is dearer to me than my life,—my honor. . . . Ever since I was a little child he has annoyed me with infamous propositions," etc., it would be difficult to imagine any way in which she could reconcile her letter and her sworn testimony, and Mr. Choate would have had the upper hand of his witness from that time on.

Furthermore, during the examination of a witness the jury invariably form their opinion of the witness's integrity, and if that opinion is in favor of the witness it is often too late to try to shake it in the summing up. It is usually, therefore, the wiser course to expose the witness to the jury in his true colors during the examination, and, if possible, prejudice them against him at the outset. In such cases, oftentimes, no summing up at all is necessary, and the closing speech becomes a mere matter of form. Many lawyers save their points in order to make a brilliant summing up, but an opinion once formed by a juror is not easily changed by a speech, however eloquent. This is the experience of every trial lawyer.

As evidence of how completely this part of Mr. Choate's case flattened out because it was left until the final argument, it is only necessary to call the reader's attention to all that was said on the subject in the summing up, viz.: "Her letter was read to the jury, which she had delivered to the defendant on the fifteenth of March, revealing her stepfather's barbarous treatment of her. When I was cross-examining her, I did it with that letter in my hand, with a view to what was written in it; so I asked her about the relations existing between herself and her stepfather, and she said he was always kind and loving and considerate, tender and gentle."

Instead of nailing this point in the cross-examination, as Sir Charles Russell, for instance, would have done, Mr. Choate turns quietly to the next subject of his examination, which is one of vital importance to his client, and to the theory of his defence.

Mr. Choate. "Can you fix the date in January when you first saw the defendant, Mr. del Valle?"

Miss Martinez. "It was on the fifteenth day of January, —either the fourteenth or the fifteenth. It was on a Thursday. I had an appointment with my dentist."

Mr. Choate. "Thursday appears by the calendar of that year to have been on the *fourteenth* of January."

Miss Martinez. "That was the day."

The supreme importance of this inquiry lies in the fact that Mr. Choate was in possession of the account books of the jeweler from whom the alleged "engagement ring" had been purchased. These records showed that the ring had been bought on the fifteenth day of January, or *one day after* the plaintiff and the defendant *first met,* and before there had been any opportunity for acquaintance or love making, or any suggestion or possibility of a proposition of marriage and presentation of an engagement ring, which, as the plaintiff said in her own story, had been given her with the express request that she should wear it until another ring should take its place.

Mr. del Valle's version of the story, which Mr. Choate was intending to develop later in the case, was that he had met the plaintiff, was pleased with her, had assisted her to her home, had met her again the following day, had suggested to her, as a little memento of their acquaintance and his coming to her assistance, that she allow him to present her with a ring, and that after lunching together in a private room at Solari's, they had gone to a jeweler's and he had selected for her an amethyst ring in commemoration of the day of their meeting. It was this ring which the plaintiff later tried to convert into an engagement ring, which she claimed was given her *three or four weeks* after she had first made the acquaintance of Mr. del Valle, and after he had repeatedly asked her hand in marriage.

Mr. Choate. "What time in the day was it that you first met Mr. del Valle on this Thursday, the fourteenth day of January?"

Miss Martinez. "About half past two o'clock in the afternoon."

Mr. Choate. "Have you any means of fixing the hour of that day?"

Miss Martinez. "Yes. I had an appointment with my dentist at three o'clock."

Mr. Choate. "Your appointment with the dentist had been previously made, and you were on your way there?"

Miss Martinez. "I was on my way there."

Mr. Choate. "It was at the corner of Broadway and 29th Street that you fell on the ice, was it not?"

Miss Martinez. "It was."

Mr. Choate. "You did not observe the defendant before you fell?"

Miss Martinez. "I did not."

Mr. Choate. "And you had never seen him before?"

Miss Martinez. "I had never seen him before."

Mr. Choate. "Did this fall render you insensible?"

Miss Martinez. "Very nearly so. I fell on my side and was lying down on the ground when Mr. del Valle raised me up. I remember there were some iron railings near there, and I was leaning against these railings while Mr. del Valle hailed a cab, assisted me into it, and took me home. He told me in the cab that he had been following me all the way up Broadway."

Mr. Choate. "Did he tell you for what object he followed you?"

Miss Martinez. "He did not. He merely told me that he was following me."

Mr. Choate. "And you did not ask him for what purpose he followed you?"

Miss Martinez. "I did not."

Mr. Choate. "Did he drive you to your home?"

Miss Martinez. "He did, and when we arrived he assisted me into the house. I had sprained my ankle. He explained my accident to my mother, and that he had brought me home. My mother thanked him and he asked if he might call again and see how I was getting along with my injury."

The plaintiff had explained that it was the serious nature of her injury which had occasioned her allowing a stranger to get her a cab and take her home. However, the clerks in the jeweler's store where the ring was bought *the day following the accident,* remembered distinctly seeing the plaintiff and the defendant together in the jewelery store for over half an hour while they were selecting the ring.

In order to involve the plaintiff in further difficulties and contradictions, Mr. Choate continues in the same vein:—

Mr. Choate. "You were somewhat seriously disabled by your accident, were you not?"

Miss Martinez. "I was."

Mr. Choate. "For how long?"

Miss Martinez. "Well, for two or three days."

Mr. Choate. "A sprained ankle?"

Miss Martinez. "My ankle hurt me very much. I had it bandaged with cold water and lay on the bed for two days. The third day I was able to limp around the room only a little, and the fourth day I could walk around."

Mr. Choate. "How long was it before you got entirely over it so as to be able to go out of doors?"

Miss Martinez. "Well, *I went out the fifth day.*"

Mr. Choate. "And not before?"

Miss Martinez. "And not before."

Mr. Choate. "So that because of the injuries that you sustained, you were confined to the house for five days?"

Miss Martinez. "I was."

Mr. Choate. "And the first day, or January 15 (this was the day she had bought the ring), you were confined to your room and lying upon the bed?"

Miss Martinez. "Yes, sir. I reclined upon my bed. I was not confined in bed as sick."

Mr. Choate. "When was the first time you were with Mr. del Valle at any time except at your mother's house?"

Miss Martinez. "Do you mean the first time that I went out with him?"

Mr. Choate. "Yes."

Miss Martinez. "It was during the week following that in which I met him. I met him on Thursday, the fourteenth, and went out with him sometime during the following week."

Mr. Choate. "What was the place?"

Miss Martinez. "We went to Delmonico's to dine."

* * * * *

Mr. Choate. "Was the ring the only present he gave you, or the first present?"

Miss Martinez. "Oh, no, not by any means."

Mr. Choate. "When did you begin to accept presents from him?"

Miss Martinez. "The first day I went out with him, when we went to Delmonico's, I accepted books from him."

Mr. Choate. "What was the book that he then presented to you?"

Miss Martinez. "Oh, well, I forget the title of it. I think it was 'Les Misérables' by Victor Hugo."

Mr. Choate. "And from that time he continued, when you went out with him, as a general thing, giving you something?"

Miss Martinez. "Giving me books and buying me candies. After we were through dining, he would stop at a confectioner's and buy me something."

Mr. Choate. "Down to the time of the first talk of marriage, which you say was about three weeks after you met, how many times did you go with him to Delmonico's or other restaurants?"

Miss Martinez. "Well, on an average of about two or three times a week."

Mr. Choate. "Where else did you go besides Delmonico's?"

Miss Martinez. "The first time I went to any place with him besides Delmonico's was at the time of the engagement, when he gave me the ring,—when he bought the ring for me."

Mr. Choate. "Where did you go then?"

Miss Martinez. "We went in University Place somewhere. I do not exactly know what street."

Mr. Choate. "What side of University Place was it?"

Miss Martinez. "On the opposite side from Christern's book store."

Mr. Choate (with a smile). "Was it a place called Solari's?"

Miss Martinez (hesitating). "I think it was."

Mr. Choate. "How many times did you go there with him before he gave you the ring?"

Miss Martinez. "I never went there before he gave me the ring. That was the first time I ever went to this place."

Mr. Choate. "How came you way down there in University Place if you live up in 56th Street? Did you make an appointment to be there?"

Miss Martinez. "He came up to the house for me."

Mr. Choate. "Came up and took you down there?"

Miss Martinez. "Yes. Didn't he come up to inquire if I had accepted him as a husband, and ask me if I had consulted with my mother, and ask me what answer I had for him, and had I not told him that I would marry him? It was then that he took me to this restaurant in a carriage, and after that he bought the ring for me."

Mr. Choate. "The same day?"

Miss Martinez. "The very same day."

Mr. Choate. "Some considerable number of weeks, you say, intervened between your first acquaintance and this dinner at Solari's,—this engagement and the giving of the ring?"

Miss Martinez. "About three weeks as nearly as I can fix the time."

Mr. Choate. "Where was this jewelery store where the ring was bought?"

Miss Martinez. "It was on Sixth Avenue. I cannot say near what street it was. I felt cold and tired that day. We walked from Solari's and it seemed to me as though the walk was rather long."

Mr. Choate. "You remember the name of the store?"

Miss Martinez. "I do not."

Mr. Choate. "Should you know the name if I told you?"

Miss Martinez. "No, I never knew the name."

This jeweler took the witness stand for the defence, and testified that Miss Martinez was present on the fifteenth of January, when the ring was bought, according to the entry made in his books, and that in consequence of the ring being too large she had ordered it made smaller, and had returned three days later herself alone, had taken the ring from his hand, and had given him a letter addressed to Mr. del Valle, asking him to deliver it when Mr. del Valle should call to pay for the ring, "although," as Mr. Choate sarcastically put it, "it had been in her fond memory as a cherished remembrance that Mr. del Valle had put it on her finger and told her to keep it there until he replaced it with another. Who does not see," said Mr. Choate, in his summing up, "that the disappearance of the ring from the case as a gift upon a promise of marriage three weeks after the first acquaintance carries down with it all this story of the return of the ring to the defendant, and the defendant's re-return of it to the plaintiff?"

Mr. Choate. "Did you ever go to this store but the one time?"

Miss Martinez. "Never went there but the one time."

Mr. Choate. "And you are sure of that?"

Miss Martinez. "I am very sure of that."

Mr. Choate. "The only time you were there was with Mr. del Valle?"

Miss Martinez. "That was the only time I have ever been in that store in my life."

Mr. Choate. "You say you looked at a solitaire diamond ring?"

Miss Martinez. "Yes, but Mr. del Valle told me that he preferred an amethyst, and I took the amethyst."

Mr. Choate. "There was a considerable difference in the cost, wasn't there, between them?"

Miss Martinez. "There was."

Mr. Choate. "Do you know the cost of the amethyst ring?"

Miss Martinez. "I think it was forty-five dollars."

Mr. Choate. "The cost of a solitaire diamond ring might be many hundreds of dollars?"

Miss Martinez. "One hundred and five dollars, one hundred and ten dollars, one hundred and fifteen dollars, —I do not know."

Mr. Choate. "Did you look at any other jewellery?"

Miss Martinez. "Mr. del Valle asked me if I wished anything else, but I did not."

Mr. Choate here deviated from his former plan of not confronting the witness with the evidence he was intending to contradict her with, and having first shown the witness the letter addressed to Mr. del Valle which she had left at the jeweler's on her second visit there, the handwriting of which the witness denied, Mr. Choate followed with this question:—[1]

Mr. Choate. "Now let me refresh your recollection a little, Miss Martinez. Didn't this visit to the jeweler's take place on the fifteenth of January, the day after you made the acquaintance of Mr. del Valle?"

Miss Martinez. "Oh, no, not by any means, sir."

Mr. Choate. "Sure of that?"

Miss Martinez. "I am very sure of it, for I was confined to my room the day after I first made the acquaintance of Mr. del Valle."

Mr. Choate. "Then you never went to that jeweler's store but once?"

Miss Martinez. "Never. I would not know the store, and do not know. I do not recollect the name or anything about it."

Mr. Choate. "There was some trouble about the ring being too large, wasn't there?"

Miss Martinez. "Yes, the ring was too large for the finger I wished it for."

Mr. Choate. "And orders were left to have it made smaller?"

Miss Martinez. "Yes."

Mr. Choate. "What arrangement was made, if any, for your getting the ring when it should be made smaller?"

Miss Martinez. "There was no arrangement made. Mr. del Valle merely said that when he called upon me again he would bring it to me, and he did bring it to me."

Mr. Choate. "About what time was that; in February?"

Miss Martinez. "It was, I should say, the first week in February. I cannot give the exact date."

Mr. Choate. "Now let me again try to refresh your

[1] This is an illustration of a practice recommended in an earlier chapter, of asking questions upon the cross-examination which you know the witness will deny, but which will acquaint the jury with the *nature of the defence* and serve to keep up their interest in the examination.

recollection. Didn't you yourself go to the jewellery store and get the ring?"

Miss Martinez. "I myself?"

Mr. Choate. "You yourself."

Miss Martinez. "I never went to that jewellery store but once in my life and that was with Mr. del Valle himself while I selected the ring."

* * * * *

On behalf of the defendant Mr. Choate was intending to swear as witnesses a Mr. Louis, who kept the store on Ninth Avenue around the corner from where the plaintiff lived in 44th Street, and a Mrs. Krank, who lived around the corner from her residence on 56th Street, who would both testify that the plaintiff had a confirmed habit of having letters left there,—letters from various gentlemen, some of them having the monogram "F. H.," the initials of Frederick Hammond, the clerk of the Hotel Royal. Mr. Choate also had in his possession a letter of the twenty-second of January, in the plaintiff's handwriting and addressed to Mr. del Valle at the inception of their acquaintance, which read, "Should you deem it necessary to write to me, a line addressed 'Miss Howard, care of J. Krank, 1060 First Avenue,' will reach me." In anticipation of this testimony, Mr. Choate next interrogated the witness as follows:—

Mr. Choate. "Did you ever go by any other name than you own father's name, Martinez, or your stepfather's name, Henriques?"

Miss Martinez. "I did not."

Mr. Choate. "Did you ever have letters left for you directed to 'Miss Howard, care of J. Krank, No. 1060 First Avenue'?" [1]

Miss Martinez. "I never did."

Mr. Choate. "Do you know No. 1060 First Avenue?"

Miss Martinez. "I do not. I have no idea where it is."

---

[1] Mr. Choate took as one theme for his summing up: "The woman who possesses an *alias* in the big cities of the world."

Mr. Choate. "Do you know what numbers on First Avenue are near to your house on 56th Street?"

Miss Martinez. "I do not. I never went on First Avenue."

Mr. Choate. "Did you ever have any letters sent to you addressed to 'Miss Howard, care of Mrs. C. Nelson,' on Ninth Avenue?"

Miss Martinez. "I never did."

Here Mr. Choate again treads upon the toes of the witness's veracity, but it is difficult to see why he did not confront her then and there with her own letter. By adopting such a course he took no chances whatever. He would have dealt her a serious blow in the eyes of the jury. Instead, Mr. Choate contents himself by putting this letter in evidence, while the defendant himself was on the witness stand, and the jury never really saw the point of it until the summing up, when their heads were so full of other things that this serious prevarication of the plaintiff probably went almost unnoticed.[1]

*   *   *   *   *

Mr. Choate. "At the meeting when Mr. del Valle brought the ring to your house, was anybody present?"

Miss Martinez. "Nobody was present."

Mr. Choate. "And I have forgotten how long you said it was that you kept the ring before returning it to him?"

Miss Martinez. "I never told you any stated time."

Mr. Choate. "Well, I would like to know now."

Miss Martinez. "I returned the ring to him when I dissolved the engagement between him and me—about a week or so after I had received the ring."

Mr. Choate. "Then it was only a week that the engagement lasted at first before it was resumed the second time?"

Miss Martinez. "Well, I think so."

The plaintiff had already read in evidence to the jury

[1] The jury remained locked up for twenty-six hours unable to agree upon a verdict, several of them voting for large damages.

a *fabricated copy* of a letter breaking her engagement to the defendant, and returning him the ring. No such letter had in fact been handed to Mr. del Valle, but the plaintiff had substituted this alleged copy for a letter, the original of which Mr. Choate had in his possession, which was the one already referred to, wherein the plaintiff had complained of the brutal solicitations of her stepfather, and had requested him not to read it until he was alone.

Mr. Choate. "Now you have spoken of the circumstances under which you returned him the ring in a letter, with injunction not to open the letter until you separated. What was your purpose in requiring him not to open the letter until he should be out of your presence?"

Miss Martinez. "Because I knew if I told him what my purpose was, he would not accept of it. He would not dissolve the engagement between us, and I wished him to see that I was determined upon it. That was my purpose."

Mr. Choate. "Was not the fact of the ring being in the letter quite obvious from the outside?"

Miss Martinez. "It was, and he asked me what it was."

Mr. Choate. "Where was it that you handed him that letter?"

Miss Martinez. "When we were dining."

Mr. Choate. "At what place? Was it this place you have just mentioned,—Solari's?"

Miss Martinez. "Yes, sir."

Mr. Choate. "How many times had you been there then?"

Miss Martinez. "We went there after our engagement very frequently."

Mr. Choate. "Was that your regular place of meeting after your engagement?"

Miss Martinez. "Sometimes we went to Delmonico's; more frequently we went to Solari's."

Mr. Choate. "And it was there that you handed him the letter? How long before going there had you written the letter?"

Miss Martinez. "It was written the day after he spoke

to me of having a compromise in Cuba. The very day after, I made up my mind to break the engagement."

Mr. Choate. "Tell me, if you please, all that he said when he spoke about this compromise."

Miss Martinez. "Well, we were coming home in a carriage, and he asked me when we should be married, and I told him I did not know; that I was not thinking of it yet for some time, and he said that when we should be married, he would like to be married privately, without anybody knowing anything about it. That he had a good many friends here in New York and people that were apt to talk, and he requested me to marry him privately and at once."

Mr. Choate. "Did he say that he already had a wife as a 'compromise'?"

Miss Martinez. "He did not."

Mr. Choate. "Did he explain in any way what this 'compromise,' as you call it, was?"

Miss Martinez. "He merely told me, 'Oh, there is no secrecy. I have a compromise in Cuba—some trouble there, for reasons best known to myself,' but that it was better to marry privately."

Mr. Choate. "Did you believe he had another wife living in Cuba?"

Miss Martinez. "No."

Mr. Choate. "What was there that you supposed could prevent a man marrying again if he loved a woman, as he said he did you, except the existence of a wife already?"

Miss Martinez. "Well, I thought perhaps he had some alliance with some woman whom he had promised to marry, or was obliged to marry, and could not marry any other woman under those circumstances."

Mr. Choate. "He did not suggest anything of that sort?"

Miss Martinez. "That was only the impression that I received at the time,—what I thought."

Mr. Choate. "And you never had any other impression but that, had you?"

Miss Martinez. "No, I had not."

Mr. Choate. "When you concluded to take him again, it was under that impression?"

Miss Martinez. "Not at all. He told me that the compromise was arranged and had been adjusted. I took him again and became engaged to him."

Mr. Choate. "Your idea of the nature of the compromise when you took him again was that he had been engaged to another woman in Cuba and promised to marry her. Is that it?"

Miss Martinez. "Yes, sir, it was something of that kind."

Mr. Choate. "Then when you concluded to take back the ring, it was upon the understanding that he had broken an engagement with a woman in Cuba. Did it not occur to you as an obstacle, when you took him again, that he had just broken a match with another woman?"

Miss Martinez. "No, not at all."

Mr. Choate. "You did not care for that?"

Miss Martinez. "No. I did not care for it, because I trusted him."

Mr. Choate. "How often did Mr. del Valle visit you at this time?"

Miss Martinez. "Four or five times a week."

Mr. Choate. "Did you and your mother keep these visits of this gentleman and the engagement a secret from your stepfather?"

Miss Martinez. "We did."

Mr. Choate. "And that because of his threat to shoot you and the man if you ever married?"

Miss Martinez. "Yes, sir."

Mr. Choate. "Had your father kept weapons ready?"

Miss Martinez. "Well, no, I do not think he did."

Mr. Choate seems to have changed his mind suddenly upon the advisability of introducing the atrocious stepfather's letter. This was the wrong time to introduce it, if at all, and the following feeble attempt was productive of nothing but a hasty retreat upon his own part.

Mr. Choate. "Did you ever make any complaint to Mr. del Valle of being harshly treated by your stepfather?"

Miss Martinez. "I never did. My father never treated me harshly."

Mr. Choate. "I want you to look at this signature and see whether that is yours on the paper now handed you" (passing a paper to witness).

Miss Martinez. "I could not say whether it is mine or not."

Mr. Choate. "What is your opinion?"

Miss Martinez. "I do not think it is. It does not look like my signature."

* * * * *

Mr. Choate. "How is it that you have produced here a copy of the letter in which you say you enclosed the ring in February or March. How is that?"

Miss Martinez. "I do not know. I merely found a copy one day in a book. I never made a practice of copying."

Mr. Choate. "When and where did you make the copy of that letter?"

Miss Martinez. "I did not make any copy of it after I had sent the letter to Mr. del Valle, but the paper upon which I wrote was defective when I wrote it to him. There was a blot or something on it, and I found the copy afterwards!"

Mr. Choate. "Then you do know exactly how you came to have a copy?"

Miss Martinez. "Yes, it was in my desk drawer, that is all, but I did not make a practice of keeping copies of all the papers."

Mr. Choate. "Did you not say a moment ago that you did not know how you came to have a copy?"

Miss Martinez. "No; I did not say I did not know how I came to have a copy."

Mr. Choate. "In what respect did this copy differ from the original enclosing the ring?"

Miss Martinez. "It did not differ. I only said there was a blot upon the paper and I put it into a drawer and wrote another one, and that paper remained blotted in the drawer for a considerable length of time."

Mr. Choate. "What part of the paper was the blot on?"

Miss Martinez. "The first page."

Mr. Choate. (handing the letter to the witness). *"Whereabouts do you see the blot?"*

Miss Martinez. "Oh, well, it is not on the copy at all."

Mr. Choate. "Oh, you sent the blotted one?"

Miss Martinez. "No, I did not. I kept the blotted one in the drawer. I did not send that."

Mr. Choate. "Where is the blotted one?"

Miss Martinez. "I have it at home. I have a copy of all these letters at home."

Mr. Choate. "Then you made a second copy from that blotted copy?"

Miss Martinez. "I did."

Mr. Choate put one question too many by asking, "Where is the blotted one?" The effect of his previous questions concerning this fabricated copy of a letter was entirely lost by allowing her a chance to reply, "I have the blotted copy at home. I have a copy of all these letters at home." The reply was false, but had she been called upon to produce the blotted copy she could have easily supplied it over night. Mr. Choate had made his point, a good one, but he did not leave it alone and so spoiled it.

All through his examination Mr. Choate skipped from one subject to another, and then, without any apparent reason, returned to the same subject again. This may have been intentional art on his part, or it may have been, as is so often the case in the excitement of a long trial, that new ideas occurred to him which brought him back to old subjects that had apparently already been exhausted. It would have been far more intelligible to the jury to have exhausted one subject at a time. It is asking too much of an ordinary juryman to shift his attention back and forth from one subject to another and expect him to catch all the points and carry clearly in his memory all that has been previously said on the subject. This mistake is almost unavoidable, unless the cross-examination is thought out thoroughly in advance, which, of course, is sometimes impracticable, as perhaps in the instant case.

It was part of the plaintiff's evidence that Mr. del Valle had induced her to leave her home and go to the Hotel Royal under an assumed name until he could engage a house in the country where she could live as the governess to his children, pending their marriage, and on a salary of $100 a month.[1] She said Mr. del Valle's object was to avoid the threat of her stepfather to shoot any man to whom she might become engaged. Mr. del Valle's own version of the story was that Miss Martinez went to the Hotel Royal of her own accord; notified him that she was there, that she had deserted her home in consequence of her stepfather's advances to her, and that she was afraid to return. She then begged him to allow her to teach his children and to live with him in the country. Evidently it was with these facts in mind that Mr. Choate cross-questioned the plaintiff as follows:—

Mr. Choate. "Now you say, Miss Martinez, that you went to the hotel on the twenty-eighth day of April?"

Miss Martinez. "I did."

Mr. Choate. "From where did you go?"

Miss Martinez. "From my own home."

Mr. Choate. "Did you know anybody at that hotel?"

Miss Martinez. "I did not."

Mr. Choate was prepared to show that the plaintiff was acquainted with the clerk of the Hotel Royal, a man by the name of Frederick Hammond, who on several occasions was seen by the bell boys in her room at the Hotel

---

[1] Mr. Choate cross-examined the plaintiff at length on this part of the case and in his summing up exclaimed, "Well, outlandish foreigners have done all sorts of things, and men have various ways of looking at the same thing, but here is a point and here is a question at which I think there are no two ways of looking, and that is that it is contrary to the common instincts of mankind, and a libel upon the common instincts of woman, that when a betrothal has taken place between a fair and unsophisticated virgin and a man of any description, that in the interval between the betrothal and the wedding ceremony, he should take her to his house and she should consent to go upon a salary of $100 a month, to serve in the capacity of a housekeeper. I leave the argument upon the point with you."

Royal, at which times the door of her bedroom was locked. The defendant's evidence subsequently showed, also, that many of the letters sent to the plaintiff under the name of Miss Howard, and addressed to different letter boxes on First Avenue, etc., had on the envelope the monogram "F. H." (Frederick Hammond).

Mr. Choate. "Did you know any of the managers or clerks at the Hotel Royal?"

Miss Martinez. "I did not."

Mr. Choate. "Did you register your name at that hotel?"

Miss Martinez. "I just merely gave my name as 'Miss Livingston.' I did not register. I suppose I was registered." (The name "Miss Livingston" registered on the hotel register was in the handwriting of this same Frederick Hammond.)

Mr. Choate. "To whom did you give your name as 'Miss Livingston'?"

Miss Martinez. "To a gentleman whom I saw before taking board there. I went to arrange for a room the day before, and he asked me my name and showed me a room and I told him my name was 'Miss Livingston,' and he put it down."

Mr. Choate. "Who was that gentleman?"

Miss Martinez. "I do not know who he was, or what he was."

Mr. Choate. "Do you know a gentleman named Frederick Hammond?"

Miss Martinez. "My receipts were signed that way, by the name of Hammond. Mr. del Valle told me that he was acquainted with some of the managers of the hotel, and it was that hotel that he suggested my going to."

Mr. Choate. "You went by his suggestion?"

Miss Martinez. "Went by his suggestion to this hotel."

Mr. Choate. "Did he tell you of Frederick Hammond?"

Miss Martinez. "He did not. He merely said that he knew some of the managers."

Mr. Choate. "You say that Hammond was the name signed to your receipt?"

Miss Martinez. "Yes, sir."

Mr. Choate. "Was that the name of the gentleman to whom you gave your name as 'Miss Livingston'?"

Miss Martinez. "I really do not know."

Mr. Choate. "Was it anybody you had ever seen before?"

Miss Martinez. "I had never seen the person before in my life." [1]

Mr. Choate. "And you do not know how or by whom your name was registered in that hotel book?"

Miss Martinez. "I do not know. The gentleman merely asked me my name and I told him. I told him the room would suit me, and I would come the next day."

Mr. Choate. "Then you went alone both days?"

Miss Martinez. "I did."

Mr. Choate. "And both times without the defendant?"

Miss Martinez. "Without the defendant."

Mr. Choate. "You selected a room that suited you?"

Miss Martinez. "I did. On the top floor. It was the only room that was available."

It was shown later that this room was a small sized hall bedroom, and yet Miss Martinez was supposed to have made this arrangement with this hotel at the request of her wealthy affianced husband. In speaking of this in his summing up, Mr. Choate says:—

"That does not look like Mr. del Valle's generous accommodations. Mr. del Valle was profuse, lavish. She had the richest meats, the finest terrapin, wines of her own choice, always, at Solari's. But here in a little four-by-ten room, in the fourth story of the Hotel Royal,—why, gentlemen, that looks to me a little more like Frederick Hammond, who wrote her name in the hotel register!"

---

[1] Mr. Choate, in his argument to the jury, said: "They went to her room on two separate occasions and found her there with Mr. Hammond with the door locked, Mr. Hammond sitting on the bed. This might have been explained, had she not already said in her cross-examination that she did not know Mr. Hammond. Now how do they meet it?"

Mr. Choate. "Did the defendant select this name of Livingston for you?"

Miss Martinez. "He merely told me to take an assumed name,—to go under some other name,—and I chose the name of Livingston."

The purpose of this line of questions was shown in the summing up to have been as follows:—

"Now, gentlemen, you have all been married, I infer from your appearance. [*Laughter.*] You have been through this mill of an engagement to be married. No matter what kind of a man he is,—he may be as bad as men are ever made, or from that all the way to the next grade below the archangels,—and I put it to you on your judgment and common sense and your conscience, that you cannot find a man who would take the betrothed of his heart, the woman whom he had chosen to be his wife, and the mother of his children,—who would take her to a hotel in the city of New York to live for a longer or shorter period under an assumed name.

"The plaintiff went to this hotel by the name of 'Livingston.' It was a good selection! She says Del Valle did not choose that name. She had already passed by the name under which she could claim the blood of all the Howards, but now she claimed alliance with the notable stock of Livingstons."

Mr. Choate. "Did you object to it when he told you to go there under an assumed name?"

Miss Martinez. "No, I did not."

Mr. Choate. "You were entirely willing to go to a strange hotel alone under an assumed name?"

Miss Martinez. "Yes. For a short while."

Mr. Choate. "I wish you would tell us again precisely what it was that induced you to go to this strange hotel under such circumstances?"

Miss Martinez. "Well, Mr. del Valle suggested that perhaps it would be better for me. He did not wish to have any trouble with my stepfather concerning my disappearance, neither did I wish to give him any unnecessary trouble if my father should take any violent steps of any kind, as he had so often threatened to do, and he suggested that I should take a room somewhere at some hotel, and see how papa would act."

Mr. Choate. "How was papa to know anything about it if you were under an assumed name?"

Miss Martinez. "Well, he certainly would know something about it when I left home."

Mr. Choate. "And the plan was that he should know about it?"

Miss Martinez. "Should know what?"

Mr. Choate. "Should know that you had gone?"

Miss Martinez. "Why, of course."

Mr. Choate. "To this hotel?"

Miss Martinez. "No, not to the hotel. He knew that I had left home, and my fear was that he would hire detectives to search for me, and of course, if he discovered me in Mr. del Valle's home, I could not answer for the consequences."

Mr. Choate. "What consequences did you apprehend?"

Miss Martinez. "I apprehended that he would kill Mr. del Valle and kill me."

Mr. Choate. "And rather than that, you were willing to go to this hotel in this manner?"

Miss Martinez. "Certainly, Mr. del Valle suggested it." [1]

Mr. Choate. "Do you know whether your father did do anything because of your leaving?"

Miss Martinez. "Yes, I know that he put a personal in the *Herald* for me."

Mr. Choate. "Did you show this 'personal' to Mr. del Valle?"

Miss Martinez. "I showed it to him."

Mr. Choate. "Did you discover it in the *Herald?*"

Miss Martinez. "I did."

---

[1] All through the discussion of the plaintiff's testimony, Mr. Choate kept exclaiming to the jury in his final argument, "What sort of an engaged young lady is this!"

Mr. Choate. "The 'personal' in the *Herald* of the second day of May, or about five days after you had reached the hotel, is contained in this paper which I now show you, isn't it?"

Miss Martinez. "Yes."

Mr. Choate. "Now after the second day of May, therefore, you knew that this 'personal' had come from your father, didn't you?"

Miss Martinez. "I did."

Mr. Choate. "After you knew that your father 'was inconsolable and would make all satisfactory,' you did not have any more fear of his shooting you or Mr. del Valle, either, did you?"

Miss Martinez. "I most certainly did. My father was not to be relied upon in what he said at all. He said a great many things which he never meant."

Mr. Choate. "Do you mean that he did not have a good reputation for veracity?"

Miss Martinez. "Not at all. But I knew that he had always threatened to shoot me and my husband, if I ever had done, and I knew that he would not make 'all satisfactory,' and that is why I did not return home."

Mr. Choate. "Did you answer this 'personal'?"

Miss Martinez. "I did not."

Mr. Choate. "Did you take any notice of your unhappy father?"

Miss Martinez. "I did not."

Mr. Choate. "Make no effort to console him?"

Miss Martinez. "I did not. I loved Mr. del Valle, and went with Mr. del Valle and trusted him. I had nothing to do with my father. My father had many others to console him."

Mr. Choate. "While you were at the Hotel Royal did you make a visit to the Central Park with Mr. del Valle?"

Miss Martinez. "Yes, frequently we went up to the Park and walked all around. It was the only chance I had of going out—when he took me up there."

Mr. Choate. "Do you remember anything you told him at that time?"

Miss Martinez. "Nothing in particular."

Mr. Choate. "Did you tell him that your stepfather had been using you brutally?"

Miss Martinez. "I did not. I never told him any such thing."

Mr. Choate. "Did you say that you had to leave home and go to the hotel because of the bad treatment of your stepfather?"

Miss Martinez. "I never did tell him so."

Mr. Choate. "Did you ever tell anybody that?"

Miss Martinez. "I could never tell any one so, because my stepfather never treated me badly."

Later in the trial Mrs. Quackenbos testified on the part of the defendant that while she was visiting Mr. del Valle's summer home at Poughkeepsie, she was introduced to the plaintiff as "Miss Henriques, the housekeeper," and that during the conversation that followed she expressed her surprise at seeing so young a lady in that position. Whereupon the plaintiff had replied that she "had a mystery attached to her life, which she would tell Mrs. Quackenbos and perhaps she would then think differently." She testified that the plaintiff had told her that her mother had married her uncle, and that she lived very unhappily at home owing to her stepfather's constant overtures to her; that her stepfather was enamored of her; that the plaintiff in making this confession had used these words, "That is why I am here, madame. My mamma asked Mr. del Valle to take me from my home." The plaintiff told Mrs. Quackenbos that it was impossible for her to remain at home; that she was almost exhausted from fighting for her honor; and that her mother had begged Mr. del Valle to take her away. In speaking of this evidence in the summing up, Mr. Choate said:—

"Why, she said, gentlemen, that she had been driven from her home by the amorous persecutions of her stepfather, and that her mother had besought Mr. del Valle to take her to his house as his governess and housekeeper. You can't rub that out, gentlemen, if you dance on it all night with India rubber shoes!"

*　　*　　*　　*　　*

Mr. Choate. "When was it that the arrangements were completed and the family moved to the summer home in Poughkeepsie?"

Miss Martinez. "The first of June."

Mr. Choate. "Did you go direct to Poughkeepsie with Mr. del Valle and his children?"

Miss Martinez. "I did."

Mr. Choate. "Now, I understand you that until the end of the first week of your stay at Mr. del Valle's house in Poughkeepsie, that is, until this 6th of June which you have spoken about, and from the 14th of January, when you first made Mr. del Valle's acquaintance, he was uniformly kind and courteous?"

Miss Martinez. "Always."

Mr. Choate. "And there was not the least symptom of impropriety in his conduct towards you?"

Miss Martinez. "Never, sir. He never offered me the slightest indignity on any occasion."

Mr. Choate. "And no approach toward impropriety on his part?"

Miss Martinez. "Never. Not on any single occasion. Not a breath of it."

Mr. Choate. "As to this occurrence of the 6th of June, I understand you to say that after breakfast you went up to your room and lay down?"

Miss Martinez. "I did."

Mr. Choate. "And I understand you to say that was your usual habit?"

Miss Martinez. "Yes, sir. It was not an everyday habit; it was more of a Sunday habit."

Mr. Choate. "What time of the day did you have breakfast on that Sunday?"

Miss Martinez. "At eleven o'clock in the morning."

Mr. Choate. "How do you fix the date?"

Miss Martinez. "I think it is a day in a woman's life that she can never forget." [1]

Mr. Choate. "And you fix it as your first Sunday in Poughkeepsie?"

Miss Martinez. "I do."

Mr. Choate. "Who were the members of the household at that time on that day? Who were they besides yourself and Mr. del Valle?"

Miss Martinez. "There were the two younger children, Mr. Alvarez, and the servants."

Mr. Choate. "How many servants were there?"

Miss Martinez. "There were seven servants."

Mr. Choate. "And your room was where?"

Miss Martinez. "My room was on the same floor with the family and Mr. del Valle's and the children's, and next to the nurse and the two younger children,—all the children, in fact."

Mr. Choate. "Now, at breakfast who were present that morning?"

Miss Martinez. "The children, Mr. Alvarez, Mr. del Valle, and myself."

Mr. Choate. "What time was it you finished breakfast?"

Miss Martinez. "About half past eleven or a quarter to twelve, perhaps twelve o'clock; I do not remember."

Mr. Choate. "And how soon after you had finished breakfast did you go to your room?"

Miss Martinez. "Immediately after."

Mr. Choate. "Did you go alone?"

Miss Martinez. "I did."

Mr. Choate. "What did you do?"

Miss Martinez. "I lay on my bed reading. I could hear the children downstairs. They were on the veranda. I heard their voices as they went away from the house with the nurse."

---

[1] Mr. Choate had in his hand at the time of this examination a letter written by Adèle, the plaintiff's sister, who had just left Poughkeepsie, where she had been making a visit, and in which she referred to her sister as being "as happy as a queen." This letter was later offered in evidence.

Mr. Choate. "You remained on your bed, did you?"

Miss Martinez. "I did. I was interested in my book and I commenced to read."

Mr. Choate. "Did you remain upon the bed from the time you first took your place upon it until Mr. del Valle had accomplished what you charged upon him yesterday?"

Miss Martinez. "I did."

Mr. Choate. "And were not off the bed at all?"

Miss Martinez. "I was not. I had partially arisen when he entered."

Mr. Choate. "The door of your room opened into the centre of the house, did it not?"

Miss Martinez. "It did."

Mr. Choate. "Did you close the door?"

Miss Martinez. "I did."

Mr. Choate. "Did you lock it?"

Miss Martinez. "I did not."

Mr. Choate. "Did you hear any other sound before Mr. del Valle appeared in your room?"

Miss Martinez. "I did not. Merely the children's receding voices in the distance."

Mr. Choate. "This was a warm summer day, was it not?"

Miss Martinez. "It was. The sixth of June."

Mr. Choate. "Were the windows open?"

Miss Martinez. "Yes."

Mr. Choate. "Did Mr. del Valle knock upon the door?"

Miss Martinez. "He did not."

Mr. Choate. "You heard the door open?"

Miss Martinez. "I did."

Mr. Choate. "You saw him enter?"

Miss Martinez. "I did."

Mr. Choate. "And were you lying upon the bed?"

Miss Martinez. "I was."

Mr. Choate. "Did you get up from the bed?"

Miss Martinez. "I just attempted to rise."

Mr. Choate. "Who prevented you?"

Miss Martinez. "He came over to me and sat down on the side of the bed."

Mr. Choate. "Did he shut the door?"

Miss Martinez. "He did."

Mr. Choate. "While he was doing that did you attempt to rise?"

Miss Martinez. "I did."

Mr. Choate. "Why didn't you rise?"

Miss Martinez. "Because I could not. He came over to me before I had partially risen."

Mr. Choate. "Do you mean to say that in the time of his coming in and presenting himself and opening and shutting the door, there was not time for you to spring up from the bed?"

Miss Martinez. "There was not, because he was already half in the room before I heard that he was in. I was engaged in reading at the time, and he had opened the door very softly."

Mr. Choate. "Was there time for you to begin to start from the bed?"

Miss Martinez. "Well, I do not know. I did not study the time."

Mr. Choate. "How long was he in your room that morning?"

Miss Martinez. "I cannot say exactly."

Mr. Choate. "You can say whether he was there an hour, or two hours, or half an hour?"

Miss Martinez. "Well, he was there about an hour."

Mr. Choate. "Did you make an outcry while he was in the room?"

Miss Martinez. "No, I did not scream."

Mr. Choate. "Did not attempt to scream, did you?"

Miss Martinez. "No, I did not attempt to scream. I remonstrated with him."

Mr. Choate. "Did you speak in a loud voice?"

Miss Martinez. "Well, not to be heard all over the house, but if anybody had been in the room he would have heard me."

Mr. Choate. "Did you speak low?"

Miss Martinez. "Lower than I am speaking now."

Mr. Choate. "You did not make any effort to make yourself heard by anybody in the house, or outside?"

Miss Martinez. "No, I was not afraid of Mr. del Valle. I did not think he came into my room to murder me, nor to hurt me."

Mr. Choate. "You found out, according to your story, what he did come for, after a while, didn't you?"

Miss Martinez. "Yes."

Mr. Choate. "And before he accomplished his purpose?"

Miss Martinez. "Yes."

Mr. Choate. "Now, didn't you speak above a low voice then?"

Miss Martinez. "Well, perhaps I did."

Mr. Choate. "Well, did you?"

Miss Martinez. "I think I did."

Mr. Choate. "Well, did you scream out?"

Miss Martinez. "I did not."

Mr. Choate. "Did you call out?"

Miss Martinez. "I did not."

Mr. Choate. "Did you speak loud enough to be heard by any of the servants below, or anybody in the hall or on the veranda?"

Miss Martinez. "I do not think anybody could have heard me."

Mr. Choate. "Why didn't you cry out?"

Miss Martinez. "Because—he told me not to."

Mr. Choate. "Oh, he told you not to?"

Miss Martinez. "Yes."

Mr. Choate. "Then it was a spirit of obedience to him."

Miss Martinez. "Just as you please to look upon it."

Mr. Choate. " 'Just as I please to look upon it'?" Well, I look upon it so. Now you say that you do not think he had any evil purpose when he came into the room?"

Miss Martinez. "No, I cannot believe he did."

Mr. Choate. "And you do not think so now?"

Miss Martinez. "Oh, I do think so now, certainly."

Mr. Choate. "You did not think so then?"

Miss Martinez. "No, I did not when he entered the room."

Mr. Choate. "There was nothing indicating an evil purpose on his part?"

Miss Martinez. "No, I do not think so."

Mr. Choate. "How long had he been there before there was anything on his part that indicated to you any evil intent?"

Miss Martinez. "About fifteen minutes."

Mr. Choate. "Before you had the least idea of any evil intent on his part?"

Miss Martinez. "Well, I did not then think he had any evil intent."

Mr. Choate. "Were you fully dressed that morning?"

Miss Martinez. "Fully dressed."

Mr. Choate. "And fully dressed when he came into the room?"

Miss Martinez. "Fully dressed."

Mr. Choate. "Just as you had been at breakfast?"

Miss Martinez. "Just the very same."

Mr. Choate. "You were lying on the bed. Where was he?"

Miss Martinez. "He was also on the bed."

Mr. Choate. "Sitting by your side?"

Miss Martinez. "Yes."

Mr. Choate. "And you and he were engaged in conversation, were you?"

Miss Martinez. "We were."

Mr. Choate. "Sometime during that hour you became partly undressed, I suppose. When was that?"

Miss Martinez. "How do you know I became partly undressed?"

Mr. Choate. "I judge so from what you have stated. I beg your pardon. Did you, or did you not?"

Miss Martinez. "No, I did not become undressed. Merely Mr. del Valle took my belt off. I had a wrapper on. I had a black silk belt."

Mr. Choate. "You had a belt? How was that secured?"

Miss Martinez. "Just merely by hook and eye. It was a black silk ribbon belt."

Mr. Choate. "And that became unhooked?"

Miss Martinez. "It did not *become* unhooked; Mr. del Valle unhooked it."

Mr. Choate. "What was it you did when he unhooked the belt? Did you cry out?"

Miss Martinez. "No, I did not cry out. I told you I made no outcry whatever."

Mr. Choate had made his point. Immediately the idea flashed across his mind that if he stopped here he had one of the opportunities of his life for the summing up. This is how he made use of it:—

"Gentlemen of the jury: This is not a story of Lucretia and Tarquin, who came with his sword. Oh, no, there was not any sword. They conversed together. There is not a word as to what was said, and after a while, the story is, he unbuckled her belt and then it was all over! On the unloosening of her belt, she went all to pieces! Gentlemen, my question to you, which I want you to take to the jury room and answer, is whether, under such circumstances, by the mere undoing of that hook and eye, and the unloosening of that belt, a woman would go all to pieces unless there was something of a very loose woman behind the belt! All the household was there. Why did she not cry out? Why did she not raise that gentle-tempered voice of hers a little? A silent seduction, by her own story!"

*   *   *   *   *

Mr. Choate. "Now, Miss Martinez, you have spoken of your father being sometime or other informed of your having gone to Poughkeepsie, and did you also understand that he was informed of your project of marriage?"

Miss Martinez. "Yes, sir, he was."

Mr. Choate. "Did he come up with his revolver?"

Miss Martinez. "He did not."

Mr. Choate. "Did he make any effort to see you?"

Miss Martinez. "No, he did not."

Mr. Choate. "Did he make any effort to see Mr. del Valle?"

Miss Martinez. "He did not."

Mr. Choate. "He appeared at Poughkeepsie after a while, did he not?"

Miss Martinez. "Yes, he did. My mother revealed the fact to him that I was at Poughkeepsie and engaged to be married to Mr. del Valle, and insisted upon his acting reasonably."

Mr. Choate. "And he did act reasonably, did he not?"

Miss Martinez. "He did."

Mr. Choate. "He came up making visits?"

Miss Martinez. "He did."

Mr. Choate. "Was Mr. del Valle at home?"

Miss Martinez. "He was."

Mr. Choate. "And you were there?"

Miss Martinez. "I was."

Mr. Choate. "Did you see the meeting between your father and Mr. del Valle?"

Miss Martinez. "I did. I introduced my father to Mr. del Valle."

Mr. Choate. "Everything was agreeable and pleasant, was it?"

Miss Martinez. "Very pleasant indeed."

Mr. Choate. "And your father stayed to dinner?"

Miss Martinez. "He did."

Mr. Choate. "Did he make any threats?"

Miss Martinez. "He did not."

Mr. Choate. "Did he exhibit any violence?"

Miss Martinez. "He did not."

Mr. Choate. "Then all your fears proved to have been unfounded, didn't they?"

Miss Martinez. "Not at all."

Mr. Choate. "You think that after all, if you had married Mr. del Valle, he would have carried his threats into execution?"

Miss Martinez. "I think he would, most certainly."

Mr. Choate. "And yet he came up pleasantly and spent

the day with Mr. del Valle and you at Mr. del Valle's house, knowing that you were living in his house?"

Miss Martinez. "Yes."

Mr. Choate. "Upon a promise of marriage?"

Miss Martinez. "He did."

Mr. Choate. "Did he try to dissuade you from marrying?"

Miss Martinez. "He did not."

Mr. Choate. "And yet you think that if you married, he would have shot you and Mr. del Valle?"

Miss Martinez. "I do most certainly think so."

* * * * *

Mr. Choate. "Miss Martinez, did you write a letter, dated September 8, to Mr. del Valle?" [1]

Miss Martinez. "I did."

Mr. Choate. "Is this the letter which I now show you?"

Miss Martinez. "Well, it may be, but I would not swear to it."

Mr. Choate. "Will you swear it is not?"

Miss Martinez. "No, I would not swear it is not."

Mr. Choate. "In this letter you say, 'I have been very happy in your house'?"

Miss Martinez. "Yes."

Mr. Choate. "That was true, was it not?"

Miss Martinez. "It was very true."

Mr. Choate. "During that period was it true that you were 'very happy' in his house?"

Miss Martinez. "Until the 6th of June, the Sunday I told you about a little while ago."

Mr. Choate. "That was four days?"

Miss Martinez. "Well, that was some time."

Mr. Choate. "You got there on the night of the first, didn't you?"

Miss Martinez. "Yes, I did."

[1] The student's attention is directed to this extremely clever use, in cross-examination, of a letter which was wholly inconsistent with the story of her stay at Poughkeepsie, which the plaintiff had already sworn to.

Mr. Choate. "And your happiness came to an end on the morning of the 6th?"

Miss Martinez. "Yes, it did."

Mr. Choate. "And that was what you meant when you wrote, 'I have been very happy in your house'?"

Miss Martinez. "I did, and up to the time when I heard of the compromise not being adjusted."

Mr. Choate. "Oh, you were very happy till then?"

Miss Martinez. "Yes."

Mr. Choate. " 'I will always think of the many happy hours spent with you.' What did you mean by 'the many happy hours'?"

Miss Martinez. "What did I mean by it?"

Mr. Choate. "Yes, what hours did you mean?"

Miss Martinez. "I meant the hours that I spent with Mr. del Valle and which were happy."

Mr. Choate. "Before the 6th of June?"

Miss Martinez. "Yes."

Mr. Choate. "And none after?"

Miss Martinez. "Not many."

Mr. Choate. "Then your object in writing this letter was to thank him for the many happy hours spent with him between the afternoon of the 1st of June, when you arrived, and the morning of the 6th of June, was it?"

Miss Martinez. "It was."

Mr. Choate. " 'And which were the only ones I have ever known.' What did you mean by that,—to compare the hours of those four days of June with all the previous hours of your life?"

Miss Martinez. "I meant with all the previous hours of my life—I had never been happy in all my life."

Mr. Choate. "As in those four days?"

Miss Martinez. "No."

Mr. Choate. "What was it that prevented your being equally happy from the time of your engagement down to the first of June?"

Miss Martinez. "Oh, I don't think it was a very happy state of mind I was in, to be engaged to Mr. del Valle and could not see him as I wished to, occasionally in the evenings. I was restricted."

Mr. Choate. "It was the restrictions that were placed upon your seeing Mr. del Valle, and yet you saw him eight times a week, I think you testified, and every day you spent hours in his company?"

Miss Martinez. "Not every day."

Mr. Choate. "Well, whenever you met?"

Miss Martinez. "Yes."

Mr. Choate. "And you were alone together?"

Miss Martinez. "We were."

Mr. Choate. "And his conduct towards you during all these hours was absolutely unquestionable?"

Miss Martinez. "Unquestionable."

Mr. Choate. "Why, then, did you say that the hours of the 2d, 3d, 4th, and 5th of June that you spent with him, were the only happy hours that you had ever known compared with the previous hours spent with Mr. del Valle?"

Miss Martinez. "It was just merely from the fact that my father's manner and way towards me made me always unhappy."

Mr. Choate. "That is, the fear that your father, if he found it out, would shoot you and your intended?"

Miss Martinez. "It was."

Mr. Choate. "You still had that fear during the 2d, 3d, 4th, and 5th of June, it seems, didn't you?"

Miss Martinez. "No, I didn't have that fear as much as I had."

Mr. Choate. "You said that was not dissipated until your father's second visit in August."

Miss Martinez. "So it was not, but I did not have as much fear then as I had before."

Mr. Choate. "Oh, because your father was in New York and you at Poughkeepsie?"

Miss Martinez. "Yes."

Mr. Choate. " 'I leave it to God to grant you the reward you so much deserve, and which is impossible for you to receive on this earth.' Reward for what, do you mean?"

Miss Martinez. "Oh, I had a conversation with Mr. del Valle before I wrote that letter to him."

Mr. Choate. "I am asking you now the meaning of this letter. What acts and conduct of his was it, taken all together, that you left it to God to reward him for, because it was impossible for him to have any reward on earth for it?"

Miss Martinez. "I did not mean at all what I wrote."

Mr. Choate. "Oh, you did not mean what you wrote?"

Miss Martinez. "No, I did not. I merely wished to keep Mr. del Valle as my friend."

Mr. Choate. "Are you in the habit now of writing what you do not mean?"

Miss Martinez. "I am certainly not in the habit."

Mr. Choate. "But this you did not mean at all, did you?"

Miss Martinez. "Oh, I meant some of it, some I didn't."

Mr. Choate. "How much of it did you mean? Did you mean that you 'left it to God to grant the reward he so much deserved'; or did you mean 'that it was impossible for him to receive that reward on earth'? Which part of it did you mean?"

Miss Martinez. "I meant no part of that."

Mr. Choate. "Did you understand that Mr. del Valle was to come and see you in New York?"

Miss Martinez. "I did, certainly."

Mr. Choate. "And so you understood when you wrote this letter?"

Miss Martinez. "I did."

Mr. Choate. "Now you began, 'My dear friend, it may be that I may never see you again.' What did you mean by that?"

Miss Martinez. "Because I doubted his word, and thought perhaps I should never see Mr. del Valle again, treating me as he had."

Mr. Choate. "You doubted his word, and you wrote him what you did not mean at all. Does that represent the real state of the relations between you at that time?"

Miss Martinez. "Well, the relations between us at the time would be very difficult indeed to define."

Mr. Choate. "I will complete the first sentence, 'still, I feel that I cannot leave your house without thanking you for all your kindness to me.'"

Miss Martinez. "Mr. del Valle always was very kind to me, always."

Mr. Choate. "And you thought that, taking his whole conduct together from the beginning to the end of your stay, it was incumbent upon you not to leave without thanking him for all his kindness to you. Is that so?"

Miss Martinez. "Yes."

Mr. Choate. "And you meant that, didn't you?"

Miss Martinez. "Well, no, I didn't mean it exactly."

Mr. Choate. "'I have been very happy in your house.' Did you mean that?"

Miss Martinez. "I was very happy in his house and I was very miserable."

Mr. Choate. "After you got to New York, Mr. del Valle did not come to see you?"

Miss Martinez. "He did not."

Mr. Choate. "And you have never seen him since until you saw him in this court room?"

Miss Martinez. "I have not."

*   *   *   *   *

Mr. Choate. "In those visits to Solari's you spoke of the other day, did you always have a private room, no one being present but yourselves and the waiter?"

Miss Martinez. "We did have a private room."

Mr. Choate. "Did you always have the same room?"

Miss Martinez. "No, not always."

Mr. Choate. "How many different private rooms should you think you had at Solari's?"

Miss Martinez. "I can't tell you how many different ones,—perhaps two or three."

Mr. Choate. "Was Mr. del Valle's demeanor to you on such occasions the same as it was when you were in your mother's house and in the street, and in public places like the opera and matinée?"

Miss Martinez. "Always the same in a private room as he was at home when my mother was not there. He used to kiss me frequently, but he never kissed me at matinées, nor did he kiss me in the street. Our intercourse and behavior, therefore, must have been different."

Mr. Choate. "Otherwise it was the same?"

Miss Martinez. "Always most respectful."

Mr. Choate. "As to his kisses, of course you made no objection?"

Miss Martinez. "None at all."

Mr. Choate. "How long were these interviews at Solari's,—these meetings when you went there and had a private room generally?"

Miss Martinez. "They varied in length. Sometimes we arrived there at two o'clock and remained until four,— sometimes we arrived there a little earlier."

Mr. Choate. "About a couple of hours."

Miss Martinez. "Two or three hours."

Mr. Choate. "What were you doing all that time?"

Miss Martinez. "We were eating."

Mr. Choate. "What, not eating all the time?"

Miss Martinez. "Eating all the time."

Mr. Choate. "Two hours eating! Well, you must have grown fat during that period!"

Miss Martinez. "Well, perhaps you eat much quicker than I do."

Mr. Choate. "You think you ate all that time?"

Miss Martinez. "Well, I do not say we gormandized continually."

Mr. Choate. "But pretty constantly eating; that was the only business?"

Miss Martinez. "First we had our dinner and then there was a digression of about half an hour before we called for dessert. That perhaps took up another hour."

Mr. Choate. "During that 'digression' what did you generally do?"

Miss Martinez. "We used to talk."

Mr. Choate. "How did Mr. del Valle progress with his English?"

Miss Martinez. "Very well indeed. Remarkably well."

Mr. Choate. "Did you practise English at Solari's?"

Miss Martinez. "Yes, frequently."

Mr. Choate. "That was a pretty constant occupation at all your meetings in those private rooms at Solari's, wasn't it,—practising or speaking English?"

Miss Martinez. "We frequently spoke about the rules of the language."

Mr. Choate. "Did his English during these intervals improve?"

Miss Martinez. "I think it did."

Mr. Choate. "And you did all you could to improve it, I suppose?"

Miss Martinez. "Undeniably so."

Mr. Choate. "You even had a book of conversation with you?"

Miss Martinez. "We had."

Mr. Choate. "And did he make great efforts at those times to improve and advance his English?"

Miss Martinez. "I believe he did."

Referring in his summing up to this part of the examination, Mr. Choate said:—

"What I am endeavoring to show you, gentlemen, is that the action of the parties does not confirm this idea of a promise of marriage, because from what you have heard of this place, from the sentiment which has made itself apparent in this court room whenever the name Solari was mentioned, I think you will bear me out in saying that it is not a place where ladies and gentlemen go for courtship with a view to matrimony. From what you know of the place, if you had made the acquaintance of a young woman and become betrothed to her, is it to Solari's you would go to do your courting with a view to matrimony? All of us, every juryman, will say 'no',—and will you not judge the defendant as you judge yourselves?

"The defendant was tickled, attracted, and pleased. Here was a woman who could speak his own language and they could pick up the broken fragments of his English and her Spanish, and put them together, and he liked nothing better, and so they went to Solari's!

"Well, gentlemen, I do not know anything about Solari's except what is shown here upon the evidence. So far as I can make out, however, people go to Solari's for all sorts of purposes. Men go there with ladies, ladies with ladies, men with men, theatre parties, family parties, matinée parties,—all sorts of parties,—and *these* parties went there together. But under the developments of this case, Solari's assumes new importance and acquires a new fame. It is no longer a mere restaurant. It is no longer a mere place for refreshment for the body, where you can get meat and wine and whatever is pleasant for the inner mind; it now attains celebrity as a new school of learning, patronized, brought into notice, by my client and the fair plaintiff as a place where you can go to drink of the Fountain of Knowledge. [*Laughter.*] They had a 'Guide to Conversation.'

"I think the fair plaintiff said that there were 'digressions' there. They ate and drank,—she thinks they ate and drank for two hours at a time, but I compelled her to say that there was an intermediate 'digression.' What there was in the digressions does not exactly appear; for one thing, there was this 'Guide to Conversation,' but there were limits even to the regions to which this Guide led them, for they both agreed that it did not bring them even to the vestibule of Criminal Conversation, which is a very important point to consider in connection with the history of these meetings at Solari's." [*Roars of laughter.*]

* * * * *

Mr. Choate. "During the period of your engagement from early in February down to the time of going to Poughkeepsie, did you ever, while with Mr. del Valle, fall in with any of his friends or acquaintances?"

Miss Martinez. "I did, on several occasions."

Mr. Choate. "Were you introduced?"

Miss Martinez. "No, but on one occasion some of his friends were at the matinée." [1]

Mr. Choate. "Were you introduced to them there, and if so, who were they?"

Miss Martinez. "I was not."

Mr. Choate. "During the period of this engagement, as you say, to you, did he introduce you at all to anybody?"

Miss Martinez. "During the period of our engagement?"

Mr. Choate. "Yes."

Miss Martinez. "No, I think not."

Mr. Choate. "Then he certainly did not introduce you to anybody as his intended wife?"

Miss Martinez. "He did not. I was not introduced to anybody."

Mr. Choate. "When you were at Poughkeepsie did any person come to the house to make a visit?"

Miss Martinez. "They did."

Mr. Choate. "Were you introduced to them?"

Miss Martinez. "I was."

Mr. Choate. "By whom?"

Miss Martinez. "By Mr. del Valle."

Mr. Choate. "How?"

Miss Martinez. "As the instructress of his children, or governess, or something of that kind."

Mr. Choate. "Never in all that time did he introduce you to anybody as his intended wife?"

Miss Martinez. "No, he did not wish anybody to know it, he said."

Mr. Choate. "When did he say that?"

Miss Martinez. "He told me so when he expected Mrs. Quackenbos' visit before she arrived."

---

[1] When speaking of this phase of the case to the jury, Mr. Choate said, "I will say this, that where there is a betrothal, the parties do give some symptoms of it sooner or later. You cannot prevent their showing it, and there is no suggestion of evidence that anybody saw these parties together acting toward each other as though they were engaged."

Mr. Choate. "That was some three months after your engagement?"

Miss Martinez. "It was."

Mr. Choate. "He did not intimate for the first three months a desire that nobody should know, did he?"

Miss Martinez. "He never said a word to me about anyone's knowing anything about it."

Mr. Choate. "And if there was any concealment, it was not on his part?"

Miss Martinez. "It was not, nor on my part either."

Mr. Choate. "Nor his desire?"

Miss Martinez. "Nor on my part either."

This gave Mr. Choate an opportunity for this final shaft at the plaintiff in his summing up:—

"You see, gentlemen, what an immense advantage it would be for her, for this family, if they could make this 'consolidated Virginia,' in the form of my client, their own. They had no possible means of support; he hove in sight, a craft laden, as they supposed, with treasure for themselves. If there had been this engagement of marriage, the world would have heard of it. I don't mean the *World* newspaper—it hears of everything—but all the world that surrounds the Henriques and Martinez family. The news would have spread that they had captured a prize and brought it into court for condemnation!"

After deliberating for twenty-six hours the jury returned a verdict in favor of the plaintiff, and assessed the damages at fifty dollars.

Chapter 19

The Cross-Examination by Henry W. Taft

of Dr. Charles Dana, Dr. Frederick Peterson and Dr. Smith Ely Jelliffe, expert witnesses, in the litigation over the will of Andrew F. Kennedy

ANDREW F. KENNEDY, a bachelor, had for more than thirty-five years prior to his death been conducting a men's clothing store in New York City. It had been a very prosperous business. At the age of sixty-seven, Mr. Kennedy suffered an apoplectic stroke. He was taken to a hospital and placed on the danger list. His right side was paralyzed and his power of speech temporarily destroyed. He remained in the hospital until his death.

On December 11, 1917, after he had been in the hospital about three weeks, Mr. Kennedy executed his Last Will and Testament. On January 5, 1918, he executed a Codicil. By these instruments he left his business of the value of about $500,000 to three of his employees, and other valuable property to friends and other employees. Small bequests were made to his two nephews and two nieces, his only next-of-kin, to whom he also left his residuary estate, which was of little or no value.

On the night of January 29, 1918, Mr. Kennedy cut his own throat with a razor which he had obtained by stealth, and on January 30th he died.

His two nieces contested the probate of the will on the ground, among others, that Mr. Kennedy at the time of making the will and codicil was lacking in testamentary capacity. To establish that fact the contestants placed on the stand three eminent alienists, none of whom had ever seen Mr. Kennedy. Their testimony was given in answer to a long hypothetical question. The question did not, however, include certain facts testified to by the witnesses for the proponents. These were (*a*) the relationship existing between Mr. Kennedy and his employees and others to whom he left the bulk of his estate; (*b*) his interest and activity in the current problems of his business during the time he was at the hospital; (*c*) that prior to the execution of the will he had told his nurse in detail the provisions of the will; and (*d*) his actions, general physical condition and mental capacity while in the hospital, as testified to by his nurses and doctors.

The hypothetical question was propounded to the three experts who were called—Dr. Charles Dana, Dr. Frederick Peterson, and Dr. Smith Ely Jelliffe—by Charles H. Tuttle, who represented the contestants. All three of these doctors had testified that in their opinion the testator had not the mental capacity to make a valid will or to comprehend the way in which he was disposing of his property. Dr. Dana at that time was one of the most plausible expert witnesses in this kind of litigation. He stood at the top of his profession as an alienist and neurologist, but he was essentially an honest witness and while he would parry with the cross-examiner as long as he could in his attempt to sustain the position taken by his side of the case, yet if properly handled by a lawyer who knew how to do it, he had too much respect for himself and his profession to swear to anything but his honest opinion. This is the way Mr. Taft handled him on cross-examination:

Mr. Taft: "Dr. Dana, it is proven in this case that at the time the testator went into the hospital he was attended by a nurse who was with him half of the day during the entire period that he was there. Just before he was to execute the will which is propounded for probate, he stated to his nurse a number of the important provisions of his will as they were contained in the paper which was just about to be executed. I will state to you the things which he stated. The principal part of his property was his business on Cortlandt Street which he had been conducting for over thirty years and that, as you will perceive by the provisions of this hypothetical question Mr. Tuttle has put to you, was left to three of his employees. You recall that, don't you?"

A. "Yes."

Q. "Now, just before he signed his will he stated to his nurse, that is, he mentioned to her, that part of the business was going to Miss Crowley, to Mr. Devinney, and to Mr. Nagel, and whatever was in the house was to be divided among them. The nurse's words were, 'I heard him speak about two of his nieces. He mentioned Harriet and Catherine, $25,000 to each; $1,000 to his nephew, and to Dominick, I do not know his last name, $2,500; to another man in the store, $2,500; to still another one $500; and to a third one $100. He also mentioned $5,000 to Miss Leighte. That is all I remember.' You will perceive that these bequests, as he informed the nurse before the act of making the will, are substantially correct as to the principal provisions of the will. Would that have any bearing upon your opinion as to his competency to dispose of his property to the persons to whom he actually did dispose of it, assuming that this evidence is correct?"

A. "I do not think it could be. Either what you say is not correct or else the hypothetical question is not correct. I mean to say that it is not possible for me to conceive of a man, who is described as being unable to articulate words distinctly and using not more than one or two words at a time, as still being able to express himself in the way you state he did if he wanted so many thousands to go to one man and so much to another. Why, of course, if that is true, I admit anything you wish. In other words, if it is proved that he was perfectly sane, intelligent, and capable of understanding the nature of his affairs, that is all there is to it."

Q. "If that is the fact then, that on the day he executed the will he repeated these provisions to the nurse, then you would be of the opinion that he had sufficient mental capacity to make a will?"

A. "It is not enough for him just to repeat it. If he said all these things voluntarily and showed by his answers and questions and his statements that he knew all about the business and knew how he was disposing of it and mentioned to whom he was distributing it, yes. There is no evidence in what you have told me that this is so. The nurse said he said it, but he could not have said it."

Q. "But the nurse testified under oath that he said it?"

A. "Well?"

Q. "You must assume that it is a fact and if it is true then I understand that your opinion is he did have capacity?"

A. "Well, we have to have things put a little differently, Mr. Taft. I mean that even if he said thus and so, I would have to know whether he articulated sentences and made these certain definite provisions, or whether the nurse said things to him to which he nodded his head and which she then interpreted in her own way. If the nurse is correct, and the evidence shows that he articulated a sentence, such as, 'I hereby wish to give so much money to John Jones, so much to Mr. Smith,' and went on talking that way, then I say he definitely did have knowledge of what he was doing, if that is what you meant by your question?"

Q. "Yes, that is what I meant. Now suppose that it appeared that from day to day he did attend to his business on Cortlandt Street, saw his people, asked them to report to him, and they did report to him figures and he kept in touch with his business all the time, would that have any effect on your judgment?"

A. "It would depend on how much he did. It would not make any difference if he just saw people from the store and gave assent to routine matters."

*   *   *   *   *

Q. "Would you give a great deal of weight as to just what he did in transacting his business for the six or eight weeks that he was in the hospital, up to the time of his death, and if you were investigating the case, would you seek to find out to what extent he attended to his affairs and was able to do so?"

A. "Yes."

Q. "And if it is proved that as a matter of fact he required his chief employees to come to the hospital and report to him the transactions of the day and caused the nurse to telephone to them concerning daily operations of his business, you would regard those facts as having a decided importance as to his capacity to deal with his business?"

A. (Still sparring.) "I do not think so necessarily. When a man is weakened mentally and depressed, it is advisable to have him pursue as much as possible his old occupations to keep him more or less interested in going through the routine measures."

Q. "But if on those occasions he did precisely the things which he was accustomed to do in the management of his business before he had the apoplectic stroke, that would have an effect upon your judgment, would it not?"

A. "If he did precisely the same things as he did when he was well, yes."

Q. "Suppose he, being the owner of real estate, himself decided to raise the rent of his tenants, would that help you in forming your opinion of his mental condition?"

A. "I do not think so, no. That might have been unwise. It might have been just silly. It would of itself indicate nothing."

Q. "You spoke a while ago of advertising?"

A. "I would think a person of a rather weak mind could revise an advertisement; that is ordinary routine work. He knows what he wants to advertise and to change a phrase would not mean anything particularly to me as regards his mental condition. I mean, he still might be very seriously deteriorated."

Q. "But if he of his own accord summoned a lawyer, saying that he wished to execute his will and then proceeded to give to the lawyer, of his own motion, instructions in detail as to what he wished inserted in his will, would that affect your judgment?"

A. "If he really did that, and voluntarily told what things he wanted; but I do not think it could be easily proved that such a thing could occur because the man's mind was deteriorated. You, Mr. Taft, are making assumptions which involve a lot of other assumptions which to my mind cannot be assumed so easily."

Q. "Now, if twenty days after the stroke, of his own motion, he caused his lawyer to be summoned and then voluntarily and without suggestion gave him material as to the provisions of the will that he wanted drawn, what would you then say?"

A. "If you propose that that be assumed, why, that is assuming that his mind is rational and normal."

Q. "If that testimony is true, it would affect your judgment?"

A. "Yes."

Q. "Which you heretofore expressed as to his capacity?"

A. "Certainly. It is practically assumed that he is normal. Therefore, I cannot state that he was not."

*   *   *   *   *

Q. "By any chance have you been influenced in your judgment as to his rationality by the provisions of his will?"

A. "Somewhat."

Q. "In other words, you have permitted your judgment as to the kind of a will which a normal man would normally make to influence you as one circumstance in forming a judgment as to this man's capacity to make a will?"

A. "Yes."

Q. "Will you please now state which of the provisions of the will you would regard as being of an abnormal character?"

A. "If you are going to ask me about these things one by one, I do not think I can answer very satisfactorily. A man makes up his mind as an expert or a specialist as to the mental condition of a person. I do not pick out single items. For example, I know from experience that a man is abnormal by the general expression of his features. One thing has affected me, that I will admit. Here is a rich man and he makes a will. It would have been perfectly possible for him, if he had intelligence, to have had his condition certified to by competent people and he did not do it. His will is certified to by a young doctor, only six months out of a medical college. It is a will which, so far as I understand it, is unjust to his blood relations and rather unexpected and unnatural as regards the disposition of his property; and it has affected me with the idea, not necessarily that he was insane, but that his mind had deteriorated."

Q. "Now you say that the will looks as if it was the will of a man not in a normal state of mind? In what respect?"

A. "Again you ask me things one by one. Is it because I think he has done an injustice to his relatives or has done more than justice to the clerks in his store?—I should think it was both of them."

Q. "Is it then because you think he had not given as much to his blood relations, as much as you think he ought to have given?"

A. "I do not know that I am here to testify as to questions of justice or injustice. I am not an expert on those things. I will say, however, so far as I can see the situation, it is not a normal will—not the will of a man who is in a perfectly normal state of mind."

Q. "And you have been influenced in forming your judgment as to his normalcy?"

A. "Yes."

Q. "By the provisions of his will?"

A. "I think that is one of the factors, yes."

Following Dr. Dana's testimony, Dr. Peterson was called by Mr. Tuttle and the same hypothetical question was propounded to him as had previously been answered by Dr. Dana, whose answers had been most pronounced in favor of the contestants. Mr. Taft, conscious of the admissions that he had already obtained from Dr. Dana, and mindful of the high standing of Dr. Peterson in his profession, wisely dismissed the witness without asking any pertinent questions.

Following Dr. Peterson, Dr. Jelliffe gave his testimony.

Dr. Jelliffe was an expert witness who at that time used to appear very frequently in our courts, and was known to be a very dangerous witness to cross-examine. However, Mr. Taft very skillfully, although the witness tried in every possible way to avoid direct answers, forced him to testify as to what he, Dr. Jelliffe, would have done had he been called as an attending physician, in an attempt to discover the mental capacity of his patient to make a will. He forced the doctor to admit that he would not only examine the patient himself, but also the regular attending physician, the nurses who waited upon him, and also the employees and friends who had talked with him. In other words, he would accept the evidence of the very people who had been called by Mr. Taft to give testimony to the normal condition of the testator's mind at the time he signed the will.

In conclusion, it is interesting to note that the Surrogate, in spite of the testimony of these three physicians, held that there was no issue to submit to a jury and admitted the will to probate, thereby practically ignoring the testimony of the three expert witnesses. There was an appeal to the appellate court, but without avail.

Chapter 20

The Cross-Examination of Richard Pigott

by Sir Charles Russell before the Parnell Commission

PROBABLY one of the most dramatic and successful of the more celebrated cross-examinations in the history of the English courts is Sir Charles Russell's cross-examination of Pigott, the chief witness in the investigating growing out of the attack upon Charles S. Parnell and sixty-five Irish members of Parliament, by name, for belonging to a lawless and even murderous organization, whose aim was the overthrow of English rule.

This cross-examination is in marked contrast with the method used by Mr. Choate in his cross-examination of the plaintiff in the Martinez case related in a preceding chapter. During the entire cross-examination of Miss Martinez, Mr. Choate carefully concealed from her the fact that he had in his possession a letter written by her, with which he intended to destroy her in his summing up. But here the opposite method was adopted by Sir Charles Russell, and after adroitly leading Pigott to commit himself irretrievably to certain absolute statements, Russell suddenly confronted him with his own letters in a way that was masterly—and deadly to Pigott.

The case is also an admirable illustration of the importance of so using a damaging letter that a dishonest witness cannot escape its effect by ready and ingenious explanations, when given an opportunity, as is often done by an unskilful cross-examiner. Attention has already been drawn to this vital point in the chapter upon the proper "Sequence of Cross-Examination." The cross-examination of Pigott shows that Sir Charles Russell thoroughly understood this branch of the art, for he read to Pigott only a portion of his damaging letter, and then mercilessly impaled him upon the sharp points of his questions before dragging him forward in a bleeding condition to face other portions of his letter, and repeated the process until Pigott was cut to pieces.

The principal charge against Parnell, and the only one that interests us in the cross-examination of the witness Pigott, was the writing of a letter by Parnell which the *Times* claimed to have obtained and published in facsimile, in which he excused the murderer of Lord Frederick Cavendish, Chief Secretary for Ireland, and of Mr. Burke, Under Secretary, in Phoenix Park, Dublin, on May 6, 1882. One particular sentence in the letter read, "I cannot refuse to admit that Burke got no more than his deserts."

The publication of this letter naturally made a great stir in Parliament and in the country at large. Parnell stated in the House of Commons that the letter was a forgery, and later asked for the appointment of a select committee to inquire whether the facsimile letter was a forgery. The Government refused this request, but appointed a special committee, composed of three judges, to investigate all the charges made by the *Times*.

The writer is indebted again to Russell's biographer, Mr. O'Brien, for the details of this celebrated case. Seldom has any legal controversy been so graphically described as this one. One seems to be living with Russell, and indeed with Mr. O'Brien himself, throughout those eventful months. We must content ourselves, however, with a reproduction of the cross-examination of Pigott as it comes from the stenographer's minutes of the trial, enlightened by the pen of Russell's facile biographer.

Mr. O'Brien speaks of it as "the event in the life of Russell—the defence of Parnell." In order to undertake this defense, Russell returned to the *Times* the retainer he had enjoyed from them for many previous years. It was known that the *Times* had bought the letter from Mr. Houston, the secretary of the Irish Loyal and Patriotic

Union, and that Mr. Houston had bought it from Pigott. But how did Pigott come by it? That was the question of the hour, and people looked forward to the day when Pigott should go into the box to tell his story, and when Sir Charles Russell should rise to cross-examine him. Mr. O'Brien writes: "Pigott's evidence in chief, so far as the letter was concerned, came practically to this: he had been employed by the Irish Loyal and Patriotic Union to hunt up documents which might incriminate Parnell, and he had bought the facsimile letter, with other letters, in Paris from an agent of the Clan-na-Gael, who had no objection to injuring Parnell for a valuable consideration. . . .

"During the whole week or more Russell had looked pale, worn, anxious, nervous, distressed. He was impatient, irritable, at times disagreeable. Even at luncheon, half an hour before, he seemed to be thoroughly out of sorts, and gave you the idea rather of a young junior with his first brief than of the most formidable advocate at the Bar. Now all was changed. As he stood facing Pigott, he was a picture of calmness, self-possession, strength; there was no sign of impatience or irritability; not a trace of illness, anxiety, or care; a slight tinge of color lighted up the face, the eyes sparkled, and a pleasant smile played about the mouth. The whole bearing and manner of the man, as he proudly turned his head toward the box, showed courage, resolution, confidence. Addressing the witness with much courtesy, while a profound silence fell upon the crowded court, he began: 'Mr. Pigott, would you be good enough, with my Lords' permission, to write some words on that sheet of paper for me? Perhaps you will sit down in order to do so?' A sheet of paper was then handed to the witness. I thought he looked for a moment surprised. This clearly was not the beginning that he had expected. He hesitated, seemed confused. Perhaps Russell observed it. At all events he added quickly:—

" 'Would you like to sit down?'

" 'Oh, no, thanks,' replied Pigott, a little flurried.

"*The President.* 'Well, but I think it is better that you

should sit down. Here is a table upon which you can write in the ordinary way—the course you always pursue.'

"Pigott sat down and seemed to recover his equilibrium.

"*Russell.* 'Will you write the word "livelihood"?'

"Pigott wrote.

"*Russell.* 'Just leave a space. Will you write the word "likelihood"?'

"Pigott wrote.

"*Russell.* 'Will you write your own name? Will you write the word "proselytism," and finally (I think I will not trouble you at present with any more) "Patrick Egan" and "P. Egan"?'

"He uttered these last words with emphasis, as if they imported something of great importance. Then, when Pigott had written, he added carelessly, 'There is one word I had forgotten. Lower down, please, leaving spaces, write the word "hesitancy." ' Then, as Pigott was about to write, he added, as if this were the vital point, 'with a small "h." ' Pigott wrote and looked relieved.

"*Russell.* 'Will you kindly give me the sheet?'

"Pigott took up a bit of blotting paper to lay on the sheet, when Russell, with a sharp ring in his voice, said rapidly, 'Don't blot it, please.' It seemed to me that the sharp ring in Russell's voice startled Pigott. While writing he had looked composed; now again he looked flurried, and nervously handed back the sheet. The attorney general looked keenly at it, and then said, with the air of a man who had himself scored, 'My Lords, I suggest that had better be photographed, if your Lordships see no objection."

"*Russell* (turning sharply toward the attorney general, and with an angry glance and an Ulster accent, which sometimes broke out when he felt irritated). 'Do not interrupt my cross-examination with that request.'

"Little did the attorney general at that moment know that, in the ten minutes or quarter of an hour which it had taken to ask these questions, Russell had gained a decisive advantage. Pigott had in one of his letters to Pat Egan

spelt 'hesitancy' thus, 'hesitency.' In one of the incriminatory letters 'hesitancy' was so spelt; and in the sheet now
handed back to Russell, Pigott had written 'hesitency,'
too. In fact it was Pigott's spelling of this word that had
put the Irish members on his scent. Pat Egan, seeing the
word spelt with an 'e' in one of the incriminatory letters,
had written to Parnell, saying in effect, 'Pigott is the forger.
In the letter ascribed to you "hesitancy" is spelt "hesitency." That is the way Pigott always spells the word.'
These things were not dreamt of in the philosophy of the
attorney general when he interrupted Russell's cross-examination with the request that the sheet 'had better be
photographed.' So closed the first round of the combat.

"Russell went on in his former courteous manner, and
Pigott, who had now completely recovered confidence,
looked once more like a man determined to stand to his
guns.

"Russell, having disposed of some preliminary points at
length (and after he had been perhaps about half an hour
on his feet), closed with the witness.

"*Russell.* 'The first publication of the articles "Parnellism and Crime" was on the 7th March, 1887?"

"*Pigott* (sturdily). 'I do not know.'

"*Russell* (amiably). 'Well, you may assume that is the
date.'

"*Pigott* (carelessly). 'I suppose so.'

"*Russell.* 'And you were aware of the intended publication of the correspondence, the incriminatory letters?'

"*Pigott* (firmly). 'No, I was not at all aware of it.'

"*Russell* (sharply, and with the Ulster ring in his
voice). 'What?'

"*Pigott* (boldly). 'No, certainly not.'

*   *   *   *   *

"*Russell.* 'Were you not aware that there were grave
charges to be made against Mr. Parnell and the leading
members of the Land League?'

"*Pigott* (positively). 'I was not aware of it until they
actually commenced.'

"*Russell* (again with the Ulster ring). 'What?'"

"*Pigott* (defiantly). 'I was not aware of it until the publication actually commenced.'"

"*Russell* (pausing, and looking straight at the witness). 'Do you swear that?'"

"*Pigott* (aggressively). 'I do.'"

"*Russell* (making a gesture with both hands, and looking toward the bench). 'Very good, there is no mistake about that.'"

"Then there was a pause; Russell placed his hands beneath the shelf in front of him, and drew from it some papers—Pigott, the attorney general, the judges, every one in court looking intently at him the while. There was not a breath, not a movement. I think it was the most dramatic scene in the whole cross-examination, abounding as it did in dramatic scenes. Then, handing Pigott a letter, Russell said calmly:—

" 'Is that your letter? Do not trouble to read it; tell me if it is your letter.'"

"Pigott took the letter, and held it close to his eyes as if reading it.

"*Russell* (sharply). 'Do not trouble to read it.'"

"*Pigott.* 'Yes, I think it is.'"

"*Russell* (with a frown). 'Have you any doubt of it?'"

"*Pigott.* 'No.'"

"*Russell* (addressing the judges). 'My Lords, it is from Anderton's Hotel, and it is addressed by the witness to Archbishop Walsh. The date, my Lords, is the 4th of March, three days before the first appearance of the first of the articles, "Parnellism and Crime." ' "

"He then read:—

" 'Private and confidential.'

" 'My Lord:—The importance of the matter about which I write will doubtless excuse this intrusion on your Grace's attention. Briefly, I wish to say that I have been made aware of the details of certain proceedings that are in preparation with the object of destroying the influence of the Parnellite party in Parliament.'

"Having read this much Russell turned to Pigott and said:—

" 'What were the certain proceedings that were in preparation?'

"*Pigott.* 'I do not recollect.'

"*Russell* (resolutely). 'Turn to my Lords and repeat the answer.'

"*Pigott.* 'I do not recollect.'

"*Russell.* 'You swear that—writing on the 4th of March, less than two years ago?'

"*Pigott.* 'Yes.'

"*Russell.* 'You do not know what that referred to?'

"*Pigott.* 'I do not really.'

"*Russell.* 'May I suggest to you?'

"*Pigott.* 'Yes, you may.'

"*Russell.* 'Did it refer to the incriminatory letters among other things?'

"*Pigott.* 'Oh, at that date? No, the letters had not been obtained, I think, at that date, had they, two years ago?'

"*Russell* (quietly and courteously). 'I do not want to confuse you at all, Mr. Pigott.'

"*Pigott.* 'Would you mind giving me that date of that letter?'

"*Russell.* 'The 4th of March.'

"*Pigott.* 'The 4th of March.'

"*Russell.* 'Is it your impression that the letters had not been obtained at that date?'

"*Pigott.* 'Oh, yes, some of the letters had been obtained before that date.'

"*Russell.* 'Then, reminding you that some of the letters had been obtained before that date, did that passage that I have read to you in that letter refer to these letters among other things?'

"*Pigott.* 'No, I rather fancy they had reference to the forthcoming articles in the *Times*.'

"*Russell* (glancing keenly at the witness). 'I thought you told us you did not know anything about the forthcoming articles.'

"*Pigott* (looking confused). 'Yes, I did. I find now I

am mistaken—that I must have heard something about them.'

"*Russell* (severely). 'Then try not to make the same mistake again, Mr. Pigott. "Now," you go on (continuing to read from Pigott's letter to the archbishop), "I cannot enter more fully into details than to state that the proceedings referred to consist in the publication of certain statements purporting to prove the complicity of Mr. Parnell himself, and some of his supporters, with murders and outrages in Ireland, to be followed, in all probability, by the institution of criminal proceedings against these parties by the Government."'

"Having finished the reading, Russell laid down the letter and said (turning toward the witness), 'Who told you that?'

"*Pigott*. 'I have no idea.'

"*Russell* (striking the paper energetically with his fingers). 'But that refers, among other things, to the incriminatory letters.'

"*Pigott*. 'I do not recollect that it did.'

"*Russell* (with energy). 'Do you swear that it did not?'

"*Pigott*. 'I will not swear that it did not.'

"*Russell*. 'Do you think it did?'

"*Pigott*. 'No, I do not think it did.'

"*Russell*. 'Do you think that these letters, if genuine, would prove or would not prove Parnell's complicity in crime?'

"*Pigott*. 'I thought they would be very likely to prove it.'

"*Russell*. 'Now, reminding you of that opinion, I ask you whether you did not intend to refer—not solely, I suggest, but among other things—to the letters as being the matter which would prove complicity or purport to prove complicity?'

"*Pigott*. 'Yes, I may have had that in my mind.'

"*Russell*. 'You could have had hardly any doubt that you had?'

"*Pigott*. 'I suppose so.'

"*Russell*. 'You suppose you may have had?'

"*Pigott*. 'Yes.'

"*Russell*. 'There is the letter and the statement (reading), "Your Grace may be assured that I speak with full knowledge, and am in a position to prove, beyond all doubt and question, the truth of what I say." Was that true?'

"*Pigott*. 'It could hardly be true.'

"*Russell*. 'Then did you write that which was false?'

"*Pigott*. 'I suppose it was in order to give strength to what I said. I do not think it was warranted by what I knew.'

"*Russell*. 'You added the untrue statement in order to add strength to what you said?'

"*Pigott*. 'Yes.'

"*Russell*. 'You believe these letters to be genuine?'

"*Pigott*. 'I do.'

"*Russell*. 'And did at this time?'

"*Pigott*. 'Yes.'

"*Russell* (reading). ' "And I will further assure your Grace that I am also able to point out how these designs may be successfully combated and finally defeated." How, if these documents were genuine documents, and you believed them to be such, how were you able to assure his Grace that you were able to point out how the design might be successfully combated and finally defeated?'

"*Pigott*. 'Well, as I say, I had not the letters actually in my mind at that time. So far as I can gather, I do not recollect the letter to Archbishop Walsh at all. My memory is really a blank on the circumstance.'

"*Russell*. 'You told me a moment ago, after great deliberation and consideration, you had both the incriminatory letters and the letter to Archbishop Walsh in your mind.'

"*Pigott*. 'I said it was probable I did; but I say the thing has completely faded out of my mind.'

"*Russell* (resolutely). 'I must press you. Assuming the letters to be genuine, what were the means by which you were able to assure his Grace that you could point out how the design might be successfully combated and finally defeated?'

"*Pigott* (helplessly). 'I cannot conceive, really.'

"*Russell.* 'Oh, try. You must really try.'

"*Pigott.* (in manifest confusion and distress). 'I cannot.'

"*Russell* (looking fixedly at the witness). 'Try.'

"*Pigott.* 'I cannot.'

"*Russell.* 'Try.'

"*Pigott.* 'It is no use.'

"*Russell* (emphatically). 'May I take it, then, your answer to my Lords is that you cannot give any explanation?'

"*Pigott.* 'I really cannot absolutely.'

"*Russell* (reading). ' "I assure your Grace that I have no other motive except to respectfully suggest that your Grace would communicate the substance to some one or other of the parties concerned, to whom I could furnish details, exhibit proofs, and suggest how the coming blow may be effectually met." What do you say to that, Mr. Pigott?'

"*Pigott.* 'I have nothing to say except that I do not recollect anything about it absolutely.'

"*Russell.* 'What was the coming blow?'

"*Pigott.* 'I suppose the coming publication.'

"*Russell.* 'How was it to be effectively met?'

"*Pigott.* 'I have not the slightest idea.'

"*Russell.* 'Assuming the letters to be genuine, does it not even now occur to your mind how it could be effectively met?'

"*Pigott.* 'No.'

"Pigott now looked like a man, after the sixth round in a prize fight, who had been knocked down in every round. But Russell showed him no mercy. I shall take another extract.

*   *   *   *   *

"*Russell.* 'Whatever the charges in "Parnellism and Crime," including the letters, were, did you believe them to be true or not?'

"*Pigott.* 'How can I say that when I say I do not know what the charges were? I say I do not recollect that letter to the archbishop at all, or any of the circumstances it refers to.'

"*Russell.* 'First of all you knew this: that you procured and paid for a number of letters?'

"*Pigott.* 'Yes.'

"*Russell.* 'Which, if genuine, you have already told me, would gravely implicate the parties from whom these were supposed to come.'

"*Pigott.* 'Yes, gravely implicate.'

"*Russell.* 'You would regard that, I suppose, as a serious charge?'

"*Pigot.* 'Yes.'

"*Russell.* 'Did you believe that charge to be true or false?'

"*Pigott.* 'I believed that charge to be true.'

"*Russell.* 'You believed that to be true?'

"*Pigott.* 'I do.'

"*Russell.* 'Now I will read this passage [from Pigott's letter to the archbishop], "I need hardly add that, did I consider the parties really guilty of the things charged against them, I should not dream of suggesting that your Grace should take part in an effort to shield them; I only wish to impress on your Grace that the evidence is apparently convincing, and would probably be sufficient to secure conviction if submitted to an English jury." What do you say to that, Mr. Pigott?'

"*Pigott* (bewildered). 'I say nothing, except that I am sure I could not have had the letters in my mind when I said that, because I do not think the letters conveyed a sufficiently serious charge to cause me to write in that way.'

"*Russell.* 'But you know that was the only part of the charge, so far as you have yet told us, that you had anything to do in getting up?'

"*Pigott.* 'Yes, that is what I say; I must have had something else in my mind which I cannot at present recollect —that I must have had other charges.'

"*Russell*. 'What charges?'

"*Pigott*. 'I do not know. That is what I cannot tell you.'

"*Russell*. 'Well, let me remind you that that particular part of the charges—the incriminatory letters—were letters that you yourself knew all about.'

"*Pigott*. 'Yes, of course.'

"*Russell* (reading from another letter of Pigott's to the archbishop). ' "I was somewhat disappointed in not having a line from your Grace, as I ventured to expect I might have been so far honored. I can assure your Grace that I have no other motive in writing save to avert, if possible, a great danger to people with whom your Grace is known to be in strong sympathy. At the same time, should your Grace not desire to interfere in the matter, or should you consider that they would refuse me a hearing, I am well content, having acquitted myself of what I conceived to be my duty in the circumstances. I will not further trouble your Grace save to again beg that you will not allow my name to transpire, seeing that to do so would interfere injuriously with my prospects, without any compensating advantage to any one. I make the request all the more confidently because I have had no part in what is being done to the prejudice of the Parnellite party, though I was enabled to become acquainted with all the details." '

"*Pigott* (with a look of confusion and alarm). 'Yes.'

"*Russell*. 'What do you say to that?'

"*Pigott*. 'That it appears to me clearly that I had not the letters in my mind.'

"*Russell*. 'Then if it appears to you clearly that you had not the letters in your mind, what had you in your mind?'

"*Pigott*. 'It must have been something far more serious.'

"*Russell*. 'What was it?'

"*Pigott* (helplessly, great beads of perspiration standing out on his forehead and trickling down his face). 'I cannot tell you. I have no idea.'

"*Russell*. 'It must have been something far more serious than the letters?'

"*Pigott* (vacantly). 'Far more serious.'

"*Russell* (briskly). 'Can you give my Lords any clew of the most indirect kind to what it was?'

"*Pigott* (in despair). 'I cannot.'

"*Russell.* 'Or from whom you heard it?'

"*Pigott.* 'No.'

"*Russell.* 'Or when you heard it?'

"*Pigott.* 'Or when I heard it.'

"*Russell.* 'Or where you heard it?'

"*Pigott.* 'Or where I heard it.'

"*Russell.* 'Have you ever mentioned this fearful matter —whatever it is—to anybody?'

"*Pigott.* 'No.'

"*Russell.* 'Still locked up, hermetically sealed in your own bosom?'

"*Pigott.* 'No, because it has gone away out of my bosom, whatever it was.'

"On receiving this answer Russell smiled, looked at the bench, and sat down. A ripple of derisive laughter broke over the court, and a buzz of many voices followed. The people standing around me looked at each other and said, 'Splendid.' The judges rose, the great crowd melted away, and an Irishman who mingled in the throng expressed, I think, the general sentiment in a single word, 'Smashed.' "

Pigott's cross-examination was finished the following day, and the second day he disappeared entirely, and later sent back from Paris a confession of his guilt, admitting his perjury, and giving the details of how he had forged the alleged Parnell letter by tracing words and phrases from genuine Parnell letters, placed against the window pane, and admitting that he had sold the forged letter for £605. After the confession was read, the Commission "found" that it was a forgery, and the *Times* withdrew the facsimile letter.

A warrant was issued for Pigott's arrest on the charge of perjury, but when he was tracked by the police to a hotel in Madrid, he asked to be given time enough to collect his belongings, and, retiring to his room, blew out his brains.

Chapter 21

The Cross-Examination of Dr. ——

in the Carlyle W. Harris case

THE RECORDS of the criminal courts in this country contain few cases that have excited so much human interest among all classes of the community as the prosecution and conviction of Carlyle W. Harris, which fell to my lot.

For years afterward there was a widespread belief among men, perhaps more especially among women, who did not attend the trial, but simply listened to the current gossip of the day and followed the newspaper accounts of the court proceedings, that Harris was innocent of the crime for the commission of which his life was forfeited to the state.

It is proposed in this chapter to discuss some of the facts that led up to the testimony of one of the most distinguished toxicologists in the country, who was called for the defence on the crucial point in the case; and to give extracts from his cross-examination, his failure to withstand which was the turning point in the entire trial. He returned to his home in Philadelphia after he left the witness stand, and declared in public, when asked to describe his experiences in New York, that he had "gone to New York only to make a fool of himself and return home again."

It is also proposed to give some of the *inside* history of the case—facts that never came out at the trial, not because they were unknown at the time to the district attorney, nor unsusceptible of proof, but because the strict rules of evidence in such cases often, as it seems to the writer, withhold from the ears of the jury certain facts, the mere recital of which seems to conclude the question of guilt. For example, the rule forbidding the presentation to the jury of anything that was said by the victim of a homicide, even to witnesses surrounding the deathbed, unless the victim in express terms makes known his own belief that he cannot live, and that he has abandoned all *hope* or expectation of recovery before he tells the tale of the manner in which he was slain, or the causes that led up to it, has allowed many a prisoner, if not to escape entirely, at least to avoid the full penalty for the crime he undoubtedly committed.

Carlyle Harris was a gentleman's son, with all the advantages of education and breeding. In his twenty-second year, and just after graduating with honors from the College of Physicians and Surgeons in New York City, he was indicted and tried for the murder of Miss Helen Potts, a young, pretty, intelligent, and talented school girl in attendance at Miss Day's Ladies Boarding School, on 40th Street, New York City.

Harris had made the acquaintance of Miss Potts in the summer of 1889, and all during the winter paid marked attention to her. The following spring, while visiting her uncle, who was a doctor, she was delivered of a four months' child, and was obliged to confess to her mother that she was secretly married to Harris under assumed names, and that her student husband had himself performed an abortion upon her.

Harris was sent for. He acknowledged the truth of his wife's statement, but refused to make the marriage public. From this time on, until the day of her daughter's death, the wretched mother made every effort to induce Harris to acknowledge his wife publicly. She finally wrote him on the 20th of January, 1891, "You must go on the 8th of February, the anniversary of your secret marriage, before a minister of the gospel, and there have a Christian marriage performed—no other course than this will any longer be satisfactory to me or keep me quiet."

That very day Harris ordered at an apothecary store six capsules, each containing 4½ grains of quinine and ⅙ of a grain of morphine, and had the box marked:

"C. W. H. Student. One before retiring." Miss Potts had been complaining of sick headaches, and Harris gave her four of these capsules as an ostensible remedy. He then wrote to Mrs. Potts that he would agree to her terms, "unless some other way could be found of satisfying her scruples," and went hurriedly to Old Point Comfort. Upon hearing from his wife that the capsules made her worse instead of better, he still persuaded her to continue taking them. On the day of her death she complained to her mother about the medicine Carlyle had given her, and threatened to throw the box with the remaining capsule out of the window. Her mother persuaded her to try this last one, which she promised to do. Miss Potts slept in a room with three classmates who, on this particular night, had gone to a symphony concert. Upon their return they found Helen asleep, but woke her up and learned from her that she had been having "such beautiful dreams,"—she "had been dreaming of Carl." Then she complained of feeling numb, and becoming frightened, begged the girls not to let her go to sleep. She repeated that she had taken the medicine Harris had given her, and asked them if they thought it possible that he would give her anything to harm her. She soon fell into a profound coma, breathing only twice to the minute. The doctors worked over her for eleven hours without restoring her to consciousness; then she stopped breathing entirely.

The autopsy, fifty-six days afterward, disclosed an apparently healthy body, and the chemical analysis of the contents of the stomach disclosed the presence of morphine but *not* of quinine, though the capsules as originally compounded by the druggist contained twenty-seven times as much quinine as morphine.

This astounding discovery led to the theory of the prosecution: that Harris had emptied the contents of *one* of the capsules, had substituted morphine in sufficient quantities to kill, *in place of* the 4½ grains of quinine (to the eye, powdered quinine and morphine are identical), and had placed this fatal capsule in the box with the other three harmless ones, one to be taken each night. He had then fled from the city, not knowing which day would brand him a murderer.

Immediately after his wife's death Harris went to one of his medical friends and said: "I only gave her four capsules of the six I had made up; *the two I kept out will show that they are perfectly harmless. No jury can convict me with those in my possession; they can be analyzed and proved to be harmless.*"

They *were* analyzed and it was proved that the prescription had been correctly compounded. But oftentimes the means a criminal uses in order to conceal his deed are the very means that Providence employs to reveal the sin that lies hidden in his soul. Harris failed to foresee that it was the preservation of these capsules that would really convict him. Miss Potts had taken *all* that he had given her, and no one could ever have been certain that it was not the druggist's awful mistake, had not these retained capsules been analyzed. When Harris emptied one capsule and reloaded it with morphine, *he had himself become the druggist.*

It was contended that Harris never intended to recognize Helen Potts as his wife. He married her in secret, it appeared at the trial,—as it were from his own lips through the medium of conversation with a friend,— "because he could not accomplish her ruin in any other way." He brought her to New York, was married to her before an alderman under assumed names, and then having accomplished his purpose, burned the evidence of their marriage, the false certificate. Finally, when the day was set upon which he *must* acknowledge her as his wife, he planned her death.

The late recorder, Frederick Smyth, presided at the trial with great dignity and fairness. The prisoner was ably represented by John A. Taylor, Esq., and William Travers Jerome, Esq., afterwards district attorney of New York.

Mr. Jerome's cross-examination of Professor Witthaus, the leading chemist for the prosecution, was an extremely able piece of work, and during its eight hours disclosed

an amount of technical information and research such as is
seldom seen in our courts. Had it not been for the witness's impregnable position, he certainly would have suc-
cumbed before the attack. The length and technicality of
the examination render its use impracticable in this connection; but it is recommended to all students of cross-
examination who find themselves confronted with the task
of examination in so remote a branch of the advocate's
equipment as a knowledge of chemistry.

The defence consisted entirely of medical testimony,
directed toward creating a doubt as to our theory that
morphine was the cause of death. Their cross-examination
of our witnesses was suggestive of death from natural
causes: from heart disease, a brain tumor, apoplexy,
epilepsy, uremia. In fact, the multiplicity of their defences
was a great weakness. Gradually they were forced to
abandon all but two possible causes of death,—that by
morphine poisoning and that by uremic poisoning. This
narrowed the issue down to the question: Was it a large
dose of morphine that caused death, or was it a latent
kidney disease that was superinduced and brought to light
in the form of uremic coma by small doses of morphine,
such as the one-sixth of a grain admittedly contained in
the capsules Harris administered? In one case Harris was
guilty; in the other he was innocent.

Helen Potts died in a profound coma. Was it the coma
of morphine, or that of kidney disease? Many of the leading authorities in this city had given their conclusions in
favor of the morphine theory. In reply to these, the defence was able to call a number of young doctors, who
have since made famous names for themselves, but who
at the time were almost useless as witnesses with the jury
because of their comparative inexperience. Mr. Jerome
had, however, secured the services of one physician who,
of all the others in the country, had apparently best qualified himself by his writings and thirty years of hospital
experience to speak authoritatively upon the subject.

His direct testimony was to the effect that—basing his
opinion upon wide reading of the literature of the subject,

and what seemed to him to be the general consensus of professional opinion about it, and *"very largely on his own experience"*—no living doctor can distinguish the coma of morphine from that of kidney disease. The theory of the criminal law is that, if the death can be equally well attributed to natural causes as to the use of poison, the jury would be bound to give the prisoner the benefit of the doubt and acquit him.

It was the turning point in the trial. If any of the jurors credited this testimony,—the witness gave the reasons for his opinion in a very quiet, conscientious, and impressive manner,—there certainly could be no conviction in the case, at most a disagreement of the jury. It was certain Harris had given the capsules, but unless his wife had died of morphine poisoning, he was innocent of her death.

The cross-examination that follows is much abbreviated and given partly from memory. It was apparent that the witness would withstand any amount of technical examination and would easily get the better of the cross-examiner if such matters were gone into. He had made a profound impression. The court had listened to him with breathless interest. He must be dealt with gently and, if possible, led into self-contradictions where he was least prepared for them.

The cross-examiner sparred for an opening with the determination to strike quickly and to sit down if he got in one telling blow. The first one missed aim a little, but the second brought a peal of laughter from the jury and the audience, and the witness retired in great confusion. Even the lawyers for the defence seemed to lose heart, and although two hours before time of adjournment, begged the court for a recess until the following day.

Counsel (quietly). "Do you wish the jury to understand, doctor, that Miss Helen Potts did not die of morphine poisoning?"

Witness. "I do not swear to that."

Counsel. "What did she die of?"

Witness. "I don't swear what she died of."

Counsel. "I understand you to say that in your opinion the symptoms of morphine could not be sworn to with positiveness. Is that correct?"

Witness. "I don't think they can, with positiveness."

Counsel. "Do you wish to go out to the world as saying that you have never diagnosed a case of morphine poisoning excepting when you had an autopsy to exclude kidney disease?"

Witness. "I do not. I have not said so."

Counsel. "Then you have diagnosed a case on the symptoms alone, yes or no? I want a categorical answer."

Witness (sparring). "I would refuse to answer that question categorically; the word 'diagnosed' is used with two different meanings. One has to make what is known as a 'working diagnosis' when he is called to a case, not a positive diagnosis."

Counsel. "When was your last case of opium or morphine poisoning?"

Witness. "I can't remember which was the last."

Counsel (seeing an opening). "I don't want the name of the patient. Give me the date approximately, that is, the year—but under oath."

Witness. "I think the last was some years ago."

Counsel. "How many years ago?"

Witness (hesitating). "It may be eight or ten years ago."

Counsel. "Was it a case of death from morphine poisoning?"

Witness. "Yes, sir."

Counsel. "Was there an autopsy?"

Witness. "No, sir."

Counsel. "How did you know it was a death from morphine, if, as you said before, such symptoms cannot be distinguished?"

Witness. "I found out from a druggist that the woman had taken seven grains of morphine."

Counsel. "You made no diagnosis at all until you heard from the druggist?"

Witness. "I began to give artificial respiration."

Counsel. "But that is just what you would do in a case of morphine poisoning?"

Witness (hesitating). "Yes, sir. I made, of course, a working diagnosis."

Counsel. "Do you remember the case you had before that?"

Witness. "I remember another case."

Counsel. "When was that?"

Witness. "It was a still longer time ago. I didn't know the date."

Counsel. "How many years ago, on your oath?"

Witness. "Fifteen, probably."

Counsel. "Any others?"

Witness. "Yes, one other."

Counsel. "When?"

Witness. "Twenty years ago."

Counsel. "Are these three cases all you can remember in your experience?"

Witness. "Yes, sir."

Counsel (chancing it). "Were more than one of them deaths from morphine?"

Witness. "No, sir, only one."

Counsel (looking at the jury somewhat triumphantly). "Then it all comes down to this: you have had the experience of one case of morphine poisoning in the last twenty years?"

Witness (in a low voice). "Yes, sir, one that I can remember."

Counsel (excitedly). "And are you willing to come here from Philadelphia, and state that the New York doctors who have already testified against you, and who swore they had had seventy-five similar cases in their own practice, are mistaken in their diagnoses and conclusions?"

Witness (embarrassed and in a low tone). "Yes, sir, I am."

Counsel. "You never heard of Helen Potts until a year after her death, did you?"

Witness. "No, sir."

Counsel. "You heard these New York physicians say that they attended her and observed her symptoms for eleven hours before death?"

Witness. "Yes, sir."

Counsel. "Are you willing to go on record, with your one experience in twenty years, as coming here and saying that you do not believe our doctors can tell morphine poisoning when they see it?"

Witness (sheepishly). "Yes, sir."

Counsel. "You have stated, have you not, that the symptoms of morphine poisoning cannot be told with positiveness?"

Witness. "Yes, sir."

Counsel. "You said you based that opinion upon your own experience, and it now turns out you have seen but one case in twenty years."

Witness. "I also base it upon my reading."

Counsel (becoming almost contemptuous in manner). "Is your reading confined to your own book?"

Witness (excitedly). "No, sir; I say no."

Counsel (calmly). "But I presume you embodied in your own book the results of your reading, did you not?"

Witness (a little apprehensively). "I tried to, sir."

It must be explained here that the attending physicians had said that the pupils of the eyes of Helen Potts were contracted to a pin point, so much so as to be practically unrecognizable, and *symmetrically* contracted—that this symptom was the one *invariably* present in coma from morphine poisoning, and distinguished it from all other forms of death, whereas in the coma of kidney disease one pupil would be dilated and the other contracted; they would be asymmetrical.

Counsel (continuing). "Allow me to read to you from your own book on page 166, where you say (reading), 'I have thought that inequality of the pupils'—that is, where they are not symmetrically contracted—'is proof that a case is not one of narcotism'—or morphine poisoning—'but *Professor Taylor has recorded a case of morphine poisoning in which it* [the asymmetrical contraction of the pupils] *occurred.*' Do I read it as you intended it?"

Witness. "Yes, sir."

Counsel. "*So until you heard of the case that Professor Taylor reported, you had always supposed symmetrical contraction of the pupils of eyes to be the distinguishing symptom of morphine poisoning, and it is on this that you base your statement that the New York doctors could not tell morphine poisoning positively when they see it?*"

Witness (little realizing the point). "Yes, sir."

Counsel (very loudly). "*Well, sir, did you investigate that case far enough to discover that Professor Taylor's patient had one glass eye?*" [1]

Witness (in confusion). "I have no memory of it."

Counsel. "That has been proved to be the case here. You would better go back to Philadelphia, sir."

There were roars of laughter throughout the audience as counsel resumed his seat and the witness walked out of the court room. It is difficult to reproduce in print the effect made by this occurrence, but with the retirement of this witness the defendant's case suffered a collapse from which it never recovered.

It is interesting to note that within a year of Harris's conviction, Dr. Buchanan was indicted and tried for a similar offence—wife poisoning by the use of morphine.

It appeared in evidence at Dr. Buchanan's trial that, during the Harris trial and the examination of the medical witnesses, presumably the witness whose examination has been given above, Buchanan had said to his messmates that "Harris was a—fool, he didn't know how to mix his drugs. If he had put a little atropine with his morphine, it would have dilated the pupil of at least one of his victim's eyes, and no doctor could have deposed to death by morphine."

When Buchanan's case came up for trial it was discovered that, although morphine had been found in the stomach, blood, and intestines of his wife's body, the

[1] The reports of six thousand cases of morphine poisoning had been examined by the prosecution in this case before trial, and among them the case reported by Professor Taylor.

pupils of the eyes were not symmetrically contracted. No positive diagnosis of her case could be made by the attending physicians until the continued chemical examination of the contents of the body disclosed indisputable evidence of atropine (belladonna). Buchanan had profited by the disclosures in the Harris trial, but had made the fatal mistake of telling his friends how it could have been done in order to cheat science. It was this statement of his that put the chemists on their guard, and resulted in Buchanan's conviction and subsequent execution.

Carlyle Harris maintained his innocence even after the Court of Appeals had unanimously sustained his conviction, and even as he calmly took his seat in the electric chair.

The most famous English poisoning case comparable to the Harris and Buchanan cases was that of the celebrated William Palmer, also a physician by profession, who poisoned his companion by the use of strychnine, in order to obtain his money and collect his racing bets.

Palmer, like Harris and Buchanan, maintained a stoical demeanor throughout his trial and confinement in jail, awaiting execution. The morning of his execution he ate his eggs at breakfast as if he were going on a journey. When he was led to the gallows, it was demanded of him in the name of God, as was the custom in England in those days, if he was innocent or guilty. He made no reply. Again the question was put, "William Palmer, in the name of Almighty God, are you innocent or guilty?" Just as the white cap descended over his face he murmured in a low breath "Guilty," and the bolts were drawn with a crash.

Chapter 22

The Cross-Examination of Dr. Jelliffe

by George Z. Medalie, in a Court Inquiry into the sanity of Joseph W. Harriman

ON MARCH 14, 1933, Joseph W. Harriman, Chairman of the Board of Directors of the Harriman National Bank and Trust Company, was arrested in bed at his home at 2 East 70th Street. He was charged with having falsified the accounts of certain depositors in the Bank and with having used funds thus obtained to bolster the stock of the Bank.

He was indicted on April 6, 1933, and was arraigned five days later, despite the spirited argument of his attorneys, led by Colonel William Donovan, that Harriman's arraignment, in view of his precarious physical condition, might prove fatal.

The following month it was reported that Harriman, who had been confined pending the trial in the Regent Nursing Home, had suddenly vanished. He left a sheaf of notes, all of which were of a suicidal tenor and were to the effect that he had done his best to save the Bank, that he had failed and that there was no other way out for him.

His attorneys, physicians, and friends seized upon this escapade of Harriman as proof of his insanity. He had never recovered from the shock of his son's death in 1928. The preceding year his wife had taken a revolver away from him, sensing an intent on his part to commit suicide. His physicians announced a series of complicated diseases. Dr. Smith Ely Jelliffe, one of the most prominent psychiatrists in the country, stated that Harriman was suffering from a complication of diseases which had impaired his memory, his judgment, and his ability to transact business.

Harriman was discovered the next day at the Old Orchard Inn in Roslyn, L. I. He had arrived at Locust Valley in Long Island on Friday evening, had had dinner at the Stage Coach Inn, which the newspapers were careful to report included a $4 steak, and had then gone by taxi to the Old Orchard Inn, where he registered under an assumed name. His disappearance was climaxed by his sudden desperate attempt at suicide with a 50¢ peeling knife, made after he had been requested by the police to return with them to the City. His wounds, however, were superficial and responded to treatment in a few days.

Six weeks later, his attorneys, contending that they had been unable to obtain any coherent assistance from Harriman in preparing his defense, filed a petition for an adjudication of his insanity. The hearing began on July 8, 1933, before Federal Judge Caffey in the Southern District of New York.

It seemed fairly clear that Dr. Jelliffe would be the defendant's star witness. His international prestige and higly specialized training and experience in nervous and mental diseases were outstanding and unimpeachable.

The doctor testified that he had first treated the defendant professionally on March 24th, 1933. In the course of his inquiries, he discovered that Harriman was never quite certain about dates, but referred to occurrences as having taken place either before or after his son died in 1928. Whenever their conversation touched upon that event, the defendant, according to the witness, "lost his emotional control."

Dr. Jelliffe testified that he had tested the defendant's sensory nerves and had discovered that the reflexes of the pupils of the defendant's eyes were sluggish and irregular. He had used an ophthalmoscope to examine the retina and found that the blood vessels "showed unmistakable evidence of disease." He found evidence of arteriosclerosis, which, by creating variations in blood pressure, would tend to result in mental disease. Harriman's sense of balance had been impaired and his peculiar mincing walk indicated an "involvement of the blood vessels of the brain."

The witness then testified with respect to the tests he had used and the results he had obtained in conducting a mental examination of the defendant.

He answered various arithmetical problems correctly. He was asked various questions relating to his school knowledge and it appeared that his knowledge of things which he had learned or which had taken place long ago was better than his knowledge of recent events.

He had difficulty in constructing simple sentences out of words which the doctor gave him and tended to omit words or to unnecessarily elaborate the sentence.

The doctor testified that Harriman's "mental defect commenced to show up very nicely" when he was asked about the meaning of proverbs. When asked, for example, the significance of the proverb, "People who live in glass houses should not throw stones," his answer was, "They will get burned by the sun."

Harriman also had difficulty in distinguishing between animals. He stated that the difference between an ox and a horse was "they were both domestic animals."

He was incapable of telling a straightforward, continuous story and had difficulty in continuing sentences started by the doctor, in spelling his name backwards, and in performing other similar operations. He also had trouble in striking the "o's" out of an advertisement, missing nearly 50% of them.

The doctor testified, in conclusion, that Harriman's memory for recent events was faulty; that he was incapable of finer combinations of ideas; that his understanding of the relationship of one idea to another was defective; that his tendency to drink was the result of arteriosclerosis and was a symptom of mental degeneracy; that Harriman revealed suicidal tendencies; that he was emotionally unstrung and tended in conversation to intersperse irrelevant jocular remarks; that his conversation lacked continuity and was repetitious; that he had delusions of persecution; that he had tendencies to confabulation or the making up of fictitious stories about things which happened to him; that he had delusions as to the value of the Bank's stock; that he had no coherent idea of what the transactions involved in the indictment were about; that his flight to Roslyn, L. I., indicated his confused state of mind; that his failure successfully to commit suicide indicated the lack of continuity in his ideas; and that he was incapable of rationally aiding in his defense.

The cross-examination of this witness is recorded here as an instructive example of the power of this legal weapon when in the hands of a master of the art even against an expert witness of such international prestige and highly specialized training in court proceedings as Dr. Jelliffe.

To appreciate this cross-examination, one must keep clearly in mind the fact that the issue to be determined related solely to Harriman's comprehension of the charges made against him.

Q. "I would like again to came back to what you said to Harriman on the subject of the accusation, and I would like you, because it is important, to search your memory for what was said. Is your memory normal? I think we will agree it is. Isn't it?"

A. "I don't know. That is for you to decide."

Q. "Very good. Now, how did you go about putting his mind on this painful subject of an accusation of crime against him, who had been regarded, as you know, as a distinguished citizen?"

A. "I said, in substance—repeated some of the statements that were made in Mr. Leisure's letter to me, of information."

Q. "What did you say to him? I now want what you said to Mr. Harriman."

A. "I am now trying to tell you."

Q. "Do not say that it was Mr. Leisure's letter; say what you said."

A. "Well, I have already told you that I cannot repeat verbatim what was said."

By the Court.

Q. "We do not want verbatim. We want the substance of what you said."

A. "That is what I have tried—"

Q. "You have not told us yet."

..*A.* "Yes, the substance was that certain transactions took place."

Q. "That means nothing. What did you tell him?"

A. "I told him that he was being accused of doing certain things."

By Mr. Medalie.

Q. "What things?"

By the Court.

Q. "What things?"

A. "Namely, that certain slips were signed by him, and that certain transfers were made from one account to another, and I went over each one of them that were mentioned, and I have already testified that he did not remember the details of any of them and was not—said that he did not give orders to have that done, and, as I have already testified, he said that he had officers that he paid fifteen to twenty-five thousand dollars a year to, to attend to those details, and he expected that they would attend to them, and he had no knowledge of them. I have already said that three or four times."

The point of the examination was then made as follows:

By Mr. Medalie.

Q. "Doctor, I would like to put it this way: It is clear, then, that he knew that you were talking about the Harriman National Bank?"

A. "Yes, he knew that he had been president of the Harriman National Bank, and—"

Q. "And he knew that that was what you were talking about?"

A. "Yes, he did."

Q. "He knew that you were talking about a securities company account?"

A. "He did."

Q. "He knew that you were talking about the accounts of certain depositors?"

A. "He did not know whether they—those accounts—that they were accounts; he was not aware of those. That was a function, he said, of his underlings."

Q. "Do you mean to say that he said that he did not know of those accounts, or that he did not know of the transfers to those accounts?"

A. "I don't know that he said—I never asked him if he ever heard of those accounts. He didn't know of the transfer of those accounts."

It was quite clear at this point that Harriman had been fully aware of the charges made against him and that, in his conversation with the doctor, he had simply denied his guilt.

Dr. Jelliffe had testified that he believed Harriman to be incompetent because he was unable to confine himself to a single subject. Throughout the cross-examination of the witness he indicated a similar tendency to stray from the subject of the examination. There was a perceptible ripple of laughter in the courtroom when the witness was asked:

Q. "Did you observe any perceptions of repetition of ideas on his part, when you asked him about other matters—if you asked him about one thing he would go off to another subject and stick to the other subject?"

A. "Yes, he did that quite frequently." . . .

Q. "Now, doctor, when I ask you a question, will you please stick to the question I ask you and not go off to something else?"

The examination then touched on the tests which the doctor had made.

Q. "I want to be sure of this. I want your help. Did he say that he never heard of the National Exhibition Company? You remember that name, don't you?"

A. "I don't remember the National Exhibition Company."

Q. "Didn't Mr. ——?"

A. "I don't remember it offhand now."

Q. "I would like to ask another thing about Mr. Harriman. Has he the habit of repetition?"

A. "Very much so."

Q. "And talking at length about the same thing over and over again, so that you can't stop him at the end of one sentence?"

A. "I would not characterize it that way, no."

Q. "Was it almost that?"

A. "No, not almost that, but he repeats very frequently."

Q. "Is that a characteristic of aging persons who are normal?"

A. "Is that a characteristic of aging persons?"

Q. "Yes."

A. "Of what?"

Q. "Aging normal people."

A. "They very frequently do something like that, yes."

Q. "The mere fact that a man does it is no evidence of his imbecility, insanity or deterioration, of itself?"

A. "Of itself alone, no."

Q. "In other words, if a witness were on the stand in the courtroom and did that kind of thing, you would not say that he was mentally deteriorated?"

A. "No, on that basis of fact, no."

*   *   *   *   *

Q. "Did you question Mr. Harriman about entries made in April, 1932, to the amount of $1,600,000?"

A. "No, not specifically about $1,600,000. I only made reference to the $300,000 amount that I have already—"

Q. "Of December, 1931?"

A. (Continuing.) "—that I have testified to. Except as I have already said, that a very large amount of stock had accumulated."

Q. "Were you informed by Mr. Leisure that what Mr. Harriman was accused of specifically in the indictment was transferring the liability of the Harriman Securities Company to individual depositors of the bank without their knowledge? Did you know that at that time?"

A. "I believe on the date of my letter, which was of

April 5th, there had been no indictment handed down, so—"

..Q. "Well, did you know that that was a fact which the Government claimed or which bank examiners claimed?"

A. "I think the phrase that was used in the letter was that the Government will make such and such a claim."

Q. "Yes. Now what I am getting to, the particular claim, did you know that the claim that was to be made by the Government was that Harriman had transferred or caused to be transferred the Securities Company liability to depositors, without their knowledge? Did you know that?"

A. "I gathered that in a general sense from the letter, yes."

Q. "Well, did you call Harriman's attention to that?"

A. "Not specifically in those words."

Q. "Well, why didn't you?"

A. "I have already told you what I asked him about."

Q. "But I want to know why you did not. Why in examining him for the purpose of finding out what he understood didn't you ask him that?"

A. "I have already told you that he told me he knew nothing at all about the transaction."

Q. "Didn't you attempt to bring his mind to specific things in connection with it, in the face of his denial?"

A. "I think I have already testified to that, yes."

Q. "Never mind what you have already testified to; I want to know what you did."

A. "I think I have already told you."

Q. "Did you call his attention to the fact that the Government claimed that he had saddled these liabilities on the books on the depositors, who knew nothing about it?"

A. "I think I said that the Government was making a claim that there was $300,000 that had been transferred from one account to the other and asked him to explain it and he was unable to explain it."

Q. "You mean he said he could not explain it, knew nothing about it?"

A. "He gave me no explanation whereby I could get any further information."

Q. "What he actually did was to tell you that he knew nothing about it?"

A. "Yes, he said he knew nothing about it, he had had no information about it. He made the further remark such as I have already testified to, that he had underlings, that he had salaried men that he paid large amounts of money to, and they took care of the details."

Q. "Is it unusual for sane men charged with crime to invent a false defense which involves a pretense of absence of knowledge or information as to the matters with which they are charged?"

A. "I think it could be done, yes."

Q. "Well, don't you know from experience that that is quite frequent?"

A. "No."

Q. "You do not know that?"

A. "No, I have not had much experience of that nature."

Q. "Then you do not feel able to say whether that is a normal device of an accused person who is sane, to falsely set up a defense of no knowledge or information?"

A. "I can conceive that it might be done, yes."

The defendant's indulgence in repetition was dealt with as follows:

Q. "Do not patients with physical ailments love to tell it to the doctor? Perfectly sane people do that kind of thing?"

A. "Surely."

Q. "And in fact do to friends and relatives until friends and relatives sicken of hearing it?"

A. "Unquestionably."

Q. "And perfectly sane people do it?"

A. "Unquestionably."

Q. "That is in line with the general idea, 'Let me tell you about my operation'?"

A. "Unquestionably."

After considering several items included in the doctor's

notes, none of which were especially significant, the examination was concluded as follows:

Q. "When did you see him after that?"

A. "I have not seen him except in court."

Q. "Well, did you see him when Dr. Gregory examined him recently?"

A. "I beg your pardon; yes, I saw him with Dr. Gregory on two occasions."

Q. "That is Friday and Saturday of last week?"

A. "Yes, sir."

Q. "Did you observe any improvement in him since June 29th?"

A. "Well, not since June 29th, but certainly since March 24th."

Q. "A substantial improvement?"

A. "I would say in a sense, yes, but in another sense, no. That is, superficially and speaking in general, his narrative with Dr. Gregory was more sustained, it was clearer, it was repetitious in the same sense that I have already mentioned. He also had made jocular allusions. He also told some funny stories, some of which I do not think he would like to have repeated in court."

Q. "You mean the kind of story one tells to his intimates?"

A. "The kind of stories which, in view of the occasion, being examined by an alienist, one would hardly expect a man to tell, in view of the seriousness of the situation. In other words, distinctly out of color, in view of the whole seriousness of the whole matter, the kind of story that a person might tell you, might say at a club or a whole lot of fellows together."

Q. "Or a whole lot of directors together?"

A. "But hardly the kind of story you would expect the Judge to hear—"

Q. "We don't need to hear them. We know what those stories are, in a general way."

A "I beg your pardon, you have not heard these stories."

Q "At clubs, boards of directors meetings, aggregations

of lawyers, eminent physicians, jurists and statesmen, the same kind of stories."

A. "Oh, yes, sir, under certain circumstances but hardly the right thing under those circumstances."

Q. "You mean it was not appropriate?"

A. "Very distinctly inappropriate."

Q. "Well, a lot of normal people do inappropriate things, don't they, without affecting their mental worth or ability?"

A. "I think a great many people that pass for normal do just that sort of thing."

Q. "Can't we very well eliminate that or wouldn't we if it were not Harriman?"

A. "Not in view of the whole situation."

Q. "Did you ever hear that Abraham Lincoln used to do that sort of thing?"

A. "Dr. Brill is quite an expert on Abraham Lincoln stories. Better ask him about that."

Q. "And that Daniel Webster used to do that kind of thing?"

A. "I have heard he did."

Q. "Regardless of whether—"

A. "But I don't believe that Daniel Webster in such a situation as Mr. Harriman was in would ever tell the same things that he told Dr. Gregory."

Q. "You mean that he might not have done so on the floor of the Senate, but might have done so in the cloakroom or in the corridor?"

A. "Yes, sir. He certainly would not do it if he was being examined as to his mental competency."

Q. "Did you make Mr. Harriman aware of the fact that his mental competency was being examined into?"

A. "That I don't know, what Mr. Harriman was aware of; absolutely I don't think he was very keenly aware of what it was all about, because Mr. Harriman immediately became the salesman with Dr. Gregory. You would have thought he was more of a bond salesman going to sell Dr. Gregory something."

Q. "Is that a sign of abnormality?"

A. "It was in my opinion distinctly under the circumstances."

Q. "And is it not a fact that alienists and neurologists, like all other physicians, try as far as possible to put a patient at his ease, so that the patient is not overpowered with the importance of the occasion?"

A. "I think that is a fairly just statement, yes, sir."

Q. "In other words, the patient is made to feel that it is just a personal, friendly, helpful visit."

A. "That is what we attempt to do, put them at their ease as much as possible."

Q. "Didn't you ever tell a patient a perfectly appropriate and proper story or describe some incident to make the patient feel at ease?"

A. "It depends upon the patient."

Q. "You do that occasionally, don't you?"

A. "Occasionally, yes, sir."

Q. "Now let me understand this: Mr. Harriman is considerably improved today over what he was on March 24th?"

A. "I would say somewhat improved. I would not say considerably."

Q. "He walks a little better?"

A. "Not much."

Q. "He conducts a sustained conversation?"

A. "Somewhat sustained conversation, sometimes he does and sometimes he doesn't."

Q. "When he talked to Dr. Gregory he kept on talking?"

A. "Yes, sir."

Q. "On the subject of the bank and its condition?"

A. "Yes, sir, he kept on talking about the subject of the bank and how the bank grew up, and how he was a poor boy, etc."

Q. "Did he say anything on that occasion that struck you as abnormal or as indicating mental incompetence, either on Friday or Saturday last?"

A. "Well, I think he overemphasized the idea that there was a plot to do him, to put him on the spot, that he had been picked out as a special victim, and that they were going to get him."

Q. "You mean the bankers, the Government or the public, which?"

A. "The bankers."

Q. "The Clearing House?"

A. "Yes."

Q. "The Clearing House wanted to close his bank?"

A. "No, the Clearing House wanted to get him."

Q. "Haven't you heard that sort of thing before? Heven't read it in newspapers, as coming from financiers and industrial leaders who were out of business or were put out of business and claimed a plot of that kind?"

A. "I have."

Q. "Haven't you heard, for example, that a prominent—"

A. "I get letters once a week—"

Q. "Wait a minute."

A. (Continuing.) "—more or less, of people who make just that sort of complaint."

Q. "Haven't you heard recently that a great industrialist claimed that the banks wanted to put him out of business?"

A. "I have read it in newspapers, yes."

Q. "Do you regard him as incompetent?"

A. "I do not know whether he ever said it or not. I only read it in the newspapers. But I know what this man said and I know the manner in which he said it, and I know particularly the evidence which he gave to sustain his statement. He told in detail how it was that they wanted to do this for him, and the relationship, the proof was so trivial, that there was no relationship between them."

Q. "What is it that he said the Clearing House wanted to do to him and how he attempted to prove it?"

A. "My best recollection is he said the story goes back to 1907 when there were difficulties of a certain nature, that is in the financial world; that he had offered to help somebody of financial standing in the community; he even said at one time that he offered to give him five hundred thousand dollars and at another time he said he did give him five hundred thousand dollars, and then some time later, in 1927, 1928, and 1929, and just before the crash when speculation was so active that the brokers would bring their certifications to the Clearing House of the amounts of money that they might want to borrow in the course of the day, and that he with others or that some others persuaded him to be spokesman that the Clearing House should not get so much gravy, as he expressed it."

The Court. "So much what?"

The Witness. "So much gravy."

Q. "Meaning profit?"

A. "That is to say, that a brokerage house would bring in an uncertified—or a certain amount that they thought they might have to borrow in the course of the day, two hundred thousand, three hundred thousand, four hundred thousand dollars; they had put a certain percentage on that and at the end of the day the percentage charge was the actual amount of money that they did borrow, whereas some of the people in the Clearing House, as I understood it, see, wanted to charge them the actual amounts that they wrote in blank at the beginning of the day. Now Mr. Harriman stood as a spokesman out against that kind of procedure at that time, and said that they should only be charged for what they actually borrowed, and he stood on the floor and made his argument and they had a vote and they lost, and that was the reason they wanted to put him on the spot."

Q. "Did he tell you how they put him on the spot?"

A. "Not specifically, no."

Q. "Did you ask him?"

A. "No."

Q. "Was he referring to fact that the Clearing House had a new man to put in as president and that he was relieved of the post of president?"

A. "That was not taken up, no."

Q. "Didn't you know that was the fact?"

A. "In general, yes."

Q. "That is, that in June or July, 1932, through Clearing House influence Mr. Cooper was made president and Mr. Harriman was left with a nominal, ornamental position of chairman of the board of directors?"

A. "I think I read something like that in the newspapers, yes."

Q. "Did it sound like a normal grievance to you, with a knowledge of that fact—the kind of grievance that a loser might normally have, even though wrong in this statement?"

A. "He had a grievance, yes."

Q. "Anything unusual in normal sane people having unjustified grievances with a trivial basis of fact?"

A. "All I can say is the material given to me and the way and the manner in which it was given to me impressed me as distinctly anomalous and abnormal and not justified."

Q. "I want you to forget about Harriman for a minute and generalize with me again. Doesn't your experience and observation show that a normal or at least a competent person will have an unfounded grievance where he is the loser, that has only a trivial basis in fact?"

A. "Very frequently that is true, yes."

Q. "Is the thought of self-destruction necessarily evidence of incompetency?"

A. "The thought of it? No."

Q. "Are efforts in that direction necessarily evidence of incompetence?"

A. "In general, yes."

Q. "Then you think anybody who attempts suicide is mentally incompetent?"

A. "In general, yes."

Q. "You say that unreservedly?"

A. "Unreservedly, yes. There might be very few exceptions, but I have never met them."

Q. "You would say that everybody that you have seen who has attempted suicide was mentally incompetent?"

A. "Every person that I have ever met that I know of,

see, anything at all about, I found them to be incompetent, yes."

Q. "By incompetent you mean unable to take care of their own affairs, unable to give any normal judgment on the ordinary processes of life?"

A. "No, I don't mean that absolutely. I mean that with reference to the act that they performed."

Q. "Well, outside of the act they performed?"

A. "But that is the act."

Q. "I know. Having attempted to commit suicide, would you say that such a person is not competent to manage his own affairs—that is, give a business judgment, decide on whether to borrow money or lend money, decide on whether to make a lease or not make a lease, decide on whether to move or not to move?"

A. "During the time that he is committing that act, no, he is not."

Q. "And when it is over with?"

A. "He might return again to such a condition that you have described, yes, or he might not. It depends on the particular kind of illness that he suffers which brings about the suicide."

Mr. Medalie. "That is all."

The decision of the Court was that Mr. Harriman was of sound mind and should stand trial. About a year later, after a five-weeks' trial, he was convicted and sentenced to four and a half years in the United States Penitentiary at Lewisburg, Pa., where he is now confined. He filed a notice of appeal, but six weeks later withdrew it and decided to serve his term.

Chapter 23

The Bellevue Hospital Case

On December 15, 1900, there appeared in the *New York World* an article written by Thomas J. Minnock, a newspaper reporter, in which he claimed to have been an eyewitness to the shocking brutality of certain nurses in attendance at the Insane Pavilion of Bellevue Hospital, which resulted in the death, by strangulation, of one of its inmates, a Frenchman named Hilliard. This Frenchman had arrived at the hospital at about four o'clock in the afternoon of Tuesday, December 11. He was suffering from alcoholic mania, but was apparently otherwise in normal physical condition. Twenty-six hours later, or on Wednesday, December 12, he died. An autopsy was performed which disclosed several bruises on his forehead, arm, hand, and shoulder, three broken ribs and a broken hyoid bone in the neck (which supports the tongue), and a suffusion of blood or haemorrhage on both sides of the windpipe. The coroner's physician reported the cause of death, as shown by the autopsy, to be strangulation. The newspaper reporter, Minnock, claimed to have been in Bellevue at the time, feigning insanity for newspaper purposes; and upon his discharge from the hospital he stated that he had seen the Frenchman strangled to death by the nurses in charge of the Pavilion by the use of a sheet tightly twisted around the insane man's neck. The language used in the newspaper articles written by Minnock to describe the occurrences preceding the Frenchman's death was as follows:—

"At supper time on Wednesday evening, when the Frenchman, Mr. Hilliard, refused to eat his supper, the nurse, Davis, started for him. Hilliard ran around the table, and the other two nurses, Dean and Marshall, headed him off and held him; they forced him down on a bench, Davis called for a sheet, one of the other two, I do not remember which, brought it, and Davis drew it around Hilliard's neck like a rope. Dean was behind the bench on which Hilliard had been pulled back; he gathered up the loose ends of the sheet and pulled the linen tight around Hilliard's neck, then he began to twist the folds in his hand. I was horrified. I have read of the garrote; I have seen pictures of how persons are executed in Spanish countries; I realized that here, before my eyes, a strangle was going to be performed. Davis twisted the ends of the sheet in his hands, round and round; he placed his knee against Hilliard's back and exercised all his force. The dying man's eyes began to bulge from their sockets; it made me sick, but I looked on as if fascinated. Hilliard's hands clutched frantically at the coils around his neck. 'Keep his hands down, can't you?' shouted Davis in a rage. Dean and Marshall seized the helpless man's hands; slowly, remorselessly, Davis kept on twisting the sheet. Hilliard began to get black in the face; his tongue was hanging out. Marshall got frightened. 'Let up, he is getting black!' he said to Davis. Davis let out a couple of twists of the sheet, but did not seem to like to do it. At last Hilliard got a little breath, just a little. The sheet was still brought tight about the neck. 'Now will you eat?' cried Davis. 'No,' gasped the insane man. Davis was furious. 'Well, I will make you eat; I will choke you until you do eat,' he shouted, and he began to twist the sheet again. Hilliard's head would have fallen upon his breast but for the fact that Davis was holding it up. He began to get black in the face again. A second time they got frightened, and Davis eased up on the string. He untwisted the sheet, but still kept a firm grasp on the folds. It took Hilliard some time to come to. When he did at last, Davis again asked him if he would eat. Hilliard had just breath enough to whisper faintly, 'No.' I thought the man was dying then. Davis twisted up the sheet again, and cried, 'Well, I will make him eat or I will choke him to death.' He twisted and twisted until I thought he would break the man's neck. Hilliard was unconscious at last. Davis jerked the man to the floor and kneeled on him, but still had the strangle hold with his knee giving him additional purchase. He twisted the sheet until his own fingers were sore, then the three nurses dragged the limp body to the bath-room, heaved him into the tub with his clothes on, and turned the cold water on him. He was dead by this time, I believe. He was strangled to death, and the finishing touches were put on when they had him on the floor. No big, strong healthy man could have lived under that awful strangling. Hilliard was weak and feeble."

The above article appeared in the morning *Journal,* a few days after the original publication in the *New York World.* The other local papers immediately took up the story, and it is easy to imagine the pitch to which the public excitement and indignation were aroused. The three nurses in charge of the pavilion at the time of Hilliard's death were immediately indicted for manslaughter, and the head nurse, Jesse R. Davis, was promptly put on trial in the Court of General Sessions, before Mr. Justice Cowing and a "special jury." The trial lasted three weeks, and after deliberating five hours upon their verdict the jury acquitted the prisoner. My appearance in the case was occasioned by the deep interest taken by the late Ogden Mills, who wished to vindicate the reputation of the training school bearing his name.

The intense interest taken in the case, not only by the public, but by the medical profession, was increased by the fact that for the first time in the criminal courts of this country two inmates of the insane pavilion, themselves admittedly insane, were called by the prosecution, and sworn and accepted by the court as witnesses against the prisoner. One of these witnesses was suffering from a form of insanity known as paranoia, and the other from general paresis. With the exception of the two insane witnesses and the medical testimony founded upon the autopsy, there was no direct evidence on which to convict the prisoner but the statement of the newspaper reporter, Minnock. He was the one sane witness called on behalf of the prosecution, who was an eye-witness to the occurrence, and the issues in the case gradually narrowed down to a question of veracity between this newspaper reporter and the accused prisoner, the testimony of each of them being corroborated or contradicted on either side by various other witnesses.

If Minnock's testimony were to be credited by the jury, the prisoner's contradiction would naturally have no effect whatever, and the public prejudice, indignation, and excitement ran so high that the jury were only too ready and willing to accept the newspaper account of the transaction. The cross-examination of Minnock, therefore, became of the utmost importance. It was essential that the effect of his testimony should be broken, and counsel having his cross-examination in charge had made the most elaborate preparations for the task. Extracts from the cross-examination are here given as illustrations of many of the suggestions which have been discussed in previous chapters.

The district attorney in charge of the prosecution was Franklin Pierce, Esq. In his opening address to the jury he stated that he "did not believe that ever in the history of the state, or indeed of the country, had a jury been called upon to decide such an important case as the one on trial." He continued: "There is no fiction—no 'Hard Cash'—in this case. The facts here surpass anything that fiction has ever produced. The witnesses will describe the most terrible treatment that was ever given to an insane man. No writer of fiction could have put them in a book. They would appear so improbable and monstrous that his manuscript would have been rejected as soon as offered to a publisher."

When the reporter, Minnock, stepped to the witness stand, the court room was crowded, and yet so intense was the excitement that every word the witness uttered could be distinctly heard by everybody present. He gave his evidence in chief clearly and calmly, and with no apparent motive but to narrate correctly the details of the crime he had seen committed. Any one unaware of his career would have regarded him as an unusually clever and apparently honest and courageous man with a keen memory, and with just the slightest touch of gratification at the important position he was holding in the public eye in consequence of his having unearthed the atrocities perpetrated in our public hospitals.

His direct evidence was practically a repetition of his newspaper article already referred to, only much more in detail. After questioning him for about an hour, the district attorney sat down with a confident, "He is your witness, if you wish to cross-examine him."

No one who has never experienced it can have the slightest appreciation of the nervous excitement attendant on being called upon to cross-examine the chief witness in a case involving the life or liberty of a human being. If Minnock withstood the cross-examination, the nurse Davis, apparently a most worthy and refined young man who had just graduated from the Mills Training School for Nurses, and about to be married to a most estimable young lady, would have to spend at least the next twenty years of his life at hard labor in state prison.

The first fifteen minutes of the cross-examination were devoted to showing that the witness was a thoroughly educated man, twenty-five years of age, a graduate of St. John's College, Fordham, New York, the Sacred Heart Academy, St. Francis Xavier's, and the De La Salle Institute, and had travelled extensively in Europe and America. The cross-examination then proceeded:—

Counsel (amiably). "Mr. Minnock, I believe you have written the story of your life and published it in the *Bridgeport Sunday Herald* as recently as last December? I hold the original article in my hand."

Witness. "It was not the story of my life."

Counsel. "The article is signed by you and purports to be a history of your life."

Witness. "It is an imaginary story dealing with hypnotism. Fiction, partly, but it dealt with facts."

Counsel. "That is, you mean to say you mixed fiction and fact in the history of your life?"

Witness. "Yes, sir."

Counsel. "In other words, you dressed up facts with fiction to make them more interesting?"

Witness. "Precisely."

Counsel. "When in this article you wrote that at the age of twelve you ran away with a circus, was that dressed up?"

Witness. "Yes, sir."

Counsel. "It was not true?"

Witness. "No, sir."

Counsel. "When you said that you continued with this circus for over a year, and went with it to Belgium, there was a particle of truth in that because you did, as a matter of fact, go to Belgium, but not with the circus as a public clown; is that the idea?"

Witness. "Yes, sir."

Counsel. "So there was some little truth mixed in at this point with the other matter?"

Witness. "Yes, sir."

Counsel. "When you wrote that you were introduced in Belgium, at the Hospital General, to Charcot, the celebrated Parisian hypnotist, was there some truth in that?"

Witness. "No, sir."

Counsel. "You knew that Charcot was one of the originators of hypnotism in France, didn't you?"

Witness. "I knew that he was one of the original hypnotists."

Counsel. "How did you come to state in the newspaper history of your life that you were introduced to Charcot at the Hospital General if that was not true?"

Witness. "While there I met Charcot."

Counsel. "Oh, I see."

Witness. "But not the original Charcot."

Counsel. "Which Charcot did you meet?"

Witness. "A woman. She was a lady assuming the name of Charcot, claiming to be Madame Charcot."

Counsel. "So that when you write in this article that you met Charcot, you intended people to understand that it was the celebrated Professor Charcot, and it was partly true, because there was a woman by the name of Charcot whom you had really met?"

Witness. "Precisely."

Counsel (quietly). "That is to say, there was some truth in it?"

Witness. "Yes, sir."

Counsel. "When in that article you said that Charcot taught you to stand pain, was there any truth in that?"

Witness. "No."

Counsel. "Did you as a matter of fact learn to stand pain?"

Witness. "No."

Counsel. "When you said in this article that Charcot began by sticking pins and knives into you little by little, so as to accustom you to standing pain, was that all fiction?"

Witness. "Yes, sir."

Counsel. "When you wrote that Charcot taught you to reduce your respirations to two a minute, so as to make your body insensible to pain, was that fiction?"

Witness. "Purely imagination."

Court (interrupting). "Counsellor, I will not allow you to go further in this line of inquiry. The witness himself says his article was almost entirely fiction, some of it founded upon fact. I will allow you the greatest latitude in a proper way, but not in this direction."

Counsel. "Your Honor does not catch the point."

Court. "I do not think I do."

Counsel. "This prosecution was started by a newspaper article written by the witness, and published in the morning *Journal.* It is the claim of the defence that the newspaper article was a mixture of fact and fiction, mostly fiction. The witness has already admitted that the history of his life, published but a few months ago, and written and signed by himself and sold as a history of his life, was a mixture of fact and fiction, mostly fiction. Would it not be instructive to the jury to learn from the lips of the witness himself how far he dressed up the pretended history of his own life, that they may draw from it some inference as to how far he has likewise dressed up the article which was the origin of this prosecution?"

Court. "I shall grant you the greatest latitude in examination of the witness in regard to the newspaper article which he published in regard to this case, but I exclude all questions relating to the witness's newspaper history of his own life."

Counsel. "Did you not have yourself photographed and published in the newspapers in connection with the history of your life, with your mouth and lips and ears sewed up, while you were insensible to pain?"

Court. "Question excluded."

Counsel. "Did you not publish a picture of yourself in connection with the pretended history of your life, representing yourself upon a cross, spiked hand and foot, but insensible to pain, in consequence of the instruction you had received from Professor Charcot?"

Court. "Question excluded."

Counsel. "I offer these pictures and articles in evidence."

Court (roughly). "Excluded." [1]

Counsel. "In the article you published in the *New York Journal,* wherein you described the occurrences in the present case, which you have just now related upon the witness stand, did you there have yourself represented as in the position of the insane patient, with a sheet twisted around your neck, and held by the hands of the hospital nurse who was strangling you to death?"

Witness. "I wrote the article, but I did not pose for the picture. The picture was posed for by some one else who looked like me."

[1] It was currently reported at the time that the District Attorney's office, in conjunction with the newspapers and the specially selected trial judge, was making unusual efforts to secure a conviction.

Counsel (stepping up to the witness and handing him the newspaper article). "Are not these words under your picture, 'This is how I saw it done, Thomas J. Minnock,' a facsimile of your handwriting?"

Witness. "Yes, sir, it is my handwriting."

Counsel. "Referring to the history of your life again how many imaginary articles on the subject have you written for the newspapers throughout the country?"

Witness. "One."

Counsel. "You have put several articles in New York papers, have you not?"

Witness. "It was only the original story. It has since been redressed, that's all."

Counsel. "Each time you signed the article and sold it to the newspaper for money, did you not?"

Court. "Excluded."

Counsel (with a sudden change of manner, and in a loud voice, turning to the audience). "Is the chief of police of Bridgeport, Connecticut, in the court room? (Turning to the witness.) Mr. Minnock, do you know this gentleman?"

Witness. "I do."

Counsel. "Tell the jury when you first made his acquaintance."

Witness. "It was when I was arrested in the Atlantic Hotel, in Bridgeport, Connecticut, with my wife."

Counsel. "Was she your wife at the time?"

Witness. "Yes, sir."

Counsel. "She was but sixteen years old?"

Witness. "Seventeen, I guess."

Counsel. "You were arrested on the ground that you were trying to drug this sixteen-year-old girl and kidnap her to New York. Do you deny it?"

Witness (doggedly). "I was arrested."

Counsel (sharply). "You know the cause of the arrest to be as I have stated? Answer yes or no!"

Witness (hesitating). "Yes, sir."

Counsel. "You were permitted by the prosecuting attorney, F. A. Bartlett, to be discharged without trial on your promise to leave the state, were you not?"

Witness. "I don't remember anything of that."

Counsel. "Do you deny it?"

Witness. "I do."

Counsel. "Did you have another young man with you upon that occasion?"

Witness. "I did. A college chum."

Counsel. "Was he also married to this sixteen-year-old girl?"

Witness (no answer).

Counsel (pointedly at witness). "Was he married to this girl also?"

Witness. "Why, no."

Counsel. "You say you were married to her. Give me the date of your marriage."

Witness. (hesitating). "I don't remember the date."

Counsel. "How many years ago was it?"

Witness. "I don't remember."

Counsel. "What is your best memory as to how many years ago it was?"

Witness. "I can't recollect."

Counsel. "Try to recollect about when you were married."

Witness. "I was married twice, civil marriage and church marriage."

Counsel. "I am talking about Miss Sadie Cook. When were you married to Sadie Cook, and where is the marriage recorded?"

Witness. "I tell you I don't remember."

Counsel. "Try."

Witness. "It might be five or six or seven or ten years ago."

Counsel. "Then you cannot tell within five years of the time when you were married, and you are now only twenty-five years old?"

Witness. "I cannot."

Counsel. "Were you married at fifteen years of age?"

Witness. "I don't think I was."

Counsel. "You know, do you not, that your marriage was several years after this arrest in Bridgeport that I have been speaking to you about?"

Witness. "I know nothing of the kind."

Counsel (resolutely). "Do you deny it?"

Witness (hesitating). "Well, no, I do not deny it."

Counsel. "I hand you now what purports to be the certificate of your marriage, three years ago. Is the date correct?"

Witness. "I never saw it before."

Counsel. "Does the certificate correctly state the time and place and circumstances of your marriage?"

Witness. "I refuse to to answer the question on the ground that it would incriminate my wife."

The theory on which the defence was being made was that the witness, Minnock, had manufactured the story which he had printed in the paper, and later swore to before the grand jury and at the trial. The effort in his cross-examination was to show that he was the kind of man who would manufacture such a story and sell it to the newspapers, and afterward, when compelled to do so, swear to it in court.

Counsel next called the witness's attention to many facts tending to show that he had been an eye-witness to adultery in divorce cases, and on both sides of them, first on one side, then on the other, in the same case, and that he had been at one time a private detective. Men whom he had robbed and blackmailed and cheated at cards were called from the audience, one after another, and he was confronted with questions referring to these charges, all of which he denied in the presence of his accusers. The presiding judge having stated to counsel in the hearing of the witness that although he allowed the witness to be brought face to face with his alleged accusers, yet he would allow no contradictions of the witness on these collateral matters, Minnock's former defiant demeanor immediately returned.

The next interrogatories put to the witness developed

the fact that, feigning insanity, he had allowed himself to be taken to Bellevue with the hope of being transferred to Ward's Island, and the intention of finally being discharged as cured, and then writing sensational newspaper articles regarding what he had seen while an inmate of the public insane asylums; that in Bellevue Hospital he had been detected as a malingerer by one of the attending physicians, Dr. Fitch, and had been taken before a police magistrate where he had stated in open court that he had found everything in Bellevue "far better than he had expected to find it," and that he had "no complaint to make and nothing to criticise."

The witness's mind was then taken from the main subject by questions concerning the various conversations had with the different nurses while in the asylum, all of which conversations he denied. The interrogatories were put in such a way as to admit of a "yes" or "no" answer only. Gradually coming nearer to the point desired to be made, the following questions were asked:—

Counsel. "Did the nurse Gordon ask you why you were willing to submit to confinement as an insane patient, and did you reply that you were a newspaper man and under contract with a Sunday paper to write up the methods of the asylum, but that the paper had repudiated the contract?"

Witness. "No."

Counsel. "Or words to that effect?"

Witness. "No."

Counsel. "I am referring to a time subsequent to your discharge from the asylum, and after you had returned to take away your belongings. Did you, at that time, tell the nurse Gordon that you had expected to be able to write an article for which you could get $140?"

Witness. "I did not."

Counsel. "Did the nurse say to you, 'You got fooled this time, didn't you?' And did you reply, 'Yes, but I will try to write up something and see if I can't get square with them!' "

Witness. "I have no memory of it."

Counsel. "Or words to that effect?"

Witness. "I did not."

All that preceded had served only as a veiled introduction to the next important question.

Counsel (quietly)."At that time, as a matter of fact, did you know anything you could write about when you got back to the *Herald* office?"

Witness. "*I knew there was nothing to write.*"

Counsel. "Did you know at that time, or have any idea what you would write when you got out?"

Witness. "Did I at that time know? *Why I knew there was nothing to write.*"

Counsel (walking forward and pointing excitedly at the witness). "Although you had seen a man choked to death with a sheet on Wednesday night, you knew on Friday morning that there was nothing you could write about?"

Witness (hesitating). "I didn't know they had killed the man."

Counsel. "Although you had seen the patient fall unconscious several times to the floor after having been choked with the sheet twisted around his neck, you knew there was nothing to write about?"

Witness. "I knew it was my duty to go and see the charity commissioner and tell him about that."

Counsel. "But you were a newspaper reporter—in the asylum for the purpose of writing up an article. Do you want to take back what you said a moment ago—that you knew there was nothing to write about?"

Witness. "Certainly not. I did not know the man was dead."

Counsel. "Did you not testify that the morning after you had seen the patient choked into unconsciousness, you heard the nurse call up the morgue to inquire if the autopsy had been made?"

Witness (sheepishly). "Well, the story that I had the contract for with the *Herald* was cancelled."

Counsel. "Is it not a fact that within four hours of the time you were finally discharged from the hospital on

Saturday afternoon, you read the newspaper account of the autopsy, and then immediately wrote your story of having seen this patient strangled to death and offered it for sale to the *New York World?*"

Witness. "That is right; yes, sir."

Counsel. "You say you knew it was your duty to go to the charity commissioner and tell him what you had seen. Did you go to him?"

Witness. "No, not after I found out through reading the autopsy that the man was killed."

Counsel. "Instead, you went to the *World,* and offered them the story in which you describe the way Hilliard was killed?"

Witness. "Yes."

Counsel. "And you did this within three or four hours of the time you read the newspaper account of the autopsy?"

Witness. "Yes."

Counsel. "The editors of the *World* refused your story unless you would put it in the form of an affidavit, did they not?"

Witness. "Yes."

Counsel. "Did you put it in the form of an affidavit?"

Witness. "Yes."

Counsel. "And that was the very night that you were discharged from the hospital?"

Witness. "Yes."

Counsel. "Every occurrence was then fresh in your mind, was it not?"

Witness. (hesitating). "What?"

Counsel. "Were the occurrences of the hospital fresh in your mind at that time?"

Witness. "Well, not any fresher then than they are now."

Counsel. "As fresh as now?"

Witness. "Yes, sir."

Counsel (pausing, looking among his papers, selecting one and walking up to the witness, handing it to him).

"Take this affidavit, made that Friday night and sold to the *World;* show me where there is a word in it about Davis having strangled the Frenchman with a sheet, the way you have described it here to-day to this jury."

Witness (refusing paper). "No, I don't think that it is there. It is not necessary for me to look it over."

Counsel (shouting). "Don't *think!* You know that it is not there, do you not?"

Witness (nervously). "Yes, sir; it is not there."

Counsel. "Had you forgotten it when you made that affidavit?"

Witness. "Yes, sir."

Counsel (loudly). "You had forgotten it, although only three days before you had seen a man strangled in your presence, with a sheet twisted around his throat, and had seen him fall lifeless upon the floor. You had forgotten it when you described the incident and made the affidavit about it to the *World?*"

Witness (hesitating). "I made two affidavits. I believe that is in the second affidavit."

Counsel. "Answer my questions, Mr. Minnock. Is there any doubt that you had forgotten it when you made the first affidavit to the *World?*"

Witness. "I had forgotten it."

Counsel (abruptly). "When did you recollect?"

Witness. "I recollected it when I made the second affidavit before the coroner."

Counsel. "And when did you make that?"

Witness. "It was a few days afterward, probably the next day or two."

Counsel (looking among his papers, and again walking up to the witness). "Please take the coroner's affidavit and point out to the jury where there is a word about a sheet having been used to strangle this man."

Witness (refusing paper). "Well, it may not be there."

Counsel. "Is it there?"

Witness (still refusing paper). "I don't know."

Counsel. "Read it carefully."

Witness (reading). "I don't see anything about it."

Counsel. "Had you forgotten it at that time as well?"

Witness (in confusion). "I certainly must have."

Counsel. "Do you want this jury to believe that, having witnessed this horrible scene which you have described, you immediately forgot it, and on two different occasions when you were narrating under oath what took place in that hospital, you forgot to mention it?"

Witness. "It escaped my memory."

Counsel. "You have testified as a witness before in this case, have you not?"

Witness. "Yes, sir."

Counsel. "Before the coroner?"

Witness. "Yes, sir."

Counsel. "But this sheet incident escaped your memory then?"

Witness. "It did not."

Counsel (taking in his hands the stenographer's minutes of the coroner's inquest). "Do you not recollect that you testified for two hours before the coroner without mentioning the sheet incident, and were then excused and were absent from the court for several days before you returned and gave the details of the sheet incident?"

Witness. "Yes, sir; that is correct."

Counsel. "Why did you not give an account of the sheet incident on the first day of your testimony?"

Witness. "Well, it escaped my memory; I forgot it."

Counsel. "Do you recollect, before beginning your testimony before the coroner, you asked to look at the affidavit that you had made for the *World?*"

Witness. "Yes, I had been sick, and I wanted to refresh my memory."

Counsel. "Do you mean that this scene that you have described so glibly to-day had faded out of your mind then, and you wanted your affidavit to refresh your recollection?"

Witness. "No, it had not faded. I merely wanted to refresh my recollection."

Counsel. "Was it not rather that you had made up the story in your affidavit, and you wanted the affidavit to

refresh your recollection as to the story you had manufactured?"

Witness. "No, sir; that is not true."

The purpose of these questions, and the use made of
the answers upon the argument, is shown by the following
extract from the summing up:—

"My point is this, gentlemen of the jury, and it is an
unanswerable one in my judgment, Mr. District Attorney:
If Minnock, fresh from the asylum, forgot this sheet
incident when he went to sell his first newspaper article to
the *World;* if he also forgot it when he went to the coroner
two days afterward to make his second affidavit; if he still
forgot it two weeks later when, at the inquest, he testified
for two hours without mentioning it, and only first recollected it when he was recalled two days afterward, then
there is but one inference to be drawn, and that is, *that
he never saw it, because he could not forget it if he had
ever seen it!* And the important feature is this: he was a
newspaper reporter; he was there, as the district attorney
says, 'to observe what was going on.' He says that he
stood by in that part of the room, pretending to take away
the dishes in order to see what was going on. He was sane,
the only sane man there. Now if he did not see it, it is
because it did not take place, and if it did not take place,
the insane men called here as witnesses could not have
seen it. Do you see the point? Can you answer it? Let me
put it again. It is not in mortal mind to believe that this
man could have seen such a transaction as he describes
and ever have forgotten it. Forget it when he writes his
article the night he leaves the asylum and sells it to the
morning *World!* Forget it two days afterward when he
makes a second important affidavit! He makes still another statement, and does not mention it, and even testifies at the coroner's inquest two weeks later, and leaves
it out. Can the human mind draw any other inference
from these facts than that he never saw it—because he
could not have forgotten it if he had ever seen it? If *he*
never saw it, it did not take place. He was on the spot,

sane, and watching everything that went on, *for the very purpose of reporting it.* And if this sheet incident did not take place, the insane men *could not* have seen it. This disposes not only of Minnock, but of all the testimony in the People's case. In order to say by your verdict that that sheet incident took place, you have got to find something that is contrary to all human experience; that is, that this man, Minnock, having seen the horrible strangling with the sheet, as he described, could *possibly* have immediately forgotten it."

The contents of the two affidavits made to the *World* and the coroner were next taken up, and the witness was first asked what the occurrence really was, as he now remembered it. After his answers, his attention was called to what he said in his affidavits, and upon the differences being made apparent, he was asked whether what he then swore to, or what he now swore to, was the actual fact; and if he was now testifying from what he remembered to have seen, or if he was trying to remember the facts as he made them up in the affidavit.

Counsel. "What was the condition of the Frenchman at supper time? Was he as gay and chipper as when you said that he had warmed up after he had been walking around awhile?"

Witness. "Yes, sir."

Counsel. "But in your affidavit you state that he seemed to be very feeble at supper. Is that true?"

Witness. "Well, yes; he did seem to be feeble."

Counsel. "But you said a moment ago that he warmed up and was all right at supper time."

Witness. "Oh, you just led me into that."

Counsel. "Well, I won't lead you into anything more. Tell us how he walked to the table."

Witness. "Well, slowly."

Counsel. "Do you remember what you said in the affidavit?"

Witness. "I certainly do."

Counsel. "What did you say?"

Witness. "I said he walked in feeble condition."

Counsel. "Are you sure that you said anything in the affidavit about how he walked at all?"

Witness. "I am not sure."

Counsel. "The sheet incident, which you have described so graphically, occurred at what hour on Wednesday after noon?"

Witness. "About six o'clock."

Counsel. "Previous to that time, during the afternoon, had there been any violence shown toward him?"

Witness. "Yes; he was shoved down several times by the nurses."

Counsel. "You mean they let him fall?"

Witness. "Yes, they thought it a very funny thing to let him totter backward, and to fall down. They then picked him up. His knees seemed to be kind of muscle-bound, and he tottered back and fell, and they laughed. This was somewhere around three o'clock in the afternoon."

Counsel. "How many times, Mr. Minnock, would you swear that you saw him fall over backward, and after being picked up by the nurse, let fall again?"

Witness. "Four or five times during the afternoon."

Counsel. "And would he always fall backward?"

Witness. "Yes, sir; he repeated the operation of tottering backward. He would totter about five feet, and would lose his balance and would fall over backward."

The witness was led on to describe in detail this process of holding up the patient, and allowing him to fall backward, and then picking him up again, in order to make the contrast more apparent with what he had said on previous occasions and had evidently forgotten.

Counsel. "I now read to you from the stenographer's minutes what you said on this subject in your sworn testimony given at the coroner's inquest. You were asked, 'Was there any violence inflicted on Wednesday before dinner time?' And you answered, 'I didn't see any.' You were asked if, up to dinner time at six o'clock on Wednesday night, there has been any violence; and you answered: 'No, sir; no violence since Tuesday night. There was nothing happened until Wednesday at supper time, somewhere about six o'clock.' Now what have you to say as to these different statements, both given under oath, one given at the coroner's inquest, and the other given here today?"

Witness. "Well, what I said about violence may have been omitted by the coroner's stenographer."

Counsel. "But did you swear to the answers that I have just read to you before the coroner?"

Witness. "I may have, and I may not have. I don't know."

Counsel. "If you swore before the coroner there was no violence, and nothing happened until Wednesday after supper, did you mean to say it?"

Witness. "I don't remember."

Counsel. "After hearing read what you swore to at the coroner's inquest, do you still maintain the truth of what you have sworn to at this trial, as to seeing the nurse let the patient fall backward four or five times, and pick him up and laugh at him?"

Witness. "I certainly do."

Counsel. "I again read you from the coroner's minutes a question asked you by the coroner himself. Question by the coroner, 'Did you at any time while in the office or the large room of the asylum see Hilliard fall or stumble?' Answer 'No, sir; I never did.' What have you to say to that?"

Witness. "That is correct."

Counsel. "Then what becomes of your statement made to the jury but fifteen minutes ago, that you saw him totter and fall backward several times?"

Witness. "It was brought out later on before the coroner."

Counsel. "Brought out later on! Let me read to you the next question put to you before the coroner. Question, 'Did you at *any time* see him try to walk or run away and fall? Answer, 'No, I never saw him fall.' What have you to say to that?"

Witness. "Well, I must have put in about the tottering in my affidavit, and omitted it later before the coroner."

At the beginning of the cross-examination it had been necessary for the counsel to fight with the Court over nearly every question asked; and question after question was ruled out. As the examination proceeded, however, the Court began to change its attitude entirely toward the witness. The presiding judge constantly frowned on the witness, kept his eyes riveted upon him, and finally broke out at this juncture: "Let me caution you, Mr. Minnock, once for all, you are here to answer counsel's questions. If you can't answer them, say so; and if you can answer them, do so; and if you have no recollection, say so."

Witness. "Well, your Honor, Mr. Wellman has been cross-examining me very severely about my wife, which he has no right to do."

Court. "You have no right to bring that up. He has a perfect right to cross-examine you."

Witness (losing his temper completely). "That man wouldn't dare to ask me those questions outside. He knows that he is under the protection of the court, or I would break his neck."

Court. "You are making a poor exhibit of yourself. Answer the questions, sir."

Counsel. "You don't seem to have any memory at all about this transaction. Are you testifying from memory as to what you saw, or making up as you go along?"

Witness (no answer).

Counsel. "Which is it?"

Witness (doggedly). "I am telling what I saw."

Counsel. "Well, listen to this then. You said in your affidavit: 'The blood was all over the floor. It was covered with Hilliard's blood, and the scrub woman came Tuesday and Wednesday morning, and washed the blood away.' Is that right?"

Witness. "Yes, sir."

Counsel. "Why, I understood you to say that you didn't get up Wednesday morning until noon. How could you see the scrub woman wash the blood away?"

Witness. "They were at the farther end of the hall. They washed the whole pavilion. I didn't see them Wednesday morning; it was Tuesday morning I saw them scrubbing."

Counsel. "You seem to have forgotten that Hilliard, the deceased, did not arrive at the pavilion until Tuesday afternoon at four o'clock. What have you to say to that?"

Witness. "Well, there were other people who got beatings besides him."

Counsel. "Then that is what you meant to refer to in your affidavit, when speaking of Hilliard's blood upon the floor. You meant beatings of other people?"

Witness. "Yes, sir—on Tuesday."

The witness was then forced to testify to minor details which, within the knowledge of the defence, could be contradicted by a dozen disinterested witnesses. Such, for instance, as hearing the nurse Davis call up the morgue, the morning after Hilliard was killed, at least a dozen times on the telephone, and anxiously inquire what had been disclosed by the autopsy; whereas, in fact, there was no direct telephonic communication whatever between the morgue and the insane pavilion; and the morgue attendants were prepared to swear that no one had called them up concerning the Hilliard autopsy, and that there were no inquiries from any source. The witness was next made to testify affirmatively to minor facts that could be, and were afterward contradicted by Dr. Wildman, by Dr. Moore, by Dr. Fitch, by Justice Hogman, by night nurses Clancy and Gordon, by Mr. Dwyer, Mr. Hayes, Mr. Fayne, by Gleason the registrar, by Spencer the electrician, by Jackson the janitor, and by several of the state's own witnesses who were to be called later.

By this time the witness had begun to flounder helplessly. He contradicted himself constantly, became red and pale by turns, hesitated before each answer, at times corrected his answers, at others was silent and made no answer at all. At the expiration of four hours he left the witness stand a thoroughly discredited, haggard, and wretched object. The court ordered him to return the following day, but he never was seen again at the trial.

A week later, his foster-mother, when called to the witness chair by the defence, handed to the judge a letter received that morning from her son, who was in Philadelphia (which, however, was not allowed to be shown to the jury) in which he wrote that he had shaken from his feet the dust of New York forever, and would never return; that he felt he had been ruined, and would be arrested for perjury if he came back, and requested money that he might travel far into the West and commence life anew. It was altogether the most tragic incident in the experience of the writer.

After the disappearance of Minnock, the newspapers, in conjunction with the District Attorney, were so determined to obtain a conviction that they called as witnesses two insane inmates of the Pavilion who had read and re-read the sensational newspaper accounts of the tragedy that had been circulated there, until their diseased minds had actually adopted the story as their own and they were ready to swear to its correctness at the trial. The jury, however, never forgot the complete collapse of the People's only sane eye witness, and acquitted the defendant.

Chapter 24

Cross-Examinations by
Charles H. Tuttle

I

The Story of "Exhibit Q"

THE FOLLOWING NARRATIVE will illustrate the value of a "hunch" in the conduct of a cross-examination, and will also illustrate the spectacle of an intelligent man of affairs gradually disintegrating as a witness under cross-examination.

In 1921 there came to trial before Judge Platzek an action by a former resident of Russia to recover from a large domestic corporation, engaged in the production and sale of aluminum, commissions for bringing about certain introductions which were said in the complaint to have led to the sale to the Russian Government of 17,500,000 pounds of aluminum for war purposes.

The defense was a general denial with special stress on the claims that no introduction or real service had been performed; that no such contract, as alleged in the complaint, had been made; that, on the contrary, the aluminum had been sold to the British Government rather than to the Russian Government; and that the intermediary had been J. P. Morgan & Co. rather than the plaintiff.

At the trial the defense counsel proclaimed dramatically that the British Government had taken the unusual course of interesting itself in establishing the truth as to the issues in this law suit and was making its secret files available for production at the trial. The defense counsel also emphasized that these files could, in consequence, not be impounded or offered in evidence, and that he therefore had caused triplicate typewritten copies to be made—one set for the court, one set for Mr. Tuttle (plaintiff's counsel) and one set for himself. Through a witness called as a representative of the British Government he then produced the original files and caused the original typewritten set of copies to be marked in evidence. He furnished the second set of alleged typewritten copies to Mr. Tuttle, who found the same very voluminous.

In leafing over the numerous copies of letters, Mr. Tuttle noticed one which closed without the usual conventional ending but merely stopped at the end of a paragraph. Ordinarily, in the hurry of the moment and because of the great bulk of the correspondence, such omission might have passed unnoticed, but it aroused a "hunch" that something was wrong. Just before the representative of the British Government left the courtroom with its original files, Mr. Tuttle seized an opportunity to examine them with seeming casualness and looked particularly at the original of the said letter, the alleged copy of which had been marked "Exhibit Q." Recalling the witness for cross-examination, Mr. Tuttle then had marked for identification the remaining two alleged typewritten copies of this letter and had the witness read aloud the final paragraph in each of the three copy sets. That paragraph was, of course, the same in each copy; and it tended to confirm the impression created by the whole correspondence that the aluminum was really being bought by and for the British Government.

He then caused the witness to read aloud the final paragraph in the original letter in the British Government's files. That final paragraph, omitted from the copies, contained statements which showed that the aluminum was in fact bought by the Russian Government for its war purposes but on English credit.

This fatal disclosure and the apparent effort at deception terminated all doubt as to the outcome of the trial. Mr. Tuttle exonerated opposing counsel when it developed that the so-called copies had been made not in his office but in another office. The jury rendered a verdict for the plaintiff in the sum of $175,000.

II

The Cross-Examination of Mr. X

On the other issues of the case, the cross-examination of the defendant's president, whom we shall call Mr. X, will furnish a striking example of how a chief executive of a large corporation, who had made a favorable impression on direct examination, could go to pieces when confronted with an analysis of the inherent and hidden contradictions and inconsistencies in his own story on the witness-stand.

Q. "Mr. X, do I understand you to say that the first time you met the plaintiff was in the office of Shipley & Moore on May 19th, 1916?"

A. "The first time I recall."

Q. "Well, have you any recollection at all of ever having seen him before?"

A. "What is it?'

Q. "Have you any recollection of ever having seen him before?"

A. "No."

Q. "You say he was introduced to you at that time?"

A. "Yes."

Q. "Was he introduced to you at that time as a stranger, you didn't recognize him at all, did you?"

A. "No."

Q. "As a man you had ever seen before?"

A. "No."

Q. "Had he ever been to your office before?"

A. "Not that I know of."

Q. "Had he ever seen you at your office before?"

A. "Not that I can recall."

Q. "Now, this letter dated April 24th, 1916, to the plaintiff, Plaintiff's Exhibit 3, that letter was written you say on what day?"

A. "On the 19th of May, 1916."

Q. "You wrote that after returning to your office that day?"

A. "I dictated it, yes."

Q. "And you did that from some memoranda which you made at the conference?"

A. "Or from memory, one of the two."

Q. "You say you made no note or longhand draft at the conference?"

A. "I didn't make any longhand draft; I don't know whether I made any notes or not."

Q. "Yes, now do you remember being examined before trial under oath in this case?"

A. "I was."

Q. "And you were examined by Mr. Roulstone, my associate here, were you not?"

A. "Yes."

Q. "Do you remember being asked concerning that letter which you have there, this April 24th letter?"

A. "I was."

Q. "What?"

A. "I was asked about it."

Q. "Yes, do you remember this question being put to you, 'Did Mr. Moore introduce plaintiff to you or vice versa?' "

A. "Yes."

Q. "And do you remember your answer, 'He introduced me in his office, but plaintiff was in my office previous to that'?"

A. "Yes, sir."

Q. "You remember that answer?"

A. "I do."

Q. "Was that answer true?"

A. "To the best of my knowledge and belief at that time it was true, yes."

Q. "So at that time you thought plaintiff had been in your office?"

A. "I did."

Q. "Do you recall about what time you thought he had been in your office?"

A. "I thought at that time that these letters were written at the time they were dated and I presumed that he must have been in my office in order for me to write them."

Q. "Now, the date of your examination was on or about April 17th, 1918?"

A. "I don't recall that."

Q. "That is the date on the first page?"

A. "All right."

Q. "Now, your memory of the transaction was as good then as it is now, wasn't it?"

A. "No, it was not."

Q. "You mean that such a thing as writing those letters, the three of them together and dating them back had escaped your memory at that time?"

A. "During that time it had."

Q. "So that when that letter was shown to you as of April 24th, bearing date April 24th, you concluded that you had seen him in your office?"

A. "I took it for granted that I had dictated that letter on April 24th, and that he must have called."

Q. "After this deposition was taken down, your testimony, you read it over, signed it, and swore to it, is that right?"

A. "I read it over, yes."

Q. "Now, do you recall at what time you read it over and signed it?"

A. "I read it over a number of times; I don't recall when I signed it."

Q. "Do you recall that you signed it only last month?"

A. "I know it was only a short time ago, yes."

Q. "Well, it was last month, was it not?"

A. "I think so, yes."

Q. "Now, of course, in reading it over and before you swore to it and had it upon the files of this court, you read it all, didn't you?"

A. "Yes."

Q. "So when you swore last month you swore to the answer that 'Moore introduced me in his office, but the plaintiff was in my office previous to that'?"

A. "I did."

Q. "You didn't correct that testimony?"

A. "I did not, didn't know I had any right to."

Q. "You had had a year to think it over and this case was on the eve of being tried then, was it not, it was on the day calendar?"

A. "I had something else to do during that year besides thinking of that."

Q. "Now, let us take the next question and answer to the one I just read you: '*Q.* When? *A.* About the time that letter of April 24th was written.' Do you remember that?"

A. "Yes."

Q. " '*Q.* Was it in the morning or afternoon? *A.* I have no idea; I stated before that he must have been in my office or I would not have written those letters.' Do you remember that?"

A. "Yes."

Q. " '*Q.* What business was he there on, do you know, did he tell you? *A.* About aluminum.' Is that right?"

A. "Yes."

Q. " '*Q.* He was there about aluminum, was he? *A.* Yes'?"

A. "Yes."

Q. " '*Q.* Did anybody introduce him to you at that time? *A.* No, he sent in a card'?"

A. "Yes."

Q. "Well, now, there was nothing in this letter of April 24th, when you first saw it, as you say now on this examination, in April, 1918, that suggested about his sending in a card, was there?"

A. "No."

Q. "You got that out of some independent thought of your own, didn't you?"

A. "Likely."

Q. "Now, when you said that he sent in a card that day, did you have any recollection, did you have any vision, did you conjure up plaintiff coming in and presenting you a card?"

A. "I don't recall now what I had in mind."

Q. "You don't know where you got the card idea, do you?"

A. "I do not."

Q. " '*Q.* He walked in alone, did he? *A.* He came into my office, yes, I saw him alone.' So those were your answers to that matter and your explanation of that letter of April 24th, at the time you were examined in April, 1918?"

A. "Yes."

Q. "And the time you swore to this deposition in April, 1921?"

A. "Yes."

Q. "Now, Mr. X, so there may be no mistake about it, these other two letters, one dated May 16, 1916, and the other dated May 18, 1916, were all written by you, you say, at your office or dictated on the afternoon of May 19th?"

A. "That is right."

Q. "There had been some conversation at the office of Moore & Shipley about your writing such letters and giving them to plaintiff, had there not?"

A. "Yes."

Q. "They were for the purpose of showing to his customer, were they not?"

A. "He wanted letters to show to the party from whom he expected to get an order, yes."

Q. "Now, why did you date back the letter to April 24th and why did you date back one of the letters to May 16th?"

A. "Plaintiff told me that he had had quotations from the Export & Import Corporation, such as are outlined in these letters, and that he had submitted them and now that I had previously explained or told plaintiff that most of the aluminum had been sold and now that it was sold he wanted something to explain to his customer why it was."

Q. "Now, didn't he say at that conference that he had sent a cable?"

A. "No."

Q. "Conveying quotations?"

A. "No."

Q. "Did he say that he had already made quotations based on quotations which he had received?"

A. "He didn't put it that way. He said that he had been quoting on aluminum but he didn't say that he had been quoting on aluminum that I had quoted him on."

Q. "Yes, but now you had quoted him on aluminum?"

A. "I had not."

Q. "Now, hadn't you quoted with him and Shipley for aluminum?"

A. "I had not."

Q. "Previous to this time?"

A. "I had not."

Q. "So you say that although you had never quoted Moore and Shipley aluminum you gave plaintiff a quotation of 66 cents a pound and dated it back to April 24th?"

A. "At their request I did."

Q. "Did you think that if you had not actually quoted plaintiff, either directly or through somebody else, on or about April 24th, as to that quantity, that that might enable him to deceive somebody?"

A. "Not at all. He said he had these quotations from Moore and Shipley."

Q. "But you say he didn't have those quotations from you?"

A. "How did I know that? How did I know that Moore and Shipley didn't have?"

Q. "I thought you said a few moments ago that you had not quoted him or Moore and Shipley?"

A. "No, I misunderstood what you said. I didn't know but what Moore and Shipley had received these quotations from some broker or somebody else that had received them from me."

Q. "Do you recognize those figures as figures and prices which you had quoted on or about April 24th?"

A. "I do not."

Q. "Was that the market then for aluminum?"

A. "Yes."

Q. "66 cents a pound for that quantity?"

A. "Yes."

Q. "So that, although you didn't know that he had received any quotations at all as of April 24th from you, you were willing to give him a letter signed by you under date of April 24th, giving him a quotation as of that date for that quantity?"

A. "I did."

Q. "Now, why was the letter of May 16th dated May 16th instead of May 18th and May 19th; what is your explanation of that?"

A. "I had sold some aluminum about that time and I had told plaintiff that I had disposed of some of the aluminum that I had and he suggested that I write a letter along that line, which I did."

Q. "You had sold about 60,000 pounds?"

A. "That is what it says there."

Q. "Well, was that the fact?"

A. "I don't know."

Q. "You don't know. Now, who suggested at that conference the fact that you had sold—who mentioned the figures 60,000 pounds, or weren't they mentioned at that conference at all?"

A. "I don't recall who mentioned it but very likely I did."

Q. "So the suggestion of your having sold 60,000 pounds came from you at that conference?"

A. "Likely."

Q. "And you don't recall now whether it was correct or not?"

A. "If I said so, it was correct."

Q. "But you don't recall any such sale at the present time?"

A. "No."

Q. "Now, as I understand you to say, that although these letters were written for the purpose of being shown to the customer, that you don't recall when you got in the presence of General Sapojnikoff that those letters were produced?"

A. "They were not produced."

Q. "Even though they were written for that purpose?"

A. "On the other hand, I don't mean that exactly; I mean they were not shown to me."

Q. "Well, I am talking about whether or not in your presence they were shown to General Sapojnikoff?"

A. "I did not see those letters while I was in that conference."

Q. "Whether you saw them or not, did you see letters, yellow paper like that, being shown?"

A. "I did not."

Q. "At this conference with General Sapojnikoff did he say anything to you as to whether or not he would be able to place a large order with you?"

A. "He—plaintiff told me that after talking to the general in some language I didn't understand that if the general was sure that I could make deliveries he was interested."

Q. "Well, did he say anything about whether if you could deliver in large quantities he would place a large order with you?"

A. "I don't recall whether he said he would place any business or not."

Q. "Well, now, on your examination before trial, page 16, were you asked these questions and did you give these answers: 'Q. Did General Sapojnikoff'—not plaintiff now —but 'did General Sapojnikoff at that conference say anything to you about his Russian Government requiring aluminum?'—do you recall what your answer was to that question?"

A. "He told me—"

Q. "Do you recall what your answer was?"

A. "I do, yes."

Q. "Which was it, 'Yes' or 'No'?"

A. "Oh, I don't know about that; I know what the general told me about that."

Q. "Well, your answer here is 'Yes'; is that correct?"

A. "Yes."

Q. "Then: 'Q. What did he say? A. He said that if he

were sure I can deliver the aluminum he would give me a large order'?"

A. "Yes."

Q. "Well, now, that refreshes your recollection that he did say that, is that it?"

A. "He said that through plaintiff."

Q. "When I asked you a moment ago as to whether he said—whether he had said either directly or through plaintiff that he would give you a large order, was your answer that he had said so?"

A. "I don't recall."

Q. "You don't recall your answer of a moment ago?"

A. "I don't recall that you asked me whether it was through either one of the two."

Q. "Now, at this conference with General Sapojnikoff did you say anything about the quantities that you could furnish, of aluminum?"

A. "Yes."

Q. "What did you say?"

A. "I told him I could furnish aluminum and so far as I recall the offers I made him were on a basis of that memorandum."

Q. "Well, I am asking you now, not on the basis of the memorandum, but I am asking you what you said in the way of the amount of aluminum that you could furnish?"

A. "I told him I could supply aluminum. We didn't talk very much about definite quantities."

Q. "Did you say that you could supply half or as much or twice the amount he desired?"

A. "No, no, we never got to a point where he told me how much he desired. It was much more important to me to know about the terms; I was not bothering about the quantity."

Q. "The subject was terms with you?"

A. "Principally, yes."

Q. "And he never got to the point where he told you of quantities and you never got to the point where you quoted him quantities?"

A. "Not that I can recall."

Q. "Well, you are clear about that, aren't you?"

A. "Yes."

Q. "Now, I ask you whether on your examination before trial you recall these questions and these answers: 'Do you remember what you did say to him? *A.* Not very well, no; I used my best business ability to convince him that I could supply aluminum'; you remember that answer, do you?"

A. "Yes."

Q. " '*Q.* Did you not say that you could deliver a stipulated quantity of aluminum each month thereafter? *A.* I did.' Do you recall that answer?"

A. "I don't recall that answer, but I presume it is there."

Q. "You haven't any doubt that that was the answer which you made at the time?"

A. "Not a bit, that is the answer I gave."

Q. "And that I am correctly reading from the minutes, your counsel checking me up?"

A. "Certainly not."

Q. "Now, I ask you if you recall this answer to this question: '*Q.* What was the maximum amount of aluminum which you offered to him? *A.* I have no idea; I should think that I would have told him that I could supply twice what he required.' Now, do you remember giving that answer?"

A. "Yes."

Q. "So that that refreshes your recollection that you and he did get down to the matter of quantities and that you told him you could give him twice what he required?"

A. "I said I told him I could, very likely I did."

Q. "We will not have any 'very likely.' Doesn't that refresh your recollection that you did get down to the subject of quantity and that you told him that you could give him twice what he required?"

A. "I said I thought I would have told him that; I didn't say I told him." . . .

Q. "Did you or did you not tell him that you could deliver twice what he required?"

A. "I did not tell him that I could deliver twice; that is only a conclusion."

Q. "Now, Mr. X, you say, as I understand it and are quite clear that this letter, Plaintiff's Exhibit 1, the Sapojnikoff letter, was never shown you until this trial?"

A. "Yes, it was not."

Q. "It was not shown you until this trial?"

A. "It was not."

Q. "Plaintiff never showed it to you?"

A. "He certainly did not."

Q. "You said he showed you some letter upon which the heading was bent back and the signature was bent back and he let you just read a line or two, is that it?"

A. "That is right."

Q. "Will you tell me again what that line or two was?"

A. "In effect, it said, 'I am interested in your proposition.' That may have been the exact wording; I don't know."

Q. "When he showed you on the way down to General Sapojnikoff's office, is that it?"

A. "Yes, on Fifth Avenue, going down to 23rd Street."

Q. "Well, he didn't tell you at the time who the signer of the letter was?"

A. "Certainly not."

Q. "Although you were headed for General Sapojnikoff's office?"

A. "How did I know that?"

Q. "Oh, you didn't know that you were headed for the Russian Commission at the time you left his apartment house?"

A. "Why, no."

Q. "You say then, as I understand it, that you went up to his apartment house?"

A. "I didn't go to his apartment house."

Q. "Where did you meet him, on the morning of May 20th?"

A. "On Fifth Avenue, on the sidewalk, somewhere about 29th Street."

Q. "Not in an entrance to an apartment house?"

A. "Yes, it was in the entrance of some house or office building I thought it was."

Q. "Either an apartment house or an office building, is that it?"

A. "I didn't know about that."

Q. "Then he just took you out on an errand, and you didn't know where you were going?"

A. "He said he wanted me to go on and meet his customer."

Q. "And he didn't say who that customer was?"

A. "He did not."

Q. "And the first you knew about who the customer was, was when you arrived at suite 1801 Flatiron Building?"

A. "Well, in the Flatiron Building, I don't know—"

Q. "Yes, now, on the way down to the Flatiron Building had anything been said, was there anything said, between you two, between the two of you, about commission or compensation in any form, shape or manner?"

A. "No, in fact, we didn't talk."

Q. "He was taking you simply to an unknown customer, and you and he were going along the street without talking?"

A. "Yes, he was going like the devil, and I was trying to keep up."

Q. "You did know, however, you were going to try to make a sale of aluminum, did you not, at the other end of this visit?"

A. "Yes."

Q. "And you, you and he, you say, never discussed plans for the forthcoming conversation with this customer?"

A. "I had told him the day before what I required, and he said he thought he could do it, and that was the end of it so far as I was concerned."

Q. "Now, you can answer that question, whether going

down this street here to wherever you were going, an unknown destination, you, a shrewd man of business, did go with him without discussing in any way the plan for presenting yourself effectively to the customer?"

A. "We did not discuss any plans."

Q. "He didn't deter you, you say, in any way, but he just went along like the devil, and you trotted behind as fast as you could, is that right?"

A. "That is right, yes, sir."

Q. "Did you ever see that letter which you say was creased down at any other time?"

A. "What letter?"

Q. "The letter which was bent back, top and bottom, did you ever see it again?"

A. "No."

Q. "Now, when you got into the Flatiron Building, where was it that the light was vouchsafed to you, that you were going to see the Russian Commission?"

A. "I don't know what you are talking about. What do you mean by 'light'?"

Q. "Light, I mean information in words—when did that dawn upon you, that you were going to see the Russian Commission?"

A. "When we got to the Russian Commission offices, I knew where I was then."

Q. "And then you went right in to see the general, is that right?"

A. "Well, we were taken into the general's office, yes." . . .

Q. "You didn't consider these letters of April 24th, May 18th and May 16th as intended to be firm offers which he could show to his customer?"

A. "Those offers were not firm at this date, when the letters were written, and he had told me that he had received them previously from Mr. Moore, and it didn't make a bit of difference to me because I was not obligated in any case."

Q. "Yet you were quoting him a price of 66 cents a pound for him to show his customer?"

A. "I should say that he didn't intend to show that to his customers; that would be my interpretation."

Q. "That is the idea that that letter was dated back, so as to match a quotation which he said he had given?"

A. "To his customer."

Q. "To his customer?"

A. "Yes."

Q. "And yet that he was not going to show his customer that letter as proof that he had had that quotation?"

A. "Well, I don't know. I don't do business that way."

Q. "You wrote the letters, didn't you?"

A. "I wrote at his request, yes."

Q. "And you do business at least to this extent in that way that you were willing to sign your name to a quotation as of April 24th when you didn't know that you had given it?"

A. "I didn't say—I knew I had not given it to him, though."

Q. "To that extent you do business that way, don't you?"

A. "All right."

Chapter 25

The Cross-Examination of Russell Sage

in Laidlaw v. Sage, by Hon. Joseph H. Choate

ONE OF THE rare instances of cross-examinations to be made the subject of appeal to the Supreme Court, General Term, and the New York Court of Appeals was the cross-examination of Russell Sage by the Hon. Joseph H. Choate in the famous suit brought against the former by William R. Laidlaw. Sage was defended by the late Edwin C. James, and Mr. Choate appeared for the plaintiff, Mr. Laidlaw.

On the fourth day of December, 1891, a stranger by the name of Norcross came to Russell Sage's New York office and sent a message to him that he wanted to see him on important business, and that he had a letter of introduction from Mr. John D. Rockefeller. Mr. Sage left his private office, and going up to Norcross, was handed an open letter which read, "This carpet bag I hold in my hand contains ten pounds of dynamite, and if I drop this bag on the floor it will destroy this building in ruins and kill every human being in it. I demand twelve hundred thousand dollars, or I will drop it. Will you give it? Yes or no?"

Mr. Sage read the letter, handed it back to Norcross, and suggested that he had a gentleman waiting for him in his private office, and could be through his business in a couple of minutes when he would give the matter his attention.

Norcross responded: "Then you decline my proposition? Will you give it to me? Yes or no?" Sage explained again why he would have to postpone giving it to him for

453

two or three minutes to get rid of some one in his private office, and just at this juncture Laidlaw entered the office, saw Norcross and Sage without hearing the conversation, and waited in the anteroom until Sage should be disengaged. As he waited, Sage edged toward him and partly seating himself upon the table near Laidlaw, and without addressing him, took him by the left hand as if to shake hands with him, but with both his own hands, and drew Laidlaw almost imperceptibly around between him and Norcross. As he did so, he said to Norcross, "If you cannot trust me, how can you expect to trust you?"

With that there was a terrible explosion. Norcross himself was blown to pieces and instantly killed. Laidlaw found himself on the floor on top of Russell Sage. He was seriously injured, and later brought suit against Sage for damages upon the ground that he had purposely made a shield of his body from the expected explosion. Sage denied that he had made a shield of Laidlaw or that he had taken him by the hand or altered his own position so as to bring Laidlaw between him and the explosion.

The case was tried four times. It was dismissed by Mr. Justice Andrews, and upon appeal the judgment was reversed. On the second trial before Mr. Justice Patterson the jury rendered a verdict of $25,000 in favor of Laidlaw. On appeal this judgment in turn was reversed. On a third trial, also before Mr. Justice Patterson, the jury disagreed; and on the fourth trial before Mr. Justice Ingraham the jury rendered a verdict in favor of Laidlaw of $40,000, which judgment was sustained by the General Term of the Supreme Court, but subsequently reversed by the Court of Appeals.

Exception on this appeal was taken, among other points, to the method used in the cross-examination of Mr. Sage by Mr. Choate. Thus the cross-examination is interesting, as an instance of what the New York Court of Appeals has decided to be an abuse of cross-examination into which, through their zeal, even eminent counsel are sometimes led, and to which I have referred in a previous chapter. It also shows to what lengths Mr. Choate was permitted to go upon the pretext of testing the witness's memory.

It was claimed by Mr. Sage's counsel upon the appeal that "the right of cross-examination was abused in this case to such an extent as to require the reversal of this monstrous judgment, which is plainly the precipitation and product of that abuse." And the Court of Appeals unanimously took this view of the matter.[1]

After Mr. Sage had finished his testimony in his own behalf, Mr. Choate rose from his chair to cross-examine; he sat on the table back of the counsel table, swinging his legs idly, regarded the witness smilingly, and then began in an unusually low voice.

Mr. Choate. "Where do you reside, Mr. Sage?"

Mr. Sage. "At 506 Fifth Avenue."

Mr. Choate (still in a very low tone). "And what is your age now?"

Mr. Sage (promptly). "Seventy-seven years."

Mr. Choate (with a strong raising of his voice). "Do you ordinarily hear as well as you have heard the two questions you have answered me?"

Mr. Sage (looking a bit surprised and answering in an almost inaudible voice). "Why, yes."

Mr. Choate. "Did you lose your voice by the explosion?"

Mr. Sage. "No."

Mr. Choate. "You spoke louder when you were in Congress, didn't you?"

Mr. Sage. "I may have."

Mr. Choate, resuming the conversational tone, began an unexpected line of questions by asking in a small-talk voice, "What jewelry do you ordinarily wear?" Witness answered that he was not in the habit of wearing jewelry.

Mr. Choate. "Do you wear a watch?"

Mr. Sage. "Yes."

Mr. Choate. "And you ordinarily carry it as you carry the one you have at present in your left vest pocket?"

[1] 158 N. Y. 73, 103.

Mr. Sage. "Yes, I suppose so."

Mr. Choate. "Was your watch hurt by the explosion?"

Mr. Sage. "I believe not."

Mr. Choate. "It was not even stopped by the explosion which perforated your vest with missiles?"

Mr. Sage. "I do not remember about this."

The witness did not quite enjoy this line of questioning, and swung his eye-glasses as if he were a trifle nervous. Mr. Choate, after regarding him in silence for some time, said, "I see you wear eye-glasses." The witness closed his glasses and put them in his vest pocket, whereupon Mr. Choate resumed, "And when you do not wear them, you carry them, I see, in your vest pocket."

Mr. Choate. "Were your glasses hurt by the explosion which inflicted forty-seven wounds on your chest?"

Mr. Sage. "I do not remember."

Mr. Choate. "You certainly would remember if you had to buy a new pair?"

If the witness answered this question, his answer was lost in the laughter which the court officer could not instantly check.

Mr. Choate. "These clothes you brought here to show —you are sure they are the same you wore that day?"

Mr. Sage. "Yes."

Mr. Choate. "How do you know?"

Mr. Sage. "The same as you would know in a matter of that kind."

Mr. Choate. "Were you familiar with these clothes?"

Mr. Sage. "Yes, sir."

Mr. Choate. "How long had you had them?"

Mr. Sage. "Oh, some months."

Mr. Choate. "Had you had them three or four years?"

Mr. Sage. "No."

Mr. Choate. "And wore them daily except on Sundays?"

Mr. Sage. "I think not; they were too heavy for summer wear."

Mr. Choate. "Do you remember looking out of the window that morning when you got up to see if it was cloudy so you would know whether to wear the old suit or not?"

Mr. Sage. "I do not remember."

Mr. Choate. "Well, let that go now; how is your general health,—good as a man of seventy-seven could expect?"

Mr. Sage. "Good except for my hearing."

Mr. Choate. "And that is impaired to the extent demonstrated here on this cross-examination?"

The witness did not answer this question, and after some more kindly inquiries regarding his health, Mr. Choate began an even more intimate inquiry concerning the business career of Mr. Sage.

He learned that the millionaire was born in Verona, Oneida County, went to Troy when he was eleven years old, and was in business there until 1863, when he came to this city.

Mr. Choate. "What was your business in Troy?"

Mr. Sage. "Merchant."

Mr. Choate. "What kind of a merchant?"

Mr. Sage. "A grocer, and I was afterwards engaged in banking and railroad operating."

Mr. Sage, as a railroad builder, excited Mr. Choate's liveliest interest. He wanted to know all about that,— the name of every road he had built or helped to build, when he had done this, and with whom he had been associated in doing it. He frequently outlined his questions by explaining that he did not wish to ask the witness any impudent questions, but merely wanted to test his memory. The financier would sometimes say that to answer some questions he would have to refer to his books, and then the lawyer would pretend great surprise that the witness could not remember even the names of roads he had built. Mr. Sage said, "Possibly we might differ as to what is aiding a road. Some I have aided as a director, and some as a stockholder."

"No, we won't differ, we will divide the question," Mr. Choate said. "First name the roads you have aided in building as a director, and then the roads you have aided in building as a stockholder." The witness either would not, or could not, and after worrying him with a hundred questions on this line, Mr. Choate finally exclaimed, "Well, we will let *that* go."

Next the cross-examiner brought the witness to consider his railroad building experience after he left Troy and came to New York, whereby he managed, under the license of testing the memory of the witness, to show the jury the intimate financial relations which had existed between Mr. Sage and Mr. Jay Gould, and finally asked the witness point blank how many roads he had assisted in building in connection with Mr. Gould as director or stockholder. After some very lively sparring the witness thought that he had been connected in one way or another in about thirty railroads. "Name them!" exclaimed Mr. Choate. The witness named three and then stopped.

Mr. Choate (looking at his list). "There are twenty-seven more. Please hurry,—you do business much faster than this in your office!"

Mr. Sage said something about a number of auxiliary roads that had been consolidated, and roads that had been merged, and unimportant roads whose directors met very seldom, and again said something about referring to his books.

Mr. Choate. "Your books have nothing to do with what I am trying to determine, which is a question of your memory."

The witness continued to spar, and at last Mr. Choate exclaimed, "Now is it not true that you have millions and millions of dollars in roads that you have not named here?"

All of the counsel for the defence were on their feet, objecting to this question, and Mr. Choate withdrew it, and added, "It appears you cannot remember, and won't you please say so?"

The witness would not say so, and Mr. Choate exclaimed, "Well, I give *that* up," and then asked, "You say you are a banker; what kind of a bank do you run,—is it a bank of deposit?" The witness said it was not, and neither was it a bank for circulating notes. "Sometimes I have money to lend," he said.

Mr. Choate. "Oh, you are a money lender. You buy puts and calls and straddles?" The witness said that he dealt in these privileges. "Kindly explain to the jury just what puts and calls and straddles are," the lawyer said encouragingly. The witness answered: "They are means to assist men of moderate capital to operate."

Mr. Choate. "A sort of *benevolent* institution, eh?"

Mr. Sage. "It is in a sense. It gives men of moderate means an opportunity to learn the methods of business."

Mr. Choate. "Do you refer to puts or calls?"

Mr. Sage. "To both."

Mr. Choate. "I do not understand."

Mr. Sage. "I thought you would not" (with a chuckle).

Mr. Choate affected a puzzled look, and asked slowly: "Is it something like this: they call it and you put it? If it goes down they get the chargeable benefit, but if it goes up you get it?"

Mr. Sage. "I only get what I am paid for the privilege."

Mr. Choate. "Now what is a straddle?"

Mr. Sage. "A straddle is the privilege of calling or putting."

"Why," exclaimed Mr. Choate, with raised eyebrows, "that seems to me like a *game of chance.*"

Mr. Sage. "It is a game of the fluctuation of the market."

"That is another way of *putting* it," Mr. Choate commented, looking as if he did not intend the pun. Then he asked, "The market once went very heavy against you in this game, did it not?"

"Yes, it did," the witness replied.

Mr. Choate. "That was an occasion when your customers could *call,* but not put, eh?"

Mr. Sage looked as if he did not understand and made no reply. Mr. Choate then added: "Did you not then have a run on your office?" The witness made some reply, hardly audible, concerning a party of Baltimore roughs, who made a row about his office for an hour when he refused to admit them.

This phase of the question was left in that vague condition, and the cross-examiner opened a new subject and unfolded a three column clipping from a newspaper, which was headed, "A Chat with Russell Sage."

Mr. Choate. "The reporters called on you soon after the explosion?"

Mr. Sage. "Yes."

Mr. Choate. "One visited your house?"

Mr. Sage. "Yes."

Mr. Choate. "Did you read over what he wrote?"

Mr. Sage. "No."

Mr. Choate. "Did you read this after it was printed?"

Mr. Sage. "I believe I did."

Mr. Choate. "It is correct?"

Mr. Sage. "Reporters sometimes go on their own imagination."

It developed that the article which Mr. Choate referred to was written by a grand-nephew of the witness. When it had thus been identified, Mr. Choate again asked the witness if the article was correct.

Colonel James exclaimed: "Are you asking him to swear to the correctness of an article from that paper? *Nobody* could do that."

"No," Mr. Choate quickly responded, "I am asking him to point out its errors. *Any one* can do that."

"This," said Colonel James, "is making a *comedy* of errors."

The witness broke in upon this little relaxation with the remark, "The reporter who wrote that was only in my house five minutes."

"Indeed," exclaimed Mr. Choate, waving the three column clipping, "he got a great deal out of you, and that is more than I have been able to do."

The first extract from the newspaper clipping read as follows: "Mr. Sage looks hale and hearty for an old man, —looks good for many years of life yet."

Mr. Choate. "Is that true?"

Mr. Sage. "We all try to hold our own as long as we can."

Mr. Choate. "You speak for yourself, when you say we all try *to hold on* to all that we can."

At this Mr. James jumped to his feet again, and there was another spirited passage at arms. When all had quieted down, Mr. Sage was next asked if the article was correct when it referred to him as looking like a "warrior after the battle." He thought that the statement was over-drawn. The article referred to Mr. Sage's having shaved himself that morning, which was three mornings after the explosion; and when he had read that, Mr. Choate asked, "Did you have any wounds at that time that a visitor could see?"

The witness replied that both of his hands were then bandaged.

Mr. Choate. "You must have shaved yourself with your feet."

* * * * *

Mr. Choate. "Was it a relief to you to see Laidlaw enter the office when you were talking to Norcross?"

Mr. Sage. "No, and if Laidlaw had stayed out in the lobby instead of coming into my office, he would have been by Norcross when the explosion took place."

Mr. Choate. "Then you think Laidlaw is indebted to you for saving his life instead of your being indebted to him for saving yours?"

Mr. Sage (decidedly). "Yes, sir."

Mr. Choate. "Oh, that makes this a very simple case, then. Did you bring your clerk here to testify as to the condition of the office after the police had cleared it out?"

Mr. Sage. "I did not bring him here, my counsel did."

Mr. Choate. "I see; you do not do any barking when you have a dog to do it for you."

Lawyers Dillon and James jumped up, and Mr. James said gravely, "Which of us is referred to as a dog?"

Mr. Choate. (laughingly). "Oh, all of us."

Mr. Choate seldom reproved the witness for the character of his answers, although when he was examined by Colonel James on the redirect he was treated with very much less courtesy, for the Colonel frequently requested him, and rather roughly, to be good enough to confine his answer to the question.

Mr. Choate's next question referred to the diagram which had been in use up to that point. He asked the witness if it was correct.

Mr. Sage. "I think it is not quite correct, not quite; if the jury will go down there, I would be glad to have them,—be glad to do anything. If the jury will go down there, I would be very glad to furnish their transportation,—if they will go."

Mr. Choate. "If you won't furnish anything *but* transportation, they won't go."

Mr. Sage. "It is substantially correct. I had a diagram made and I offered an opportunity to Mr. Laidlaw's counsel to have a correct one made. I never withheld anything from anybody."

The diagram which Mr. Sage had prepared was produced, and upon examination it was seen that it contained lines indicating a wrong rule, and had some other inaccuracies which did not seem to amount to much really; but Mr. Choate appeared to be very much impressed with these differences.

"I want you," he said to the witness, "to reconcile your testimony with your own diagram."

The witness looked at the diagram for some time, and Mr. Choate, observing him, remarked, "You will have to *make a straddle* to reconcile that, won't you?"

Some marks and signs of erasures were seen on the Sage diagram, which gave Mr. Choate an opportunity to ask, in a sensational tone, if any one could inform him who had been tampering with it. No one could, and the diagram was dropped and the subject of a tattered suit of clothes taken up again.

Mr. Choate. "What tailor did you employ at the time of the explosion?"

Mr. Sage. "Several."

Mr. Choate. "Name them; I want to follow up these clothes."

Mr. Sage. "Tailor Jessup made the coat and vest."

Mr. Choate. "Where is his place?"

Mr. Sage. "On Broadway."

Mr. Choate. "Is he there now?"

Mr. Sage. "Oh, no, he has gone to heaven."

Mr. Choate. "To heaven where all good tailors go? Who made the trousers?"

Mr. Sage. "I cannot tell where I may have bought them."

Mr. Choate. "Bought them? You do not buy ready-made trousers, do you?"

Mr. Sage. "I do sometimes. I get a better fit."

Mr. Choate. "Get benefit?"

Mr. Sage. "No; better fit."

Mr. Choate. "Where is the receipt for them?"

Mr. Sage. "I have none."

Mr. Choate. "Do you pay money without receipts?"

Mr. Sage. "I do sometimes."

Mr. Choate. "Indeed?"

Mr. Sage. "Yes; you do not take a receipt for your hat."

The vest was then produced, and two holes in the outer cloth were exhibited by Mr. Choate, who asked the witness if these were the places where the foreign substances entered which penetrated his body. The witness replied that they were, and Mr. Choate next asked him if he had had the vest relined. Mr. Sage replied that he had not. "How is it, then," Mr. Choate asked, passing the vest to the jury with great satisfaction, "that these holes do not penetrate the lining?" The witness said that he could not explain that, but insisted that that was the vest and it would have to speak for itself. Mr. Choate again took the vest and counted six holes on the cloth on the other side, and asked the witness if that count was right. Mr. Sage replied, "I will take your count," and then caused a laugh by suddenly reaching out for the vest, and saying, "If you have no objection, though, I would like to see it."

Mr. Choate. "Now are not three of these holes moth-eaten?"

Mr. Sage. "I think not."

Mr. Choate. "Are you a judge of moth-eaten goods?"

Mr. Sage. "No."

Mr. Choate. "Where is the shirt you wore?"

Mr. Sage. "Destroyed."

Mr. Choate. "By whom?"

Mr. Sage. "The cook."

Mr. Choate. "The cook?"

Mr. Sage. "I meant the laundress."

The vest was passed to the jury for their inspection, and the jurymen got into an eager whispered discussion as to whether certain of the holes were moth-eaten or not. There was a tailor on the jury. Observing the discussion, Mr. Choate took back the garment and said in his most winning way, "Now we don't want the jury to disagree." He next held up the coat, which was very much more injured in the tails than in front, and asked the witness how he accounted for that.

Mr. Sage. "It is one of the freaks of electricity."

Mr. Choate. "One of those things no fellow can find out."

The witness could not recall how much he had paid for the coat or for any of the garments, and after an unsuccessful attempt to identify the maker of the trousers by the name of the button, which proved to be the name of the buttonmaker, the old clothes were temporarily allowed to rest, and Mr. Choate asked the witness how long he had been unconscious. He replied that he thought he was unconscious two seconds.

Mr. Choate. "How did you know you were not unconscious ten minutes?"

Mr. Sage. "Only from what Mr. Walker says."

Mr. Choate. "Where is he?"

Mr. Sage. "On the Street."

Mr. Choate. "On Chambers Street, downstairs?"

Mr. Sage. "No, on Wall Street."

Mr. Choate. "Oh, I forgot that *the* street to you means Wall Street. Were you not up and dressed every day after the explosion?"

Mr. Sage. "I cannot remember."

Mr. Choate. "You did business every day?"

Mr. Sage. "Colonel Slocum and my nephew called upon me about business, and my counsel looked after some missing papers and bonds."

Mr. Choate. "You then held some Missouri Pacific collateral trust bonds?"

Mr. Sage. "Yes."

Mr. Choate. "How many?"

Mr. Sage. "Cannot say."

Mr. Choate. "Can't you tell within a limit of ten to one thousand?"

Mr. Sage. "No."

Mr. Choate. "Nor within one hundred to two hundred?"

Mr. Sage. "No."

Mr. Choate. "Is it because you have too little memory or too many bonds? How many loans did you have out at that time?"

Mr. Sage. "I cannot tell."

Mr. Choate. "Can you tell within two hundred thousand of the amount then due you from your *largest* creditor?"

Mr. Sage. "Any man doing the business I am—"

Mr. Choate. "Oh, there is no other man like you in the world. No, you cannot tell within two hundred thousand of the amount of the largest loan you then had out, but you set up your memory against Laidlaw's?"

Mr. Sage. "I do."

Mr. Choate. "Were you not very excited?"

Mr. Sage. "I was thoughtful. I was self-poised. I did not believe his dynamite would do so much damage, or that he would sacrifice himself."

Mr. Choate. "Never heard of a man killing himself?"

Mr. Sage. "Not in that way." [1]

[1] Extracts from *New York Sun.* March, 1894.

Chapter 26

The Cross-Examination of
Louis H. Perlman

*in Perlman Rim Corporation v. Firestone
Tire & Rubber Co., by Martin W. Littleton*

IN A SUIT to sustain a patent, the general effect of which,
if successful, would be that the entire automobile industry
of the United States would have to pay royalty to Louis
H. Perlman or his corporation for the right to manufacture
and sell demountable rims, the issue depended upon the
credibility of plaintiff's chief witness, the alleged inventor
Perlman. Could Perlman successfully prove that he conceived the invention in 1903? The evidence in support of
this proposition was necessarily Perlman's own testimony,
corroborated by such circumstances as he could summon,
but in the last analysis the question was: "Was Perlman
worthy of belief?"

The defendants, represented by Martin W. Littleton,
were well aware that Perlman was a crafty, resourceful
and nimble witness, for he had testified on other occasions.
They were in possession of facts showing that he, at a
considerably earlier date, had been engaged in a fake
medicine business, and that while in London conducting
a fake medicine company, he with his associates had de-
vised a scheme which was generally called a "word competition," which was to induce a great number of persons
to send sums of money to Perlman and his associates, for
which the sender never received any return. The defense
was also in possession of the fact that Perlman was arrested for this by an inspector of Scotland Yard, had an
examining trial in Bow Street before Justice Bridges, was
represented by eminent counsel, was locked up for two
months in jail and finally released on a cash bail and had
become a fugitive from justice.

In cross-examining Perlman a less skilled counsel might have submitted all of this matter to him, and he might easily have admitted all of the facts and still have claimed that it did not reflect in anywise upon his ability to invent. In other words, it might simply have passed off as an unpleasant episode, that took place some twenty years before.

The object of Mr. Littleton, therefore, was to see if the witness Perlman would actually commit perjury under the very eye of the Court. If he did this, the Judge who was to pass upon his credibility would, of course, reject his evidence as a whole. If Perlman were convinced that the cross-examiner had all of the facts and data concerning the events in London he would probably admit them, but if he could be sure that the cross-examiner did not have these data but was simply striking in a blind fashion, he could and would with safety deny or evade by pretending not to remember the events.

In order to give the witness confidence in himself and to make him feel that he was master of the situation, counsel first devoted almost a whole day to a cross-examination regarding the invention, the structure of the wheels, the embodiment of the idea of the patent in the wheels and all of the technical details of its construction, whether by Perlman or otherwise. It was evident that the witness got the better of the lawyer during this examination, so much so, that there was a manifest impatience on the part of the Court toward counsel for apparently prolonging the examination unnecessarily.

Toward the late afternoon, counsel, weary from his cross-examination and apparently outwitted and outgeneraled, picked up his papers in a careless manner from the table and proceeded to ask the witness questions concerning the various enterprises in which he had been engaged. This was done for the purpose of eliciting his memory at and about the period when the events in London transpired and to show, without the witness realizing it, that he did have a clear memory of all these events. This examination disclosed that the witness had been engaged in the publishing business and in the vending or advertising of proprietary medicines and in the sale of pills, which was a kindred business to the one which he had conducted in London and on account of which he had gotten into criminal courts. Finally the cross-examiner asked the witness:

Q. "When did you leave Jersey City to go to any other place in business?"

A. "I do not recall the date."

The witness had now begun to answer in a most indifferent and self-confident fashion that he did not recall this, that and the other, and to make it appear that the cross-examiner was engaged in an idle and vain cross-examination.

Q. "Did you not go to London in 1895?"

A. "I may have."

Q. "Well, did you not? Do you not remember if you did?"

A. "I do not remember."

Q. "Did you not go to London with, or there to meet, Edward Ames Webber, in 1895?"

A. "I may have."

Q. "Well, surely, you know whether you went to Europe in the year 1895?"

A. "I do not remember."

Q. "You have never been since 1895, have you?"

A. "I believe I have."

Q. "To London?"

A. "I believe so."

Q. "Did you not go to London in 1895 and there organize or take with you as an organization the American Oxyzone Syndicate?"

A. "I have no recollection of it."

Q. "Did you not stop at the First Avenue Hotel, Holburn, first? Doesn't that refresh your recollection?"

A. "I may have stopped at the First Avenue Hotel."

Q. "Well, do you not know that you did, Mr. Perlman?"

A. "I do not recall."

Q. "Is it not a fact that you went to the First Avenue Hotel, Holburn, and there you occupied Room 800 in that Hotel and Edward Ames Webber also occupied in the hotel Room 805?"

A. "I do not recall."

This question, with its particularity with reference to the room, was asked because the cross-examiner thought that the witness would be convinced that the room numbers were the invention of the cross-examiner and only for the purpose of entrapping him, because it must always be remembered that this was a very experienced witness.

Q. "And did you not then organize and send out notices of the organization of the American Oxyzone Syndicate, on or about the 16th of January, 1895, or in the preceding December or November, 1894?"

A. "I have no recollection of it."

Q. "Do you not know that shortly after your arrival in England you and Webber inserted advertisements in the London and country papers regarding a word competition —maybe that will refresh your recollection—and issued circulars relating to the competition?"

A. "I have no recollection of it."

The witness was still thoroughly convinced that all that the cross-examiner had was merely the advertisements of the Oxyzone Syndicate and that he could afford to pretend that he had forgotten these.

Q. "Do you not know that the advertisements and circulars contained particulars of word competitions and that a prize of four pounds was offered to every person who could supply the full list of correct answers to four skeleton words? Does that refresh your recollection?"

A. "It does not."

Q. "That the four skeleton words were given in the advertisement and it was stated no entrance fee was charged but that if the person sending in the guess or solution would send ten shillings and sixpence along he would receive a can or tin of Oxyzone and later on receive three pounds ten shillings and sixpence, which would be the equivalent of the original advertisement for four pounds, which was the first reward? Does that help your recollection any?"

A. "It does not."

Q. "You did not do that?"

A. "I have no recollection of it."

Q. "You did not publish such a scheme in London at that time?"

A. "I have no recollection of it."

Q. "Do you know Edward Ames Webber?"

A. "I do not recall having knowing him."

Q. "Do you mean you never recall having known a man of the name of Edward Ames Webber?"

A. "I knew Guy Webber."

Q. "Did you know a man by the name of Edward Ames Webber, a younger man?"

A. "I do not recall having known him."

Q. "Do you know a man by the name of Henry Marshall?"

A. "I do not."

The questions asked with reference to Edward Ames Webber were obviously answered by the witness in pursuance of a plan of the witness to pretend to have no memory regarding the fraudulent scheme for which he was arrested and held in London.

Q. "Did you not give your address as J. B. Quint, in care of Gibbs, Smith & Company, 10 High Holborn, London, and in the circular as G. Webber, Treasurer?"

A. "I have no recollection of it."

Q. "To bring it to your recollection, do you not know that you were visited at your rooms in the First Avenue Hotel by Henry Marshall, the inspector of police, who took you down to the Bow Street Station?"

A. "I have no recollection of it."

Hereupon, counsel, seeing that the witness was prepared to go through by taking refuge under the oft repeated answer that he "had no recollection," determined to group a number of questions in one, as follows:

Q. "Do you not know that thereafter, after that examination, you and Webber were indicted for larceny, cheating and deceit, under the law, and put in jail and you finally furnished bail and you fled your bail, and that you are now a fugitive from justice?"

A. "I have no recollection of that incident."

This was a high point in the cross-examiner's plan. The witness had answered that he did not remember being indicted, that he did not remember giving bail and he did not know that he was a fugitive from justice and had been in jail, and all in one question. The reason for the fashion of the question, otherwise objectionable in the manner in which it was put, was a fear on the part of the cross-examiner that the counsel on the other side might object to the mere question as to whether he had been in jail or been indicted, and counsel felt that if he could couple with it a question as to whether or not the witness had not fled his bail and was not now a fugitive from justice, he might make the question at least to that extent competent. But counsel on the other side, who were highly respectable gentlemen and wholly unaware of the record of their client, were so thunderstruck at these disclosures that they did not find their feet or their tongues to object. Immediately the cross-examiner thundered at the witness, *"Do you deny it?"* The witness did not get an opportunity to answer. By this time the Court had observed what the cross-examiner had intended to bring out,—that the witness was committing perjury under his very eye,—and the Court said:

Q. "You have no recollection of that incident?"

A. "I have not."

Q. "Do you mean to sit there, sir—Do you deny it?"

A. "I have no recollection of it, your Honor."

Q. "Do you mean to sit there, sir, and tell me that that may have happened and you do not recollect it?"

A. "I have answered the question to the best of my ability."

Q. "Answer that question to me, sir, now. Do you mean to sit in that chair and tell me that these things which have been said to you may have happened to you and that you do not recall them?"

A. "I do not know that they ever happened. I have no recollection of it."

Q. "And yet, you do not deny it?"

A. "I cannot recall them."

Q. "Do you deny them, sir?"

A. "I cannot recall them."

Q. "Do you deny them?"

A. "I will not deny them; I do not recall them."

Here Counsel resumed his examination and began to surround the witness with other circumstances taking place at the time, in Bow Street Court, in London, with a view of revealing the utter falsity of his claim that he did not remember, by showing that he could not have forgotten.

Q. "Mr. Perlman, do you remember that you had counsel of the name of Wetner in the court?"

A. "I do not remember."

Q. "Do you remember that you were in jail for two months in London?"

A. "I do not recall the incident."

Q. "Do you mean to say that you deny you were in jail for two months in London?"

A. "I do not remember that I was."

Q. "Do you take the position that what I am presenting here is something that is false and that I am wrongfully accusing you when I present you these documents and ask you these questions?"

A. "I have no recollection of what you have outlined."

Q. "Do you think you may have been in jail in London two months and forgotten it?"

A. "It is not possible for me to tell."

Counsel read to the witness Perlman in detail the charge that had been presented against him in the Bow Street Court, reading him the formal language of the charge, which set forth the exact character of his crime.

Q. "Was that not read to you by the Magistrate and to Edward Ames Webber, on the 17th day of January, 1895?"

A. "I have no recollection of ever having heard anything like that."

Thereupon, counsel read to the witness the testimony of Henry Marshall, Inspector of Police, taken in his presence in the Bow Street Court, reciting the charge and the conversation that the Inspector had had with Perlman, the accused, in detail.

Q. "Does that refresh your recollection?"

A. "It does not."

Q. "Did that happen?"

A. "I have no recollection of it."

Q. "Do you deny that what I read was said in your presence and hearing in the Bow Street Police Court, in London?"

A. "I have no recollection of it."

The Court then asked:

Q. "You can answer the question, whether you deny it?"

Then the witness Perlman answered: "I do not deny it, because I do not recollect it."

Q. "You say you will not deny it?" (No answer to that.)

The Court said: "He will not deny it."

The cross-examiner then proceeded to bring to the attention of the witness Perlman all of the details of his operations in London, with merchants and with banks and bankers, as to all of which the witness answered:

"I have no recollection of it."

Q. "You certainly remember so distinguished a person as Sir Edward Carson, don't you? He is now a member of the cabinet."

A. "I have heard of him."

Q. "And Sir Edward Clark, K. C., who was a leader of the London bar for years?"

A. "I have heard of Sir Edward Clark."

Q. "Did they not finally come in as counsel for you and Webber?"

A. "I have no recollection of their ever having come in as counsel for me."

Q. "Do you deny that they did?"

A. "I have no recollection of having met them."

Q. "Do you not know that at the last minute, after you had been in jail two months, Sir Edward Carson and Sir Edward Clark appeared and said that your witness, an important witness, known as the Treasurer, was needed, and you procured bail, got an adjournment, and fled and your bail has been forfeited? Don't you know that?"

A. "I have no recollection of such an incident."

By the Court:

Q. "You have no recollection of any part of what he has told you?"

A. "I have not."

Q. "And you will not deny it in whole or in part? I do not understand that."

A. "I cannot deny what I do not remember to have happened."

Q. "So that I understand, in respect of all this testimony, that it may have happened to you but you do not recollect it, is that it?"

A. "I have no recollection of any such thing as that."

Q. "Please answer my question. It may have happened to you but you do not recall it. Can you not recall it?"

A. "I cannot admit that it happened to me because I do not remember it."

Q. "I do not ask you whether you admit it. I said, your position is that it may have happened to you but you do not recall it, is that your position?"

A. "No, sir."

Q. "It is not your position?"

A. "It is not my position."

Q. "Your position is, then, that it did not happen, it could not have happened?"

A. "I have no recollection of any such incident as that happening."

Q. "You keep taking refuge in that, which as you know perfectly well by now is not what I want you to answer, and is not what I mean by my question. I press you again, is it your position that this may have happened to you but you do not recall it?"

A. "Had it happened I would have recalled it."

Q. "If it had happened you would have recalled it?"

A. "I would have remembered it."

Q. "So therefore you deny that it happened, do you?"

A. "I cannot state that it happened, because I have no recollection of it."

Q. "Very good, you say it could not have happened to you?"

A. "It could not have happened without my remembering it."

Q. "It could not have happened without your remembering it, is that your position?"

A. "It would not appear so to me."

Q. "I do not know what would appear to you. I want you to think now, as you are on your oath, whether it could have happened to you and you have forgotten it; because I shall take that as an equivalent to a denial, which it certainly is. Now I ask you, is it your position that that could not have happened to you, and therefore did not happen to you?"

A. "Well, your Honor, I have no recollection of any such occurrence as that."

Q. "Now, if you continue to trifle with me I shall have to take some action on it. I shall have to commit you until you answer the question as I put it to you. I will give you plenty of opportunity. I say, is it your position that the things, the arrest and the general circumstances that Mr. Littleton has told you, could not and did not happen to you?"

A. "I cannot say that they did not happen."

Q. "They might have happened to you and you have forgotten it? Take your time."

A. "If they happened, I do not remember them."

Q. " Might they have happened and you have forgotten them? I will give you two more chances, and if you do not answer I shall commit you."

A. "Possibly it may have happened and I do not remember them."

Q. "Is it your position that you might have been arrested in England, under the circumstances detailed to you, and you have forgotten it, forgotten all about it?"

A. "It may be."

The witness was further examined in great detail, to further surround him with incontestable facts and circumstances, to all of the questions concerning which he merely replied that he did not remember.

When the cross-examiner had concluded, the counsel for the plaintiff arose and said: "I would like to make an observation, if I may. I hope your Honor will believe that this attack on the plaintiff's principal witness is as unexpected to counsel as to the Court.

The Court. "Absolutely."

Plaintiff's Counsel. "And I feel that my duty to my client, Perlman Rim Corporation, and my duty to the Court requires that I should immediately make an investigation and for that purpose will ask you to adjourn the proceeding till tomorrow."

The following day the counsel for the plaintiff asked leave to take a nonsuit. The Court entirely absolved the counsel for the plaintiff from any part or parcel of any aspect of the witness's predicament, assuring counsel that the Court had the utmost faith in the integrity and high mindedness of counsel. The Court permitted the nonsuit to be taken and impounded all of the exhibits, documentary and otherwise, and the matter was sent to the Grand Jury.